Ministry in the Anglican Tradition from Henry VIII to 1900

ANGLICAN STUDIES

Series Editor

Sheryl A. Kujawa-Holbrook, Claremont School of Theology

This series responds to the growing need for high-quality and innovative research in Anglican Studies made available to the scholarly and ecclesial communities. Anglican Studies as expressed here is an interdisciplinary field, including Anglican history, theology, liturgy, preaching, postcolonial studies, ecclesiology, spirituality, literature, missiology, ethics/moral theology, ministry, pastoral care, ecumenism, and interreligious studies. Studies that engage global Anglicanism, as well as studies related to individual contexts are welcome. The series seeks monographs and edited volumes which explore contemporary issues and forge new directions in interdisciplinary research.

Titles in the series

Ministry in the Anglican Tradition from Henry VIII to 1900, by John L. Kater

A Eucharist-shaped Church: Prayer, Theology, and Mission, edited by Daniel J. Handschy, Donna R. Hawk-Reinhard, and Marshall E. Crossnoe

Ministry in the Anglican Tradition from Henry VIII to 1900

John L. Kater

LEXINGTON BOOKS/FORTRESS ACADEMIC
Lanham • Boulder • New York • London

Published by Lexington Books/Fortress Academic
Lexington Books is an imprint of The Rowman & Littlefield Publishing Group, Inc.
4501 Forbes Boulevard, Suite 200, Lanham, Maryland 20706
www.rowman.com

86-90 Paul Street, London EC2A 4NE, United Kingdom

Copyright © 2022 by The Rowman & Littlefield Publishing Group, Inc.

All rights reserved. No part of this book may be reproduced in any form or by any electronic or mechanical means, including information storage and retrieval systems, without written permission from the publisher, except by a reviewer who may quote passages in a review.

British Library Cataloguing in Publication Information Available

Library of Congress Cataloging-in-Publication Data Available

ISBN 9781978714823 (cloth) | ISBN 9781978714847 (pbk.) | ISBN 9781978714830 (epub)

Contents

1. Reformations: The Beginnings of Ministry in the Anglican Tradition — 1
2. Settlement: Ministry in the Reign of Elizabeth — 21
3. Unsettlement: Ministry after Elizabeth — 39
4. Divergence: Ministry after the Restoration — 59
5. Stirrings: The Beginnings of Overseas Anglicanism — 85
6. Reconsiderations: Anglican Ministry in England and Ireland, 1800–1860 — 113
7. Pioneers: Mission and Ministry in North America, 1800–1860 — 135
8. Missions: Global Anglican Ministry in the Early Nineteenth Century — 155
9. Tremblings: Ministry in the Church of England, 1860–1900 — 181
10. Britannia: Ministry in the British Empire, 1850–1900 — 197
11. Evangelism: Global Anglican Ministry, 1850–1900 — 221
12. Tensions: Anglican Ministry in the United States of America, 1860–1900 — 249
13. Visions: The Future(s) of Mission and Ministry in the Anglican Tradition — 281

Bibliography — 289
Index — 307
About the Author — 323

Chapter One

Reformations

The Beginnings of Ministry in the Anglican Tradition

The distinctively Anglican understanding of the Church's ministry reflects the peculiar legacy of the English Reformation and its aftermath. It reveals the strongly political dimension of that process as it occurred in England, as well as the heritage of Roman Catholic Christianity in Britain, the impulses and currents of the Reformation on the European continent, and serious, sometimes bloody conflicts among the English Reformers themselves. The understanding of ministry that emerged shares a great deal with other Christian churches, but it also includes a specifically Anglican perspective that appears nowhere else and continues to shape how ministry is perceived by contemporary Anglican Christians as well as their relationships, formal and informal, with other bodies.

The mission of the Church on the eve of the Reformation seemed clear to any Christian who thought to ask. The Church existed to provide the means by which humankind could achieve its ultimate union with God, a destiny interrupted by the fact of original sin but also a possibility restored through the sacrifice of Christ. Its mission was carried out by providing the means by which individual Christians could access the benefits of Christ's self-offering, and by safeguarding the order of the world as God intended it. The Church's ministry was accomplished by its ordained leaders, who celebrated the sacraments without which no one could achieve salvation; by its engagement with the principalities and powers of the world to ensure that society itself was organized in accordance with Christian norms, and by the intercessions of those who had dedicated themselves to a life of prayer and service through the many religious orders for both men and women that had proliferated over the centuries. Ordinary Christians participated in the Church's ministry through their own prayers, acts of service to those in need, care of the church buildings in which they worshiped, and the offerings, voluntary or otherwise, which provided financial support for the vast infrastructure of the medieval Church. In the course of what came to be the Reformation, every one of those aspects of the Church's mission and ministry would be challenged.

HENRY VIII: RELUCTANT REFORMER

The great upheavals that shook Western Christendom beginning in the fifteenth century and continued to convulse the churches for the next three hundred years produced widely varied results among different peoples. In England, the sixteenth century was the time of the Tudors, a relatively short-lived dynasty that nevertheless permanently marked the history of both English church and people.

In fact, the distinction between the English nation and its church would have been incomprehensible in the Tudors' day; the Church of England *was* the English people as they stood as a nation before God. When Henry VIII assumed the throne in 1509, the English church (*Ecclesia Anglicana*) was conceived as both a recognizable entity with its own liturgical rites and also an integral part of the Catholic Church. The ultimate authority of the Pope was assumed. While some scholars claim to detect a particularly English quality to both the worship and spirituality of the time, others note the deep devotion that English Christians shared with other Roman Catholics through the cult of the Virgin Mary and other saints. The great shrines at sites such as Walsingham and Canterbury were not only centers of piety but also produced vast amounts of income from faithful pilgrims who expressed their prayers or thanksgivings with generous alms.

Some English Christians had been involved in the religious conflicts that provide the historical background of the Reformation. In the fourteenth century, the Oxford scholar John Wycliffe was identified with the translation of the Bible into English and attacks on fundamental doctrines of Roman Catholic Christianity as well as the Church's wealth. He generated a movement of followers (the "Lollards") who embraced his ideas and who continued to struggle against many of the most treasured tenets of Roman Catholic Christianity. The dramatic religious conflicts unleashed by Martin Luther and others, which rocked Europe in the early decades of the sixteenth century, were noted and discussed by the learned academics of the English universities but otherwise had little immediate impact in England. King Henry VIII had no use for Luther's attack on Catholic sacramental theology; his book entitled *Declaration of the Seven Sacraments Against Martin Luther* went through some twenty editions. Henry was rewarded by a grateful Pope Leo X with the title "Defender of the Faith."

Henry's concern to defend Catholic sacramental teaching against Luther's arguments demonstrates the central position for Christian faith and practice occupied by the sacraments in medieval Roman Catholicism. Although the doctrine of transubstantiation had not yet been made part of the body of Catholic dogma, it was central to popular belief. It held that in the sacrifice of the Mass, the bread and wine of the Eucharist are changed into the substance of the body and blood of Christ, in such a way that the priest represents Christ's sacrifice for the spiritual benefit of those who are present or for whom it is offered. Indeed, the priestly power to realize this miracle and to celebrate the sacraments was perceived to be the most significant aspect of all ministry and the foundation of Roman Catholic worship and spirituality.

The Sarum (or Salisbury) Use which shaped the liturgical life of the Church of England called for considerably more elaborate ritual than the worship of Catholics on the European continent. Like other Roman Catholic ordination rites, it emphasized the power to offer the Eucharistic sacrifice, but it also underlined the special holiness of the priestly vocation. Both dimensions of priesthood were stressed symbolically in the liturgy: the bestowal of the priestly stole as a symbol of personal holiness, and the delivery of the vessels of Holy Communion by the ordaining bishop with the words, "Receive the power to offer sacrifice to God and to celebrate Mass, both for the living and the dead."[1]

For ordinary English Christians, the practice of their faith was focused on attendance at Mass and the occasional reception of the sacrament of Holy Communion, always preceded by confession and absolution; the frequent festivals that marked the great events of the Christian Year; and the special services of the Church that marked birth, marriage, and death. The parish church was the focus of the community, providing a setting for worship and other momentous events of the cycle of human life. As in other parts of Europe, medieval churches in England were lavishly decorated with images, wall paintings, vestments and altar hangings. Providing and maintaining the objects used in worship or in the decoration of the church was a highly respected way by which parishioners could demonstrate their loyalty to the Church and their devotion to God and the Saints, and most congregations had a large number of guilds dedicated to the decoration and upkeep of the church and especially of the various images that decorated it. Guilds also prayed for their departed members and provided a strong sense of community, not only among the living but between the living and the dead. The records of one English village parish, Morebath in Somerset, reveal that

> from 1529 onwards, most of the imagery in the church was replaced or else revamped by being gilded, repainted and installed in new or redecorated tabernacles. . . . The image of the Virgin was a special focus for piety in later

medieval England, and appealed particularly to women. . . . [T]he symbolic force of gifts of kerchiefs, girdles, beads and gowns conveyed much the same sense of intimacy, as do bequests of flowers and [candles] to burn before the specified images between first vespers and mass—that is, all night long—on feast days.[2]

Bequests to the local parish church (as well as to institutions such as alms-houses, priories, colleges and other institutions where prayers for departed benefactors would have played a regular part in worship) were a common feature of piety on the eve of the Reformation. Parishioners who remembered the parish in their wills could expect their names to be added to the parish Bede-roll, assuring them of the future prayers of the congregation, and making of the parish what one historian calls a "self-help association" which transcended death and the passage of time.[3]

Just as every village in the countryside and every urban neighborhood featured its parish church, the broader English landscape was dominated by the great religious houses established by monastic orders of men and women. In Henry VIII's time these establishments were centers of great wealth, owning vast tracts of land as well as treasures amassed over the years. The monastic life provided an option for dedication to a committed life of prayer; ordinary medieval Christians saw the monks and nuns as spiritual allies whose prayers benefited those whose practice of faith must inevitably be compromised by the demands of everyday life.

While invention of the printing press had made the communication of ideas vastly easier in the sixteenth century, many ordinary English Christians of Henry VIII's time would have been illiterate. Furthermore, the language of both church and academy was Latin. The subtleties of Catholic liturgy were largely inaccessible to English churchgoers during Henry's reign, and the piety of ordinary Christians was often mingled with folk beliefs and practices that antedate the arrival of Christianity.

Such reformation of English Christianity as occurred under Henry reflects the emphases and the limitations of his personal conflict with the Papacy as well as the interests and concerns of two of his closest advisors, Thomas Cranmer, Henry's Archbishop of Canterbury after 1533, and Thomas Cromwell, named as Vicar-General and Vice-Gerent in Spirituals a year later. It was Cromwell, who, in Diarmaid MacCulloch's words, was the "mastermind" of the "moves which decisively and permanently asserted" the priority of English common law over the Church's own canon law, paving the way for Henry to claim his position as "Supreme Head on earth of the Church of England."[4] Scholars and church leaders traveled frequently to the continent and could hardly escape participating in the controversies shaking the church there. The influence of the European Reformers on Cromwell and Cranmer is seen early on; even before Cranmer's nomination by Henry as Archbishop and the Pope's approval of his appointment, he had married a relative of the German reformer Osiander—a fact he kept carefully hidden from the king. Although Henry was reticent about making significant changes to the Church of England, the nature of his rupture with the Papacy, the impact of that break and subsequent actions on the king's part did in fact drastically alter the Church's understanding and practice of ministry, especially by identifying and affirming a dramatically expanded role for the monarch in the leadership of the Church. The immediate issue behind the rejection of papal authority was, of course, the Pope's refusal to accede to Henry's well-known desire for an annulment of his marriage to his first wife, Catherine of Aragon. The failure of Henry's appeal for an annulment of his marriage was followed by Parliament's Act of Supremacy in 1534, affirming the king's position as the Church of England's supreme head.

Subsequent events would demonstrate that at least for Cranmer, this was not a matter of political chicanery but a deeply held belief. It was based on an imperial model of the Church, dating back in its original form to the days of the Roman Empire and the establishment of Christianity as the imperial state religion. That model saw the role of the emperor as a God-given vocation that conveyed ultimate responsibility for the material *and spiritual* well-being of the whole people. The logic of the Royal Supremacy was based on the claim that England was itself an empire, Henry VIII was its emperor, and therefore held not only temporal but spiritual authority over his realm. Christian princes, wrote Cranmer, have "the whole cure of all their subjects as well concerning the administration of God's Word for the cure of souls, as concerning the ministration of things political and civil governance." They are responsible for "bishops, parsons, vicars and other such priests as be appointed by his highness to that administration." Furthermore, he asserted, government is itself a God-given vocation: Those who exercise political power and have responsibility for government, whether the monarch and Parliament or local justices of the peace, act just as surely in God's name and under God's Providence as the bishops and clergy of the Church of England. "Equal grace," he claimed, "is given to civil and ecclesiastical ministers."[5] But if Henry claimed supreme headship over the Church of England, what then of the thousands of monks and nuns who lived under the various monastic rules of their orders? What of the Church's ordained ministry? And how did Henry's newly asserted authority affect the practice of ministry across England?

The answer to the first of those questions came fairly quickly. Recognizing both the enormous wealth of the monastic houses and the implicit threat to his authority they represented, Henry soon moved against them. He appointed a royal commission to investigate conditions in the religious houses, which (predictably and perhaps erroneously) determined that they were hotbeds of vice and corruption. Shortly after receiving the report, Henry made one of the most far-reaching changes to the life of the Church of England of his reign: he began abolishing the religious houses, dismissed their members and effectively brought an end to monasticism in the Church of England, taking their resources of land and other material possessions for the Crown. Henry's dissolution of the monasteries provoked the worst crisis of his reign, even as it demonstrated that at the time popular support for the kind of reforms already undertaken on the continent remained limited, especially in the north of England. First in Lincolnshire and then in Yorkshire, bands of irate citizens gathered to demand the restoration of the religious houses. In Yorkshire, the movement, known as the "Pilgrimage of Grace," grew to some thirty thousand, armed and prepared to do battle with the king if necessary to procure the reestablishment of the monasteries. Faced with certain defeat, Henry agreed to the crowd's demands and they dispersed. The King then declared martial law, arrested and ultimately executed many of the leaders. The religious houses remained closed; more than three centuries would pass before the monastic life was restored to the Church of England.

Related to Henry's seizure of the religious houses was another action which had dramatic consequences for English Christians. In 1538, injunctions forbade pilgrimages and offerings to the shrines which were to be found all over England, generally in conjunction with the monasteries. Only images not associated with either pilgrimages or offerings were permitted in churches. The destruction of the great English shrines yielded another source of income for the Crown. "2621 ounces of gold, 4285 ounces of silver, gold, and a great number of pearls and precious stones" were taken from the shrines at Lincoln Cathedral alone. In the same year, parishes were required to deliver all relics in their possession for destruction.[6]

Cranmer wrote that the office of a bishop is "to preserve the peace of the Church and the purity of the truth of the Gospel," which implies for both priests and bishops great care so that "no erroneous doctrine, or superstition, or idolatry, or anything which could diminish the glory of Christ, or harm Christian piety, . . . should be introduced into the Church either by themselves or others."[7] But in Cranmer's mind, the continued presence of an ordained ministry in no way challenged or compromised the monarch's authority and responsibility for oversight of the church. In 1540 he argued that princes "supervised not only the civil service but also the ministry of the Word and care of souls. Princes were empowered to elect, assign and appoint all ministers, civil and ecclesiastical, in their realms." Ceremonies of ordination and installation, while attractive and useful, are not necessary, and no more convey any special grace than does taking on a civil office.[8]

Certainly Henry VIII behaved as if overseeing the Church's life were his prerogative, so that "no erroneous doctrine, or superstition, or idolatry, or anything which could diminish the glory of Christ, or harm Christian piety, . . . should be introduced into the Church either by themselves or others." Dabbling in the theological controversies of his time and influenced by Cranmer, Cromwell and others with sympathies for the European Reformation, he permitted a lengthy dialogue with representatives of the German Lutherans over a three-year period. In 1536, the so-called Ten Articles were published, with the stated purpose of achieving "unity and concord in religious opinions" through the exercise of royal authority, and to "repress" and "utterly extinguish" all opposing viewpoints. The same year saw an injunction against indulgences, once a significant source of income for the Church and an important dimension of popular piety.[9]

The subtle influence of advisors influenced by the European Reformation can be seen in the Ten Articles' affirmation of the authority of the Bible, along with the three Ecumenical Creeds and the first four Ecumenical Councils, as well as in a cautious acceptance of the doctrine of justification by faith on which Luther's own theology was based. Nevertheless, the wording of the doctrine in the Ten Articles makes it clear that it does not contradict the traditional Catholic emphasis on the necessity of good works on which much traditional piety depended. A year later, the king authorized an English translation of the Bible, and in 1538 each parish was ordered to have a copy accessible in the church. A similar cautious opening to Protestant ideas can be perceived in the "Bishops' Book," *Institution of a Christian Man,* published by a group of bishops in 1537 (though without the king's approval). By 1539, however, Cranmer's influence had waned and Henry veered sharply towards a more narrowly Catholic perspective. The Six Articles, issued under his authority in 1539, affirmed the doctrine of transubstantiation and made denying it a capital offense. They also prescribed continuing the Catholic practice by which only the priest received the consecrated wine at Communion; clerical celibacy; vows of chastity or widowhood; private masses; and auricular confession to a priest. In 1543 an "Act for the Advancement of the True Religion" restricted the reading of the Bible to the upper classes; women were allowed to read it only in private. In the same year, the "King's Book," *A Necessary Doctrine and Erudition for any Christian Man,* replaced the discredited "Bishops' Book" and articulated a thoroughly Catholic understanding of the Church and its ministry, except that the king's authority was substituted for that of the pope. Its most significant innovation for the practice of ministry in the Church of England came from Henry's decision that it was not necessary to offer masses for the dead to help them earn release from purgatory. Such masses had been an important part of popular spiritual practice as well as a significant source of income for congregations and clergy. The "King's Book" did not reject prayers for the dead altogether, but it interpreted them as acts of charity rather than an important part of the process by which the departed achieve salvation.[10]

Like many of those who had played a significant part in Henry's reign, Thomas Cromwell ultimately fell into disfavor with the king and was executed in 1540. Thomas Cranmer managed to survive Henry, though his freedom to carry out more significant reforms was severely limited and Henry's autocratic personality required him to be a cautious advocate of further change. Long eager for worship in the English language, he was successful in persuading Henry to allow a Litany in English, but throughout Henry's reign the services of the Church of England continued to be in Latin, with no significant changes from the worship of the Roman Catholic Church. Indeed, at times the process appears to have been a delicate dance, with Cranmer and others pushing gently for more significant theological and liturgical reform against the nearly instinctive resistance—and absolute power—of the king.

By the time of Henry's death in 1547, the influence of the Reformation was much greater, and its ideas had spread widely among the Court and the great families of England; indeed, Henry's sixth (and last) wife, Katherine Parr, was herself deeply committed to the Evangelical (Protestant) understanding of Christian faith—a commitment which at one moment nearly cost her life. In fact, in his last years almost all the people closest to King Henry can be identified as supporters of the evangelical reforms.[11] Henry's nine-year-old son, who succeeded to the throne as Edward VI, gave his name to the brief but volatile period of more wide-reaching reform which forever changed the Church of England as well as its practice of ministry.

EDWARD VI: EAGER REFORMER

The Privy Council, which provided governmental oversight on behalf of the young king, began mandating a series of changes that must have seemed nearly overwhelming to the ordinary churchgoer of the mid-sixteenth century. Only a year after Henry's death, the Council issued detailed instructions affecting the worship and piety of the English Church. It ordered clergy to instruct their congregations that prayers should be directed only to God and to warn them that veneration of saints or images can lead to "idolatry and superstition." The epistle and gospel at the principal Sunday service were to be read in English, and Bible reading was encouraged for both clergy and laypeople. Priests were to instruct their congregations to learn the Lord's Prayer, the Creeds and the Ten Commandments in English, and only those with specific license to preach were permitted to do so. Clergy were ordered to "take away, utterly extinct, and destroy all shrines, all tables, candlesticks, trundles or rolls of wax, pictures, paintings, and all other monuments of feigned miracles, pilgrimage, idolatry and superstition." Each church was to have a "comely and honest pulpit" for the preaching of the Word, and a "strong chest" for donations.[12] Cranmer suggested that what people previously "were wont to bestow upon pardons, pilgrimages, trentals [sets of thirty masses], masses satisfactory, decking of images, offerings of candles, giving to friars, and upon other like blind devotions" should now be given as offerings for the poor.[13] In the same year, Parliament ordered that at all services, communicants should be given the chalice along with the bread at Holy Communion. Original preaching by most clergy was replaced by the *Book of Homilies*, a collection of twelve sermons written by some of the most illustrious of the Reformers, which first appeared in 1547 and guaranteed that what congregations heard was what their bishops wanted them to hear. Later in 1548, all preaching licenses were revoked after word reached the Privy Council that clergy were using the sermon to criticize the reforms being undertaken.[14]

But if these early actions of the regents shook the practice of many English Christians, surely the effect of the appearance of the first liturgy in English in 1549 made even more impact. While the *Book of Common Prayer* directed the celebration of the "Supper of the Lorde and the Holy Communion, Commonly called the Masse" as the chief service of worship on Sundays, Cranmer had effectively removed all references to the sacrificial nature of the service, emphasizing that Christ's own self-offering was "a full, perfect and sufficient sacrifice for the sins of the whole world." The only sacrifice that Christians could, or should, make to God was the "pure, holy and living" offering of "ourselves, our souls and bodies."[15]

In the *Book of Common Prayer,* Cranmer had also adapted and simplified the complicated service books of daily offices into two services, Daily Mattins (Morning Prayer) and Evensong. These services were designed to be read daily not only by clergy but by the Christian community gathered in their parishes, and included lengthy readings from both the Hebrew and Christian scriptures (the entire Bible was designed to be read through in a yearly cycle), with the Psalms assigned to be read through monthly. The 1549 Prayer Book also changed the practice of Confirmation, now no longer considered as one of the sacraments of the Church and administered to very young children but transformed, probably under Lutheran influence, into a rite of maturity required for adolescents who had attained "the age of reason" to be admitted to the status of communicant. The new service required the bishop presiding to examine the candidates for confirmation using the Church's Catechism provided for that purpose, in order to assure that the knowledge and reverence necessary to safeguard the holiness of receiving Communion were clearly demonstrated. Cranmer also added several lengthy warnings to be read to congregations prior to the celebration of the Eucharist, in order to clarify the danger of receiving the sacrament "unworthily," that is, without proper repentance, preparation and understanding of its significance.

But one of the most dramatic changes in the religious life of ordinary Christians was surely the elimination of the practice of confession to a priest. If receiving the sacrament of Communion required attention to the state of one's soul, it also affirmed the belief that life with God depends entirely on God's mercy rather than on the behavior of the Christian. This doctrine of "justification by grace through faith" sets apart all Reformation Christianity from the Roman Catholic practice of confessing one's sins to a priest in order to receive absolution, which, in the Reformers' view, tended to legalism. Public worship included a corporate confession of sinfulness, followed by an affirmation of God's forgiveness; for cases of troubled conscience, and in time of serious illness, Cranmer also allowed for priests to hear private confessions, but the purpose of the absolution was not so much to *forgive* sins as to convey assurance of *God's* forgiveness.

Cranmer followed the work of liturgical revision with a new English Ordinal. In providing for the ordination of bishops, priests and deacons, he declined to accept the pattern of most of the Reformed churches of Europe, which had collapsed the episcopate into the ministry of presbyters on the ground that there is no clear distinction between the two orders in the New Testament. On the other hand, in adapting the old Sarum ordinations rites for the Reformed English Church, Cranmer carefully eliminated whatever he considered to represent later additions, accretions and abuses from Roman Catholic practice, as well as any reference to the Eucharist as a "propitiatory sacrifice."[16]

The 1549 Prayer Book required the use of the surplice by parish clergy at Morning and Evening Prayer; at cathedrals and colleges, academic hoods could also be worn. Bishops were to preside at the Holy Communion in rochet, surplice or alb, cope or "vestment" (presumably a chasuble), and with their pastoral staff at hand. Traditional Catholic gestures such as "kneeling, crossing, holding up of handes, knocking upon the brest" were made optional.[17]

Yet another significant change enacted in 1549 was the somewhat grudging approval by Parliament of the right for the Church's clergy to marry. Clearly Parliament continued to share Henry's distaste for married clergy; the act underlined their belief that it is "better for . . . priests and other ministers in the church . . . to live chaste sole and separate from the company of women and the bond of marriage" and to avoid being troubled with "the charge of household . . . [and] the care and cost of finding wife and children. . . ." However, Parliament affirmed that scripture clearly permitted clerical marriage and recognized that many clergy had already opted against celibacy.[18]

Historians disagree on the impact of such rapid and dramatic changes on the life of ordinary English Christians. Massed gatherings of farmers encamped to protest incursions on common land by great landlords clearly identified their aspirations with the Reformed religion. Diarmaid MacCulloch speaks of the Reformation accomplished under Edward VI as "a movement of hope and moral fervour, capable of generating a mood of intense excitement, so that by 1549 thousands of people all over southeast England gathered in what was called 'the camping time' . . . This was a time of apparently infinite possibilities, when ordinary people believed that they could themselves influence the future."[19]

Meanwhile, on the other side of England, in the counties of the southwest, thousands of people were also encamped, but their purpose was to protest vehemently the changes forced upon them by the new decrees and to demand a return to the Latin mass, clerical celibacy and the rites and rituals they had always known. Eamon Duffy views the process of Reformation as a "stripping of the altars,"[20] and in his study of the people of the Somerset parish of Morebath, he describes the reforms of Edward's time as "a force which threatened the foundation of their world."[21] Detailed analyses of the contemporary sources available confirm the judgment that the changes to everyday religious practice, and the ways in which the Church of England exercised its ministry, had both spiritual and institutional effects. The number of ordinations declined significantly, and the parish guilds withered and died as the Reformation progressed.[22] Richard Rex notes a dimension of irony in the fact that "the late medieval church in England was . . . hugely popular," yet "the parishes of England acquiesced in the Henrician assault with startling promptness and obedience."[23]

There was sufficient opposition to clerical marriage to prompt Parliament to take note of the frequent occasions when people "spake slanderously of such marriages, and accounted the children begotten in them to be bastards," with the effect that "the word of God was not heard with due reverence. . . ." A second Act approved in 1552 declared unconditionally that clergy marriages were valid and "the children begot in them should be inheritable according to law."[24]

One effect of the Reformation was to change the status of laypeople and their relationship to the clergy. MacCulloch calls attention to the fact that the widespread religious discussion initiated by the process of reform "involved laity as well as clergy. The heresy commissions issued by the Edwardian government included beside the predictable leading clergy some prominent informed laity . . . and one of the functions of these commissions was to argue heretics out of their error: the lay people would be part of the discussion."[25]

English Reformed Christianity shared many doctrinal or theological emphases with the reformed churches of Europe, all of them ultimately related to the assertion that the Bible occupies a unique place in establishing Christian faith and practice. From that fundamental assertion comes the profound emphasis on hearing and receiving God's Word through the Bible as the privileged medium by which the promise of salvation reaches sinful human beings. Medieval Catholic Christians were exposed to sermons from a variety of sources, but the purpose of preaching was very different from that which evolved among the Reformers. Catholic sermons were at pains to provide "proper doctrinal information" to counteract ideas that might lead the unsuspecting into heresy or worse.[26] They were also seen as means to awaken sinful Christians to the reality of their sins, and to move them to avail themselves of the sacrament of penance by which God's forgiveness would be assured to them. Reformed preachers, on the other hand, believed that the sermon provides Christians with their primary encounter with God. Christ makes himself present in and through the preached Word, challenging each hearer to come to faith in him. Paul Avis notes that this perspective was also that of the English Reformers: "the primary mark of the Church is the word of God." Avis considers this affirmation to be the heart of the common theology shared by the Reformers, whatever their differences:

> Where the Gospel is, Christ is; and where Christ is, there is the Church. All that is necessary to authentic "Churchhood" is the possession of the gospel . . . If the gospel alone validates the Church, it validates the Church's ministry too. Other considerations may have to be introduced to define a regular ministry and to safeguard good order in the Christian community, but that is a separate question over and above the primary question of the validity of a ministry.

This Reformed understanding of the presence of the Word as definitive for the Church can also be seen in the re-statement of the place of the sacraments for the Christian life. The *Book of Common Prayer*'s frequent references to clergy as "ministers of Word and Sacrament" hint at a perception that sees in the sacrament the "acted-out" Word of God just as the scripture and sermon provide the "preached" or "proclaimed" Word. The immediate relationship between the gospel and the sacraments can be seen in Cranmer's revised Prayer Book of 1552, when the priest who delivers the elements of Communion says, "Take and eat this in remembrance that Christ died for thee, and feed on him in thy heart by faith with thanksgiving."

The revised service of Holy Communion fits well with the alterations to church buildings already mandated by the Reformation: stone altars were required to be removed and replaced with wooden tables for the celebration of the sacrament. "For the use of an altar," Cranmer wrote, "is to make sacrifice upon it: the use of a table is to serve for men (sic) to eat upon."[27]

The second edition of the *Book of Common Prayer*, which appeared in 1552, responded to both Protestant critics in Europe, who considered it only halfway to a genuinely Protestant document, and also to the assertions of Catholic-minded Anglicans who claimed that the 1549 Prayer Book remained a Catholic liturgy. The changes made in the second Book left no doubt as to its Protestant character. References to "The Masse" were now removed (the Eucharistic liturgy is described as "The Order for the Administration of the Lordes Supper, or Holye Communion").[28] Kneeling for reception of the sacrament was still permitted, but a new rubric (the "Black Rubric," so called not because of its content but because unlike other rubrics it was printed in black rather than red) made it clear that the gesture was not meant to imply any presence of Christ in the elements of Communion, a viewpoint reinforced by directing that whatever Eucharistic bread remained after the service was to be taken home for the priest's dinner.

In the first Book, the words to be recited when delivering the elements to the congregation had implied, or at least permitted, belief in the real presence of Christ in the sacrament ("The Body of Our Lord Jesus Christ which was given for thee preserve thy body and soul unto everlasting life"). In the 1552 Book they were replaced with a sentence emphasizing that eating and drinking the bread and wine of the Communion are an act of "remembrance" of Christ's sacrificial death in which believers are fed spiritually.[29]

Similar changes can be found in the revised ordination services that appeared in 1552. All references to vestments associated with the Catholic orders of episcopate and priesthood were eliminated, as was the delivery of the chalice and paten to the priest and the pastoral staff to the bishop. In each case, the newly ordained was now presented with a Bible. In the opinion of Roman Catholic historian Edward Echlin, these changes are "a clear instance of where an omission is more indicative of the rite's intended signification than what was retained."[30]

Yet, in spite of the significant changes in understanding of the ordained ministry represented by the various stages of the English Reformation and what MacCulloch calls "Edward's revolution: the on-going construction of a new church," the Church under Edward retained an ordained ministry structured, under God and the monarch, according to the three ancient orders of bishops, priests and deacons. Cranmer's "Preface" to the Ordinal made it clear that these distinctions dated from the time of the apostles, and the reformed English Church had no intention of abolishing them, in spite of considerable pressure, especially from Europe, to do so. At the same time, it is important to recall that it was the king who appointed bishops, and who continued to have ultimate oversight over the well-being of the Church; far from being the apostolic figures they became in later centuries, English bishops at the time of the Reformation were "governors in a settled society: Justices of the Peace, members of the upper house of Parliament—in other words, great magnates of the realm."[31]

The last significant act of Reformation came towards the end of Edward's short life, in 1553, with the publication of the "Forty-Two Articles of Religion." The Articles served as a summary of the Reformed faith of the Church of England as Cranmer and his reforming colleagues understood it. As a document, its purpose was not unlike the "Confessions" which played such an important part in the definitions (and conflicts) among Protestants on the European continent; its difference rested in the fact that the Articles were binding only on clergy, not the laity.

The "Forty-Two Articles" made explicit as matters of faith a number of the decisions taken over the years by the king, Parliament, the Church Convocation and, of course, Cranmer and the other clerical leaders who were an integral part of those decisions. They were also at pains to offer a justification for many of the actions that shaped the Reformation, and to explain why they considered some doctrines held by Christians of other churches to be wrong or at least irrelevant to the Church of England.

One of the most important of the Articles in laying down the *principles* by which the Church altered its worship, its polity and its practice of ministry is to be found in Article 34 of the Thirty-nine Articles which were the later heirs of the original forty-two.

> XXXIV. Of the Traditions of the Church. It is not necessary that the Traditions and Ceremonies be in all places one, or utterly like; for at all times they have been divers, and may be changed according to the diversity of countries, times, and men's manners, so that nothing be ordained against God's Word. Whosoever, through his private judgment, willingly and purposely, doth openly break the Traditions and Ceremonies of the Church, which be not repugnant to the Word of God, and be ordained and approved by common authority, ought to be rebuked openly, (that others may fear to do the like,) as he that offendeth against the common order of the Church, and hurteth the authority of the Magistrate, and woundeth the consciences of the weaker brethren. Every particular or national Church hath authority to ordain, change, and abolish. Ceremonies or Rites of the Church ordained by man's authority, so that all things be done to edifying.[32]

The Article is of special significance because it not only articulates a rationale for the appropriateness of the Church's structuring of its own practice of the faith and the criterion for measuring the correctness of the steps it might take; it also insists on a principle of liturgical diversity (mirrored, in most Anglican minds of the day, by a diversity of ministry and structure) that assumes that other national churches will reach different decisions.

The Article is also significant because it takes an essentially *functional* rather than *theological* approach to defining the correctness of a church's internal life. It opts for this position on the basis of its observation that in fact, Christians have *always* exhibited differences in their traditions and ceremonies. The criterion for evaluating called-for changes is not some absolute Catholic or Protestant principle, such as papal authority or scriptural mandate; rather, the question to be asked is whether the practices reflect countries, times and customs—we might say the *context*—and at the same time whether they contribute to "edifying," or building up the faith and life of the community and its people. In keeping with the Biblical emphasis of the Reformers, the only guideline demanded is that the traditions and ceremonies not contradict the scriptures.

So basic is this principle to their understanding of the process of Reformation that gave birth to the reformed Church of England that the authors of the Article point out that, under the rubric of strengthening the community of faith, all humanly conceived aspects of the Church's life may be changed or abolished by the Church. At the same time, the Article notes that individual Christians whose own opinions lead them to ignore or willingly break the legally accepted norms established by the Church in such a way as to lead others to do the same are to be publicly reprimanded for offending against the Church's good order, undermining the authority of the civil law that upholds the Church's ways, and wounding the conscience of weaker members.

Against the fractious nature of English society as Edward's health failed, Article 34 was a stern warning of the importance of a clear national consensus on the practice of religion if peace was to prevail, as well as a clear statement of the principles on which the Reformation had been accomplished. Future generations of Anglicans have looked back to it as something of an icon of a style of Christian faith and practice that assumes both diversity among Christians and the ways in which that diversity reflects the distinct contexts in which Christians live out their lives. But the "Forty-Two Articles of Religion" were to have a limited lifespan as a confessional statement of the Church's faith, for on July 6, 1553, Edward VI died.

MARY: REFORMATION UNDONE

Although Henry had named his three children—Edward, Mary and Elizabeth—as his heirs, and Parliament had approved the order of succession, he had of course hoped that his son would continue the Tudor dynasty and his two daughters would be passed over. Edward's death at the age of fifteen, and his illegal designation of his young Protestant cousin, Lady Jane

Grey, as his successor, created a brief but ugly interlude in what would have in any case been a tumultuous succession. Jane herself opposed the plan that would have made her queen, and wore the crown in misery for only nine days before Mary's arrival in London, backed by an army intent on placing her on the throne. Given the passions and the political realities of the day, Jane's execution at the Tower was inevitable.

Mary's reign, shorter than her brother's, was marked primarily by her eager attempts to restore the Church of England to papal allegiance. Even she realized the impossibility of restoring the religious houses, long since dissolved and their wealth dispersed; but she was determined to undo the rest of the reforms undertaken by Henry and Edward. By early 1554, the Latin Roman Catholic liturgy had become the proscribed usage of the Church of England. Clergy who had married were forced to leave their parishes, and to choose between their ministry and their family; those who renounced their marriage and did public penance were allowed to take other congregations. Mary repudiated the Royal Supremacy, and the papal legate Cardinal Pole pronounced absolution over a kneeling monarch and Parliament. In parishes throughout England, congregational life began taking its traditional form and "the laudable and honest ceremonies which were wont to be used, frequented and observed in the Church" were now commanded to be restored. By Easter, 1554, at Morebath, Somerset,

> the high altar was rebuilt and the communion table banished. The Palm Sunday "general dirige of this churche" had once more been sung for the parish dead, and for the Holy Week celebrations the parish unearthed the Easter Sepulchre, concealed during the Edwardine destructions. . . . Another parishioner, Richard Timewell, presented a box to keep the Blessed Sacrament in, and the parish paid 4d for wire and cord to hang the canopy over it.[33]

Parish guilds were reorganized, the financial footing of the congregation was regained and gifts were made for redecorating of the church in accordance with Roman Catholic usage; the English Bible and Erasmus' *Paraphrases*, required by the Reforms, were now sent off to diocesan authorities and replaced by (costly) Latin missals. Restoring parish churches to meet Mary's injunctions proved as expensive as the alterations mandated by the Reformers a few years before, but fortunately many of the items that had been banished from churches had been guarded in secure hiding places and were now restored to use.[34]

Just as the reforms of the previous twenty-plus years had been imposed from above, so the restoration of Roman Catholic Christianity under Mary was accomplished by royal fiat. In neither process were ordinary Christians, whether clergy or laypeople, consulted about their preferences. It is certain that throughout the process of reformation, there were Christians at every level of society who supported the changes, while others passionately opposed them. Failure to obey the letter and spirit of the royal decrees and the Acts of Parliament that enforced them was a treasonable offense. While the majority of English Christians acquiesced in decisions over which they considered themselves to have no options and often declined to make their personal feelings known, on both sides there were noteworthy gestures of spiritual disobedience by individuals who considered it impossible to accept the violation of their conscience imposed by the religious and political authorities.

Once it became clear that Mary intended to suppress the Reformation, four bishops, seventy-four clergy and ninety-nine divinity students fled to Protestant countries in Europe, where they were welcomed by the Reformed churches as co-workers and in many cases exercised a pastoral ministry, especially among English-speaking congregations.[35] Shortly after coming to power, Mary ordered the arrest of three of the bishops who had been the most outspoken defenders of the Reformation: Hugh Latimer, bishop under Henry VIII whose evangelical sympathies had led him to resign his see when Henry imposed the Six Articles; Nicholas Ridley, Bishop of Rochester; and the Archbishop of Canterbury, Thomas Cranmer. Imprisoned in 1553, the three participated in a disputation with a group of Roman Catholic theologians held in Oxford in 1555. Shortly thereafter, Ridley and Latimer were condemned to death, and were executed on October 16, 1555. Cranmer struggled hard with the demands of his faith in the light of Mary's accession to the throne, and his vacillations prolonged his life. Believing as he did in the Royal Supremacy, he wrestled with the possibility that his Christian duty was to offer her unquestioning obedience even though he strenuously disagreed with the direction she was leading the Church. He attempted to recant his participation in the Reformation, but Mary mistrusted him, and at last formally relieved him of his title as Archbishop of Canterbury. At the time of his execution on March 21, 1556, he renounced his recantation and declared himself loyal to the principles of the Reformation.

The three martyred bishops were among a total of 277 persons executed under Mary's reign for failing to be reconciled to the Roman Catholic Church. Many English Christians were exhausted by nearly thirty years of often bloody religious conflict and troubled by the spectacle of bishops and other Christians burned at the stake. Mary's popularity began to evaporate, not only because of the fierceness of her struggle against Reformed Christianity but because she insisted on contracting a highly unpopular marriage with Philip, heir to the Spanish throne. By the time of her death in 1558, the population was eager to welcome her half-sister Elizabeth, daughter of Anne Boleyn, as queen of England.

NOTES

1. Edward P. Echlin, *The Story of Anglican Ministry* (Slough: St. Paul Publications, 1975), 8.
2. Eamon Duffy, *The Voices of Morebath: Reformation and Rebellion in an English Village* (New Haven: Yale University Press, 2001), 76.
3. Clive Burgess, "London Parishioners in Times of Change: St. Andrew Hubbard, Eastcheap, c. 1450 – 1570," *Journal of Ecclesiastical History* 53 (January 2002), 47–51.
4. Diarmaid MacCulloch, *All Things New: The Reformation and its Legacy* (Oxford: Oxford University Press, 2016), 102.
5. Paul Avis, *The Church in the Theology of the Reformers* (London: Marshall and Scott, 1981), 140–141.
6. Robert Whiting, "Local Responses to the Henrician Reformation," in D. MacCullough, ed., *The Reign of Henry VIII: Politics, Policy and Piety* (New York: MacMillan and Co., 1995), 217–219.
7. Thomas Cranmer, "De Ordine, Injunctions given by the most Excellent Prince, Edward the Sixth . . . in earth under Christ of the Church of England and of Ireland the Supreme Head . . .," in J. E. Cox, ed., *Miscellaneous Writings and Letters of Thomas Cranmer* (Cambridge: Cambridge University Press, 1846), 484.
8. Echlin, *The Story of Anglican Ministry*, 59–60.
9. Richard Rex, *Henry VIII and the English Reformation* (New York: St. Martin's Press, 1993), 90.
10. MacCulloch, "Henry VIII and the Reform of the Church," *The Reign of Henry VIII*, 177.
11. MacCulloch, "Henry VIII," 179.
12. Thomas Cranmer, "Injunctions given by the most Excellent Prince Edward the Sixth . . . in earth under Christ of the Church of England and Ireland the Supreme Head . . . ," in Cox. ed., *Miscellaneous Writings and Letters of Thomas Cranmer*, 498–503.
13. Thomas Cranmer, "ARTICLES to be inquired of in the visitations to be had within the Diocese of Canterbury . . . ," 1548. Quoted in Cox, ed., *Miscellaneous Writings*, 155.
14. Thomas Cranmer, "Letters Missive from the Council to the Bishops of the Realm Concerning the Communion to be ministered in both Kinds," in Cox, ed., *Miscellaneous Writings*, 511.
15. *The First and Second Prayer Books of Edward the Sixth* (London: J. M. Dent and Sons, 1957), 212.
16. Echlin, *The Story of Anglican Ministry*, 1–3.
17. *First and Second Prayer Books*, 288–289.
18. Richard M. Spielmann, "The Beginnings of Clerical Marriage in the English Reformation: The Reigns of Edward and Mary," *Anglican and Episcopal History* LVI (September 1987), 252.
19. Diarmaid MacCulloch, *Tudor Church Militant: Edward VI and the Protestant Reformation* (London: Allen Lane, 1999), 126.

20. Eamon Duffy, *The Stripping of the Altars: Traditional Religion in England, 1400–1580* (New Haven: Yale University Press, 2005)

21. Duffy, *The Voices of Morebath*, 141.

22. Whiting, "Local Responses," in MacCulloch, ed, *The Reign of Henry VIII*, 209–211.

23. Rex, *Henry VIII*, 101–102.

24. Rex, *Henry VIII*, 253.

25. MacCulloch, *Tudor Church Militant*, 132.

26. Avis, *The Church in the Theology of the Reformers*, 66.

27. Cranmer, "Reasons why the Lord's Board should be rather after the form of a Table . . . than of an altar," in Cox, ed., *Miscellaneous Writings*, 524–525.

28. *First and Second Prayer Books of Edward the Sixth*, 377.

29. MacCulloch, *Tudor Church Militant*, 192.

30. Echlin, *The Story of Anglican Ministry*, 107–108.

31. MacCulloch, *Tudor Church Militant*, 183.

32. *The Book of Common Prayer* (Oxford: Oxford University Press, undated), 708.

33. Duffy, *The Voices of Morebath*, 159–160.

34. Duffy, *Voices*, 159–162.

35. Hugh Ross Williamson, *The Beginning of the English Reformation* (New York: Sheed and Ward, 1957), 79. Williamson points out that fifteen of these exiles would become archbishops and bishops under Elizabeth.

Chapter Two

Settlement

Ministry in the Reign of Elizabeth

Elizabeth's long reign of forty-three years marks the period of the consolidation of Reformed English Christianity and the establishment of its ministry in a form recognizable to most Anglicans today. But it would have been difficult to imagine that outcome when she ascended the throne in 1558, inheriting as she did a country shaken by inter-religious conflict and violence, political intrigue, threats from abroad, and uncertainty, even doubt, about her ability to govern a people threatening to spiral out of control. Circumstances and history, of course, revealed that she was eminently capable of rising to the challenge and restoring order if not unanimity to her troubled realm.

Like all her Tudor relatives, Elizabeth took for granted that social order depended upon religious unity, and she realized from the beginning of her reign that if a civil war was to be avoided, the church must provide a common frame of reference for national identity. To that end, she and Parliament set about establishing guidelines that would provide sufficient breadth to make it possible for Christians of varying opinions to participate in the national Church.

SETTLEMENT: FOUNDATIONS

The three foundations on which this "Elizabethan Settlement" rested were the Act of Supremacy and the Act of Uniformity, approved by Parliament in 1559, and the Thirty-Nine Articles of Religion, adopted by the Convocations of the Church's two provinces, Canterbury and York, in 1563.

The Act of Supremacy decreed that anyone holding public office was required to affirm the Queen as "Supreme Governor," a title which applied not only to her temporal power but her spiritual and ecclesiastical authority. The Act of Uniformity re-imposed the *Book of Common Prayer* as the official liturgy of the Church of England and required every male subject to attend church weekly under pain of a fine of twelve pence. The Thirty-Nine Articles represented a revision of the Forty-Two Articles from Edward's reign; all clergy were required to attest that they accepted them as an accurate statement of Christian doctrine. The Settlement avoided the extreme Protestant position represented by the 1552 Prayer Book by making several small but significant changes at Elizabeth's insistence.[1] The so-called "Black Rubric," which formally denied any presence of Christ in the sacramental bread and wine of the Eucharist, was omitted, and the words used to deliver the elements of Communion from the 1549 and 1552 Prayer Books were combined, in effect making room for two widely divergent understandings of the Eucharist. The rubric from the 1549 Prayer Book proscribing the vestments to be worn by the clergy was restored. Coupled with Elizabeth's willingness to abandon Henry and Edward's claim to be "supreme head on earth of the Church of England" in favor of the more modest title of "supreme governor," these changes reflected the hope that much of the opposition from Catholic sympathizers to a reformed Church would be weakened. As the philosopher Francis Bacon observed, it was not Elizabeth's desire to "make windows into men's souls";[2] what concerned her was acceptance of the political and religious facts of life that would make it possible or England to enjoy peace. Just six years after Queen Mary had mandated the restoration of altars and images, the Injunctions imposing the newly revised Book of Common Prayer now required their destruction. Parishes all over England found themselves scrambling to purchase the new Prayer Book, the English Bible, Litany and Psalter, and a copy of Erasmus' *Paraphrases* which were once again ordered to be in the possession of each church.[3]

1563 also marked the re-publication of the *Book of Homilies*, a collection of sermons which originally appeared in 1547 but which was now augmented by the addition of six new sermons. Like its predecessor, Elizabeth's *Book of Homilies* was required to be used in every parish church in England. The Homilies immediately became an important instrument for re-educating people after the tumult of the previous reigns; they articulated the Church's "official" teaching on a number of practical aspects if Christian life, including prayer, the sacraments, and the appropriate use of scripture. The Homilies were another effort by the Queen and her appointed leaders to quiet dissension and lessen the potential for critical pulpit attacks by clergy dissatisfied with aspects of the Settlement. Commenting on the effect of the Homilies, Brian Hartley writes that they

> provided a framework, a rhetoric and a pattern that was meant to lead to both faithful hearing and faithful living. In the end, it contributed as well a key

rhetorical tool for the stabilization of the Elizabethan regime—but, perhaps even more importantly, for the reordering of a church, a people and a nation.[4]

But in fact, the goals of the Elizabethan Settlement were only partially realized. While it probably prevented (or at least postponed) open and violent civil strife, it did not resolve the enormous differences of religious opinion on which English Christians were divided. The end of Mary's reign meant that large numbers of exiled clergy, who had been welcomed by European churches dominated by the ideas of John Calvin, now returned home as convinced "Puritans," convinced that the English Reformation remained unfinished and the work of 'purifying' the Church of England must continue. Theirs was a perspective that Elizabeth heartily opposed.

SETTLEMENT: COMMON GROUND

In spite of their differences, at least among the educated classes, supporters and opponents of the Elizabethan Settlement shared much in common: belief in the authority of scriptures as a guide to Christian living; confidence in God's providence and intervention in everyday experience; a sense of the well-ordered society in which each person's faithfulness involved acceptance of their state in life, however exalted or humble it might be; the habit of regular attendance at worship; reading the Bible and devotional books; attention to the needs of the poor, the sick and the old.[5] The Christian family was considered to be the appropriate setting for the practice of faith, mirroring as it did the image of the "God-fearing Englishman and the pious matron."[6] In his magisterial study of the English family, Lawrence Stone describes this "new emphasis on the home and on domestic virtues" as "perhaps the most far-reaching consequence of the Reformation in England. The household," he declares,

> was the inheritor of many of the responsibilities of the parish and the Church; the family head was inheritor of much of the authority and many powers of the priest. . . . [P]ublic ceremonies were at least partially replaced or reinforced by family prayers. These took place in the home, a prominent feature of which was now the Holy Bible on a lectern in the hall, or taken from a bible-box. It was a book which also, significantly enough, often served at all levels of society to record the family genealogy. Thus the Word of God was to some degree removed from the parish church and transferred to the private home: the Holy Spirit was partly domesticated.[7]

Indeed, one of the sermons added in Elizabeth's time to the *Book of Homilies* demonstrated clearly the changed attitude of the Church of England towards the relative value of marriage and celibacy. While the Homilies of 1547 encouraged any who "feel in themselves a sufficiency and ability . . . to lead a sole and continent life, let them praise God for his gift," the 1563 "Homily of the State of Matrimony" provided "a warm advocacy of 'the friendly fellowship' that is marriage." It also affirmed a sternly patriarchal model of the family, in which the husband, as head of the household, is the voice of reason and authority in governing his wife, "a weak creature, not endowed with like strength and constancy of mind, therefore—sooner disquieted . . . more prone to all weak affections and dispositions of mind . . . and more vain in the phantasies and opinions."[8]

It was this model of marriage that was commended not only to English congregations but also the burgeoning number of clergy homes as priests began to marry in large numbers. Elizabeth shared the disdain of both her father and her sister Mary towards the idea of a married clergy, and was known to be rude and offensive both to the unwary clergy wives who crossed her path and to those members of the clergy who exercised their right to marry, The historian Anne Barstow comments that

> it is not surprising that the record gives no sixteenth century evidence of "leadership" among clergy wives. . . . Given the official and popular hatred unleashed in the 1540s and 1550s, the first clerical wives did well to remain alive, to remain married, and to found families. Even after the legal restrictions against them were lifted, they still faced several generations of suspicion and hostility from many sides.[9]

The assumptions shared alike by Puritans and supporters of Elizabeth's Settlement called for qualified and educated clergy to provide pastoral care and scriptural teaching. Rosemary O'Day's study of the emergence of a professional clergy under Elizabeth and her immediate successors confirms an "acute shortage of clergy in the Reformation period," which "seriously undermined the prospects of pastoral care and spiritual education of the laity which both the lay and the clerical leaders of Protestantism envisaged as the ideal."[10] O'Day observes that "late sixteenth-century and early seventeenth-century Europe in general seems to have been obsessed with the ideal of a resident, parochial clergy." She considers that one of the results of this development was a shift in the clergy's self-understanding of their role from service to the state to the pastoral care of their congregation.[11]

The relationship with their clergy to which English laypeople now became accustomed could hardly have been more different than that which they had experienced prior to the Reformation, when compulsory confession had been the primary context for encounters with the clergy. As more and more priests exercised their privilege of marrying, their congregations came to understand that their guidance in family matters was now based on the clergy's own experience of married life. Clerical families were expected to be a model for the congregation, demonstrating the attention to family prayer, Bible reading, and study that formed the heart of household piety in Elizabeth's time. The priest was assumed to exercise a role in the parish not unlike the one he held in his own household. He was charged with seeing that children were taught the rudiments of Christian faith and, once having reached the "years of discretion, presented to the bishop for confirmation. He was responsible for disciplining the wayward, especially adulterers and women who had given birth to children out of wedlock." And it was his presence that brought comfort in time of illness, as he reminded the sick that their suffering could be a trial of their faith or a correction for their sins: "Repentance, patience, trust in God's mercy, gratitude for his fatherly visitation, and complete submission to [God's] will, would help the invalid forward to everlasting life." Indeed, the Reformed cleric was expected to remind the sick or dying that there is "no greater comfort . . . than to suffer as Christ had suffered."[12]

But the ordained leadership of the Church of England had been battered by the persecutions and conflicts of Queen Mary's reign. When Matthew Parker, Elizabeth's appointee as Archbishop of Canterbury, assumed his position, more than half the parishes in the diocese of Canterbury had no incumbent clergy. Among those still occupying posts in the diocese, he found not only sympathizers with both Roman Catholicism and more radical Reform; he also encountered priests who claimed occult powers, and others who were perceived as "drunkards, blasphemers, sexual offenders, scolds, tale-bearers, and 'singers of songs that [were] vile or unclean.' The youth had to be educated, charity and wills proved. . . . [T]he quality of the clergy had to be raised."[13] Alarmed by the threat posed by incompetent or dissident clergy who might influence opposition to her Settlement, Elizabeth almost immediately revoked almost all preaching licenses.[14]

The lack of educated clergy was heightened by the gross inequality of clerical incomes. Late in Elizabeth's reign, only six hundred of the more than nine thousand clerical livings provided sufficient income to support a "learned minister"; some clergy depended on their private incomes or support from a wealthy patron, while others supplemented their income as teachers, preachers, merchants or craftsmen.[15]

Archbishop Parker preferred to avoid ordaining those of "base occupation or non-clerical background," but he performed the astonishing number of 233 ordinations in his first eight months, mostly with minimal examination of the candidates' academic preparation.[16] In his first decade, only one of the 282 persons ordained in the diocese of Chester was a university graduate.[17]

Faced with the enormous need for qualified ministers, Parker proposed a plan for providing alternative pastoral care until more clergy could be recruited and trained.

> The scheme involved the employment of readers or lectors, usually laymen, empowered to read the prayerbook services, but not to administer the sacraments. . . . Parker fully intended the readers to have some status, envisaging something akin to an ordination ceremony. He saw the "order" of lectors as more than a temporary expedient: they would be used not only in parishes devoid of clergy, but as assistants to incumbents and to curates. . . . Seventy-one lectors served in Canterbury diocese alone between December 1550 and 1662. . . . After this, the appointment of lectors was left to the discretion of individual bishops and they were employed on an ad hoc basis, never again forming part of a coherent scheme.[18]

O'Day notes that Parker's experiment represented the first time that "laymen were admitted, indeed invited, to an active role in the ministry."[19]

It was not, however, the only ecclesiastical role played by the laity during Elizabeth's reign. Royal Commissions charged with rooting out and eliminating more traditional religious habits were staffed with "religiously trustworthy and influential local laymen as well as clergy," though that practice declined in the latter decades of her reign.[20] Furthermore, many of the beneficed "livings" which bestowed the right to exercise clerical ministry in a particular parish remained in the hands of prominent laypeople or institutions such as colleges, and the power of bishops to intervene in the placement of clergy was therefore often minimal.[21]

In spite of the multiple developments in the relationship between clergy and congregations, neither the Reformation nor the Elizabethan Settlement altered the ancient process by which clergy were appointed to their duties. Long before Henry's break with Rome, the Church of England had developed the principle of *advowson*, or right of nomination to the rectorship of a parish. Originally derived from the founding or financial support of local congregations, it evolved into a highly diverse network of lay, clerical and institutional patronage which conferred the privilege of naming local clergy. Advowsons held by monasteries before their dissolution were distributed to royal favorites or courtiers. Holders of an advowson presented their candidate to the bishop for *collation*, the granting of spiritual responsibility for the parish (or *living*) and induction, by which the priest received the temporal rights to which he was entitled, including both the salary and life tenure rights in all the parish properties.

These two actions, collation and induction, were performed by the bishop of the diocese in which the parish church was located, in exercise of his function as the Ordinary, a title applied to the bishop when exercising various extra-ecclesiastical duties, including inducting clerics into the rectorship of parishes. A bishop could deputize another person to serve as the Ordinary in his diocese. This deputization was quite common in Plantagenet and Tudor times as bishops were frequently called to court to take up positions in the royal household or sent on diplomatic missions abroad.[22]

O'Day's careful study of the conditions of the clergy in Elizabeth's time adds important information to our understanding of how the Tudor church practiced its ministry in the later years of Elizabeth's reign. The range of income provided by livings throughout the Church of England was extreme. While a few prominent members of the clergy held multiple benefices, spent much of their time in London and hired "curates" to care for the congregations for which they were nominally responsible, most clergy lived in far different circumstances. Rural clergy depended on the property attached to the living (the "glebe") for both housing and income, which was augmented by stipulated percentages of the produce of other farms in the neighborhood, gathered yearly into "tithe barns" for the support of the clergy. Many clergy raised cattle, while others owned pigs, poultry, horses and oxen; glebes also produced wheat and hay, as well as flax and peas in some areas. Clerical rights to tithes of other farmers' produce inevitably created hostility among some parishioners, particularly when drought or other natural disasters reduced production; to many, it seemed that they were providing their parish clergy with unearned income, while the priest argued that tithes represented both obedience to the scriptural injunction to "render to God what belongs to God" and payment for the essential ministries which only clergy could provide.[23]

O'Day considers that whatever the social background of the clergy (and some belonged to the minor gentry while others were farmers), their growing common professional interests tended to make them a clearly defined social group. Clergy were set apart from the laity they served by the nature of their income, by their literacy and their familiarity with books and intellectual pursuits, and even by the presence of a "study" in the rectory. The continued use of clerical vestments and dress emphasized the "separateness" of the clergy as a special order of society.[24] The growing assumption by the clergy of a professional identity and status within English society must be considered in the light of the multiplicity of duties they undertook and the roles they occupied. The historian David Cressy points out that "the relationship of clergy and laity in post-Reformation England was complicated by social, cultural, religious and financial transactions."[25]

Whatever their position on the great conflicts of the day, the clergy shared common professional interests, among them the belief that ordination required learning in order to carry out the preaching and teaching they took so seriously. Two Cambridge colleges were founded during this period specifically to provide academic training for Puritan-minded clergy. Puritans also concurred in the appropriateness of the tithe, considering it to be justified by scripture.[26]

Whether they approved of them or not, the rhythms of the Prayer Book shaped the life of English Christians. Church attendance was mandatory, and all the great moments of life—childbirth, baptism, confirmation, marriage, illness, death itself—were marked by the ministrations of the local parish clergy. "For parishioners at home in their local community," Cressy observed, "their minister could appear as an overweening or incomprehensible outsider. In a world of tradesmen, artisans and agriculturalists, academic clerics (no matter what their taste in theology) were inevitably alien."[27] No doubt the fact that congregations had no role in the selection of their clergy also contributed to the distance between priest and people.

Besides differences of class, status, and the sometimes-tense issue of tithes, the relationship between clergy and parishioners was further complicated by the fact that clergy often occupied the position of local magistrate in a court system that proscribed penalties for infractions of moral norms and acts of blasphemy—including verbal attacks on the clergy. Lawrence Stone points out "the luxuriant growth of neighbourly activity and scrutiny" as a fact of life for Elizabethan Anglicans. And, he notes,

> during the late sixteenth and early seventeenth centuries, this intrusive scrutiny actually intensified due to the rise of ethical Puritanism and the increased activity of the Church courts in controlling personal morality. Everyone gossiped freely about the most intimate details of domestic relations, and did not hesitate to denounce violations of community norms to an archdeacon's visitation enquiry, so that people were constantly testifying in court about the alleged moral peccadilloes of their neighbours.[28]

Indeed, so pervasive was the role of the clergy and the church courts in enforcing moral strictures that Stone believes that "the family life of the poor was more heavily regulated by public pressures between 1580 and 1660 than at any time before or since."[29]

One of the most severe aspects of the community discipline enforced by the Church during Elizabeth's reign was the revival of public penance for behavior judged to be sinful. This custom, which dated back to the late thirteenth century, but had fallen into disuse by the time of Henry VIII, reappeared in a number of places throughout England in the period immediately following Elizabeth's accession.[30] In Nottingham, one man who was judged to be guilty of "sexual incontinence and fornication" was required to stand in the market place "bareheaded, bare legged, and bare footed in his shirt onlye," with a sheet tied around his middle and a white rod in his hand. In the first thirty years of Elizabeth's reign, seventy-six people were thus humiliated for sexual misconduct in the Archdeaconry of Essex alone. In such cases, the clergy were often the accusers and in some places, magistrates allowed the clergy to impose public penance on misbehaving parishioners.[31]

SETTLEMENT: DISSENT

Relations between clergy and laity were complicated still more when rectors or vicars and congregations stood on opposite sides of the issues that divided English Christians throughout Elizabeth's reign and beyond. Those disagreements often escalated to verbal and even physical abuse. Cressy documents a number of such attacks during Elizabeth's long reign. In 1592, after calling his parish priest "a prattling fool," a layman in Sandon, Essex, then threw kneeling cushions at the parish sexton—presumably a Puritan expression of disagreement with the prescribed custom of kneeling in English churches—"and thereby brake his head."[32] On the other hand, there are also frequent examples of congregations bringing charges against their more Puritan-minded clergy, especially when they refused to make the sign of the cross in baptism as prescribed by the Prayer Book, made unauthorized alterations to the Prayer Book services, refused to wear the surplice, denied Communion to parishioners who insisted on kneeling, or refused to administer Communion or baptism in homes to those who were seriously ill.[33]

Not all the growing differences between supporters and opponents of Elizabeth's Settlement affected the practice of ministry so dramatically; other, less violent expressions of dissent were also in evidence. Unhappy that the Church of England provided only monthly or quarterly sermons, many congregations began hiring "parish lecturers" in an effort to increase the opportunity to hear preaching. (Not all lecturers were Puritans, but the majority were chosen to counteract the preaching and teaching of parish clergy who disapproved of the pressure for more radical reform and who believed that preaching should not be separated from the celebration of the Eucharist.) Many opponents of the parish lectureships were concerned that members of the congregation who funded the lecturers had more power over them than the parish clergy. O'Day considers that through the movement to establish lectureships, "Puritan laity were trying to subvert the Elizabethan Settlement."[34]

Another way in which Puritans sought to shape the practice of ministry in the Church of England was through informal gatherings known as "prophesyings," in which several clergy would meet together to preach to each other and to whoever chose to join them. The initiative for these events was invariably local, and they often occurred without the approval of the bishop. Thomas Bentham, Bishop of Litchfield and Coventry, considered the movement a positive development for both clergy, whose preaching skills and knowledge of the Christian faith could only be strengthened by the exercise, and also for laypeople, for whom it provided a form of catechetical education.[35] The Queen, however, viewed the prophesyings with alarm, seeing in them a possible setting for plotting conspiracies and agitation for further reform. She ordered Edmund Grindal, who had succeeded Matthew Parker as Archbishop of Canterbury in 1576, to suppress them. Grindal was himself an ardent Reformer who had fled England during Mary's reign. As Archbishop of York, he had been a firm enforcer of the Act of Uniformity against its opponents (mostly Roman Catholics in the north of England). But the Archbishop showed himself much less willing to take action against the Puritan prophesyings, and voiced his disagreement with the Queen. As a result, he was removed from his jurisdiction and placed under a form of house arrest. He later apologized to the Queen and was allowed to resume his ecclesiastical duties but died in 1583.

The Queen's conflict with Archbishop Grindal was perhaps the most serious example of the evolving relationship between the monarchy and the bishops of the time. In fact, in the course of her long reign both the bishops' way of life and their ministry changed considerably. The expropriation of land previously attached to the bishops' sees, which began under Henry, reduced the bishops' income significantly, while the cost of living had risen substantially. During Elizabeth's reign, some sixty-seven episcopal palaces were granted or leased away. One study of the period observed that "as a consequence, the households of the Elizabethan bishops were smaller than those of their medieval counterparts, their hospitality more restrained, and their funerals generally less lavish. They tended, therefore, to live and die in the style of a modest nobleman or gentleman, rather than that of a great lord or prince." The same study emphasizes the change in their function within the Church. No longer chosen to occupy high state offices, their governmental duties apart from membership in the House of Lords were more likely exercised on the local level in roles such as justices of the peace. On the other hand, their pastoral duties received much more attention than those of their predecessors, for they were now "required to be theologians and biblical scholars rather than administrators or lawyers."[36]

In Elizabeth's time, the Royal Supremacy was generally accepted across the theological spectrum of theological opinion and ministerial practice. In 1570, the Puritan Edward Dering, preaching before the Queen, proclaimed that the monarch's "greatest duty [is] to be careful for religion, to maintain the gospel, to teach the people knowledge and build his whole government with faithfulness."[37] Bishop John Jewel, a staunch supporter of the ministry of bishops, concurred, calling monarchs "nursing fathers for the church . . . ; neither for any greater cause hath God willed governments to exist, than that there might be always some to maintain and preserve religion and piety."[38] But the Puritan clergy, many of whom had been willing to accept the episcopate as a temporary aspect of the Settlement that restored Reformed Christianity to England, now grew increasingly restive as the bishops followed Elizabeth's directives in attempting to enforce ministerial discipline to which they were opposed, such as the clergy's use of the surplice in worship and strict adherence to the Prayer Book liturgies. The last decades of her reign were marked by increasing conflict between two diverging attitudes towards the ministry of the Church: the Puritans, who wished for a Church of England without bishops and more closely conformed to the Presbyterian model of the European Reformed churches, and those supporters of the uniquely English model of Reformation Christianity, who continued to value the liturgy of the *Book of Common Prayer* and to argue for the episcopate as apostolic in origin. For some Puritan clergy, many ordinary members of the Church seemed to be functionally atheists due to their passive obedience to authority and acceptance of familiar traditions that harked back to Rome and, in their opinion, had no place in a godly reformed Church of England.[39]

SETTLEMENT: ADVOCATES

The growing conflict in the Church of England had one major and perhaps unforeseen consequence. The early stages of the controversies had been spelled out primarily in sermons and pamphlets; now, several accomplished theological scholars undertook much more detailed apologetic writing on behalf of the English Church as it had been established under Elizabeth. The first of these was John Jewel, Elizabeth's Bishop of Salisbury, whose *Apology, or Answer, in Defense of the Church of England* appeared in English in 1567.

Jewel sought to chart a course for Anglicanism as a "middle way" (*via media*) between the two poles of Christian faith that challenged English Christians, the Roman Catholic and Reformed/Presbyterian traditions. Jewel argued that the rapid spread of Reformed Christianity could be interpreted as such clear evidence of God's support for the reformation that even popes would realize that God "doth from heaven laugh at their enterprise."[40]

Jewel's commendation of the Church of England was pragmatic as well as theological: "Go, I pray you, into those places where at this present, through God's goodness, the gospel is taught. Where is there more majesty? Where is there less arrogancy or tyranny? Where is the prince more honoured? Where is the people less unruly? Where hath there at any time the commonwealth or the church been more quiet?" Against the Puritans who would eliminate the office of bishop, Jewel insisted that "there be divers degrees of ministers in the church, whereof some be deacons, some priests, some bishops; to whom is committed the office to instruct the people, and the whole charge and setting forth of religion." The power given to them "to bind, to loose, to open, to shut" is found in their authority to declare God's forgiveness to the penitent and reconciliation for those who have "banished and made themselves strangers from the common fellowship and from the body of Christ." In Jewel's view, this authority did not imply that priests should hear private confessions, but that they should "teach, they should publish abroad the gospel."[41]

H. F. Woodhouse sees Jewel's understanding of the ministry of the clergy as both *essential* and *representative*: "In the Word and Sacraments the living reigning Christ is present and the ministry of both represents him."[42] Jewel himself wrote that the purpose of the ordained ministry is "to preach the Word, administer the sacraments, and to feed the flock . . . Through the [ordained] ministry God gathers to himself an acceptable people, and makes them obedient to the gospel of Christ. . . . The principal part of the ministerial office is to preach repentance."[43]

The theologian considered as Jewel's most able successor and the primary advocate of the Anglicanism achieved in the Elizabethan Settlement was Richard Hooker. Indeed, many consider him to be the most outstanding theologian the Anglican Communion has ever produced. Hooker wrote towards the end of Elizabeth's reign and the latter volumes of his multi-volume treatise on Anglicanism were published long after her death and his own. The title of Hooker's work could not be more apt: *Of the Laws of Ecclesiastical Policy* proposes that we understand our faith through the ways in which the Christian community is organized in accordance with God's laws.

Hooker is perhaps best remembered for his reliance on the triad of scripture, tradition and reason. Like all the Reformers, he considered the Bible to be the ultimate authority for Christians; with many of his Anglican colleagues, he believed that the scripture provides neither an infallible guide nor an answer to every doubt, and that its meaning and significance must be interpreted. By *tradition*, Hooker understood the long history of interpretation by which Christians have wrestled with the scriptures; *reason* is the particular human attribute that makes such wrestling and interpretation possible.

Hooker affirmed the belief spelled out in the "Articles of Religion" that Christian worship and the practice of faith have always exhibited diversity because they reflect the differences of time and circumstance that inevitably mark the church. He distinguished between the core proclamation of the Gospel, which he considered binding on all Christians, and what he termed "things indifferent."[44] For example, all Christians are required by Christ's commandment to share in the Eucharistic meal of bread and wine, about which Jesus said, "Do this in remembrance of me." But the *form* by which the

Eucharist is celebrated is not mandated by scripture, and we need not search the Bible to discover a uniquely privileged set of liturgical practices. Indeed, much of Book V of Hooker's *Laws* is devoted to a carefully argued defense of the appropriateness of Anglican worship against Puritan objections that it is unscriptural.

Like most of his Anglican contemporaries, Hooker recognized that while Christ called together a group of apostles and shared with them the gift of the Holy Spirit for guiding the Church, there is no direct commandment establishing the threefold order of bishops, priests and deacons. He accepted that the apostolic succession of bishops cannot be said to respond to a command from God, but rather reflects the practice of the church in the age of the apostles. Nevertheless, he insisted, the fact that this tradition has endured down through the ages and has proven to be an efficient and appropriate way of governing the Christian community, can lead us to assume that its development represents God's will for the church; hence the Puritan desire to eliminate the episcopate is in error.[45]

Hooker assumed that the order exhibited by both church and society reflects the divine order established by God and accessible to humankind through the exercise of our God-given reason. Indeed, in Hooker's work the passion Elizabeth brought to restoring peace and harmony to England is given a divine sanction. Like Calvin, Hooker believed that society was meant to reflect Christian values; he also believed that all people, whatever their state in life, are called to a life of holiness or union with God.[46] Hooker agreed with his European Protestant colleagues that the possibility of growth in holy living begins with our justification by God's free gift; in that sense, he as a thorough-going Reformer.[47] But he parted company with the Puritans when he asserted that we encounter God's grace to grow in holiness primarily through the sacraments and not, as the Puritans believed, through preaching.[48] Jewel had affirmed that Christ "doth truly and presently give himself in his sacraments" although his presence is a spiritual one;[49] Hooker goes further: "Such as will live the life of God must eat the flesh and drink the blood of the Son of man, because this is a part of that diet which if we want we cannot live." Hooker considered that "the real presence of Christ's most blessed body and blood" is not to be found in the bread and wine of the Eucharist, but in "the worthy receiver of the sacrament" since its very purpose is to deepen our life in Christ. But he also suggested that the disputes among Christians over theories explaining how Christ's presence is to be understood are issues about which "we need not greatly to care or inquire."[50]

The achievements of theologians such as Jewel and Hooker are only part of a nationwide effort of religious instruction that involved both clergy and laypeople. Its strength can be measured by the fact that some half a million copies of official catechisms and three quarters of a million of unofficial alternatives were circulating among a population of four million.[51] In his own lifetime, Hooker's defense of Anglicanism was challenged by powerful Puritan clergy, including his colleague Walter Travers, who served as Lecturer at the Temple Church of which Hooker was the Master.

By the end of Elizabeth's reign, other Anglicans were responding to the continuing Puritan attacks by making stronger claims for an episcopal form of government. In 1593, Thomas Bilson, later Bishop of Winchester, published *The Perpetual Government of Christ's Church*, called by one historian "the most exhaustive treatment of episcopacy in sixteenth century Anglican literature."[52] Bilson argued that it was appropriate that bishops should be selected by monarchs, since he hoped that "the gravity and prudency of the magistrate may worthily be preferred to the rashness and rudeness of the many."[53] He considered bishops to be the direct successors of the apostles, holding their authority directly from Christ and enjoying the "infallible direction by the Holy Ghost."[54]

SETTLEMENT: CONSEQUENCES

The English historian E. T. Davies dates the last decades of the sixteenth century as the crucible from which modern Anglicanism emerged.[55] Given the circumstances of the period, that might seem a rash assumption. When Elizabeth died in 1603, bringing to an end more than a century of Tudor rule, the conflict between Puritans and the supporters of the Elizabethan Settlement had not been put to rest; it had, if anything, become more acrimonious. Indeed, the next century would usher in not only a new dynasty but a religious establishment determined to push the Church of England in a direction diametrically opposed to the Puritans' goals and to make it ever more difficult for them to remain in it. Vicious struggles between a Parliament increasingly dominated by Puritans and a king and prelates convinced of their divine prerogatives eventually brought both church and state to the breaking point and for a time it must have seemed that Anglicanism as Elizabeth had conceived it was dead. Nowhere did that struggle take a more terrible toll than on the Church's ordained leadership. But in fact, the Church of England that emerged from a bloody time of testing was indeed recognizable as the Church of the Elizabethan Settlement. In that sense Davies is surely right. The Church of England does still bear many of the marks it assumed in Elizabeth's reign. Even Anglicanism in its global identity is clearly descended from the Church as Elizabeth knew it, insofar as it continues to be both constructed and defined in term of *national* churches. Paul Avis argues that "the idea of a national church belonged to the essence of historical Anglicanism," and continues to be "integral to the Anglican understanding of the Church."[56] For the Tudors,

Anglican meant "English," and the English character of the church they crafted was so much a part of its identity that they could not have conceived of another, broader definition. Centuries later, Anglican theologians would continue to assume, as Richard Hooker did, that nations were "natural," part of God's own design, their very existence a sign of God's care of the human family. The 1930 Lambeth Conference noted that one of the "distinguishing marks of those churches that make up the Anglican Communion" is that "they are particular or national churches, and as such, promote within each of their territories a national expression of Christian faith."[57]

Avis points out that while the *English* model of national church has been intimately linked with the unique relationship to the state which it has enjoyed since Tudor times, and the very concept itself is a legacy of Tudor Anglicanism, national churches need not be establishments of the state, nor is the concept related to either size or percentage of the population. Rather, he considers the concept to be directly related to "a nationwide mission of the gospel and nationwide service to the community." A national church, he affirms,

> understands that its mission is to the whole nation, to the whole population considered as a great community (or community of communities). It is committed to providing a ministry of word, sacrament and pastoral care to every sector of the population. It has a close and sympathetic relationship to national culture and, more locally, to regional expressions of that culture.... It expects to make its contribution to the articulation of public doctrine, particularly in social and educational policy and to the principles of wide acceptation that underlie it. It aims to project its message, its values and its presence at every level of national life.[58]

At the time of its Reformation, the Church of England understood ministry to be intimately linked to the context of its own society, and to perceive the public dimension of ministry as a calling in which both clergy and laypeople participate. Nor can we draw a sharp line between the liturgical and the administrative, the pastoral and the institutional. Laypeople—from Crown and Parliament to the churchwardens and clerks of the humblest country parish—participated in ministry alongside the Church's ordained leadership, because they were understood to be called by God to do so and because the well-being of the People of God is the responsibility of all those who "in this transitory life are in trouble, sorrow, need, sickness or any other adversity."[59]

Insofar as Anglicans in other places embrace a perspective that takes to itself our world in all its brokenness and possibility, that treasures the rich diversity with which God has blessed the human family and our "fragile island home," and that believes in God's call for the healing of the nations, they continue to be moved by the same sense of mission and ministry that shaped the church that Elizabeth knew. Insofar as Anglicans treasure a *living* heritage, and hold in a wonderful tension both the global vision of all the nations of this world made by God of one blood, and the here and now with which we are graced—the universal and the local, the past and the present, the catholic and the contextual—they are all Elizabeth's heirs.

NOTES

1. E. Echlin, *The Story of Anglican Ministry*, 115.
2. Diarmaid MacCulloch, *The Reformation: A History* (New York: Viking, 2004), 282.
3. E. Duffy, *The Voices of Morebath*, 170–171.
4. Brian T. Hartley, "The Liturgical Reordering of the *Ecclesia Anglicana*: Faithful Understanding of the Elizabethan Homilies of 1563," *Anglican and Episcopal History*, LII (March 1983), 12–13.
5. A. Tindal Hart, *The Man in the Pew: 1558–1660* (London: John Baker, 1966), 189, 198.
6. Hart, *The Man in the Pew*, 186, 205.
7. Lawrence Stone, *The Family, Sex and Marriage in England 1500–1800* (New York: Weidenfeld and Nicolson, 1977), 141–142.
8. Anne Llewellyn Barstow, "The First Generations of Anglican Clergy Wives: Heroines or Whores?" *Anglican and Episcopal History*, LII (March 1983), 12–13.
9. Barstow, "The First Generations," 15.
10. Rosemary O'Day, *The English Clergy: The Emergence and Consolidation of a Profession 1558–1642* (Leicester: Leicester University Press, 1979), 30.
11. O'Day, *The English Clergy*, 143.
12. Ralph Houlbrooke, "The Family and Pastoral Care," in G. R. Evans, ed., *A History of Pastoral Care* (London: Cassell, 2000), 272–276.
13. J. I. Daeley, "Pluralism in the Diocese of Canterbury during the Administration of Matthew Parker, 1559–1575," *Journal of Ecclesiastical History*, XVIII, 1, 1967, 33–49.
14. Diarmaid MacCulloch, *The Later Reformation in England 1547–1603* (London: MacMillan Press, 1990), 133.
15. Rosemary O'Day and Felicity Heal, eds., *Continuity and Change: Personnel and Administration in the Church of England 1500–1642* (Leicester: Leicester University Press, 1976), 57.
16. O'Day and Heal, *Continuity and Change,* 56.
17. O'Day and Heal, *Continuity and Change,* 61.
18. O'Day, *The English Clergy*, 130.
19. O'Day, *The English Clergy,* 30.
20. MacCulloch, *The Later Reformation,* 110.
21. O'Day, *The English Clergy,* 113.

22. Philip M. Jelley, "Power, Authority and Conflict: How the Virginia Colonists secured, exercised and defended the rights of their local Church of England Parish Vestries to select their clergy," unpublished paper, 2007.

23. O'Day, *The English Clergy,* 181–183.

24. O'Day, *The English Clergy,* 190.

25. David Cressy, *Agnes Bowker's Cat: Travesties and Transgressions in Tudor and Stuart England* (Oxford: Oxford University Press, 2000), 139.

26. O'Day, *The English Clergy,* 134.

27. Cressy, *Agnes Bowker's Hat,* 140.

28. Stone, *Family, Sex and Marriage,* 93.

29. Stone, *Family, Sex and Marriage,* 146.

30. Dave Postles, "Penance and the Market Place: A Reformation Dialogue with the Medieval Church c. 1250-c.1600," *Journal of Ecclesiastical History,* 54 (July 2003), 443.

31. Postles, "Penance," 452–458.

32. Cressy, *Agnes Bowker's Cat,* 140.

33. Judith Maltby, "By this book: parishioners, the Prayer Book and the established Church," in Peter Marshall, ed., *The Impact of the English Reformation 1500–1640* (New York: Oxford University Press, 1997), 260–267.

34. O'Day, *The English Clergy,* 99–100, 103.

35. O'Day, *The English Clergy,* 47.

36. Susan Doran and Christopher Durston, *Princes, Pastors and People: The Church and Religion in England 1529–1689* (London: Routledge, 1991), 131.

37. Quoted in H. G. Reventlow, *The Authority of the Bible and the Rise of the Modern World* (London, SCM, 1984), 136–137.

38. Quoted in Norman Sykes, *Old Priest and New Presbyter: Episcopacy and Presbyterianism in the Reformation with special relation to the Churches of England and Scotland* (Cambridge: Cambridge University Press, 1956), 6.

39. See, e.g., Timothy Scott McGinnis, *George Gifford and the Reformation of the Common Sort: Puritan Priorities in Elizabethan Religious Life* (Kirksville, MO: Truman State University Press, 2004).

40. John Jewel, *An Apology, or Answer, In Defense of the Church of England, with a brief and plain declaration of the true religion professed and used in the same* (1567 English edition) in J. Ayres, ed., *The Works of John Jewel, Bishop of Salisbury* (Cambridge: Cambridge University Press, 1848), Vol. III, 55.

41. Jewel, *Apology,* pp. 59–61.

42. H. F. Woodhouse, *The Doctrine of the Church in Anglican Theology 1547–1603* (London: SPCK, 1954), 78.

43. Jewel, *Apology,* 59.

44. Richard Hooker, *Of the Laws of Ecclesiastical Polity,* Volume I, Book III, ii.1–2 (Cambridge: Cambridge University Press, 1977), 246–248.

45. Hooker devoted almost the entirety of Book VII of the *Laws* to the defense of the episcopate in the Church of England. *Laws*, Volume III (Cambridge: Cambridge University Press, 1981), 143–312.

46. Hooker, *Laws*, Book I, xi, 3 in *Laws*, Volume I, 112–114.

47. Hooker, "Virtus Sacramenti et Dei gratia," Dublin Fragments 16–17, in John Booty ed., *Richard Hooker, Of the Laws of Ecclesiastical Polity: Attack and Responses* (Cambridge: Cambridge University Press, 1982), 117–119.

48. Hooker, *Laws*, Book V, xxii, 10–12 in Laws, Volume II, 97–100.

49. Ayre, ed., *The Works of John Jewel,* Volume III, 63.

50. Hooker, *Laws*, Book V, lxvii, 5–6, in *Laws*, Volume II, 247–248.

51. MacCulloch, *The Later Reformation,* 167.

52. E. T. Davies, *Episcopacy and the Royal Supremacy in the Church of England in the XVI Century* (Oxford: Basil Blackwell, 1950), 33.

53. Thomas Bilson, *The Perpetual Government of Christ's Church* (Oxford: Oxford University Press, 1842), 441.

54. Davies, *Episcopacy*, 33.

55. Davies, *Episcopacy*, 55.

56. Paul Avis, *Church, State and Establishment* (London: SPCK, 2001), 14.

57. Lambeth Conference 1930, Resolution 49b.

58. Avis, *Church, State and Establishment,* 15.

59. *The Book of Common Prayer* (New York: Seabury Press, 1979), 329. This phrase from the "Prayers of the People" in Rite I first appeared in both the 1549 and 1552 Prayer Books.

Chapter Three

Unsettlement
Ministry after Elizabeth

Elizabeth's forty-five-year reign began with the hope that the Church of England might serve as an important instrument of national unity for a people deeply divided by issues of religion. But while the force of her own character and personality and the legal strictures which reinforced conformity succeeded in holding her Settlement in place throughout her lifetime, the hope of a national church in which all English people could find a comfortable home never came even close to being reality. While Richard Hooker was using the pulpit of London's Temple Church on Sunday mornings to spell out a vision of *Ecclesia Anglicana* to which every English subject would be united through baptism, the same pulpit was occupied every Sunday afternoon by Walter Travers, the congregation's Lecturer, whose fiery defense of Puritan Christianity and his attacks on Elizabeth's Settlement continued until the Archbishop of Canterbury prohibited him from preaching. The conflict between Hooker and Travers is symptomatic of the continued conflict over the nature of the church and its ministry between those who accepted the broad contours of Elizabeth's church and those who continued to press for more drastic reform, a conflict which Elizabeth's death did nothing to resolve.

Elizabeth was the last of the Tudor monarchs to reign over England. As the descendant of Henry VII, founder of the Tudor dynasty, Elizabeth's cousin Mary Stuart, Queen of Scots, would have been next in line to inherit the throne. But her devotion to Roman Catholicism, her own scandal-ridden reign in Scotland which forced her to abdicate in favor of her infant son, and Elizabeth's fears that Mary was plotting to usurp her throne, led to Mary's imprisonment and ultimately to her execution for treason fifteen years before Elizabeth's death. When Elizabeth died in 1603, Mary's son, Scotland's king James VI, was proclaimed as James I, king of England.

JAMES I AND THE CHURCH'S MINISTRY

James' own religious upbringing had been in the Church of Scotland, which had passed through a much more severe reformation than the Church of England. While the church preserved the order of bishops appointed by the monarch, the Scottish Reformer John Knox and others had succeeded in creating an independent Church Assembly which governed the church and continued to press for a fully presbyterian system.

Like the Tudors, James took theology with great seriousness. He himself authored two books in which he spelled out his belief in the doctrine of the "divine right of kings," arguing that monarchs exercise a God-given vocation. Years before he inherited the English throne, he had increased the number of Scottish bishops, and considered that the Church of England's structure, by which the monarch governed the church through its bishops, was highly preferable to a Church Assembly over which he had little or no control.

Many English Puritans had hoped that his Scottish heritage would make James more sympathetic to their requests to remove what they considered undesirable remnants of the Church's Roman Catholic past. Whether they identified themselves as Puritans or not, most English Christians in James' time as in that of Elizabeth were sympathetic to many aspects of Calvin's teaching. But James was every bit as determined as Elizabeth to enforce conformity to Prayer Book worship and to maintain the authority of the bishops as a fundamental part of the English Church. His commitment to the role of bishops was integral to his understanding of his own role as king. Without bishops, James remarked, "I know what would become of my supremacy. . . . No bishop, no King. When I mean to live under a presbytery I will go to Scotland again."[1] In spite of strong objections, he was successful in restoring a Scottish diocesan system which restored some of the bishops' authority.

If the Puritans within the Church of England were fearful of what they had always considered to be regrettable holdovers of the Church's medieval past, that fear was only fed by the awareness that Jesuit and other Roman Catholic clergy continued to operate within England as they had throughout Elizabeth's reign. Indeed, a remarkable network of "safe houses" scattered throughout the country assured that families who continued, often at great peril, to hold to their ancestral faith were served by priests in hiding. Aware that their life might well be forfeited if they were discovered, both priests and their lay protectors were determined to maintain their Church's presence and ministry in a land that considered them both wrong-headed and treacherous. Both opinions were strengthened by the discovery of the so-called Gunpowder Plot of 1605, by which the House of Lords was to have been blown up during Parliament's Opening Ceremony. While contemporary historians question many of the assertions made by the government at the time, there is no doubt that the threat was real and narrowly averted the death not only of King James but of the other members of the House of Lords, including the bishops of the Church of England. The wave of tortures and executions that followed did little to remove the anxieties of those whose religious allegiance was with the English rather than with the Roman Church.[2]

Early in his reign, James summoned a conference to respond to the demands of Puritan elements within the Church of England. But the Hampton Court Conference, at which a number of bishops and the Archbishop of Canterbury discussed concerns with a smaller group of distinguished Puritan clergy, failed to achieve the hoped-for consensus. One positive outcome of the event, however, was the proposal to initiate a new translation of the scriptures into English, a task in which Anglicans of all persuasions could and did participate. The completed translation, which appeared in 1611, immediately replaced the so-called "Bishops' Bible," which dated from Elizabeth's reign, and provided an alternative to translations which were considered to be prejudiced in favor of Calvinist teaching.[3] But while some moderate Puritans played an important role in the translation process, the guidelines by which it was undertaken made it clear that "the old ecclesiastical words" such as *church* and *bishop* were to be employed in preference to terms such as "congregation" and "superintendent," which would have been more congenial to the Puritan participants. As Adam Nicolson points out in his account of the translation commissioned by James, "The Church of England, like the Church of Rome, but unlike the more fully reformed churches of Europe, relied for its understanding of the often complex tests of scripture on the ancient traditions of Christianity . . ."[4]

If Elizabeth considered the bishops as strategic agents of her rule, James saw them as at once pillars of the state, supporters on whom he could depend for wise advice, astute administrators of their dioceses, guardians of the king's supremacy and Prayer Book worship, enforcers of social and spiritual discipline, and chief pastors of their diocese.[5] In general, James' bishops took those duties with great seriousness; in spite of their role in government (all but two of the bishops were members of the House of Lords), most spent the greater part of each year in their dioceses.[6] Then as now, the chief encounter between bishops and congregations was through the bishop's visitation, when the rite of Confirmation was administered—often to more than a thousand persons in one service—and issues of church discipline were aired and resolved. Tobias Matthew, Archbishop of York for most of James' reign, preached 550 sermons during his eleven years as Bishop of Durham, and 721 in his first fifteen years as Archbishop.[7]

Not surprisingly, James' conviction about the absolute power of the monarchy was a source of concern for the English Parliament, which took its own governmental prerogatives with great seriousness. As a result, James' reign was marked by frequent tension between them. That tension was of course reflected in congregational life, nowhere more than in the passionate preaching in which clergy and lecturers of every opinion regularly indulged.

Like Elizabeth, James was anxious about the effect of preaching over which he had no control; late in his reign, he issued "Directions Concerning Preachers" in which he attempted to end the use of the pulpit as a platform for controversy. The document drew a sharp distinction between the latitude permitted to bishops, cathedral and university deans on one hand, and ordinary parish clergy, whose preaching was restricted to the doctrines specifically spelled out in the Articles of Religion and the Books of Homilies published in Edward's and Elizabeth's reigns. Preachers at evening services, often the favored venue for Puritan lecturers, were commanded to limit their topics to the Catechism, Creed, Ten Commandments and Lord's Prayer, and parish clergy were to avoid altogether the controversial doctrines such as predestination which continued to occasion theological division in the Church. No preacher, of whatever status, was to "fall into bitter invectives, and indecent railing speeches against the persons of either papists or puritans"; their errors should rather be addressed "modestly and gravely." Nor was any preacher to be permitted to "declare, limit, or bound out . . . the power, prerogative, jurisdiction, authority or duty of sovereign princes, or otherwise meddle with these matters of state and the references betwixt princes and the people . . . but rather to confine themselves wholly to those two heads of faith and good life, which are the subject of the ancient sermons and homilies."[8]

James blamed the bishops for allowing church life to become so mired in conflict, and demanded that they exercise more care in licensing preachers, particularly those (mostly Puritan) lecturers "severed from the ancient clergy of England, being neither parsons, vicars or curates."[9]

The king's directive on preaching demonstrated his intention to use the prerogatives of his role as Supreme Governor of the Church of England to contain and lower the volume of the perennial controversy affecting it. At the same time, he was determined to stifle the Puritan clergy's criticism of his reign by separating spirituality and politics, theology and matters of state. His intent was effectively to eliminate the English congregation as a focus of conflict. The content of the "Declarations" demonstrates how intertwined were the religious and political dimensions of that conflict, and the seriousness of the continuing doctrinal disagreement in the Church of England.

Calvinist doctrines of election and predestination, on which much Puritan theology depended, were already being challenged by the Dutch theologian Jacob Arminius, who argued that Christ died not just for some but for all and that Christians have the freedom to accept or reject their salvation. Most Calvinists saw his teaching as dangerously close to the Roman Catholic assertion that Christians help determine whether they are saved, undermining Calvin's insistence that salvation depends entirely on Christ's election. But Arminius' work found a ready audience among those Anglicans who emphasized the sacraments over the preached Word; some, indeed, even dismissed the sermon as merely preparation for the act of worship, not part of worship itself.[10]

Puritans, on the other hand, did all in their power to emphasize the sermon, and often made use of the position of parish lecturer, hired by the congregations themselves, to subvert the "official" teaching of the parish clergy, many of whom in any case continued to be poorly educated and preached only rarely.

In her study of the English clergy under Elizabeth and the Stuarts, Rosemary O'Day notes that the important role played by laypeople in the conflicts over doctrine and ministry during Elizabeth's reign continued under the Stuarts. The Puritan agenda was often pushed by congregations rather than their clergy.[11] And while bishops struggled to enforce conformity on an increasingly resistant church, large numbers of parish clergy continued to be appointed to their positions by lay patrons over whom the bishop had little or no control.

Meanwhile, the parish continued to be what it had been since the Middle Ages: the "basic territorial unit" of England, a "unit of administration and pastoral care," required by the state to serve a variety of secular as well as pastoral purposes, including not only responsibility for the poor and sick who lived within its boundaries, but also the collection of taxes and the maintenance of local roads and bridges.[12] While the clergy obviously played a primary role in administration, lay leaders also had significant tasks. It was the Churchwardens, elected by the congregation, who customarily presented the parish's financial report to its members, as well as managing gifts made to the congregation. Sidesmen functioned as a local council of oversight, and numbered from between four and six to as many as twenty-four or even thirty. Each parish had a paid Clerk, who was literate enough to sing the congregational responses in the service, and employed a sexton who also served as gravedigger.[13]

In many places, one of the sources of parish income was the traditional "church-ale," commonly held around Whitsunday, when the parish brewed large quantities of ale or beer for sale to its members along with food to accompany the drink. Puritans generally opposed the church-ale, considering it a frivolous and inappropriate means of supporting the parish; they preferred the rental or sale of pew-space in the church. Bell-ringing at weddings and funerals and burials themselves also served as important sources of income for the congregation.[14]

In the seventeenth century, most clergy lived in medieval hall-houses, some with no more than a floor of beaten earth, and a few still constructed around a central hearth. Clerical travel was generally by horse; widespread use of carriages by the church's ordained leaders did not appear until the nineteenth century.[15]

Concern over the consequences of an inadequately educated clergy led James to give increasing attention to assuring that they had access to a university education, and the Church of the seventeenth century was noteworthy for the intellectual and academic skills of its ordained leaders. Writing in 1623, Joseph Hall, then Dean of Worcester, could describe the Anglican clergy as *stupor mundi* ("the wonder of the world"). "So many learned divines, so many eloquent preachers, shall in vain be sought elsewhere this day, in whatever region under the cope of heaven."[16] (However, one contemporary historian points out that they arrived at that position "through a series of crises and disasters, compromises and processes of accommodation that appeared far from wonderful.")[17]

In O'Day's view, the raising of standards for clergy education was one of the factors contributing to the formation of a distinctive clerical class which was increasingly distanced from parishioners, with its own "professional training, interests and habits," distinctive dress, a sense of the importance of the clerical calling, and the "hereditary nature of the profession."[18]

King James himself was responsible for encouraging John Donne, one of the best-known and most remembered clerics of his time, to seek ordination. Donne would have seemed an unlikely candidate for priesthood; in his youth, some members of his family were punished for practicing Roman Catholicism, and his own early life was marked by behavior best described as profligate. He spent time as a soldier in Spain and the Azores, contracted a clandestine marriage which enraged his wife's prominent family, and was widely known to be the author of a body of poetry that was as noteworthy for its celebration of sensuality as for its fashionable use of metaphor and artifice. Politically and socially ambitious, he served briefly as a member of Parliament and in spite of his colorful past continually sought advantages by lurking at the edges of the highest levels of the Court. James, however, made it clear that he would give him no preferment except as a royal chaplain, an appointment he received immediately after his ordination.[19]

Donne's own experience and his keen powers of rational analysis kept him all too aware of the fleeting nature of worldly success, and both his poetry and his sermons reveal just how much the spirituality of his time was shaped by the pervasiveness of death. His years as a soldier, the early death of five of his twelve children and of his wife at the age of thirty-three, provided ample evidence that "[n]o man is an island, entire of itself; every man is a piece of the continent, a part of the main; . . . any man's death diminishes me, because I am involved in mankind, and therefore never send to know for whom the bell tolls; it tolls for thee."[20] Donne was appointed Dean of London's St. Paul's Cathedral in 1621, and for ten years he preached to the most diverse congregations imaginable, including Parliament and the Court, two kings, and the Cathedral's poor neighbors.

Unlike many of his Puritan-minded contemporaries whose sermons emphasized teachings to be applied to family life, Donne's sermons almost never offered such practical advice. Even when he preached at weddings, he tended to speak of the ways in which marriage pre-figures the relationship between Christ and the individual soul. He commended chastity and believed that married couples should live in "sober constancy," remembering that the primary purpose of marriage is the procreation of children.[21]

John Donne is one of a large number of noteworthy clergy who helped to shape the nature of the Church of England's ministry during the seventeenth century. Some, like Donne, were best known for their skilled preaching; many left behind a literary legacy that to later generations seems to outshine their ministry. The same extravagant use of metaphor and verbal "conceits" that so marks English poetry of the period was amply displayed in their sermons, and the frequent use of Latin and Greek, not always translated, reminded hearers of the preacher's academic abilities while complementing the congregation's ability to understand the references (whether or not the complement was based on reality).

Other clergy of the period demonstrated a passion for pastoral ministry, while still others contributed to the development of a uniquely Anglican spirituality. Most of the best known are identified more closely with the reigns of James' two successors, his son and grandson, Charles I and II. Their ministries are all the more remarkable given the cataclysmic events that shook the English church and nation for the better part of the century.

One of the most memorable of the clerics of James' reign, whose work provides a bridge between Elizabeth's Church and that of the Stuarts, was Lancelot Andrewes. Already a popular preacher and writer in Elizabeth's time, he was appointed by James to be bishop of Chichester and later of Winchester. Andrewes was the epitome of the learned clergy at whom some marveled; a frequent preacher at Court, he also wrote *A Manual of Private Devotions* that appealed to laypeople who shared his commitment to a sacramentally based spirituality. Much to the dismay of the Puritans, Andrewes was prepared to agree with Roman Catholics that the Eucharist can properly be called a sacrifice, and his theology can serve as a preface to the more aggressive high-church position of Archbishop William Laud. While Andrewes had no use for the Roman Catholic doctrine of transubstantiation or any other theory that proposed to explain the nature of Christ's presence in the sacrament, he insisted that the "real presence" of Christ in the Eucharist is an integral part of the Church of England's teaching. Andrewes died shortly after the death of King James; five years later, Charles I ordered a collection of his sermons to be published.

CHARLES I AND OLIVER CROMWELL: MINISTRY IN A TIME OF WAR

While James obviously took his prerogatives as Supreme Governor of the Church with great seriousness, the policies of his son Charles I, who succeeded him in 1625, demonstrated an even greater concern for "order and obedience, authority and deference."[22]

In establishing his policies towards the Church, Charles relied for much of his reign on his Archbishop of Canterbury, William Laud, whom he appointed in 1633. Laud was a convinced Arminian and already well known as a supporter of "high-church" theology and practices over against the Puritanism of so many of his contemporaries. Like Cranmer and Hooker before him, he considered that "the Church can have no being except in the Commonwealth, and the Commonwealth can have no blessed and happy being but by the Church."[23]

> Church and State are so nearly united together that they may seem to be two bodies, yet in some relations they may be accepted but as one in as much as they are both made up of the same men which are differenced only in relation to Spiritual and civil ends. This nearness makes the Church call on the help of the State to succor and support her, whensoever she is pressed beyond her strength. And the same nearness makes the Church call in the help of the State, both to teach that duty which her members know not and to exhort them to, and encourage them in the duty that they know.[24]

Puritans found Laud's strong support of the Established Church troubling if not surprising; but they were horrified when he ordered that Communion tables be restored to their traditional place at the east wall of the church and be fenced off with a chancel rail to emphasize his belief that the altar is "the greatest place of God's residence on earth." Laud was a passionate defender of liturgical worship and considered Calvinism to be "fundamentally subversive of the institutional structures of state as well as church." He saw liturgical ceremonies as "the hedge that fence the substance of religion from all the indignities which profaneness and sacrilege too commonly put upon it."[25] He also oversaw the expulsion of non-conformist clergy from their parishes and attacked the Puritan custom of strict observance of Sunday as the Christian Sabbath.[26] Given his partisan and polarizing leadership, it is not surprising that he has been described both as "among the greatest archbishops of Canterbury since the Reformation" and "the greatest calamity ever visited upon the Church of England."[27]

Laud's emphasis on the "beauty of holiness" and the liturgical practices he favored had never entirely disappeared from the Church of England. Much of his theology was already present in the work of Lancelot Andrewes. Moreover, throughout the reigns of Elizabeth and her successors, London's Westminster Abbey had continued to use unleavened wafers for Holy Communion, its clergy had worn copes and other vestments commonly associated with its Roman Catholic past, and its choral services had preserved a rich heritage of English liturgical music. The Abbey was "not necessarily the cradle of Laudianism," comments one historian, "but it certainly acted as one of the midwives."[28] However, the vast majority of the Church of England's members had never experienced worship in the Abbey. Laud's attempt to make such practices universal, his constant attacks on the Calvinist religion of much of England, and his willingness to make use of the full power of the state to enforce his decrees, made him extremely unpopular, even hated. His support came chiefly from "learned scholars, able theologians and saintly priests."[29]

But not all the life of the Church during Charles' reign was conflict. Figures like George Herbert can serve as a reminder of the faithful ministry undertaken by many who chose to remove themselves from the increasingly divided centers of church life. Herbert could have been, and indeed briefly was, part of that world, serving as a member of Parliament for two years before retiring from politics and seeking ordination.

Herbert was quite capable of producing the kind of sophisticated poetry for which Donne is remembered, but his literary output was entirely religious. From the time of his ordination at the age of 36 until his death three years later, he served as a parish priest in the little community of Bemerton, near Salisbury. He was noted during his life for his generous spirit and unflagging commitment to his pastoral responsibilities. His understanding of the nature and obligations of ministry in the countryside was summarized in a collection of poems, *The Temple: Sacred Poems and Private Ejaculations,* published shortly after his death, and in *A Priest to the Temple or The Country Parson*, which first appeared when the practice of the Church of England as Herbert knew it had been abolished by law.

For Herbert, the priest was primarily a *pastor,* placed in the midst of a congregation as "the deputy of Christ for the reducing of Man to the Obedience of God." He found the term "parson" to be particularly apt for his understanding of the clerical role: the parson is the "person" of the parish, around whom the community of faith is formed and who functions as its primary guide, both by teaching and (in Herbert's view) especially by example. Herbert undoubtedly had an extremely high view of the calling to ordained ministry, considering the priest to be acting out Paul's description of his own ministry as completing Christ's work on behalf of the Church. "Out of this Charter of the Priesthood may be plainly gathered both the Dignity thereof, and the Duty: The Dignity, in that a Priest may do what Christ did, and by his authority, and as his Viceregent. The Duty, in that a Priest is to do that which Christ did, and after his manner, both for Doctrine and Life."[30] On the eve of his ordination he had written, "I will be sure to live well, because the virtuous life of a clergyman is the most powerful eloquence to persuade all that see it to reverence and love, and at least to desire to live like him. And this I will do, because I know we live in an age that hath more need of good examples than precepts."[31]

Herbert had a strong sense of the ways in which the *context* of ministry defines and orders its priorities; because "country parsons" live among people whose work is hard and whose rewards are often meager, they must take special care to live simply, to speak honestly, to give no hint of greed, and above all to avoid the abuse of alcohol, "because it is the most popular vice."[32] He commended the use of stories and sayings over what he called "exhortation" when preaching to "Countrey people; which are thick, and heavy, and hard to raise to a point of Zeal, and fervency, and need a mountaine of fire to kindle them."[33]

George Herbert was one of the early practitioners of a discipline closely associated with the clergy of the seventeenth century: the guidance of his parishioners in making the most appropriate decision in matters of conscience. Even his poetry reflects the teaching function of the pastor. Although the poems are often rhetorically addressed to God, they "'teach' by moving the reader to an affective response and therefore ultimately to a change of life."[34]

While Herbert described an intimate relationship between the country parson and the members of the congregation, he also insisted on the priest's duty to model an appropriate piety—and never to accept less from other worshippers. High-ranking parishioners are no more to be excused for inadequate behavior in church than the most humble.

> What [The Parson] exacts of them all possible reverence, by no means enduring either talking, or sleeping, or gazing, or leaning, or half-kneeling, or any undutiful behavior in them, but causing them, when they sit, or stand, or kneel, to do all in a strait, [sic] and steady posture, and every one, man, and child, answering aloud both Amen, and all other answers, which are on the Clerks and people's part to answer; which answers also are to be done not in a hudling, or slubbering

fashion, gaping, or scratching the head, or spitting even in the midst of their answer, but gently and pausably, thinking they say . . .³⁵

Herbert considered that "the life and spirituality of the Church . . . was based firmly on corporate prayer." He described the *Book of Common Prayer* as "*the* primary guide for the development of right belief, right attitude and right action." Liturgical leadership was the primary place where the pastor's teaching ministry was to be practiced, and though he took the priest's preaching duties seriously, he also affirmed that "praying's the end of preaching." Herbert also believed that in his role as parson, the parish priest should take an active role in physical healing—what Philip Sheldrake describes as "a holistic model of pastoral care." Ideally, the priest would also be a physician, and Herbert recommends that both the parson and his wife be skilled in the healing powers of plants and herbs.³⁶

The seriousness with which George Herbert took his calling was, he believed, an obligation which extended to the life of a clerical household and indeed the households of the congregation. That such an ideal was actually put into practice can be seen in the example of the Little Gidding community, organized by the Farrer family in rural Huntingdonshire.

Like George Herbert, Nicholas Farrer and his family had enjoyed a conventionally successful life in London; both he and his older brother were officers of the Virginia Company until its charter was revoked, and Nicholas Farrer served briefly in Parliament. Facing a financial crisis, the family, led by the brothers' widowed mother, purchased a manor in the country, where they set out to establish as a community of disciplined prayer.

Nicholas Farrer was ordained as a deacon with the understanding that he would not subsequently be ordained to the priesthood. He became the chief liturgical officer of the household, which came to number at least thirty people, including twenty family members, a number of servants and three schoolmasters.³⁷ The community provided housing for poor widows, a dispensary and infirmary, and undertook rudimentary religious education for the children of the village. Its round of prayer was rigorous: Morning Prayer at 6 a.m., the Litany at 10 a.m., Evensong at 4 p.m., and voluntary night vigils from 9 p.m. to 1 a.m., at which time Nicholas Farrer would rise. The family was divided into teams for hourly prayers and recitation of the Psalms (the entire Psalter was recited every twenty-four hours). Sunday worship was at the parish church, to which the entire community walked in procession. Prayer Book fast days were observed, and the food that was saved was passed on to the poor. Young women customarily wore black dresses and veils.³⁸

Little Gidding was the first attempt by Anglicans to establish a disciplined community of prayer since the abolition of the religious orders by Henry VIII. Not surprisingly, given the intense religious conflict of the times, it attracted considerable attention, and one historian suggests that those who visited Little Gidding to see this strange phenomenon must have numbered in the thousands. The Bishop of Lincoln made at least four visits, and King Charles I visited twice. Puritans were scandalized and spread rumors about the community, culminating in the publication of a scurrilous book, *The Arminian Nunnery,* of which thousands of copies were circulated.[39]

In a much-respected study which re-awakened interest in the Anglicanism of the seventeenth century, H. R. McAdoo noted that Caroline theologians "visualized moral and ascetic theology as one integrated science, the aim of which was not simply the interpretation and application of law, but the edification of the spiritual life and the salvation of the soul of man."[40] This perception of the ultimate unity between moral behavior and spirituality set the Church of England apart from the other great European Reformed traditions and provides an approach which unites liturgy and worship, prayer and the informed moral choices made by ordinary Christians. One of the practical results of this perspective was a flourishing of manuals of devotion and practical piety that achieved enormous popularity in their day and made clear that the goal of union with God should shape the life of every faithful Christian. In its time, none was more popular than Jeremy Taylor's *The Rule and Exercise of Holy Living* and its companion volume, *The Rule and Exercise of Holy Dying*; Taylor invited his readers to consider that "there is not one moment of our lives (after we come to the use of reason), but we are or may be doing the work of God, even then when we most of all serve ourselves."[41] Taylor's own spirituality was tested by circumstances, including the death of four of his children and the suffering that befell him in the early years of his ministry: the loss of his parish, exile and imprisonment. *Holy Living* offered pastoral guidance for those who were living through similar times of trouble and dislocation.

The disciplined piety commended by figures like Herbert, Taylor and the Farrer family reflected an Anglican spirituality that had matured over the course of nearly a century. But its profound love of order could not ultimately prevail against the chaos that was looming in England. Like his father, Charles I was a firm believer in the divine right of kings, convinced that he was ultimately accountable to no one but God. His attempts to ignore or bypass Parliament in the conduct and financing of foreign policy led to an eleven-year period of "personal rule" in which the king relied on questionable and widely despised tactics to raise money without the approval of Parliament. In 1637, Charles attempted to impose a *Book of Common Prayer* on the Church of Scotland, even though most Scots were staunch Calvinists who longed for the removal of their bishops and the establishment of a presbyterian church. The Scottish Prayer Book was drawn not from Cranmer's second, more Reformed book of 1552, but the earlier version of 1549. It was vehemently opposed across Scotland, and late in 1638 the General Assembly of the Church of Scotland expelled its bishops and rejected all of the king's demands.

The first skirmishes of a lengthy period of armed conflict were unleashed by Scottish opposition to Charles I. Charles was forced to call Parliament into session, and it soon became clear that the balance of power had passed from the king's hands. One of its early actions was to order the arrest of Archbishop Laud on charges of treason; five years later, it ordered his execution.

Charles' own stubbornness, supported by his firm belief in his God-given prerogatives, led to increasing hostility in both England and Scotland, while the Roman Catholic majority in Ireland, which England had been attempting to subdue and convert for over a century, rose in full revolt. The king's defense of Archbishop Laud and others who were critical of Calvinist theology and insistent on highly ceremonial worship led many to see him as a potential advocate of Roman Catholicism, a suspicion strengthened by the fact that Charles' queen was a French Roman Catholic. An unsuccessful attempt by Charles to arrest his chief opponents in Parliament led to a complete breakdown in the relationship between the two and made civil war nearly inevitable. Both Charles and Parliament raised armies, and the first battle between them was fought late in 1642.

The following year, the English Parliament passed a "Solemn League and Covenant," in which it agreed to adopt the Scottish system of church government. It invited 151 people to form a Westminster Assembly and oversee the further reform of the Church. Although most participated at least nominally in the life of the Church of England and a few of its members supported the episcopate, others were Independents who wanted to replace the national Church with a system of local congregational autonomy; most were Presbyterians by theological preference. It was this body which ultimately produced the Westminster Confession, a "Larger Catechism" and a "Shorter Catechism." All three documents were meant to replace the Church of England's "Articles of Religion" and other formularies and to provide guidelines for its further reform, the Puritans' long-hoped-for goal. The Westminster Confession was adopted by the Scottish Church Assembly as its declaration of faith in 1647, and in the following year by both the Scottish and English Parliaments.

In 1645, the English Parliament abolished the *Book of Common Prayer*, replacing it with a *Directory of Public Worship* based on the Scottish Reformer John Knox's *Book of Common Order* from a century earlier. The new book, which never enjoyed universal usage, attempted to follow the more extreme Puritan principle that only what is clearly spelled out in scripture is to be included in public worship. Worship was to be focused on the reading and preaching of scripture. Advocates of the *Book of Common Prayer* mourned the absence of any form of prescribed liturgy, uniformity of language, lay participation through hymns and congregational responses, kneeling to receive Holy Communion, the use of the sign of the cross in Baptism and of a wedding ring in marriage, the calendar of Church seasons and feast days, and any form of burial service at all.

In 1646, the English Parliament formally abolished the episcopate and the Church of England became *de facto* a Presbyterian church. The bishops, deprived of their positions, went into retirement. While a large number of clergy accepted the new church order, nearly six thousand, including 2,425 parish priests, were either sequestered from their positions or harassed without being expelled.[42] Worship according to the *Book of Common Prayer* was clandestine, although widespread.

In the early stages of the Civil War Parliament had relied on local militias, but in 1645 some of its most radical leaders established the New Model Army as a more professional and therefore more dependable fighting force. It was this new body that eventually defeated Charles' forces. Many in the New Model Army were Independents who considered the establishment of a presbyterian church order nearly as unacceptable as government by bishops.

In 1647 Charles found himself in the hands of his adversaries. Escaping briefly from his confinement, he was soon re-captured by his opponents. He continued unsuccessfully to try to negotiate a settlement which would allow him to retain some measure of power. Fighting began again in 1648, and by January 1649, Parliament had put him on trial. Ten days later he was executed. On the same day, Parliament abolished the monarchy and the House of Lords and established England as a "commonwealth." By this time, Oliver Cromwell, who had been a leader in the Parliamentary forces, was the most powerful man in England, and was named to chair the Council of State created by the House of Commons to govern the country.

While Parliament had been responsible for the creation of the New Order Army, the relationship between the two deteriorated rapidly. The early years of the Commonwealth were marked by aggressive military campaigns to subdue rebellions in both Ireland and Scotland, and increasing frustration by Cromwell and others at Parliament's behavior. In 1653, Cromwell declared Parliament dissolved; later in the year, he and other Army officers appointed a body charged with designing a new political structure. After it failed to reach agreement on the question of tithes for the clergy, it voted itself out of existence. The stage was set for the Council of State to design its own structure, which it adopted in December of 1653. While establishing new guidelines for Parliament, it also created the position of Lord Protector, to be elected for life. Oliver Cromwell was installed in this position the day after its approval.

The Parliament elected under the new government proved totally ineffective, and once its term had expired, Cromwell divided England into military districts; while local officials continued to perform their duties, ultimate authority was now in the hands of the Army. However, a new Parliament refused to approve taxes for the Army's permanent support, and instead offered the Crown to Cromwell. While he declined the title of king, he accepted the right to nominate his own successor.

Throughout his life, Oliver Cromwell's military and political behavior was a reflection of his religious beliefs. Like many of the Army from which he emerged, he himself supported the Independents, but shared the Puritan goal of a "godly society." His hatred of Roman Catholicism led him to use terror in putting down the rebellion in Ireland early in his rule. England under Cromwell was a repressive society, and much of the negative significance of the word "Puritanical" stems from his time as Lord Protector. Theatres and other places of entertainment were closed, and in 1652 the celebration of Christmas was formally forbidden. His armies were notorious for the destruction of religious art and architecture, which they understood to be left-over signs of idolatry lingering from the Roman Catholic past.

Cromwell is sometimes honored as an early proponent of religious freedom, and it is true that people of many and varied opinions found a place under his leadership. But the tolerance he espoused was itself a function of his deep belief in the correctness of his own faith, and his willingness to wait until the Lord should lead others to the same understanding. To a Scottish Presbyterian, he argued that "we look at ministers as helpers of, and not lords over, the people . . . You say that you have just cause to regret that men of civil employments should usurp the calling and reemployment of the ministry, to the scandal of the Reformed Kirks. Are you troubled that Christ is preached?"[43]

But Cromwell's tolerance did not extend to either Roman Catholics or the Anglicans who publicly and steadfastly refused to compromise with the new order, all of whom he considered to be disturbers of the peace of the godly society he was intent on establishing. To Cromwell, that peace seemed sometimes to be tested by Presbyterians as well.

In 1654, Cromwell appointed a group of clergy and laymen to a commission of "triers," charged with deciding on appointments of parish clergy and lecturers. A similar commission of "ejectors" was assigned the task of approving—or dismissing—those already serving as parish clergy. Both groups were made up of Independents, Presbyterians and Baptists, whom Cromwell believed should together form the church of the English people. Meanwhile, wrote one historian, "the greater part of the old Church was quietly absorbed into the Cromwellian establishment."[44]

Cromwell's hopes for an established church incorporating distinct groups who shared a commitment to Calvinist Christianity foundered on a number of issues and conflicts, in response to which he assumed increasing personal control over church policy. Ironically, his vision of a church was ultimately contradictory: as one biographer comments, "the doctrine that only the elect constitute the church cannot be reconciled with a national church." In the end, "the wide toleration which he had advocated had to be sacrificed for reasons of state."[45]

In 1655, Cromwell moved against the Anglican clergy in a decisive way. The diarist John Evelyn, a member of the small minority who remained not only a faithful supporter of the king but also of the king's Church, described with sorrow a visit to London on Christmas Day, 1655,

> where Dr. Wild preached the funeral sermon of Preaching, this being the last day; after which Cromwell's proclamation was to take place, that none of the Church of England should dare either to preach, or administer Sacraments, teach schools, etc., on pain of imprisonment, or exile. So this was the most mournful day that in my life I had seen, or the Church of England herself, since the Reformation; to the great rejoicing of both Papist and Presbyter. So pathetic was his discourse, that it drew tears from many of the [hearers]. Myself, wife, and some of our family, received the Communion, God make me thankful, who hath hitherto provided for us the food of our souls as well as bodies! The Lord Jesus pity our distressed Church, and bring back the captivity of Zion![46]

Two years later, Evelyn described the raiding of a clandestine Anglican celebration of the Christmas Eucharist.

> Sermon ended, as [Mr. Gunning] was giving us the Holy Sacrament, the chapel was surrounded with soldiers, and all the communicants and assembly surprised and kept prisoners by them, some in the house, others carried away. It fell to my share to be confined to a room in the house . . . In the afternoon, came Colonel Whalley, Goffe, and others, from Whitehall, to examine us one by one; some they committed to the marshal, some to prison. When I came before them, they took my name and abode, examined me why, contrary to the ordinance made, that none should any longer observe the superstition of the nativity (so esteemed by them), I durst offend, and be at common prayers, which they told me was but the mass in English, and particularly pray for Charles Stuart [the exiled son of the executed Charles I]: for which we had no scripture. I told them that we did not pray for Charles Stuart, but for all Christian kings, princes, and governors. They replied, in so doing we prayed for the king of Spain too, who was their enemy and a Papist, with other frivolous and ensnaring questions, and much threatening; and . . . dismissed me with much pity for my ignorance. These were men of high flight and above ordinances, and spoke spiteful things of our Lord's nativity. As we went up to receive the Sacrament, the miscreants held their muskets against us, as if they would have shot us at the altar; but yet suffering us to finish the office of Communion, as perhaps not having instructions what to do, in case they found us in that action. So I got home late the next day: thanks be to God![47]

Less than a year later, Oliver Cromwell was dead. His son Richard assumed the title of Protector, but after only seven months the Army removed him from office and re-convened the reduced Parliament which had sentenced Charles I to death. Following a brief period of factional conflict, the Army recalled the full Parliament, which had last met in 1640. Negotiations began with Charles II, who was declared by Parliament to have been the lawful king since the death of his father, and on May 29, 1660 Charles returned to London in triumph.

John Evelyn, who had been prevented by illness from accepting an invitation to accompany the party that went to Holland to bring the king back to England, described the homecoming in his diary.

> This day his Majesty, Charles II, came to London, after a sad and long exile and calamitous suffering both of the King and the Church, . . . with a triumph of above 20,000 horse and foot, brandishing their swords, and shouting with inexpressable joy; the ways strewn with flowers, the bells ringing, the streets hung with tapestry, fountains running with wine; the Mayor, Aldermen, and all the companies, in their liveries, chains of gold and banners; Lords and Nobles, clad in cloth of silver, gold and velvet; the windows and balconies, all set with ladies; trumpets, music, and myriads of people flocking. . . .
>
> I stood in the Strand and beheld it, and blessed God. And all this was done without one drop of blood shed, and by that very army which rebelled against him; but it was the Lord's doing, for such a restoration was never mentioned in any history, ancient or modern, since the return of the Jews from their Babylonish captivity; nor so joyful a day and so bright ever seen in this nation.[48]

Not everyone shared John Evelyn's joy. While most of those who had participated in the Commonwealth were pardoned, those who had been directly involved with the trial and execution of Charles I were tried, found guilty and condemned to death or life imprisonment. Though he had been dead since 1658, Oliver Cromwell's body was taken from its tomb in Westminster Abbey and subjected to a posthumous beheading, the fate which would have befallen him had he still been alive. His head was placed on a pole outside Westminster Abbey, where it remained for nearly twenty-five years as a grisly reminder of one of the most chaotic decades in the history of the English church and people.

NOTES

1. David H. Willson, *King James VI and I* (London: Jonathan Cape Ltd., 1963 edition), 198, 207.

2. See Alice Hogge, *God's Secret Agents: Queen Elizabeth's Forbidden Priests and the Hatching of the Gunpowder Plot* (London: Harper Perennial, 2005).

3. See Alister McGrath, *In the Beginning: The Story of the King James Bible and How It Changed a Nation, a Language and a Culture* (New York: Random House, 2001).

4. Adam Nicolson, *God's Secretaries: The Making of the King James Bible* (New York: HarperCollins, 2003), 75–76.

5. Kenneth Fincham, *Prelate As Pastor: The Episcopate of James I* (Oxford: Clarendon Press, 1990).

6. Fincham, *Prelate*, 41.

7. Fincham, *Prelate*, 89.

8. James I, "Directions Concerning Preachers" (1622) in Henry Gee and William Hardy, eds., *Documents Illustrative of English Church History* (New York: The Macmillan Company, 1896), 516–517.

9. James, "Directions," 518.

10. O'Day, *The English Clergy*, 103. On the other hand, Judith Malthy notes that early in James' reign, in Manchester there was "an articulate group of conformist laity, demanding worship according to the Book of Common Prayer and willing to go to law to discipline their minister . . . a pattern we find repeated elsewhere time and again." Judith Malthy, "'By the Book': Parishioners, the Prayer Book and the Established Church," in Fincham, ed., *The Early Stuart Church*, 1603–1642, 109–110.

11. O'Day, *The English Clergy*, 103. On the other hand, Judith Malthy notes that early in James' reign, in Manchester there was "an articulate group of conformist laity, demanding worship according to the Book of Common Prayer and willing to go to law to discipline their minister . . . a pattern we find repeated elsewhere time and again." Judith Malthy, "'By the Book': Parishioners, the Prayer Book and the Established Church," in Fincham, ed., *The Early Stuart Church*, 1603–1642, 109–110.

12. N. J. G. Pounds, *A History of the English Parish: The Culture of Religion from Augustine to Victoria* (Cambridge: Cambridge University Press, 2000), 3–4.

13. Pounds., *History*, 187–190.

14. Pounds, *History*, 241–244.

15. Pounds, *History*, 178, 181.

16. Joseph Hall, "Columba Noae, with a Translation," in Philip Wynter, ed., *The Works of the Reverend Joseph Hall, D.D.* (Oxford: Oxford University Press, 1843), X, 29.

17. Felicity Heal, *Reformation in Britain and Ireland* (Oxford: Oxford University Press, 2003), 5.

18. O'Day, *The English Clergy*, 189–190.

19. John Stubbs, *John Donne: The Reformed Soul: A Biography* (London: Viking Press, 2007).

20. John Donne, "*Nunc lento somitu dicunt, morieris,* XVII. MEDITATION," *Devotions Upon Diverse Occasions,* in Robert Coffin and Alexander Witherspoon, eds., *Seventeenth Century Prose and Poetry* (New York: Harcourt Brace, 1957), 68.

21. Houlbrooke, "The Family and Pastoral Care," in G. R. Evans, ed., *A History of Pastoral Care,* 286.

22. Kenneth Fincham and Peter Lake, "The Ecclesiastical Policies of James I and Charles I," in K. Fincham, ed., *The Early Stuart Church, 1603 – 1642* (London: The Macmillan Press, 1993), 24.

23. Charles Carlton, *Archbishop William Laud* (London: Routledge and Kegan Paul, Ltd., 1987), 44.

24. Carlton, *Laud*, 63.

25. Kenneth Hylson-Smith, *High Churchmanship in the Church of England from the 16th Century to the Late Twentieth Century* (Edinburgh: T. and T. Clark, 1993), 30.

26. Nicholas Tyacke, "Archbishop Laud," in Fincham, ed., *The Early Stuart Church, 1603 – 1642,* 61, 65.

27. Peter Marshall, *Reformation England 1480–1642* (London: Arnold, 2003), 202.

28. J. F. Merritt, "The Cradle of Laudianism? Westminster Abbey, 1558–1630," *Journal of Ecclesiastical History,* 52, 4 (October 2001), 625–634.

29. Robert S. Bosher, *The Making of the Restoration Settlement: The Influence of the Laudians 1649–1662* (London: Dacre Press, 1951), 2.

30. Ronald Blythe, ed., George Herbert, *A Priest to the Temple or The Country Parson with Selected Poems* (London: SCM-Canterbury Press, Ltd., 2003), 4.

31. Quoted in Kenneth Hylson-Smith, *High Churchmanship in the Church of England from the Sixteenth to the Late Twentieth Century* (Edinburgh: T. and T. Clark, 1993), 52.

32. Herbert, *The Priest to the Temple,* 7.

33. Herbert, *The Priest to the Temple,* 15.

34. Philip Sheldrake, *Love Took My Hand: The Spirituality of George Herbert* (Cambridge, MA: Cowley Publications, 2000), 16.

35. Herbert, *The Priest to the Temple,* 12–13.

36. Philip Sheldrake, "George Herbert and *The Country Parson,"* in Evans, ed., *A History of Pastoral Care,* 299–300, 307–308.

37. Henry Collett, *Little Gidding and Its Founder: An Account of the Religious Community Established by Nicholas Farrer in the XVIIth Century* (London: SPCK, 1925), 15–16.

38. Collett, *Little Gidding,* 20–24.

39. Collett, *Little Gidding,* 25–34.

40. H. R. McAdoo, *The Structure of Caroline Moral Theology* (New York: Longmans, Green and Co., 1949), 15.

41. Jeremy Taylor, *The Rule and Exercise of Holy Living* (New York: Harper and Row, 1970), 8.

42. Bosher, *The Making of the Restoration Settlement,* 5.

43. Quoted in George Drake, "The Ideology of Oliver Cromwell," *Church History,* 35, 3 (September 1966), 259–260.

44. Bosher, *The Making of the Restoration Settlement,* xiv.

45. Ethyn W. Kirby, "The Cromwellian Establishment," *Church History,* 10 (June 1941), 158.

46. William Bray, ed., *The Diary of John Evelyn* (New York: M. Walter Dunne, 1901), I, 307–308.
47. Bray, *The Diary of John Evelyn,* I, 319.
48. Bray, *The Diary of John Evelyn,* I, 332–333.

Chapter Four

Divergence

Ministry after the Restoration

The grisly sight of Cromwell's severed head that greeted worshippers at Westminster Abbey served as a grim reminder of the violence that had shaken the English church and people for two decades. That bloody history had permanent effects on English Christianity, in ways that could not have been predicted beforehand. Most of the Church of England, both clergy and laypeople, had made their peace, however unhappily, with the Commonwealth and the disappearance of the Prayer Book and their bishops. For a century, the Anglican assertion that it was the Church of the English people held together in uneasy communion people whose understanding of Christian faith was much marked by differences as well as by elements they shared. Nostalgia for the early days of the Reformation co-existed with passions for change; Arminians and Calvinists knelt—willingly or unwillingly—side by side to receive Communion.

With whatever zeal Archbishop Laud defended his understanding of the nature of Anglican Christianity, he never deluded himself that everyone agreed with his reading of its identity. But as the armed conflict and its aftermath ran its course, it was the minority who defended Laudian-style Anglicanism—people like John Evelyn and the priests and prelates who had been forced underground or into imprisonment or exile—who came to see themselves as the exclusive guardians of authentic English Christianity. Robert Bosher, whose study of the Restoration remains an important interpretation more than half a century after its writing, commented that

> the role of a self-conscious and vocal Anglicanism had entirely devolved on the minority which had maintained a separate and independent existence. In the crucial years before and during the settlement, the Anglican cause was effectively represented only by this well-organized group of High Churchmen. It was one of the rare occasions when the Church of England was able to act as a unity,

free of inner tension; its babel of voices was stilled, and only one voice spoke in the silence.... They were not conscious of being one party among several; they thought of themselves rather as the faithful remnant of a persecuted Church.[1]

During the worst years of Cromwellian persecution, the only visible segment of this remnant existed in Europe, where small gatherings of exiled Anglicans continued to worship according to the *Book of Common Prayer*.

HOME AGAIN: THE RESTORATION AND THE CHURCH OF ENGLAND

In the aftermath of the return of King Charles II, the future of the Church of England and its relation to the events of the recent past demanded early resolution. Charles had indicated his willingness to follow policies that would restore order and, insofar as it was possible, to reconcile old differences. The first years of his reign were marked by constant political and ecclesiastical maneuvering. Bishops were appointed to most of the sees which had been vacated by death. In the spring of 1661, a new Parliament was elected which solidly supported the restoration of the old Church.

It was at this point that the future of the Church of England's ordained ministry hung in the balance. Many of the parish clergy who had been installed during the Commonwealth not only opposed the use of the *Book of Common Prayer*; in many cases, they had not been ordained by bishops. Even before the king had arrived in England, he had been approached by Puritan leaders asking that the Prayer Book and the use of the surplice not be re-imposed on the Church. Charles promised an opportunity to consider their requests, a promise kept with the meeting of the Savoy Conference early in 1661. It brought together twelve bishops and twelve distinguished Puritan clergy, each attended by a team of nine consultants.

The Puritans presented a proposal for a Reformed alternative to the Prayer Book. Reflecting long-standing complaints, most of them dating back to the time of Elizabeth, they asked that a number of aspects of Prayer Book piety be made optional. These included the use of the wedding ring; congregational participation in worship beyond adding its "Amen" to the pastor's prayers; reference to vestments of any kind; the custom of godparents; and the rite of Confirmation administered by bishops. The bishops rejected almost all the Puritan proposals, and while some historians disagree, Bosher contends that the Anglican side never really intended to accept changes which would have made reconciliation with the Puritan side possible.[2]

The Parliament of 1661, which Bosher categorized as "the most Royalist and Anglican legislature that ever sat in England," undertook a series of actions that affirmed the impossibility of reconciliation.³ The Corporation Act required anyone holding civil, military or corporate office to be an annual communicant of the Church of England, to swear the Oaths of Allegiance and affirm the monarch's position as supreme governor of the Church of England, and to renounce the Covenant which nearly twenty years before had imposed a presbyterian system on the Church of England. The following year, Parliament approved a new revision of the *Book of Common Prayer* which continues to be the official liturgy of the Church of England to this day.

St. Bartholomew's Day, August 24, 1662, was set as the final date by which clergy were to affirm their conformity to the newly re-established Church of England. On that day, about two thousand clergy retired from their positions as parish clergy, an event which has come to be known as the "Great Ejection." Over the next few years, Parliament continued to pass harsh measures aimed at eliminating or controlling "dissent" or "non-conformity." The Conventicle Act of 1664 outlawed gatherings of more than five people for worship not conducted according to the *Book of Common Prayer*; a year later, the Five-Mile Act prohibited dissenting clergy from living within a radius of five miles of their previous congregation.

These harsh policies greatly affected the Church's ministry. Large numbers of laypeople followed their non-conforming clergy out of the Church of England, ending forever the possibility of considering it as "the Church of the English people." From now on, its legally established status would continue to guarantee its close relationship to the State, but a sizeable minority of the population would no longer consider themselves participants in its life. Bosher notes another consequence: Conformity was now the responsibility of Parliament, not the Church. "The political strength of the High Church party was bought with a price—the Church surrendered to Parliament its last shred of independence."[4]

Figures from the diocese of Canterbury reveal that the clergy who remained part of the Church of England's ordained ministry represented a broad spectrum of the society they served. 23 percent were the children of clergy, 28 percent were from gentry families and nearly half were from backgrounds with lower social status.[5] They understood their ministry as agents of stability in parishes that had been ripped asunder by the Restoration. The historian Jeremy Gregory sums up the clergy's mood as a reaction to the events of the last decades: "[B]ecause religious preoccupations were deemed to be central to social, political, and intellectual order, any religious experience which threatened that order needed to be anaesthetized. . . ." [The Church's] primary objective was "to be an instrument of religious, and thereby social and political, stability, by preaching with Anglican doctrine and by supporting the forces of order."[6]

No one understood that function of ministry better than the anonymous author of a work published shortly before the end of Cromwell's rule, which underwent multiple reprintings and enjoyed immense popularity among ordinary Anglicans for more than a century. Its primary purpose was summarized in its lengthy title, *The practice of Christian graces, or, The Whole Duty of Man, laid down in a plain and familiar way for the use of all, but especially the meanest sort* . . .[7] It was divided into seventeen chapters designed to be read by families, one each Sunday, allowing for the book to be read through three times in a year. It began with an impassioned argument for the importance of each individual's care of the soul given the disordered nature of each of its functions—the understanding, the will and the affections. Its Anglican perspective was underlined by its insistence that the Christian life is defined by obedience to God's will as it is revealed in both nature and scripture, and by its reminder that such a life of obedience also requires faithfulness to each of the ordered and hierarchical relationships which define every human life: between the subject and the monarch, between husband and wife, parents and children, servants and masters.

The contemporary reader of works such as *The Whole Duty of Man* might struggle to see why dutiful conformity to the rigorous social mores and distinctions that marked English society in centuries past should be considered an integral part of the Christian life; but to faithful members of the Church of England in the aftermath of conflict, it was simply a reflection of the divinely mandated order that held together the distinct elements of church and state and guaranteed that the chaos of the last century might be laid to rest at last. Harmony between faith and order would remain an unexamined pillar of Anglican ministry for the next three hundred years.

UNEASY RESTORATION: THE CHURCH OF SCOTLAND

The results of the return of the Stuart monarchy in Scotland were quite different than in Charles' other realms of England, Ireland and Wales, since the Church of Scotland had a longer history of presbyterian polity and strong support for it remained intact. The Restoration would prove to bring little stability to parishes north of the border. When Charles returned to Britain in 1660, he assured the Synod of Edinburgh that he intended to maintain the Scottish Church as it had been established by law. But if its Presbyterian members assumed that Charles meant to leave the Church's structures unchanged, they were mistaken. The Scottish Parliament proved just as eager as its English counterpart to undo the actions of previous decades, declaring that all the acts establishing a presbyterian polity in the years leading up to Cromwell's Commonwealth were null and void. It ordered reparations to be paid to

Episcopal clergy deprived of their parishes and to the heirs of those who had died; Scotland's Lord Chancellor, the Earl of Glencairn, summed up the mood when he reviled "the insolence of the Presbyterians" and asserted that the overwhelming majority of the Scottish people "longed for Episcopacy, by which no rebellion was ever hatched; . . . whereas [Calvinism] and Presbytery had never been introduced without blood and rebellion."[8]

Charles indicated his intention to re-establish the Church of Scotland with an episcopal polity, although only one of its bishops from the period before the Civil War had survived. By the end of 1661, presbyteries had lost their authority to induct clergy into parishes, and soon after, synods and kirk sessions, the agencies by which the Scottish Church had been governed, were abolished. Four new bishops were consecrated in England for the Scottish Church, including James Sharp as Archbishop of St. Andrew's and primate of Scotland. Sharp's consecration was a particularly bitter pill, since he had previously been opposed to episcopacy, and was therefore "execrated by the Presbyterians as their *Judas, traitor and betrayer*."[9]

The Earl of Glencairn's reading of the mood of the Scottish population proved to be overly optimistic; a few years after his consecration, Archbishop Sharp was the target of an assassination attempt, from which he emerged unscathed but which permanently injured Bishop Honeyman of Orkney, who was at his side. Preachers opposed to the new church order and its liturgical practices began inciting opposition by preaching outdoors to farmers, leading the government to declare such preaching illegal. Conflict over worship and polity wracked the Scottish church throughout Charles' reign. In spite of substantial loyalty to a dynasty still identified with Scottish national identity and a significant number of supporters of his religious policies, strong and militant opposition remained, culminating in a successful attack on Archbishop Sharp's life in 1679, in which he was fatally shot sixteen times while traveling with his daughter; she herself was robbed and slightly injured in the attack.

RESTORATION: UNRAVELING

Parliament's efforts to impose a strict Anglican conformity on society were ultimately in vain, and in England the principal challenges came from an unexpected quarter: the royal family itself. In some ways, Charles squandered the support of a Parliament that had been intent on restoring the role and power of the monarch.

Shortly after Charles II returned to England, he married a Portuguese princess, and his subjects soon discovered that he was deeply embroiled in European political intrigues and the wars that often accompanied them. Not only had he never shared Parliament's fear of Roman Catholicism; he had in fact signed a secret agreement with the king of France expressing his intention to accept it when circumstances permitted. In 1672, he issued a Declaration of Indulgence, setting aside the restrictions on dissenters established at the time of his restoration to the throne. Parliament was incensed, and forced the king not only to withdraw the declaration but to assent to the first of the Test Acts, further marginalizing religious dissent by limiting government service to communicants of the Church of England.

While Charles fathered a dozen illegitimate children, many of whom were awarded titles, he and his Portuguese queen had no children and his heir apparent was his Roman Catholic brother, James, Duke of York. The last years of Charles' reign were marked by increasing anxiety over the possibility of another Roman Catholic monarch and rumors of a plot to kill the king. While Charles ignored them, those fears resulted in Parliament's consideration of an Exclusion Bill which would have prohibited Roman Catholics from occupying the throne. In 1679, Charles suspended Parliament and reigned as an absolute monarch for the rest of his life. He died in 1685; on his deathbed, he was received into the Roman Catholic Church, though the circumstances of his conversion have often been questioned.

It was Charles II who laid a firm foundation, to a far greater extent than any of his predecessors, for Britain's overseas imperial ambitions. Those ventures had highly significant consequences, not only for the British Empire but for the history of Anglican Christianity, its global mission and ministry. Through a series of charters he gave permission to the British East India Company to acquire territory in the Indian subcontinent as well as to maintain its own military forces, wage war, take responsibility for civil and criminal jurisdiction in those areas it controlled, mint currency—in other words, to function as a surrogate government for the English crown. Charles also chartered the Hudson's Bay Company, which began as an enterprise to develop the Canadian fur trade but eventually controlled some three million square miles of North American territory.

JAMES II AND THE "GLORIOUS REVOLUTION"

In spite of his unpopularity, Charles' brother James succeeded him to the throne in 1685. James was the father of two daughters, both of whom had been raised as members of the Church of England, and who were his heirs. His elder daughter Mary was married to her first cousin, Prince William of Orange, hereditary ruler of five of the provinces that made up the Dutch Republic and a staunch member of the (Calvinist) Dutch Reformed Church.

Following the death of his first wife, James married Mary of Modena, an Italian princess who was also Roman Catholic. James was determined to make it possible for Roman Catholics to practice their faith openly, and in 1687 he issued another Declaration of Indulgence, which was revised and renewed early in the following year. Seven bishops, including Archbishop Sancroft of Canterbury, opposed the Declaration, for which they were imprisoned and brought to trial; their stand won them great popularity and they were acquitted of all the charges brought against them.

The fears of a Roman Catholic dynasty gained strength when, early in 1688, Mary of Modena gave birth to a son who would take precedence over his two Anglican half-sisters as his father's heir. On the day that the bishops' acquittal was announced, a letter from the Bishop of London and six highly placed political leaders reached William of Orange, asking that he intervene to prevent what they considered a political and religious disaster. A series of hasty negotiations followed, and William landed in the south of England with a force of four thousand cavalry troops and eleven thousand foot soldiers. James soon realized that he could not hope to prevail against the incursion; alarmed that even his own troops were deserting to the other side, he fled the country in December of 1688.

Early the following year, William convened a "Convention Parliament" which determined that by leaving England, James II had abdicated the throne. William and Mary, who were invited to reign jointly as King and Queen, agreed to a number of conditions that permanently changed the nature of the English government and also had significant consequences for the Church and its future ministry. In effect, their decision to accept the limitations on royal power imposed by Parliament and their acceptance of an English Bill of Rights established England as a constitutional monarchy, in which the sovereign's power was severely limited and the initiative of government passed to Parliament.

But while English history describes the events of 1688 and 1689 as the "Glorious Revolution," it was a time of renewed crisis for the Church and its ministry, not only in England but throughout the British Isles. Indeed, its consequences were most dramatic in Scotland.

THE "NON-JURORS"

The Church of the Restoration had fervently embraced the divine right of kings and the Christian obligation to obey divinely appointed authority was an important tenet of its preaching. The strictures by which the Church and its bishops had been restored under Charles II included solemn oaths of allegiance to the monarch by all those who held its offices. Not surprisingly, William and Mary expected the same oath once they had assumed the throne. But the peculiar circumstances of James' departure and his continued survival in exile, from where he insisted that he remained the duly crowned and anointed king, created a serious problem of conscience for many clergy. In Scotland, national loyalty to the Stuart dynasty was also a factor. When the new monarchs demanded that all clergy pledge their allegiance to them, nine bishops of the Church of England, including the Archbishop of Canterbury and four others who had been imprisoned by James II, declared that they were unable to take such an oath. They were joined in their refusal by one bishop in Ireland and all the Scottish bishops, as well as some four hundred English clergy, many Scottish priests, and a large number of laypeople.

Not surprisingly, the King and Queen had little patience with these "Non-Jurors," and they were warned that unless they acquiesced by taking the oath, they would be deprived of their posts and deposed. Three of the original non-juring bishops had died before the deadline passed, but in February 1690, the survivors were removed from office, their posts declared vacant, and new bishops and clergy assigned in their place.

The Non-Jurors were secure in the rightness of their actions and believed that by remaining faithful to the anointed monarch, they represented in fact the "true" Church of England, while the much larger number of clergy and laypeople who accepted the new king and queen were guilty of schism. This argument failed to move William and Mary; although William had accepted membership in the Church of England when he took the throne, in fact he personally hoped for complete religious freedom for all, including Roman Catholics, in order to strengthen political alliances with several European Catholic powers. But while the 1689 Act of Toleration provided for the licensing of non-conforming clergy and the opening of dissenting places of worship, it excluded Roman Catholics, Quakers and Unitarians, continued to require the oaths of allegiance and supremacy, and maintained the rigorous exclusion from public office required by the Test Act. In general, the clergy and bishops who now assumed power in the Church of England supported this limited tolerance, and in general they demonstrated a more relaxed, even indifferent, posture towards doctrines and practices that seemed to them to divide rather than unite people on both the local and the international level. These "latitudinarians" tended to stress the familiar Anglican value of reasoned order, and many participated freely in the wealth of scientific and philosophical investigation and speculation that so marked the Britain of the eighteenth century.

While the latitudinarians are sometimes viewed as uninterested in pastoral ministry, in fact their perspective was often the result of their analysis of the current reality of English religion, which they recognized had reached a critical state of disunity. Gilbert Burnet, who served as bishop of Salisbury in the years immediately following the Glorious Revolution, combined a concern for addressing the situation of those outside the Established Church with a deep interest in pastoral ministry. He condemned what he called "the neglect of discipline and the careless abuses of clergy," especially the widespread situation of clergy with multiple cures and absence from their parish. Convinced that the problems of the Church on the local level were primarily the result of poor theological education, he began a training program for clergy in the diocese of Salisbury. Burnet urged priests to break with "the world, wealth and pleasure," and to avoid augmenting their income by teaching or farming, which he considered distractions from their primary duties. Their task, he believed, was "working for reconciliation between neighbours, admonishing those of rank who set ill examples (preferably by letter!), visiting the sick, preparing the dying for judgment, going from home to home and getting to know his people."[10]

In Scotland, William and Mary's policy towards the Non-Jurors led to quite different consequences. The resistance of the bishops provided an opportunity for the Scottish Presbyterians to argue for the permanent elimination of the episcopate and the re-establishment of a presbyterian polity. The monarchs acceded to this request, and the non-juring bishops and clergy, along with their lay followers, withdrew from what became the now-presbyterian Church of Scotland. To some extent the separation reflected larger divisions within Scottish society; many of the nobility and gentry were Episcopalians, while the Presbyterians were drawn mainly from the urban and merchant middle class.[11]

For a brief period, the Scottish Non-Jurors hoped that their exclusion would be a temporary one, but when it became clear that the hold of William and Mary on the throne was secure and that James' exile would be lengthy and perhaps permanent, they took steps to establish what was later described as "the Catholic remainder of the antient (sic) Church of Scotland" and which survives to this day as the Scottish Episcopal Church.[12]

The existence of Non-Jurors in England, formerly part of the Established Church but now organizing themselves into dissident congregations, and in Scotland, where they created a new Episcopal alternative to the Scottish church, challenged the previously held concept of the nature of a national church. Within a few years, the surviving non-juring bishops in England had consecrated new bishops to assure the survival of what they continued to believe was the "true" Church of England; with the passage of time, the Scottish bishops also took steps to ensure the continuation of bishops in apostolic succession. No longer able to preside over dioceses, since only the monarch could appoint bishops to their sees, they consecrated new bishops as members of what was considered an "Episcopal college," with joint responsibility for the non-juring church.

Reduced to meeting under strange and restrained circumstances, often in private homes, the Non-Jurors in both England and Scotland preserved the characteristics which had already marked the Stuart church: a profound commitment to the episcopate as a guarantee of the authenticity of the Church's ministry and its apostolic nature; an emphasis on sacramental worship; a deeply felt and earnestly practiced piety; belief in the divine right of monarchs, and an often passionate loyalty to the exiled James and his young son over against William and Mary.

In 1701, James died, but the Non-Jurors' hopes that his son might become heir were dashed when the Act of Settlement prohibited a Roman Catholic from occupying the throne. Six years later, England and Scotland, which had maintained separate governments while sharing monarchs, agreed to an Act of Union; henceforth, Scottish representatives sat in the British Parliament, although the Church of Scotland maintained its independence and its presbyterian governance.

Over the next decades, the fate of the Stuart claimants became part of the complex and conflicted relationship between France, which continued to recognize and support them, and Britain. The "Old Pretender," James' son James Francis Edward Stuart, led an invasion of Scotland in 1715, but his anticipated support failed to materialize and a year later he retired to France. In 1743, he named his son, Charles Edward (known in legend and folklore as "Bonnie Prince Charlie") as regent. The young Charles attempted another invasion in 1745, but enjoyed no more success than his father.

Queen Anne, who succeeded William and Mary on the throne, allowed clergy ordained by English or Irish bishops (but not Scottish bishops) to exercise a public ministry in Scotland, but following Charles Edward's invasion of 1745, in which many Episcopalians were charged as conspirators, a series of repressive measures were approved. Systematic espionage was directed at Episcopal services, Scottish Episcopal holy orders were declared illegal, even family prayers could include no more than five persons unrelated to the family, and only "ministers, elders, or preachers of the Established Church of Scotland" could serve as chaplains to noble families. Episcopal worship took place, one commentator reported, "in the dens and caves of the earth, in secluded woods, and on the mountainside." Over the years, the persecution had its effects: four decades later, there were only four bishops and forty clergy who identified themselves with the Episcopal Church of Scotland; its members numbered no more than five percent of the population.[13]

As the years passed and it became obvious that the Stuarts would never again occupy the throne, most of the English Non-Jurors gradually found their way back to the Church of England. Eighteenth century bishops were dominated by the latitudinarians appointed by William and Mary and their successors, while the clergy tended to remain more loyal to the values and practices of the Restoration. Meetings of the Church Convocation became so heated between the two houses that the government suspended it in 1717; it was not summoned again for nearly a century and a half.

The Non-Jurors themselves were not exempt from controversy. Their principal advocates wrote in defense of a high view of the episcopacy which distanced them theologically from those latitudinarian bishops who, following Hooker, considered the ministry of bishops to be a "thing indifferent." George Hickes, one of the Non-Jurors consecrated as bishop to continue the apostolic succession, believed that "the true essence of Catholicity on earth resides in episcopacy. . . . Any other form of Church Order set up by men is only 'another government, another mission and another ministry of their own divising, against the government and ministry set up by divine authority for the Catholic Church.'"[14]

In time, some Non-Jurors came to believe that the revisions Cranmer had made to his own 1549 *Book of Common Prayer* had resulted in a deficient Eucharistic liturgy that failed to reflect adequately the practice of the ancient Church that he had claimed to restore. The "usages" that had been eliminated were the mixing of water and wine in the chalice, prayers for the departed, the *epiclesis,* or invocation of the Holy Spirit on the bread and wine of the Eucharist, and a prayer of oblation or offering. These elements had been added by Laud to the Scottish liturgy in 1637; some Non-Jurors, who came to be known as "Usagers," insisted on restoring them for their own use. But others considered that changing the Prayer Book amounted to rejecting the historic Church of England by which they identified themselves. For nearly fifteen years various Non-Jurors declared themselves out of communion with others, and well into the eighteenth century a few stubborn people continued to insist that only their version of the Church fully represented the Catholic heritage of the ancient Christian community. Isolated from both the Established Church and the Protestant dissenters, they held tenaciously to a sacramental piety that sought to color all of life.

William Law, who was ordained a deacon in the Church of England but made a priest by the Non-Jurors, understood that alienation from the ordinary folk who surrounded them was to be an inevitable result of seeking to live faithfully. His best-known work, *A Serious Call to a Devout and Holy Life,* is reminiscent of similar books produced a century earlier; in spite of Law's own somewhat marginalized status, the book enjoyed enormous popularity and influence for many years after its publication in 1728. Law stood apart from many of his non-juring associates in paying little attention to worship but emphasizing an all-encompassing spirituality bordering on the ascetic and even the mystical.

If contempt of the world and heavenly affection is a necessary temper of Christians, it is necessary that this temper appear in the whole course of their lives, in their manner of using the world, because it can have no place anywhere else. If self-denial be a condition of salvation, all that would be saved must make it a part of their ordinary life. If humility is a Christian duty, then the common life of a Christian is to be a constant course of humility in all its kinds.[15]

Law considered that laypeople, like clergy, are called to the highest standard of Christian behavior; each calling makes special demands on faith, but all are equally meant to issue in holiness.

> For all the virtues of the Christian life, its perfect purity, its heavenly tempers, are as much the sole rule of your life as the sole rule of the life of a bishop. . . . For there is no reason why you should think the highest holiness, the most heavenly tempers to be the duty and happiness of a bishop, but what is as good a reason why you should think the same tempers to be the duty and happiness of all Christians.[16]

The high moral standards preached by non-juring clergy like Law were reflected in the lives of exemplary laypeople who followed them out of the Established Church. One of the best known of his time was Henry Dodwell, briefly a professor at Oxford but deprived of his post when he refused to take the oath to William and Mary. Although he eventually returned to the Church of England, he wrote extensively and critically about the English Reformation, considering that the church in the time of Henry VIII had erred in "placing the church's future in the hands of the State" and reserving especially harsh criticism for Thomas Cranmer, whom he considered a "sycophant who gained advancement in the church and preserved his own life by doing the king's bidding."[17] But Dodwell's stern and passionate defense of a concept of a Church of England related to but independent of the monarchy was reflected in his own deeply committed personal piety: he refused ordination, which cost him a fellowship at Trinity College, Dublin, because of a profound sense of personal unworthiness. A colleague once wrote of him that while some called him obstinate, "obstinacy, (if it may be so called) is always laudable; and I wish that all men would observe and follow it, especially those of the clergy; and I heartily wish moreover that half the clergy, nay that one tenth part of them, had the fortieth part of the integrity, learning and holiness of this lay-man . . ."[18]

MINISTRY IN THE EIGHTEENTH CENTURY

The somber spirituality commended by the Non-Juror clergy to their followers was sometimes found among the leaders of the Established Church as well. However, the eighteenth-century Church of England is generally considered to have been primarily concerned with the role of its ministry in undergirding what was believed to be a God-given social order: "Humility, reverence, submission to moral authority and submission to social superiors continued to be the message of the pulpit and ... of *The Whole Duty of Man*."[19]

Much of the Church's ministry was rooted in the English countryside where the overwhelming majority of the population lived. This meant that most clergy continued to depend on the tithe; their sustenance therefore depended on the economic health of England's farmers. "The clergy," one historian wrote, "were rural men leading rural lives; their attitudes were rural, their lives were rural, and even their hatreds were rural."[20] Studies of the eighteenth century demonstrate that in its early decades, the Church of England's clergy shared a common culture, in part the result of a common educational background, generally a grammar school or private tutor followed by Oxford or Cambridge. Apart from the standard classical education offered by the university, theological preparation was mostly limited to a course of twelve lectures by a Divinity professor and a set of examinations on the works of William Paley, whose approach has been described as "rationalistic" in piety and "provok[ing] little deep questioning concerning the fundamental matters of faith ... Dissent—even comment—was not asked for, nor was it expected."[21]

The diaries of those country clergy often provide revealing glimpses into the practice of the Church's ministry among ordinary Anglicans. Most provided the services they were expected to perform, including attention to the needs of the poor of the parish; many, however, also seem to have spent a good deal of their energy enjoying (and recording) the social life to which their position as principal persons of the parish entitled them. One of the best known of the diarists, James Woodforde, described the welcome he offered to the local farmers when, early in December, they gathered to pay their tithes:

> I gave them a good dinner, sirloin of Beef rosted, a Leg of Mutton boiled and Plumb Puddings in plenty. Recd. To-day only for Tithe and Glebe of them ... [236 pounds two shillings]. ... They all broke up at about 10 at night. Dinner at 2. Every person well pleased, and were very happy indeed. They had to drink Wine, Punch and Ale as much as they pleased; they drank of wine 5 bottles, of Rum 1 gallon and half, and I know not [how much] ale. ... Some dined in the Parlour and some in the Kitchen 17 dined etc. that paid my Tithe.[22]

On Christmas day, Parson Woodforde received the hind quarter of a London lamb from his upholsterer and commented that "prodigious fine it was indeed." He invited seven poor people to dine with him and then accompany him to church; to each he gave a shilling and "by God's grace I intend doing the same next Christmas Day. Gave old Richard Bates an old black coat and waistcoat. I had a fine sirloin of Beef rosted and Plumb Puddings. It was very dark at Church this aft. I could scarcely see . . . " Soon afterwards, he joined a weekly dining club, where he enjoyed "a Leg of Mutton boiled, a butter Pudding, and a couple of Ducks." In the afternoon he played Quadrille, lost one shilling and threepence, and noted, "I gave nothing at all to the Servants."[23]

It would, however, be a mistake to assume that the Church of England's parish clergy were uniformly an idle lot. The diaries of clergy like William Cole, rector of Bletchley, Buckinghamshire for fifteen years at mid-century, permit a glimpse into the ordinary events of eighteenth-century country life as well as the style and nature of their ministry.

> Sunday 9. Thaw. After Matins I went to the other End of the Town to administer the Sacrament to Robert Ashby & to pray by Wm. Bradbury. I lent 6 Pounds to Joe Holdom the Butcher, & as many to Mr. Cartwright about a Fortnight ago . . .
>
> Tuesday, 20. Cold and dry. . . . I went in my Chaise to Eaton to pray by the wife of Robert King; from thence to West Blecheley on the same Errand to the Wife of Robert Mollard, very ill with a Cancer on her Thigh from thence to Robert Ashby, who is better, but I prayed by him, as I did also with Wm. Bradbury, who was very ill of Consumption. I wrote to Mr. Etheridge of Simpson, Brother-in-Law to Farmer Turner, who died at West Blecheley yesterday of the Small Pox, to let him be put into the Grave this Evening, & I would read the Burial Service over him to-morrow; as hardly any of the Parish had had the Distmper [sic] & few of the Clergy could be got to bury him; as even those who had had it themselves, were afraid of carrying the Infection to their Wives & Children. He readily assented to my Proposal; Mrs. Willis so alarmed, that she went out of the Parish for a week or two.[24]

Perhaps it was Parson Cole's own dedication to his ministry (and to the station in life it presupposed) that led him to cast a critical eye towards those who did not measure up to his self-imposed standards. He criticized his own bishop with vehemence:

> [T]he clownish Carriage & Want of Behaviour and Manners in the present Bp. Was so notorious at his last Visitation that every one was scandalized at it, & among all my Acquaintance I never heard him mentioned but with the utmost Disrespect. . . . Indeed, the Bp's ungainly, awkward, splay-footed Carriage and Yorkshire Dialect is a full Indication of his humble Education and mean Extraction . . . With what Face can the Church of England abuse the Popish Church & Hierarchy for Nepotism and Pluralities? when they are equally if not greatly more guilty of the same & other Faults, as pretending to a greater Purity, than the other?[25]

Parson Cole was not the only person in the Church of England who was concerned about "pluralities," the custom of multiple livings concentrated in the hands of one clergyman. While it was sometimes defended on the grounds that it made it possible for the Church to "stretch its limited resources to provide . . . a minimum of pastoral oversight," it was particularly condemned when one priest held several well-endowed livings and their geographical location made it impossible for him to tend them all. Absenteeism, and the provision of minimal care by hiring underpaid, perhaps resentful curates, plagued the Church for many years, and provoked Archbishop Thomas Secher to remind his clergy that "it is only by living amongst your People and knowing them thoroughly that can show you what is level to their Capacities and suited to their Circumstances and what will reform their Faults and improve their hearts in true Goodness. Yet unless this is your Business with them and unless you perform it Everything else is Nothing."[26]

In both rural and urban parishes, it was the clergy's responsibility to maintain their own rectories; if they allowed them to fall into disrepair, their successors expected them or their heirs to negotiate a financial settlement or face legal action. Peter Virgin's study of the clerical life in this period describes a work load consisting of "taking Sunday services, catechizing the young, preparing candidates for confirmation, visiting the sick and elderly, and being responsible for 'rites of passage'" and observes that, except for towns where the entire population belonged to one parish, the list is "neither long nor . . . heavy."[27] A review of two deaneries in the eastern county of Norfolk reveals that the Eucharist was never celebrated more than four times a year, and in most congregations fewer than ten persons actually received the Sacrament at any given service. One church went for seven years without a celebration of the Eucharist because no laypeople could be found to receive Communion.[28]

Meanwhile, in the cities, those clergy with learning and time sufficient to allow them leisure were active participants in the explosion of scientific knowledge and philosophical speculation that characterized urbane London society. At the very end of the seventeenth century, two important lay voices had challenged the nature of traditional belief: John Locke published his *Reasonableness of Christianity* in 1695, and a year later John Toland wrote *Christianity Not Mysterious*. Both works were the subject of considerable speculation and anxiety on the part of more traditional Christians, who were alarmed by their skeptical attitude towards biblical "signs and wonders" and to any truth taught by scripture but unproven by empirical observation or rational analysis. Less than twenty years later, Benjamin Hoadley, the bishop of Bangor, Wales, attacked what he considered to be the narrow-minded dogmatism of the Non-Jurors, arguing that the scriptures contain no information or guidance whatsoever about the structures of the institutional church.

Each in his own way advocated a more relaxed ecclesiastical body that could encompass a wide variety of belief and practice but still provide the underpinning for a stable and harmonious social order.

In spite of the Church of England's commitment to an orderly society, the eighteenth century witnessed the beginnings of profound changes that would ultimately convulse both church and society. Much of the population of the countryside either worked as tenants on the great estates or owned holdings too small to provide for their household. Fortunately, those holdings were complemented by great tracts of publicly owned or "common" land on which farmers could graze their flocks or herds. Removing common land from public use by fencing or "enclosing" it for sale to private owners was a process requiring the approval of Parliament, but in difficult economic times, it was always an attractive way of providing income for the State. Its consequences for the farmers were, however, severe, and often resulted in reducing rural families to penury. Employment opportunities for those displaced by enclosure tended to be either in the towns or in the mines scattered across much of central and northern England. In both settings, the wages were minimal and the working conditions tended to be unspeakable by any standards.

While enclosure became much more prevalent in the second half of the eighteenth century, the process of urbanization and industrialization was already evident long before. The essentially conservative culture of the countryside continued to hold most of the population within the fold of the Established Church, but the relationship between the poor and the Church's leadership became increasingly more problematic, especially when poverty-stricken farmers struggled to pay their tithes to clergy whose social standing set them apart. The growing custom of renting or selling pew-space to those who could afford it also identified and marginalized those whose very presence at worship depended on the free seating that might or might not be sufficient to hold the numbers who needed it. Not only was there insufficient free seating in most parishes; the growth rate for many English towns was so rapid that the Church could not begin to keep up with the need for new church buildings. It is small wonder that many of those with few economic resources found their way to Dissenting chapels in towns where they were available. In Merthyr Tydfil, a mining town in Wales, three quarters of the population identified themselves as Non-conformists. One Welsh observer who lamented the decline of the Established Church described it as "ruined," with many churches offering little in the way or preaching, catechizing or celebrations of the Eucharist. "Such is the faint shadow that remains among us of the public sense of religion," he wrote.[29]

Poverty in both rural and urban settings became a significant issue for eighteenth-century English church and society, not least because it had become more obvious and therefore more problematic. While a series of Poor Laws pretended to provide public relief for the most abject suffering, in 1723 the Workhouse Test Act condemned the able-bodied poor to workhouses, and the stage was set for the evolution of a culture of poverty that flourished in the following century and was portrayed in all its misery by novelists like Charles Dickens. "Wealth and poverty were national obsessions in late eighteenth century Britain," wrote Deborah Valense, "because both were manifestly proliferating."[30]

The Church of England has frequently been criticized for failing to respond adequately to the constantly growing tension and social dislocation, and it is certainly true that many of its leaders and spokespersons limited their actions to vague calls for civility, appropriate deference and acceptance of their lot on the part of the poor, and compassionate charity from the more prosperous. There were, however, some whose attitude was more direct, none more outspoken than William Law, who considered greed, ostentation and concern for comfort and luxury to be the marks of superficial faith and held both rich and poor to the same standard of modesty, humility and attention to the needs of others. Although a Non-Juror, his influence is evident among those members of the Church of England who were troubled by what they perceived as their Church's widespread spiritual apathy, lack of concern to improve the lot of the poor and unwillingness to address the conditions in which they lived.

It was perhaps inevitable that movements would appear on the scene to address the presumed need of attention to the poor, of energized commitments, personal engagement and perhaps even genuine church reform. The early eighteenth century was a time of growing awareness of the need for ministry with people for whom Christian faith and the life of the Church that promoted it were often unknown. With the new century a number of reform-minded societies were formed to address the vices associated with poverty: prostitution, promiscuity, alcoholism, stealing, and disrespect for the norms of "polite" society. These societies for the reform of manners flourished especially among the well-born and prosperous young, who often became quite passionate on their behalf; one skeptical observer described such groups as societies "of worthy gentlemen, who seem to prosecute vice with as much pleasure as others commit it, to their mortal horror be it mentioned." But they can also be seen as yet another expression of the impulse to create England as a "godly society," in which its people display "real holiness of heart and life."[31]

There is certainly plenty of evidence to indicate that many active participants in the Church of England did in fact respond with generosity to the needs of the poor. The Wardens of the Church of St. John the Baptist, Chester, opted to record representative gifts on wall tablets mounted near the entrance to the church, where worshippers might be encouraged to similar acts of compassion:

> H.S. of this City, gave to ye poor of this Parish ten pounds, ye interest thereof to be given by ye Min[iste]r & Ward[en]s to 20 poor old Maids or widows 6d. a peice [sic], none to be taken into ye numb[e]r under 60 years old, & such as are & have been of good behavior, & members of ye Church of England. ... The above said Mrs. Hellena Salmon, late of this City, by her last Will and Testament, as added to her former Legacy, Given to the Poor of this Parish, the sum of Ten pounds, the Life of it to be given to Poor House-keepers, inhabiting in and belonging to this Parish, at the discretion of the Church-Wardens of this Parish, for the time being on the 10th Day of April Anually for ever.[32]

Contemporary scholars have done much to correct the image of a Church totally devoid of spiritual vitality or a sense of mission. One sympathetic historian considers that the problem lay, not with the lack of conscientious clergy but with the organization of the Church itself.

> The Church of England was not lacking in good or even great men as once was thought.... The problem lay rather in the structure of the church.... There was no central body to think strategically for the church. There was no structural potentiality for concerted action on any matter.... The bishops spent months at the House of Lords, yet lacked the power to effect meaningful change. Dioceses and parishes tended to go their separate ways and to act congregationally rather than regionally or nationally. They existed mainly in southern England away from the growing areas of population.[33]

It was into such a church and world that the Wesley brothers, who profoundly challenged the Church's ministry, were born and came of age.

A NEW REFORMATION?

John and Charles Wesley, whose ministries were so closely joined that it is impossible to separate their influence, were born into a clerical family; their father was rector of Epworth, Lincolnshire. Both grandfathers were ejected from the Church at the time of the Restoration as Dissenters; both parents found their way back to the Church of England, and at the time of the "Glorious Revolution," their mother supported the Non-Jurors (much to the disgust of their father). The Wesley household included ten children; at least six others had died. John Wesley was born in 1703 and his brother Charles was four years younger. Both brothers studied at Oxford, and John Wesley briefly served as his father's curate before returning to the University as a Fellow of Lincoln College.

The Wesley brothers became the nucleus of a small group of young men whose piety was shaped by such rigorous spiritual mentors as William Law, and who were dubbed the "Holy Club" or "Methodists" because of their strict spiritual discipline, including weekly attendance at the Eucharist, daily Morning and Evening Prayer, Bible study, fasting, and "good works" such as visits to prisons.[34] In 1735, their commitments took them as missionaries to the North American colony of Georgia. Their ministry in Georgia was in every sense a disaster, but it was on their outward journey that they first met a group of Moravian Brethren, whose piety combined liturgical discipline with a simple and highly emotive personal faith. Within a few years, both Wesley brothers had experienced a mystical awareness of the gracious presence and call of God, experiences which provided them with a sense of religious certainty that they had been seeking and which they had first encountered among the Moravian Brethren. John Wesley later broke with the Moravians and confessed privately that he suffered perennial doubts, but they never intruded upon his preaching. For the rest of their lives, both Wesley brothers dedicated themselves to striving for personal holiness and to awakening a similar commitment in others.

Nor were they alone in this commitment. George Whitefield was perhaps the best known of the English church leaders who were beginning to find dramatic responses to their preaching among the poor. Other groups, such as the Moravian Brethren themselves, were popularizing a style of Christian faith and practice which emphasized an emotive piety that stood in sharp contrast to the ordered worship and prayer of the Church of England. But it is the Wesleys who soon found themselves at the center of a movement which swept across England, creating conflict within the Church even as it fired enthusiasm in the crowds of the poor who welcomed their message with noisy and often unruly ecstasy.

Whitefield, already known for his habit of preaching in the fields to the colliers of Bristol, knew John Wesley's work from Wesley's presentations on behalf of several religious societies, and invited him to participate in his ministry. Like Whitefield, Wesley discovered that his powerful presentation of the gospel as free grace produced ecstatic behavior: hearers regularly fainted, spoke in tongues, and otherwise exhibited dramatic religious behavior unknown in the ordered liturgical life of the eighteenth-century Church of England. Charles Wesley, always close to his older brother in his spiritual journey, discovered a talent for writing hymns, and in the course of his lifetime produced many thousands. Some remain popular to this day, while others have long since disappeared from use; most are written to celebrate and embrace God's love and graciousness to sinners.

> Outcasts of men, to you I call,
> Harlots and publicans and thieves!
> He spreads his arms t'embrace you all

> Sinners alone his grace receives:
> No need of him the righteous have;
> He came the lost to seek and save.[35]

Both Wesleys took their role as priests of the Church of England with great seriousness, and treasured its liturgical life, especially the Eucharist; indeed, in 1745 Charles Wesley published a collection of over one hundred *Hymns on the Lord's Supper*. But the decision to participate in the kind of ministry Whitefield was already conducting meant that they were inevitably distanced from ordinary congregational life. John Wesley described his first experience of open-air preaching:

> At four in the afternoon I submitted to be more vile [sic] and proclaimed in the highways the glad tidings of salvation speaking from a little eminence adjoining [Bristol] to about 3000 people. The Scripture on which I spoke was this (is it possible that anyone should be ignorant that it is fulfilled in every true minister of Christ?), "The Spirit of the Lord is upon me, because he hath anointed me to preach the Gospel to the poor."[36]

Parish clergy responsible for the spiritual life of their communities were often incensed that priests of the Church would presume to intrude within their parish's borders without permission or invitation; bishops were not only alarmed at the implications for good parish order, but at the Wesleys' apparent disdain for the services of the *Book of Common Prayer* in their public meetings.

The Wesleys ultimately broke with Whitefield over the issue of predestination, which both brothers rejected. Ironically, a phenomenon which began in unstructured revival soon became, under John Wesley's leadership, a highly organized institution. One author describes this Methodist movement as "a kind of missionary society," but meant to function within the broad boundaries of the Church of England.[37] Wesley himself described the United Societies as "a company of men having the form and seeking the power of godliness, united in order to pray together, to receive the word of exhortation, and to watch over one another in love, that they may help each other to work out their salvation."

> [E]ach society is divided into smaller companies, called *classes,* according to their respective places of abode. There are about twelve persons in every class; one of whom is styled the *Leader.* It is his business, (a) To see to each person in his class once a week at least, in order to inquire how their souls prosper; to advise, reprove, comfort, or exhort, as occasion may require; to receive what they are willing to give toward the relief of the poor; (b) to inform the Minister of any that are sick, or of any that walk disorderly, and will not be reproved' to pay to the Stewards what they have received of their several classes in the week

preceding; and to show what each person has contributed. . . . There is one only condition previously required in those who desire admission into these societies—a desire *to flee from the wrath that is to come, to be saved from their sins.*[38]

Wesley assumed that members would demonstrate their continuing commitment "to evidence their desire of salvation." This would be evidenced by "avoiding evil of every kind," such as profaning the Lord's Day, swearing, drinking, fighting, quarreling, speaking evil of authority, giving in to the desire for luxury; "by doing good, by being, in every kind, merciful after their power," and by regular attendance at worship, including the Eucharist, family and private prayer, reading the scripture, and fasting.[39]

In addition to the classes, Wesley also established *Bands*, with an even more rigorous set of rules and a regular discipline of mutual confession. In the face of the movement's rapid growth, John Wesley began licensing lay preachers—another challenge to the Established Church and its good order, since only bishops had the authority to issue licenses for preaching. One contemporary considered that "Methodism as to its external form is such a deviation from the rule and constitution of the Church of England that all attempts to render them consistent must be in vain."[40] John Wesley himself demonstrated his disdain for canonical structures when he judged them to impede the cause of mission: "I look upon all the world as my parish"; he declared, "thus far, I mean that in whatever part of it I am, I judge it meet and right and my bounden duty to declare unto all that are willing to hear the glad tidings of salvation."[41]

It is clear that wherever the Methodist movement spread—and it extended throughout England and even in the North American colonies—it introduced a distinctive form of ministry. Gordon Wakefield describes it as a form of spiritual direction, "revolutionary"

> not only because it is social, a matter of fellowship, but that it is lay. Christians of suitable gifts, graces and dedication, but otherwise ordinary people of no particular education or social cachet, have the power to be spiritual guides and to exercise the priestly office of the remission of sins . . . [T]he Methodist laity are to be consulted not only in matters of doctrine, they are to be pastors of the flock. The minister, itinerant, is the [pastor of pastors], responsible for their training in priesthood. But behind this remarkable institution of dedicated lay leaders was the autocratic figure of John Wesley, whom his contemporaries often nicknamed "Pope John."[42]

In spite of the innovative nature of the Wesleys' ministry, their attitude to the political dimension of Christian faith was remarkably Anglican. Writing on the eve of the American Revolution, John Wesley described himself as "an High Churchman," "bred up from my childhood in the highest notion of passive obedience and non-resistance," and rejected the idea that civil authority is derived from the people rather than from God.[43]

The focus of the Wesleys' movement on the English working class and the poor, and the exuberance of its gatherings, meant that it never overcame its lack of popularity among middle-and upper-class members of the Church of England. Nevertheless, there were aspects of the religious revival of which they were leaders that did appeal to both clergy and laypeople of higher social status: its inherent social and political conservatism, its emphasis on the reform of vices considered endemic in England at the time, and its insistence on both personal holiness and an active participation in social reform. Ironically, just as those aspects of his spirituality and ministry were beginning to be accepted by many active participants in the Church of England, John Wesley took actions that ultimately led to the rupture between the Methodist societies and the Established Church.

In the aftermath of the American Revolution, which left Anglicans in the former colonies bereft of half their clergy and took a terrible toll on the Church's resources, John Wesley decided to take matters literally into his own hands. He had already come to agree with the Puritans that the episcopate as a separate order was not an essential part of the New Testament church; in 1784, with the imposition of hands he "set apart" Thomas Coke, an Anglican priest, as Superintendent for ministry in the United States and also ordained two of his lay preachers as missionary clergy for America. The eighty-year-old John defended his actions against the fury of Charles Wesley, who considered that his brother had been led astray by the ambitions of Thomas Coke. But the consequences of those actions were dramatic and rapid; within a relatively short time, the Methodist societies had withdrawn from the Church of England and were on their way to becoming Dissenters in England and a new denomination on American soil.

THE EVANGELICALS

The Evangelical Movement as it developed apart from the Wesleys was more a phenomenon of the middle and upper classes of English society. It derived much of its influence from the untiring efforts of a group of prominent English laypeople in association with a few clergy to commend a deeper form of Christian commitment and serious engagement with what they perceived as dire social evils—especially a cruel penal system and an even more horrific traffic in human lives through the slave trade. This group came to be known as the Clapham Sect because most of its members lived in that village just south of London and were associated with its parish church.

The group's best-known members were undoubtedly William Wilberforce and Henry Thornton, both members of Parliament and tireless campaigners on behalf of the abolition of the slave trade. In a 1789 speech to Parliament, Wilberforce insisted that "the Slave Trade, in its very nature, is the source of . . . tragedies. . . . It is a trade in its principle inevitably calculated to sow the seeds of every mischief, to inspire enmity, to destroy humanity . . . [It has] had the effect in Africa of carrying misery, devastation and ruin wherever its baneful influence has extended."[44]

In 1797, Wilberforce published *A Practical View of the Prevailing Religious System of Professed Christians in the Higher and Middle Classes in this Country, Contrasted with Real Christianity.* Its ponderous title aptly summarizes Wilberforce's intention to critique what he considered the superficial nature of the Christianity of England's privileged classes and to invite his peers and colleagues to a more committed practice of their faith.

Three generations of the Venn family also played an active part in the Clapham group: Henry Venn, who had served as curate of Clapham Parish and who is considered the group's founder; his son, John Venn, rector of the parish; and the younger Henry Venn, closely identified with the work of the Church Missionary Society. The group also included Hannah More, who with her sister Martha dedicated herself to the cause of education and health care for the rural poor, and Katherine Hankey, who later served as a missionary. More's Mendip Schools, begun in Cheddar to provide church-sponsored education for poor children, were teaching three thousand children in twelve parishes within the space of ten years.[45] Other prominent members of the Clapham Sect included a Governor-General of India; the chair of the Board of Directors of the British East India Company; a Governor of the Bank of England; and Charles Simeon, known for his active support of overseas mission.

But while the Evangelical Movement generated enormous energy on behalf of the incipient Anglican missions in other parts of the world, perhaps its greatest legacy was associated with Parliament's approval of the Slave Trade Act of 1807, outlawing traffic in enslaved persons by British subjects and throughout Britain and its possessions. Its approval by Parliament was the result of the tireless efforts on its behalf over a ten-year period by Wilberforce and his allies and also the outpouring of popular sentiment generated by the growing Evangelical influence in the Church of England.

By the dawn of the nineteenth century, the movement which the Wesleys had served through their long lifetimes had spread far beyond the bounds of the Church to which they themselves were loyal, and their legacy is most closely identified with the Methodist churches now found throughout the world. Yet the Evangelical Movement also took root in the Church of England

and became a major force for spiritual revival and social reform. Its early growth was charged with conflict. As one historian observes,

> The parish of the late eighteenth century served as a crucible for the many varieties of revival which sprang up during this period. Although a strong thrust within the Church of England eventually integrated order with gospel preaching and restored balance, the arena was a scene of confusion and disruption for several decades. The enthusiastic methodists were often quite effective and most certainly produced results. Yet their methods and irregularity also caused unnecessary confusion. The evangelical movement emerged in this generation by initiating a vital sense of order and propriety while retaining a clear commitment to gospel preaching.[46]

In the years ahead, the evangelical movement would motivate countless zealous missionaries to carry their faith wherever British Christianity was established. Inviting and affirming the dedicated work of laypeople from all social strata, it permanently broadened the practice and understanding of Anglican ministry in the process.

NOTES

1. Bosher, *The Making of the Restoration Settlement: The Influence of the Laudians 1649–1662* (London: Dacre Press, 1951), xiv.

2. Bosher, *Restoration Settlement*, 218.

3. Bosher, *Restoration Settlement*, 221.

4. Bosher, *Restoration Settlement*, 281.

5. Jeremy Gregory, *Restoration, Reformation and Reform 1660–1828: Archbishops of Canterbury and their Diocese* (Oxford: Clarendon Press, 2000), 73.

6. Gregory, *Restoration*, 4.

7. Richard Allestree, *The practice of Christian graces, or, The Whole Duty of Man, laid down in a plain and familiar way for the use of all, but especially the meanest sort* . . . (London: SPCK, 1870).

8. John Parker Lawson, *The Episcopal Church of Scotland* (Edinburgh: Gallie and Bayley, 1844), 671.

9. Lawson, *Episcopal Church*, 676.

10. David Cornick, "Pastoral Care in England: Perkins, Baxter and Burnet," in G. R. Evans, ed., *A History of Pastoral Care*, 320–322.

11. H. M. Luckock, *The Church in Scotland* (London: Wells, Gardner, Barton &Co., 1892), 240.

12. Philip H. E. Thomas, "Unity and Concord: An Early Anglican 'Communion,'" *Journal of Anglican Studies* (June 2004), 9.

13. Luckock, *The Church in Scotland*, 277.

14. George Tavard, *The Quest for Catholicity: A Study in Anglicanism* (New York: Herder and Herder, 1964), 101.

15. William Law, *A Serious Call to a Devout and Holy Life* (New York: Paulist Press, 1978), 51.

16. Law, *Serious Call,* 147.

17. Obert D. Cornwall, "Divine Right Monarchy, Henry Dodwell's Critique of the Reformation and Defense of the Deprived Nonjuror Bishops," *Anglican and Episcopal History* (March 1999), 44, 57.

18. Thomas Hearne, quoted in Cornwall, "Divine Right Monarchy," 42.

19. J. C. D. Clark, *English Society 1688–1832: Ideology, social structure and political practice during the ancient regime* (Cambridge: Cambridge University Press, 1985), 126.

20. Peter Virgin, *The Church in an Age of Negligence: Ecclesiastical Structures and Problems of Church Reform* (Cambridge: James Clarke and Co., 1989), 109.

21. Virgin, *Age of Negligence,* 131, 133.

22. Michael Brander, *The Country Divine* (Edinburgh: The St. Andrew Press, 1981), 114.

23. Brander, *The Country Divine,* 115.

24. Brander, *The Country Divine,* 91–92.

25. Brander, *The Country Divine,* 92.

26. Gregory, *Restoration,* 121–122.

27. Gregory, *Restoration,* 151.

28. Gregory, *Restoration,* 155.

29. William Gibson, ed., *Religion and Society in England and Wales, 1989–1800* (Leicester: Leicester University Press, 1998), 7, 64–65.

30. Deborah Valense, "Charity, Custom and Humanity: Changing Attitudes towards the Poor in Eighteenth-Century England," in Jane Garnett and Colin Matthew, eds., *Revival and Religion Since 1700: Essays for John Walsh* (London: The Humbledon Press, 1992), 60.

31. Joseph Woodward, quoted in *Religion and Society in England and Wales, 1689–1800,* 53.

32. Church of St. John the Baptist, Chester, UK, Narthex.

33. Frank Whaling, "Introduction," *John and Charles Wesley: Selected Prayers, Hymns, Journal Notes, Sermons, Letters and Treatises* (New York: Paulist Press, 1981), 25.

34. Gordon Wakefield, "John and Charles Wesley: A Tale of Two Brothers," in Geoffrey Rowell, ed., *The English Religious Tradition and the Genius of Anglicanism"* (Oxford: Ikon Productions, Ltd., 1992), 171.

35. Wakefield, "John and Charles Wesley," 176.

36. Wakefield, "John and Charles Wesley," 177.

37. Whaling, "Introduction," *John and Charles Wesley,* 34.

38. John Wesley, "The Nature, Design, and General Rules of the United Societies," in Whaling, ed., *John and Charles Wesley,* 108–109.

39. John Wesley, "The Nature, Design, and General Rules of the United Societies, in London, Bristol, Kingswood, Newcastle-upon-Tyne, etc., 1743," *John and Charles Wesley,* 109–110.

40. Adam of Winteringham, quoted in Whaling, "Introduction," *John and Charles Wesley,* 54.

41. Wakefield, "John and Charles Wesley," 177.

42. Wakefield, "John and Charles Wesley, 186.

43. Clark, *English Society 1688–1832,* 236–237.

44. William Wilberforce, Speech to Parliament, May 12, 1789, in Klaus Koschorke, Frieder Ludwig, and Marianne Delgado, eds., *A History of Christianity in Asia, Africa, and Latin America, 1450–1990: A Documentary Sourcebook* (Grand Rapids, MI: William B. Eerdmans Publishing Co., 2007), 180.

45. S. C. Carpenter, *Church and People, 1989 – 1889: A History of the Church of England from William Wilberforce to "Lux Mundi"* (London: SPCK, 1933), 39.

46. Wesley Balda, "Ecclesiastics and Enthusiasts: The Evangelical Emergence in England 1760 – 1800," in *Anglican and Episcopal History,* XLIX (September 1980), 231.

Chapter Five

Stirrings

The Beginnings of Overseas Anglicanism

The Church of England's unique insistence on the *national* character of its structures and ministries not only shaped its own life and self-understanding; it had a profound effect on how English Christians approached the task of Christian mission and ministry. Roman Catholic missionaries might probe the far reaches of Asia and the Americas in search of converts; their practice of ministry was defined by the Vatican and their concept of church transcended national boundaries. But English Christians believed that the practice of faith is defined by *nationhood*; English Christianity, then, belonged to those parts of the world where English people made their home.

ENGLISH CHRISTIANS ABROAD

Once English merchants joined the scramble to establish sources of raw materials in other parts of the world, chaplains also accompanied ships sailing to Asia, and by 1635, chaplains had been appointed for the British trading stations in the Ottoman Empire. The earliest Anglican baptisms on North American soil took place in 1587 on Roanoke Island, England's first American colony and now part of North Carolina, when Manteo, a Native American "friend and guide" to the English settlers and Virginia Dare, daughter of two colonists, were baptized.[1] "Where the English traveled," observed the British historian W. M. Jacob, "they took their reformed practice of the Christian faith and liturgy with them." In 1578 the island of Newfoundland was established as a colony of the British crown; its charter forbade any laws that restricted "the true Christian faith or religion now professed in the church of England."[2]

When the English began establishing overseas colonies, other European powers had already been engaged in widespread colonizing for nearly a century. The outpost established by royal charter at Jamestown in 1607 gave the English company founded to establish a North American colony unrestricted right within a vast expanse of territory to "all the Lands, Woods, Soil, Grounds, Havens, Ports, Rivers, Mines, Minerals, Marshes, Waters, Fishings, Commodities, and Hereditaments, whatsoever." This more than generous gift from King James I to a group of "loving and well-disposed subjects," comprised of "certain Knights, Gentlemen, Merchants, and other Adventurers," had the declared intention of

> so noble a Work, which may, by the Providence of Almighty God, hereafter tend to the Glory of his Divine Majesty, in propagating of Christian Religion to such People, as yet live in Darkness and miserable Ignorance of the true Knowledge and Worship of God, and may in time bring the Infidels and Savages, living in those parts, to human Civility, and to a settled and quiet Government. . . .[3]

Hence the company of settlers who established the Jamestown Colony on the coast of Virginia a few months later was accompanied by a chaplain, the Reverend Robert Hunt, who can be identified as the first Anglican missionary to serve a permanent English settlement in North America.

Doubtless the English colonists were sincere in their intention to share their Christian faith and its undoubted consequences, the ordered benefits of a government founded on the principles of English civilization and culture. But the reason those Native peoples, previously ignored by English Christians, now became the object of their missionary intentions, was not only their presumed status of spiritual neediness, but the fact that they had now become, at least in the minds of the English, subjects of the Crown, and therefore potential members of the Church of England. Before many years had passed, the number of non-Christian subjects perceived to be in need of baptism and "civilization" was augmented by the arrival, in 1619, of the first of the enslaved Africans to appear in the colony. The story of the Church of England's mission within English territories in the New World is henceforth complicated by a triple challenge: ministering to the ever-growing population of English settlers (many—perhaps most—of whom ignored or rejected it); converting and ministering to the multiplicity of Native peoples; and evangelizing enslaved people who had been wrenched unwillingly from their homelands through human treachery and cupidity, and transported by people who may well have identified themselves as adherents of the same Church which the enslaved were now being urged to embrace.

The Church of England found itself radically unprepared to undertake all three challenges. Nothing in its history had prepared it to practice its ministry in the unknown circumstances of the North American wilderness, nor had it ever before encountered the need to address peoples who were not already Christian. Sharing the Gospel with non-Christians in the hope of their conversion called for skills and perspectives for which even the conflicts associated with the Reformation had not prepared them.

Indeed, the original settlers of the Jamestown Colony must have taxed the abilities of their clergy, since a few years after its establishment an early governor found it necessary to rely on martial law to ensure church attendance; the officers of the little garrison of soldiers were charged with assuring that "Almighty God be duly and daily served" by twice-daily attendance at services, and blasphemy, impious speaking against the Trinity, and unlawful oaths were to be severely punished. Misusing God's name or speaking against Christian doctrine was punishable by death. The clergy were responsible for daily Morning and Evening Prayer, weekly preaching and catechizing, and were also required to appoint four of the "most religious and best-disposed persons in their parishes" to act as informants on church members, to maintain church buildings, and to keep records of baptisms, marriages and deaths. Newly arrived colonists must report to the clergy on the condition of their faith; those judged insufficiently devout were required to submit to instruction under penalty of whipping. William Manross, the venerable historian of the Church in the American colonies, remarks that if

> the severity of the penalties (which were harsh even when judged by contemporary standards) had not forced them into [disuse], their disregard of the actual conditions of colonial life would have done so, for they presupposed an effective Church Establishment in a community where there were probably not more than two clergymen, ministering to a handful of scattered and ignorant settlers. For many of the colonists, attendance at daily services would probably have been not so much a hardship as an impossibility . . .[4]

The stringent laws by which a naïve governor attempted to recreate the "godly society" longed for by many Christians in England were soon revised to reflect more adequately the new reality which English colonists now called home. As increasing numbers of settlers made the dangerous crossing to what they viewed as a land of opportunity, the territory controlled by the British presence was divided into "corporations," each with its own glebe lands reserved for the support of the resident clergy, and church buildings and cemeteries were established. Clergy received their stipends in the form of a portion of the colony's chief crops, tobacco and corn. Disparaging the clergy was punished by fines and public humiliation, but the clergy were also held to account: absence from a parish for more than two months was punishable by loss of half a year's stipend. By 1630 parishes had both Vestries and Churchwardens.

These early attempts at ordering the life of the Church of England in Virginia reveal a well-meaning attempt to replicate, as far as possible, the circumstances to which it was accustomed; but at home, it ministered to a settled population and made use of all the trappings and safeguards of a Church intimately bound to the institutions of State. In the new circumstances, some of the requisite characteristics of the Established Church were notably absent, most significantly the presence of bishops who might have overseen the orderly growth of the Church's presence in the New World, stimulated the Church's ministry with the Native population and the ever-increasing number of enslaved people arriving from Africa, and addressed the not infrequent problems of clergy misbehavior. (Many of the clergy who found their way to the North American colonies dedicated themselves to the daunting responsibilities they believed they had been given. But others found the isolation of their situation, the absence of any effective oversight, and the reality of a setting for which neither experience nor training had prepared them, to be overwhelming. Reports of inappropriate behavior, especially the abuse of alcohol, appear all too frequently in contemporary comments about the colonial clergy.) The presence of bishops in the American colonies would have meant that native-born candidates would not have been required to make the long, costly and dangerous journey to England in order to receive ordination, and the chronic shortage of suitable clergy which afflicted the colonial church would have been eliminated or at least minimized. But both political and theological issues stood in the way.

The diversity of the charters under which the thirteen colonies of the Atlantic coast were governed, and the disparate religious principles that provided one of the motives for their establishment, meant that the episcopate as it had been ordered at the time of the English Reformation, and which was restored after the Commonwealth, would have been inconceivable in the American colonies. In New England and elsewhere, the Presbyterian and Congregationalist heirs of the Puritan faction, who had agitated for the abolition of the episcopate in England, were militantly opposed to the introduction of bishops into North America. In the absence of local bishops, the Bishop of London gradually assumed ultimate responsibility for the colonial congregations, although that responsibility was always more implicit than official. After 1689, the Bishop delegated some responsibilities to resident clergy known as "Commissaries." In the eighteenth century, in all the colonies where the Church enjoyed some sort of legal establishment, the royal governor served as the "Ordinary," assuming the bishop's right to investigate clergy credentials and to induct rectors into the temporal privileges of their parishes.

But by that time, at least in Virginia where the Church of England was most firmly established, parishes had become accustomed to a quasi-independent existence under what Manross calls "long immunity from ecclesiastical discipline." Vestries were empowered by law to choose a "godly layman" to lead services when no clergy were on hand, and even when resident clergy were present, the Holy Communion was celebrated only three or four times a year.[5]

The most significant innovation in Anglican ministry in Virginia was the gradual development of the Vestry's role and responsibilities on the congregational level. Prerogatives which had been carefully guarded in England through the practice of "advowson" were challenged, and as a result Anglican ministry in the New World developed unique characteristics.

As early as 1611, the Governor of the Virginia Colony had required that in each parish, the clergy should be assisted by four appropriately pious laymen who exercised duties similar to the Churchwardens in English congregations. These included not only the care of church property but soon included administrative tasks such as maintaining parish records and helping "prevent all ungodly disorders."[6] Within less than twenty-five years, these groups of lay congregational representatives had expanded into Vestries similar to those in English parishes, and had assumed one duty which no English congregation would have claimed: the right to select their own clergy. Furthermore, the colonial legislature acquiesced in this radical change, recognizing the Vestry as the "basic parochial governing entity," though it reserved to itself the power to remove clergy who failed in the adequate performance of their ministry.[7]

While the intent of this legislation was to allow vestries to present their choice of rector to the royal governor, who would act as the Ordinary and induct him into the prerogatives of his office, many congregations declined to follow this procedure, instead offering their clergy yearly contracts. The effect of this custom was to create substantial instability in the relationship between clergy and congregation, since any parish priest who offended the parish Vestry could find himself without employment and thousands of miles from home. It is not surprising that the Virginia clergy complained bitterly about the custom.

The erosion of the relative power of the clergy in the colonies is also noted in a recent study of baptism and marriage as practiced in the plantation societies of the southern American colonies and especially in the West Indies. In such settings, English colonists preferred to celebrate both rites in their homes in spite of the Anglican tradition specifying the church as their appropriate setting. Nicholas Beasley, its author, considers that

> the celebration of both rites at home kept the power of marriage and baptism under lay control. . . . The Church of England's clergy in the plantation regions

were thus constantly reminded that they served very much at the pleasure of their lay masters. . . . further undermining the already limited independence of clergy and any possibility that the English church might find any prophetic stance between slaves and their owners.

Beasley also notes that for free persons of color, baptisms and marriages in the church legitimized their status and set them apart from the enslaved population, who rarely had access to either, becoming part of "processes that regulated the diffusion of power throughout the social hierarchy."[8]

The chaos of the Civil War and the Commonwealth left the Church in the colonies relatively unscathed, and the period following the Restoration of the monarchy and episcopate was marked by efforts to regain control over the system of clergy selection which had created significant power on the part of parish vestries at the expense of the clergy. But those efforts were largely unsuccessful, and gradually parishes throughout the American colonies claimed the right to participate in the selection of their clergy for granted. Even Anglicans in New York City, where the Church of England was established, enjoyed that privilege, guaranteed by their Royal Charter in 1697.[9] In Marblehead, Massachusetts, a parish Vestry was organized two years before the congregation's first missionary arrived from England to take up his duties.[10]

The situation for Anglican churches in New England was quite different from that in Virginia and the other colonies to their south. Anglican congregations in Massachusetts and Connecticut were tiny minorities in colonies where Congregational churches were established by law. In Massachusetts, it was not until 1691 that the monarchs decreed freedom of religion to all except Roman Catholics, though the issue of whether Anglicans were required to pay taxes to support the established Congregational church involved many early vestries in both Massachusetts and Connecticut in heavy controversy. The chief responsibility of the vestries in New England was the financial support of their own congregation; as was common in other American colonies, renting pew space proved to be the chief source of funds.[11] Congregations were expected to provide their clergy with a house and glebe and, if possible, part of his stipend. Conflicts in New England parishes were often between American Vestries and English clergy, who judged "a dependency of the Clergy upon the People" as "a great obstruction to the progress of the Church here and Religion in general."[12]

The experience of the Church of England's first century in the New World reveals a struggle between the impulse to replicate its traditional ministry in the new setting, and the attempt—successful or unsuccessful—to shape a new style of ministry more appropriate to the rugged frontier context of the North American colonies. Commenting on the frequent conflict between the colonial clergy and those responsible for their incomes, the English historian H. G. G. Herklots notes that "neither side to the dispute was speaking the language of the frontier, but that of settled lands, or of lands becoming settled." In the churches themselves, rigid social hierarchies were maintained by wealthy families who assumed the same social prerogatives that their cousins in England claimed as rights.[13]

But in fact, the situation in which clergy performed their ministry in the colonial setting was challenging and difficult, and provided opportunities both for devoted service and for debauchery. The commissary of Maryland complained that "one Holt, a scandalous and enormous wretch, who had lately been deprived of his Living in Virginia by [the Commissary], because of his Adulteries, Drunkenness and fightings, was come into Maryland and placed in one of the best parishes."[14] On the other hand, the growth of Anglican Christianity in the American colonies depended on the initiative of both clergy and laypeople who were determined to preserve the church they had inherited, and who lived and worked faithfully to see that it survived in the strange new setting to which it had been brought. While acknowledging that clergy who accepted colonial appointments were often unsuited for ministry in England, the American historian John Woolverton considered that in general, the colonial clergy demonstrated "high standards of conduct and in the majority of cases unremitting dedication."[15]

The isolation of many colonial Anglican congregations affected other aspects of church life as well. "In many ways," wrote W. M. Jacob, "Anglicanism in North America was developing along congregational lines . . . There was no unifying factor between the congregations of each colony nor was there any unifying factor between the congregations within each colony."[16] Such an impulse to unity would occur only after thirteen of the colonies declared their independence and struggled successfully to create a new church out of the ruins of the old one.

THOMAS BRAY AND THE SOCIETY FOR THE PROPAGATION OF THE GOSPEL

The dawning of the eighteenth century marked a notable new advance in the Church of England's overseas ministries, and it was primarily due to the work of one remarkable mission-minded priest named Thomas Bray.

Bray was appointed Commissary for Maryland in 1695, but chose to spend the early years of his appointment learning about the condition of the colonial churches and attempting to put in place the institutional support that had so far been lacking. He first turned his attention to the need for an educated clergy, noting that missionary priests rarely had sufficient resources to buy the books they needed. He launched an appeal for funds for "encouraging Learning and Religion in the Foreign Plantations" and succeeded in establishing thirty-nine libraries in the American colonies and eighty in England; one was located in Gravesend, where clergy bound for America and waiting for their passage could spend their time in study. In 1698, Bray and four laymen, who shared his belief in the importance of religious education for the well-being of society, established what was to become the Society for the Promotion of Christian Knowledge (SPCK), soon to function as an important source for books and other educational resources for clergy in the colonies. In 1699, Bray finally made a brief visit to Maryland, where he worked to improve the lot of the clergy, established libraries, and held a "Visitation" of the clergy intended to prevent scandals, encourage them in their clerical duties, and "to propagate the true Religion in the neighbouring Provinces."[17] Upon his return to England after only three months, he dedicated himself to establishing a serious and permanent structure to provide support for Anglican ministry overseas. In 1701, the Society for the Propagation of the Gospel in Foreign Parts (SPG) received a royal charter stipulating that the Archbishops of Canterbury and York as well as a number of other distinguished bishops and clerics would be members of its governing body. While the peculiar relationship between the English Church and State prevented its official status as an agency of the Church of England, its composition and the participation of the Archbishop of Canterbury as its president guaranteed that it would enjoy an especially close relationship with the Church. For the next century and a half, most of the work of carrying Anglican Christianity to the far reaches of the British Empire was carried out by English missionaries supported by the SPG. Indeed, its foundation has been called "a turning-point in the development of the Anglican Communion."[18]

By the time the SPG began its work, the British presence had already extended well beyond the thirteen colonies of the American coast. The eighteenth century saw an enormous increase in the need for Anglican missionaries, as French Canada passed to British control in mid-century and the islands of the West Indies which, like the southern colonies of North America, were populated by both English colonists and large numbers of enslaved Africans, assumed increasing importance for Britain. Within a decade of its founding, SPG determined that its first priority should be "the conversion of heathen and infidels."[19] But early encouragement by the Church of England for evangelizing enslaved people was often resisted by slave owners out of fear that baptism might be interpreted to imply secular freedom. In an effort to allay this fear, a number of colonial legislatures enacted laws affirming that baptism did not affect the status of slaves.[20] Beyond the inherent cruelty of the institution itself, there were obvious contradictions between the practice of Christian faith and the institution of slavery as it was practiced in the British colonies, most notably in the widespread custom of ignoring or forbidding marriages between slaves and the severing of family units through sale of individual slaves, whatever their family status or obligations. Voices in the Church of England frequently reminded slave owners that as Christians, they had the duty to provide for both the physical and spiritual well-being of enslaved persons, even as they also preached obedience and acquiescence to those who were enslaved. The "Associates of Dr. Bray" was a group established in 1723/24 to support the evangelization of Black inhabitants of the colonies. They sent books to colonial clergy and between 1758 and 1765 established schools for Blacks in Philadelphia, New York, Williamsburg, Newport, Rhode Island and Fredericksburg, Virginia.[21] The contradiction between the intentions and efforts of the Church and the inhuman realities of slavery as it was practiced are poignantly illustrated in a letter received by the Bishop of London in 1723. An enslaved man in Virginia wrote a description of how "wee are commanded to keep holey the Sabbath day and wee doo hardly know when it comes for our task mastrs are as hard with us as the Egpttions was with the Chilldann of Issarell. . . ." He pleaded with the bishop to "settell one thing upon us which is that our childarn be broatt up in the way of the Christtian faith and our desire is that they may be Larnd the Lords prayer the creed and the ten commandments and that they may appear Every Lords day att Church."[22]

In 1743, a Maryland clergyman, Thomas Bacon, preached and published four sermons "addressed to masters and servants," which were popular enough to be augmented and published seventy years later by William Meade, then Bishop of Virginia (and himself a slaveowner). Bacon argued that it was in the masters' interest to evangelize the enslaved, since those who consider their servitude to be a God-given state with a duty to obedience require less supervision and oversight and are much less likely to try to escape. Sermons addressed to the enslaved themselves emphasized the value of obedience on earth in securing the rewards of heaven after death.[23]

Where large numbers of enslaved persons were converted, church buildings accommodated their presence either by seating at the rear of the congregation or, if space permitted or required, in a second-story gallery at the rear of the church. Many churches constructed in the eighteenth and nineteenth centuries, especially in the southern United States, still retain their old galleries. At the infrequent times when Holy Communion was celebrated, the congregation approached the altar in the order of their social status, with the enslaved receiving the sacrament after all the white members had completed their communion.

In 1680, Morgan Godwyn, who had served as a missionary in Virginia, published *The Negro's and Indian Advocate*, which strongly criticized the failure of slave-owners to support the conversion of "those Myriads of hungry and distressed Souls abroad . . . our Peoples [sic] Slaves and Vassals, but from whom also the Bread of life is most sacrilegiously detained."[24] It was just such concern that prompted the SPG to give special emphasis to ministry among the enslaved population of the colonies. An overwhelming amount of information—two million documents, including twenty thousand manuscript documents such as missionary reports—remains in the SPG archives.[25]

The Society was a persistent and significant voice in the unsuccessful effort to obtain a bishop for the American colonies, and in 1717 it established the American Colonial Bishop's Fund. Indeed, the historian Daniel O'Connor observed that the SPG's high-church ethos took for granted the Church of England's duty to ensure that all British subjects received the ministry of "Orthodox Clergy in Foreign Parts," and the Society and SPCK were to become an important *locus* of this tradition throughout the eighteenth century and onwards. Their work was undergirded by a political theology which took for granted the intimate relationship between Church and state, conceived as two aspects of one national reality.[26]

The relationship between the SPG and the Church of England was articulated on a regular basis through the sermons preached in London by distinguished clergy to mark significant events and anniversaries in the Society's life. One of the recurring themes of those sermons was the importance of the conversion of the Native people, "advocating education and a civilizing mission, and identifying the rapacity of the settlers as the chief obstacle to [their] conversion." Another primary concern was slavery: In a sermon preached only six years after the Society's charter, William Beveridge declared that God surely permitted slavery only as a means for converting Africans who could return to their own continent and effect its evangelization. The SPG also recognized that its missionaries were charged with guiding the English settlers who had made their home in the colonies from their "former Rudeness . . . [t]o become a religious, sober and Polite People."[27]

In spite of its commitment to the conversion of the rapidly growing number of enslaved Africans to be found throughout Britain's American and Caribbean colonies, and although some of its preachers and spokespersons considered the slave trade to violate both divine and human law, as an organization SPG did not promote the principle of emancipation.[28] Its acceptance of slavery as an institution was due in part to the widespread fear among eighteenth century Anglicans of any sort of disorder, a fear heightened by the religious and broader social dislocations produced by the Great Awakening of the 1730s and afterward. But it also reflected the peculiar and ironic situation in which the Society found itself at once committed to the conversion of enslaved people and also the owner and operator of a plantation run with slave labor.[29]

Christopher Codrington, a generous benefactor of the Society and a third-generation sugar planter as well as governor of the Leeward Islands, was so impressed with its purposes that he left the Society two sugar plantations and three hundred enslaved persons. His will directed the SPG to run the plantations, located on the island of Barbados, as model establishments and to use their profits to establish a community living under monastic vows for the training of future evangelists. As a result of this curious bequest, the SPG found itself forced to "endure the hazards of the sugar economy if it wished to reap profits from its inheritance and to Christianize the West Indies." As a result, one hundred and twenty years of plantation operation under the slave regime were ahead for the society, years checkered by financial loss and the disappointments of unfulfilled hopes.[30]

Sadly, the conditions under which the Society's own enslaved people lived and worked at Codrington differed little from those found on other plantations. For eight years between 1724 and 1732, all were branded with the word "Society" and those considered "sickly, Lazy, Runaways or otherwise useless" were sold. Nor did the missionary clergy, many of whom were themselves slave owners or received slave labor as part of their salary, necessarily provide positive examples of benevolent care: clerical correspondence of the period describes whipping and selling of the enslaved as punishment for disobedience. Not surprisingly, efforts at their evangelization rarely matched hopes or expectations. It was only in the last decades of the eighteenth century that significant numbers of voices within the SPG expressed support for the abolition of the slave trade, a campaign that already motivated many Anglicans to make their voices heard.[31]

The historian Rowan Strong believes that the sermons related to the SPG provide an important source for understanding the role of the Church in the development of the nascent British Empire. Furthermore, he writes, "an official and conscious Anglican concern for empire, and for missions by the Church of England, dates continuously from the foundation of the [SPG] in 1701."[32] He considers that the "relgous and national identity" with "an imperial dimension in the eighteenth century" was due to "wars with Catholic France for overseas territories and to the transatlantic connection of Britain with her North American colonies."[33] Travis Glasson affirms Strong's position, arguing that the

> first generation of SPG supporters envisioned the Church of England as a global institution, a supranational church with a reach commensurate with England's expanding power.... Convinced that Episcopal Protestantism was the best form of Christianity and that a close alliance between the church and the state was essential to the health of both, the Society's backers saw the Atlantic world as a field of intense religious competition.[34]

During the decades prior to independence Anglican ministry continued to adapt itself, often uncertainly, to frontier conditions beyond the more settled coastal regions of the colonies. Early in the 1730s the first "Great Awakening" began to emerge as a new challenge to both the Church of England and the other Reformed churches that had established themselves in the colonies, promoting a highly emotional style of worship and preaching drawn from the frequent "revivals" associated with the movement. The historian Winthrop Hudson comments, "People everywhere were caught up in the movement, and its influence as spread by innumerable local pastors, passing itinerants, and lay exhorters."[35] While Anglican Evangelicals like George Whitefield and the followers of the Wesleys are often associated with the Awakening, much of the movement's passion occurred outside the established churches and resulted in the formation of local congregations, often led by poorly educated leaders whose authority came more from their charismatic appeal than any formal ordination. Most Anglican clergy lamented the ways in which the enthusiasm of the Awakening took a toll on their congregations as members abandoned them or challenged the stately and restrained tradition of Anglican worship. Devereux Jarrett was one of the very few Anglican clergy sympathetic to the movement: "From the 1760s to the 1780s, during the period of the Great Awakening in Virginia, he carried on an indefatigable circuit-riding ministry to almost thirty counties in Virginia and North Carolina. Preaching in homes and plantation fields, and on weekdays as well as Sundays, he attracted the common people far more than his fellow clergy in the established church."[36]

ANGLICAN MISSION AND NATIVE PEOPLES IN NORTH AMERICA

The Church of England's attempts to convert the Native peoples of North America were even more problematic than its ministry to enslaved Africans. The motives themselves were not always positive; the Native American (Choctaw) historian Owanah Anderson notes the importance given to establishing a "bulwark against the Papists" already present in large numbers among the Native people in the Spanish and French colonies, and quotes one early advocate of evangelism, Robert Gray, who argued that conversion was preferable to genocide, "if the land can then be taken peacefully." Early intentions by the Virginia legislature to provide a school for Native education and broader efforts to convert the original inhabitants of Virginia foundered after an uprising in 1622.[37]

Efforts at evangelization among Native people revealed that the missionaries generally understood their task to include not only their religious conversion but the destruction of Native culture and the imposition of English "civilization." Indeed, Rowan Strong argues that by the 1730s, Anglicans were advocating "'civilization' as a preliminary to conversion" both for the enslaved and for Native peoples. In 1757, the secretary of the SPG commented that "they must be reduced from their barbarity . . . , and be made Men [sic], that is, rational, considerate Creatures, before they will become good Christians."[38]

One notable exception to the effort to impose British "civilization" on Indian peoples was an effort by Robert Hicks and John Evans to educate Native students at the College of William and Mary, located at the colonial capital of Williamsburg, Virginia. They urged that an Indian man accompany the students in order to ensure that they did not forget their native language. But Anderson observes that suspicion, dislike of English culture and the inevitable alienation from family and tradition meant that efforts to educate Native students from the immediate region were soon abandoned. The College next turned its attempt at recruiting Indian students to the Seneca tribe whose territories were far to the north. But the chiefs sent a definitive—and ironic—reply:

> We know that you highly esteem the kind of learning taught in these colleges. But, you who are wise must know that the different nations have different conceptions of things; and you will not, therefore, take it amiss if our ideas of this education happen not to be the same with yours.
>
> Several of our young men were formerly brought up at the colleges of the Northern provinces . . . but when they came back to us they were bad runners, ignorant of every means of living in the woods, unable to bear either cold or hunger, knew neither how to build a cabin, take a deer or kill an enemy; spoke our language imperfectly—they were, therefore, neither fit for hunters, warriors nor counselors. They were totally good for nothing.

While formally declining the College's invitation the chiefs did, however, offer to train a dozen sons of Virginia gentlemen, "instruct[ing] them in all that we know, and make men of them."[39]

In spite of the difficulties almost universally encountered by Anglican missionaries in their work with Native tribes, many continued to believe what the Bishop of St. Asaph had pronounced at mid-century: God had blessed British commerce and colonization "as a divine method of bringing the barbarous natives of North America to Christianity."[40] By century's end, the close of the eighteenth century, the SPG had undertaken work with no fewer than forty-six Native tribes, sponsored schools for indigenous children in New Brunswick, Nova Scotia, New England, and several mid-Atlantic colonies and the *Book of Common Prayer* had been translated into the Mohawk and Micmac languages.[41]

AMERICAN INDEPENDENCE AND ANGLICAN MINISTRY

In the latter half of the eighteenth century, the broad diversity of religious allegiances present in the North American colonies had not prevented Anglican Christianity from prospering. On the eve of the American Revolution, the Church of England was not only the second largest of all the churches present in the colonies; it was also among those experiencing rapid and sustained growth. In Connecticut, where there had been thirty Anglican churches in 1761, by 1774 there were forty-seven, with twenty more congregations meeting in public spaces such as schools.[42] But for Anglicans, the end of the War of Independence that erupted on North American soil in 1776 terminated the Church of England's missionary efforts in the new nation and left a struggling but autonomous church eager to affirm its own American identity.

In the course of the war and its aftermath, half of the Anglican clergy at work in the thirteen American colonies abandoned their ministry; many returned to England, while others made their way to either Canada or the British possessions in the West Indies. Those who remained, accompanied by strong and committed laypeople, permanently changed and broadened not only the definition of what it means to be "Anglican" but also the ways in which Anglican Christians, lay and ordained, practiced their vocation to ministry. David Holmes' extensive research on the effects of the War indicates that it was more divisive for Anglicans than for any other body of Christians in the colonies. He has demonstrated that in those colonies where Anglicanism was weak and in areas where there was strong support for an American episcopate, where "high-church" ideas prevailed, where clergy were supported by the SPG and where the population included large numbers of recent arrivals from England and Scotland, clergy were likely to support the British in the War. With the exception of the clergy of Maryland, where Anglicanism was a strong colonial presence, wherever "low-church" or latitudinarian positions were popular, where there was little support for an episcopate and where parishes tended to be self-supporting, clergy tended to support the Revolution. There was also a significant geographical component to the conflict. In New England, only two clergy were "patriots," in New York only one, while in the middle colonies the clergy were divided, with the exception of Maryland, where two-thirds supported England. In Virginia, on the other hand, three-quarters of the clergy clearly supported independence.[43]

One of the issues that had led to the English Civil War more than a century earlier was also a factor in determining the colonial clergy's behavior in a time of unrest and revolt. In her study of clergy during the Revolution, Nancy Rhodes notes that those who sided with the patriots tended to accept the Calvinist belief that when rulers disobey God's will, their Christian subjects have the right to resist and even replace them. The loyalist clergy, on the other hand, often identified with the perspective on which the Stewart kings had depended, that Christians owe passive obedience and non-resistance to God's anointed monarch.[44]

Bound by their ordination oaths, most clergy considered themselves in principle sworn "to be loyal to the King, to pray publicly for him and for his family and government each Sunday, and so to be guilty of treason in the colonies" where such activities had been decreed by Congress to be a criminal offense.[45] In the face of such a conflict, those clergy who did not leave their parishes did however usually halt services, performing pastoral duties such as baptisms, marriages and funerals as they could. Many suffered at the hands of their patriot congregations and local authorities, including prison, exile or house arrest, "with many clergy losing their life's possessions, others being separated from their families, and still others acquiring bodily infirmities that remained with them for life." Anglican church buildings were commandeered as hospitals, barracks and stables. Holmes describes the hostile acts by which many churches were damaged: "Common mischief for boys of the Revolutionary years in Salem, Massachusetts, was going to 'rock the Tory Church,'" while in Newport, Rhode Island, "colonial troops ripped out and used for target practice the ornate altar piece of Trinity Church, on which the Arms of Great Britain were prominent."[46]

Rhodes considers that one of the effects of the conflict was what she calls the "depoliticization of the Colonial Anglican clergy" who remained in their posts, their withdrawal from speaking on any subject judged to have political overtones. Of the twenty-three Anglican clergy in Connecticut, all were loyal to the Crown, but most remained quietly at work in their assigned parishes.[47]

Nor were the clerical supporters of the British cause the only Anglicans who suffered as a result of the War of Independence. A large memorial plaque in the crossing of England's Chester Cathedral commemorates the life and death of Frederick Philipse, Esq.,

> late of the Province of New York; a gentleman in whom the various social, domestic and religious Virtues were eminently united. . . . Firmly attached to his Sovereign and the British Constitution, he opposed, at the Hazard of his Life, the late Rebellion in North America; and for this faithful Discharge of his Duty to his King and Country, he was Proscribed, and his Estate, one of the largest in New york (sic), was Confiscated by the Usurped Legislature of that

Province, . . . and came to England leaving all his Property behind him; which Reverse of Fortune he bore with that Calmness, Fortitude and Dignity which had distinguished him through every former Stage of Life.[48]

Numbers of other laypeople who had supported the British found themselves in similar positions, and either returned to England or emigrated to one of its other possessions. On the other hand, some Loyalist clergy and laypeople decided to make their peace with the new republic, and remained to help in the formation of what became the Protestant Episcopal Church in the United States of America. Not all made the transition easily; Thomas Ellison, rector of St. Peter's Church in Albany, New York, was described by his famous parishioner James Fenimore Cooper as the

> epitome of the national prejudices, and in some respect the national character' of England . . . particularly severe on the immoralities of the French Revolution, and though eating our bread, was not especially lenient to our own; . . . [He was] particularly tenacious of the ritual and of all the decencies of the Church; detested a democrat as he did the devil; cracked his jokes daily about Mr. Jefferson . . . prayed fervently on Sunday, and decried all morals, institutions, churches, manners, and laws but those of England from Monday to Saturday. [49]

AN AMERICAN CHURCH

When the War formally ended in 1783, the Anglican churches of the thirteen colonies were in nearly desperate condition: funding from the SPG had ended, there were no replacements for the clergy and laypeople who had left, congregations had gone for years without public worship, many church buildings were in ruins, and it was by no means clear where funds would come to restore the damage.[50]

But the story of ministry in the new nation was not all bad. Frederick Mills observed that "at the very time the parish vestries were enlisting men for Holy Orders, rebuilding or repairing their churches, developing financial resources, and revitalizing their [educational-humanitarian] institutions, delegates from these same parishes were busy forming state conventions and one convocation which in turn selected representatives to a national convention."[51]

The immediate task confronting Anglicans in the newly independent nation was to devise a way to maintain their heritage of faith and order while adapting to the radically changed political situation in which they found themselves. The historian Frank Sugeno has emphasized the challenge for Christians who had inherited a belief that the Church was an integral part of national identity, but for whom the English established state-church model was not an option: "The idea of having the Church of England serve as the spiritual component of the life of each colony was not possible in most colonies where other Christian traditions dominated. . . . The question of the church's identity in a non-Anglican nation had to be faced."[52] Two early voices in the process of establishing an American identity and in developing an indigenous style of ministry suited to the new nation were William White and Samuel Seabury.

In 1782, White, chaplain of the Continental Congress and rector of Christ Church in Philadelphia, published *The Case of the Episcopal Churches in the United States Considered,* in which he argued that the new nation required a church that would play the same role in providing the spiritual dimension of national identity that the Church of England did for the English nation. Such a church would reflect both the worship and order inherited from its predecessors and also those peculiarly American characteristics that were being enshrined in its founding documents. In order for such a national church to come into being, he realized that the Anglican congregations, many of which had no formal relationships with other parishes, would need to organize themselves into state entities, which could then meet to adopt a structure for a national church. Concretely, White argued for a church that would preserve the threefold ordained ministry of bishops, priests and deacons, but that would also be democratically governed, providing for the full participation of laypeople. In proposing an American episcopate, White acknowledged that "there cannot be produced an instance of Laymen in America, unless in the very infancy of the settlements, soliciting the introduction of a bishop."[53] (Nancy Rhodes notes that proponents of an American episcopate argued that opposition was based on a mistaken understanding of just what such bishops would and would not *do.*)[54]

In Pennsylvania and in six other states, principles proposed by White formed the basis of the new structures supporting the Church's ministry, among them the assurance that "no power was to be delegated to a general ecclesiastical government which a local congregation or vestry could exercise," a principle that guaranteed the fundamental role of laypeople in shaping the Church's life and work.[55]

But the first bishop of the new church came not from Pennsylvania or from one of the colonies where the War of Independence had received substantial support, but from a state where all the clergy had been Loyalists: Connecticut. In 1782, even before the signing of the peace treaty that formally ended the War of Independence, ten clergy met and elected one of their number, Samuel Seabury, to seek ordination as a bishop and ensure the episcopal character of the Church in Connecticut. Seabury accordingly set off for England, bearing testimonials from a group of clergy who supported him and also a document stating his hope to continue work as an SPG missionary in the city of New London as well as functioning as a bishop.[56]

Seabury's request to the Archbishop of Canterbury was denied, not because the Church of England wished to withhold the episcopate from the now independent Americans but because they were not free to perform ordinations without the mandatory oath of allegiance to the sovereign. When it became clear that he would not be consecrated in England, he appealed to the non-juring Episcopal Church of Scotland, who acted favorably on his request. On November 14, 1784, Seabury was consecrated a bishop by the Bishop and Coadjutor of Aberdeen and the Bishop of Moray and Ross. The following day, Seabury and the Scottish bishops signed a concordat in which they acknowledged commitment to "a free, valid and purely ecclesiastical Episcopacy" and a common understanding of the Gospel. They also affirmed a shared understanding of the Church, in which bishops exercise their "sacred office . . . independent of all lay powers," and committed themselves to a relationship of full communion between the "Catholic remainder of the ancient Church of Scotland and the now rising Church in the United States of America." The Scottish bishops also expressed their hope that Seabury would use "gentle methods of argument and persuasion" to ensure that American Episcopalians would adopt the Scottish Eucharistic Prayer, which included several elements not found in the English *Book of Common Prayer* of 1662: an oblation, or offering, of the bread and wine to God, a prayer invoking the Holy Spirit on the elements, and a commemoration of the saints.[57]

Upon his return to Connecticut, Seabury again took up his duties at the parish in New London (though without the financial support of the SPG), as well as his new work as bishop. Two years later, at the urging of the English bishops who feared the formation of another Episcopal Church with no relationship to the Church of England, Parliament voted to permit the ordination of bishops whose ministries would be carried out beyond the British Empire, provided they performed no ministerial functions on British territory.

In 1787, William White, who had been elected bishop of Pennsylvania, and Samuel Provoost, rector of Trinity Church, New York City, who had been chosen first bishop of New York, took advantage of Parliament's actions and were consecrated as bishops in Canterbury. Over the course of the next years, Episcopalians in the new republic were able to put in place the structures on which the Protestant Episcopal Church in the United States of America was constitutionally established. The church was established as a federation of dioceses, with oversight in the hands of a bicameral legislature, the General Convention, which would meet triennially. In the House of Deputies, each diocese would be represented by an equal number of lay and clergy delegates; the House of Bishops would meet separately, but all major decisions affecting the Church as a whole would require approval of both Houses. The structure as it finally emerged represented a compromise reached after lengthy and often spirited discussions that fully satisfied neither side. Seabury and some high-church representatives were uncomfortable with the role given to laypeople in the governance of the Church; others would have preferred that the bishops simply form a "third order" in a one-chamber legislature.

One of the early actions on which the Church was required to take action was the approval of an American *Book of Common Prayer,* which was first published in 1789. In its preface, the authors noted their belief that American independence was providential, and that no longer bound to the Church of England, Episcopalians in the United States now enjoyed the same liberty to shape their own worship as English Christians had appreciated at the time of the Reformation. While expressing gratitude to their English forebears for "her first foundation and a long continuance of nursing care and protection," the Episcopalians claimed their liberty, not only in drafting new prayers to respond to their changed political situation, but "to take a further review of the Public Service, and to establish such other alterations and amendments therein as might be deemed expedient." Furthermore, although they affirmed that they were "far from intending to depart from the Church of England in any essential point of doctrine, discipline, or worship; or further than local circumstances require," they also recognized their freedom "to model and organize their respective Churches, and forms of worship and discipline, in such manner as they might judge most convenient for their future prosperity."[58] Bishop Seabury was more successful in influencing the revision of the Prayer Book than he had been in attempting to limit the role of laypeople; the 1789 Book and every subsequent version of the American Prayer Book has in fact included the Scottish Eucharistic Prayer as requested by his consecrators.

The last bishop to travel to England for consecration was James Madison, cousin of the president of the same name and himself president of the College of William and Mary.[59] Madison was chosen to be the first bishop of Virginia, and consecrated in Canterbury in 1790. Two years later, the four American bishops, including Seabury, met at Trinity Church in New York to consecrate the first bishop ordained on American soil, Thomas Claggett of Maryland.[60]

With the ability to carry on its own institutional and liturgical life assured, the Episcopal Church had little communication with the Church of England in the years that followed. In 1822, William White, who was serving as Presiding Bishop, was asked to write a letter of introduction for an American priest who intended to visit England. He was forced to decline because he knew no one to whom he might write. As one historian noted, "American priests and bishops who visited England were treated officially as laymen, admitted to the sacraments, but forbidden any clerical function. They felt the humiliation deeply. . . . Not only was the Church of England legally indifferent to the American church, but also there was little communication on any level."[61]

The American Church historian Robert Bosher identified five ways in which the Episcopal Church re-visioned its heritage from the Church of England. For the first time, the authority of the bishops was clearly defined and limited by means of a written Constitution, and the laity were given a role in their election; no diocese held metropolitical authority over another; the government of the church rested in the hands of a two-house legislature in which both houses had equal power; laypeople had a significant role in the legislative and administrative processes of the Church; and it depended upon voluntary contributions for its financial resources. But beyond these important innovations, he also noted that the American Episcopal Church was of extreme significance for the future definition of Anglicanism as a concept (and, he might have added, for the evolution of distinctive forms of ministry). Before its creation, he observed, the word *Anglican* "described a particular church, identified with the national life, traditions and institutions of the English people." After the War of Independence, that earlier concept had become an anachronism: *English* and *Anglican* were no longer equivalent terms.[62]

The English bishop Samuel Wilberforce's history of the Episcopal Church, written in 1844, demonstrated that the distinctly American characteristics of the Episcopal Church were of interest to English Anglicans, even if they did not approve of them. In Wilberforce's view, they were due in part to the poor quality of many of the clergy who ministered in the American colonies prior to independence. "The clergy who came out were those least fitted for a work which, far more than that of ordinary stations, required the highest gifts of holy zeal and knowledge." A lack of discipline within the colonial Church also contributed, he asserted, to a situation in which "the Vestry was now the master of the clergy" and lay readers "from a lower class than the clergy" and natives besides, were "insinuating themselves into the regard of the congregation."[63]

Wilberforce considered that the absence of bishops in the English colonies had contributed to a precipitous and violent rupture with England by weakening people's loyalty to the mother country and her church; if there had been a colonial episcopate, he believed, "the colonies might now, perhaps, have been as much an independent nation; but they might have reached that state by a gradual progress to a national maturity [and] their youthful affections might never have been torn from us; and England, America and the world, might have been spared those bitter sufferings with which they have been visited in the war of independence, and its clear consequence, the French Revolution."[64]

THE CHURCH OF ENGLAND IN CANADA

The English Church and State responded to the loss of the American colonies and the rupture with American Anglicans by trying to ensure that the same sort of events did not disturb the colonies to the north. In 1787, Charles Inglis was appointed the first bishop of the Church of England on the North American continent. Although he was designated Bishop of Nova Scotia, his responsibility also included Prince Edward Island, Upper and Lower Canada (Ontario and Quebec), Bermuda and Newfoundland.

Inglis had first come to North America as an SPG missionary assigned to Delaware; he was later curate at Trinity Church, New York City, and when the British occupied the city he became its rector. An outspoken loyalist, when the British Army left New York he returned to England before being appointed as bishop.

Like Seabury, Inglis considered the bishop's relationship with the clergy to be of primary importance for the Church's ministry; both relied on regular gatherings of the clergy for purposes of communication and, when necessary, encouragement and discipline. The sheer immensity of the territory under Inglis' authority made it necessary to appoint clergy to act as commissaries in his name in Quebec, Upper Canada (Ontario), and New Brunswick.

But in fact the clergy of Canada were as unaccustomed to having the direct oversight of a bishop or his representative as the clergy to their south, and the impression they made on Inglis was hardly positive. He informed the Archbishop of Canterbury that of the eleven missionaries serving in Nova Scotia, "four are diligent, useful clergymen—three are indifferent, neither doing much good or harm, and as for the remaining four, it would be happy for the Church if they were not in her orders."[65]

The Anglican clergy under Inglis' charge worked under conditions not unlike those experienced by missionaries on the American frontier: "Scarcity of supplies, inflation and the challenges of carving settlements out of virgin forest made life in many parts of Bishop Inglis' diocese a harsh reality indeed. . . . To note only one index of the situation, despite funds earmarked for the construction of parsonages, [two clergy] had to construct their own homes at their own expense."[66] On the other hand, the SPG continued to support its missionary clergy with financial assistance, and unlike the Episcopal Church, the Church of England in Canada was established by law. But its numbers were small; Anglicans comprised twenty percent of the population of New Brunswick, but a tiny minority in the French-speaking colony of Quebec. Furthermore, Inglis found himself in power struggles with some of the royal governors of the colonies, who were used to exercising temporal authority in the established church and gave up their prerogatives with little grace.[67]

Financial support from the SPG and the British government was taken for granted by Anglican settlers in Upper Canada, where the first resident missionary cleric arrived in 1785. Few records survive from the early days of Ontario Anglicanism; Canadian church historian Robert Black reports that

> One gets a shadowy glimpse of worship led by prominent laity at which printed sermons were read for edification, and of the practice of baptism by midwives—perhaps, it was suspected, according to ceremonially deficient forms, and often unrecorded in parishes. Clergy never turned down requests for ministrations, but for precious income were allowed to charge for making it a record in the register. . . . [F]ew settlers of the Loyalist era bothered with the expense.

Bishop Inglis required that missionary clergy appoint two wardens and a clerk, and to hold a yearly parish meeting for setting pew rents. Black writes, "Worship was generally non-eucharistic, and any offering during the quarterly or monthly Holy Communion was for many years applied (as in England) for poor relief. Clergy did not view themselves as beholden to their people or dependent on their gifts, but as servants of their bishop and through him of the governor and the sovereign."[68]

It is clear that the Church's intention in Ontario was to replicate the established-church model of the Church of England; in 1790, one-seventh of all Crown lands to be opened in the future were designated as "Clergy Reserves," to be used for the support of the Anglican clergy. In 1793, a separate diocese of Quebec was established, and oversight of Upper Canada was assigned to its bishop, Jacob Mountain. But like the church to the south, Canadian Anglicans eventually came to realize that the parish structure as they had known it in England was impossible to maintain in the vast northern wilderness. Black cites the distance between parishes, the scarcity of settlements and of clergy, and the relative strength of Dissenting denominations with structures more easily adapted to the wilderness. And, he adds,

> Church leaders were frequently reluctant to modify historic English practice to accommodate Upper Canadian realities even when the effectiveness of their ministry was at stake . . . Bishop Mountain rejected [the governor's proposal to encourage lay readers to lead Morning Prayer and read printed sermons] decisively, as he believed that the laity were properly recipients of the Church's ministrations, not leaders. To encourage unsupervised religious meetings could, in Mountain's view, tend only to foster congregationalism and democracy—the roots, perhaps, of some future replay of the American Revolution.[69]

No doubt it would have been hard for Bishop Mountain to imagine a worse outcome; and indeed, the specter of revolution shaped the Church of England's ministry for many years to come.

ANGLICAN MINISTRY IN AUSTRALIA: BEGINNINGS

Like the North American colony of Georgia, Australia was first occupied by the British as a site for a penal colony to which criminals could be exiled, either for a fixed sentence or permanently. The Eclectic Society was a group of Evangelical clergy and laypeople in London who met regularly to discuss the Church's mission, many of whose members would later be among the founders of the Church Missionary Society. Some of its members, including William Wilberforce, were concerned that an Evangelical chaplain accompany the prisoners and the soldiers and civil officials who traveled with them. They were able to secure the appointment of Richard Johnson. Johnson was appointed chaplain to the prison colony in New South Wales, in southeastern Australia, in 1786, and landed at Botany Bay in 1788.

Some of the special emphases of his ministry can be identified from a publication he wrote in 1792 and published at his own expense. It was entitled "An Address to the Inhabitants of the Colonies Established in New South Wales and Norfolk Island" and dedicated "to all Inhabitants, and especially to the unhappy prisoners and convicts established at Port Jackson and Norfolk Island, ... by their very sincere and sympathizing friend, and faithful servant, in the Gospel of Christ." The document was written in two parts. In the first, Johnson spoke from a clearly Evangelical perspective, expressing fears that most of his audience had not in fact been converted, and appealing to them to consider the importance of accepting Christ and his Gospel lest they face sure damnation. It is followed by a catalogue of actions Johnson recommended for those of his readers who wished to live faithfully. The first was constant attention to the Bible (and he urged those who could not read to consider learning, in order to have access to God's Word). He warned of the particular danger of dishonoring the Lord's Day, to which he attributed the early death of some members of the colony. Christians are meant to begin each Sunday with prayer, and to participate in both morning and afternoon worship. He also reminded those residents who were either settlers or had already completed their sentences that they were just as obligated to practice their faith as the "unhappy prisoners."[70] Johnson also called attention to the necessity for faithful Christians to avoid profanity, sexual immorality, theft, and idleness and reminded them that God had decreed that some people occupy positions of authority while others are called to be subject to them. He made clear his awareness that the environment of a penal colony is not the ideal setting to practice Christian piety, but on the other hand, he insisted that his hearers had responsibility for the well-being of their own souls, and reminded them that whatever their station, their actions affected their families and also served as an example—positive or negative—to the Aboriginal population who were witnesses to their actions.[71]

The Australian historian Brian Fletcher observes that the government had a significant interest in the ministry of the Church of England in New South Wales:

> The fact that the convicts were expected to remain in the colony after completing their sentences made it even more desirable for them to be purged of their criminal tendencies. The Church of England, as the only branch of the Christian faith officially recognized in England, was the instrument naturally chosen to implement the government's objectives. Clergy could convey the appropriate message and set an example through the purity of their own lives. In England they served as magistrates and in this capacity could readily assist the hard-pressed civil administration of New South Wales.[72]

While Anglican ministry in Australia would grow significantly in both activity and complexity during the following century, its roots—and its relationship to the development of Australian culture and national identity—lie with the remarkable collection of individuals who, whether by their own choice or not, found themselves at the other end of the world from the church to which they had pledged their faithfulness.

By the end of the eighteenth century, Anglican ministry was being undertaken in ways and settings that Thomas Bray could not have imagined when he founded the SPG a hundred years earlier. The spread of English Christianity had been erratic and marked by failures as well as successes, and it had been shaken by conflicts of personality, theology and politics. But however tentative and threatened its witness in many places, there was no mistaking its identity and its heritage. The ministry of a national church had embraced a worldwide mission. That mission had nurtured and strengthened a constantly growing passion for empire. Within another hundred years, ministry in the Anglican tradition would be found in countless settings and in circumstances even more unimaginable than those of the century that now drew to a close.

NOTES

1. "North Carolina commemorates baptisms of Manteo and Virginia Dare," *The Historiographer* (Fall 2008), 1, 19. The inhabitants of the colony on Roanoke Island disappeared and twenty years passed before a permanent English settlement was established a Jamestown, Virginia.

2. W. M. Jacob, *The Making of the Anglican Church Worldwide* (London: SPCK, 1997), 37.

3. The Avalon Project (Documents in Law, History and Diplomacy), Yale University Law School, http://avalon.law.yale.edu/17th_century/va01.asp. Accessed on July 22, 2011.

4. William W. Manross, *A History of the American Episcopal Church* (New York: Morehouse-Gorham Co., 1950), 9.

5. Manross, *A History of the American Episcopal Church,* 17–18.

6. Jelley, "Power, Authority and Conflict," 27.

7. Jelley, "Power, Authority and Conflict," 32–34.

8. Nicholas Beasley, "Domestic Rituals: Marriage and Baptism in the British Plantation Colonies, 1650–1780," *Anglican and Episcopal History,* 76 (September 2007), 353–354, 357.

9. Jelley, "Power, Authority and Conflict," 59–60.

10. Borden W. Painter, Jr., "The Vestry in Colonial New England," *Historical Magazine of the Protestant Episcopal Church,* XLIV (December 1975), 382.

11. Painter, "Vestry," 392.

12. Mr. Price of King's Chapel, Boston, quoted in Painter, "Vestry," 403.

13. H. G. G. Herklots, *Frontiers of the Church: The Making of the Anglican Communion* (London: Ernest Benn, 1961), 47.

14. Herklots, *Frontiers,* 46.

15. John Woolverton, *Colonial Anglicanism in North America* (Detroit: Wayne State University Press, 1984), 23, 27.

16. W. M. Jacob, *The Making of the Anglican Church Worldwide,* 56–57.

17. Herklots, *Frontiers,* 51.

18. Herklots, *Frontiers,* 54.

19. J. W. C. Wand, ed., *The Anglican Communion: A Survey* (London: Oxford University Press, 1948), 11.

20. Maryland adapted such a statute as early as 1639; Virginia followed in 1667, and Prince Edward Island over a century later, in 1781. New Jersey, New York, North and South Carolina had similar laws.

21. Edward L. Bond, "Colonial Virginia Mission Attitudes toward Native Peoples and African-American Slaves," in Amos Yong and Barbara Brown Ziklund, eds., *Remembering Jamestown: Hard Questions About Christian Mission* (Eugene, OR: Pickwick Publications, 2010), 87.

22. Bond, "Colonial Virginia Mission Attitudes," 87–88.

23. William Meade, *Sermons Addressed to Masters and Servants, and Published in the Year 1743, by the Rev. Thomas Bacon . . . Now Republished with Other Tracts and Dialogues on the Same Subject, and Recommended to All Masters and Mistresses to Be Used in their Families* (Winchester, VA: John Heiskell, Printer, 1813).

24. Marcus W. Jernegan, "Slavery and Conversion in the American Colonies," *American Historical Review,* 21 (April 1916), 509.

25. Brenda Hough, "The Archives of the Society for the Propagation of the Gospel," *Historical Magazine of the Protestant Episcopal Church,* 46 (September 1977), 309.

26. Daniel O'Connor et al., *Three Centuries of Mission: The United Society for the Propagation of the Gospel 1701–2000* (London: Continuum, 2000), 7–8.

27. O'Connor, *Three Centuries of Mission*, 10, 12.

28. O'Connor, *Three Centuries of Mission*, 11.

29. Travis Glasson, *Mastering Christianity: Missionary Anglicanism and Slavery in the Atlantic World* (Oxford: Oxford University Press, 2012, 6). Glasson notes that "over the course of the eighteenth century, the SPG owned more people as slaves than it employed as missionaries."

30. John A. Schutz, "Christopher Codrington's Will: Launching the S.P.G. into the Barbadian Sugar Business," *Pacific Historical Review*, 15 (March 1946), 192.

31. Glasson, *Mastering Christianity*, 101, 118, 156. In 1783, Beilby Porteus, Lord Bishop of London's Annual Sermon to the Society was "a clear, dramatic, and forceful condemnation of the slave trade and a detailed criticism of colonial slavery." Glasson, 210.

32. Rowan Strong, *Anglicanism and the British Empire c. 1700–1850* (Oxford: Oxford University Press, 2007), 6.

33. Strong, *Anglicanism and the British Empire*, 21.

34. Glasson, *Mastering Christianity*, 4.

35. Winthrop A. Hudson, *Religion in America: An Historical Account of the Development of American Religious Life* (third edition) (New York: Charles Scribner's Sons, 1981), 76.

36. David L. Holmes, "Foreword," in Devereux Jarrett, *The Life of Devereux Jarrett* (Cleveland: The Pilgrim Press, 1995), ix.

37. Owanah Anderson, *Jamestown Commitment: The Episcopal Church and the American Indian* (Cincinnati: Forward Movement Publications, 1988), 18.

38. Strong, *Anglicanism and the British Empire*, 50.

39. Owanah Anderson, *400 Years: Anglican/Episcopal Mission Among American Indians* (Cincinnati: Forward Movement Publications, 1997), 8–9.

40. Strong, *Anglicanism and the British Empire*, 62.

41. Strong, *Anglicanism and the British Empire*, 17.

42. David L. Holmes, "The Episcopal Church and the Revolution," *Historical Magazine of the Protestant Episcopal Church*, LVII (September 1978), 261; Nancy L. Rhodes, *Revolutionary Anglicanism: The Colonial Church of England Clergy during the American Revolution* (New York: New York University Press, 1999).

43. Holmes, "The Episcopal Church and the Revolution," 264–268.

44. On the other hand, Rhodes also notes that some Loyalist clergy rejected passive obedience and non-resistance, using the Glorious Revolution as a precedent, but still considered that English rule, however imperfect, was preferable to an unknown and possibly chaotic future. Rhodes, *Revolutionary Anglicanism*, 64, 73.

45. Holmes, "The Episcopal Church and the Revolution," 270.

46. Holmes, "The Episcopal Church and the Revolution," 277–278.

47. Rhodes, *Revolutionary Anglicanism*, 88–89.

48. Memorial Tablet, Frederick Philipse (1720–1785), Cathedral Church of Christ and the Blessed Virgin Mary, Chester, UK.

49. Robert Bruce Mullin, *Episcopal Vision/American Reality: High Church Theology and Social Thought in Evangelical America* (New Haven; Yale University Press, 1986), 9.

50. Holmes, "The Episcopal Church and the American Revolution," 283.

51. Frederick V. Mills, Sr., "The Protestant Episcopal Churches in the United States 1783–1789: Suspended Animation or Remarkable Recovery?" *Historical Magazine of the Protestant Episcopal Church,* XLVI (June 1977), 165.

52. Frank E. Sugeno, "The Establishmentarian Ideal and the Mission of the Episcopal Church," *Historical Magazine of the Protestant Episcopal Church,* LIII (December 1984), 286.

53. Quoted in David L. Holmes, *A Brief History of the Episcopal Church* (Valley Forge, PA: Trinity Press, International, 1993), 51.

54. Rhodes, *Revolutionary Anglicanism,* 37.

55. Mills, "The Protestant Episcopal Churches in the United States," 167.

56. Bruce Steiner, *Samuel Seabury 1729–1796: A Study in the High Church Tradition* (Athens, OH: Ohio University Press, 1971), 191.

57. William Stevens Perry, ed., *Journals of General Conventions of the Protestant Episcopal Church in the United States of America,* III: Historical Notes and Documents (Claremont, NH: The Claremont Manufacturing Co., 1874), 236–239.

58. *The Book of Common Prayer and Administration of the Sacraments and Other Rites and Ceremonies of the Church,* "Preface" (New York: The Seabury Press, 1979), 9–11.

59. Madison was not the first choice to serve as bishop of Virginia. David Griffith was elected as bishop but was unable to raise the funds required for the trip to and from England. Robert Prichard, *A History of the Episcopal Church* (revised edition) (Harrisburg, PA: Morehouse Publishing, 1999), 86.

60. Bishop Claggett was also the second choice to occupy his position. William Smith had been elected in 1783 but "because of his reputation for consumption of alcohol, he was unable to gain the endorsement from General Convention required by the [Episcopal Church's] new constitution." Prichard, *A History of the Episcopal Church,* 86.

61. Roland Foster, "Seabury and the Anglican Communion," in Robert G. Carroon, ed., *A New Heart, A New Spirit: Sermons and Addresses Commemorating the Bicentennial of the Consecration of Samuel Seabury, First Bishop of the American Episcopal Church* (Wilton, CT: Morehouse-Barlow, 1988), 24–25.

62. R. Bosher, *The American Church and the Formation of the Anglican Communion, 1823–1853* (Evanston, Illinois: Seabury-Western Theological Seminary, 1962), 4.

63. Samuel Wilberforce, *A History of the Protestant Episcopal Church in America* (London: James Burns, 1844), 138–139.

64. Wilberforce, *History,* 184.

65. Quoted in Ross N. Hebb, "Bishop Charles Inglis and Bishop Samuel Seabury: High Churchmanship in Varying New World Contexts," *Anglican and Episcopal History,* LXXVI (March 2007), 67.

66. Hebb, "Inglis and Seabury," 80.

67. Hebb, "Inglis and Seabury," 80–82.

68. Robert M. Black, "Stablished in the Faith: The Church of England in Upper Canada 1780 – 1867," in Alan L. Hayes, ed., *By Grace Co-Workers: Building the Anglican Diocese of Toronto 1780 – 1989* (Toronto: Anglican Book Centre, 1989), 24.

69. Black, "Stablished in the Faith," 26.

70. Richard Johnson, "An Address to the Inhabitants of the Colonies, Established in New South Wales and Norfolk Island" (printed by the author, 1792).

71. Johnson, "Address."

72. Brian Fletcher, "The Anglican Ascendancy 1788–1835," in Bruce Kaye, ed., *Anglicanism in Australia: A History* (Melbourne: Melbourne University Press, 2002), 8.

Chapter Six

Reconsiderations

Anglican Ministry in England and Ireland, 1800–1860

At the dawning of the nineteenth century, Anglican ministry was being undertaken not only in the British Isles but wherever the church had accompanied English merchants and settlers. An autonomous Episcopal Church in the United States had changed forever the meaning of "Anglican" and developed its own unique style of ministry, but in general the Church of England continued attempting to transplant the patterns of ministry it had developed for itself into radically new settings. By the end of the century, the burgeoning British and American empires would carry Anglican Christianity to the farthest reaches of the planet, and the practice of ministry would evolve in response to widely diverse contexts.

THE CHURCH OF ENGLAND: MINISTRY IN TRANSITION

For the English church, the American War of Independence and the chaos of the French Revolution that followed it by a few years were seen as warnings of the unpredictable consequences of popular discontent and uprisings. The cries of "Liberty, Equality and Fraternity" that marked the French Revolution, like the patriotic slogans that had earlier moved Americans to support independence, seemed to challenge the carefully maintained sense of order and hierarchy so valued by the English church and nation.

Yet that order and the hierarchy hallowed by tradition which supported it were threatened by rapid social changes occurring across England. The enclosure of public lands, which began in the mid-1700s and had a drastic impact on the well-being of poor farmers who had depended on common land for grazing their animals, reached an average of eighty a year in the first two decades of the nineteenth century, producing an exodus from the countryside just as the burgeoning factories identified with the Industrial Revolution were creating a new class, the urban proletariat.[1] In the absence of any meaningful legal protection for their workers, the factories of the nineteenth century had free rein to keep them underpaid, living and working in squalid conditions where they were victims of misery, disease, and uncompensated injury. The Church of England found itself challenged to minister to both the rural and newly urban poor, as well as their affluent patrons and employers.

Meanwhile, the changes occurring throughout English society were having an impact on the church's ordained leadership. Those clergy who depended upon tithes and rents for their income found the early decades of the nineteenth century difficult indeed, and an 1835 survey noted a median income of £235 for clergy in charge of parishes, an amount generally considered to be insufficient to maintain a household, especially given the considerable social demands placed on the clergy. Assisting clergy usually fared much worse. Rural England generally relied on clergy whose own background was from the countryside; while some twenty percent were aristocrats and another twenty percent were from non-gentry clerical households, the bulk of the clergy were drawn from the professional class.[2]

A survey conducted in 1835 also revealed that nearly three thousand parishes had no housing for their clergy; among those that did, there were great discrepancies. Some were quite grand; others judged to be too small were enlarged in the nineteenth century. The renovated rectory of Bemerton, Salisbury, housed the rector and his wife, four daughters, ten indoor servants, two gardeners and two stablemen. The more modest parsonage in which the Brontë sisters grew up boasted two floors with four rooms on each and was cared for by two servants. Rectories were often used as schoolhouses, since clergy found that establishing schools was a viable way to augment their meager income. Many clergy reported problems with their water supply due to the proximity of the parish cemetery.[3]

The many roles clergy were called upon to fill continued to provoke frequent conflicts of interest. Particularly in the first third of the nineteenth century, clergy often had a major role in county government, especially by serving as Justices of the Peace. This meant that clergy sometimes found themselves in the position of sentencing someone to prison while providing pastoral care to the family left behind.[4]

Like their predecessors in earlier centuries, nineteenth century English clergy often remained in one post for their entire ministry. The parish of Berwick, Surrey had only two rectors between 1797 and 1906. As the century progressed, clerical living standards improved steadily; by mid-century, most had servants. Mary Sumner, founder of the Mother's Union and wife of a country rector, was reported "never to have put on her own stockings in her life," and one of the Sumner household's servants spent every morning on the task of trimming and filling forty oil lamps. It was often servants who functioned as go-betweens between the clergy and the poor, who would never have presumed to approach the parish priest through the front door.[5]

The lifestyle of some clergy mimicked that of the gentry; early in the nineteenth century, there were twenty priests in the diocese of Exeter who kept packs of hounds for foxhunting. Rectory mealtimes frequently followed the schedule of the aristocracy: breakfast at ten in the morning, a luncheon, often of cold meat, at mid-day, and dinner in the late afternoon—4:30 or, for the most fashionable clerical households, still later—5, 6 or even 6:30 p.m. As in any gentry household, ladies customarily withdrew to the drawing room for coffee after dinner until the gentlemen joined them. In the evening, a light supper might be served on a tray. As the century progressed, fashion changed; breakfast was taken earlier, and dinner was at 1, 3 or 5 p.m.[6]

The nineteenth century would see great changes in how Anglicans understood the nature of ministry, but in its early decades the worship of the Church continued much as before. Faithfulness to the pattern of worship assumed by the *Book of Common Prayer* required a two-hour service in the morning, and an hour and a half in the afternoon. In spite of a resurgence of interest in sacramental worship, Mattins and Evensong continued to be the normative services for Sundays; as late as mid-century in the diocese of York nearly half the churches had fewer than twelve celebrations of the Eucharist per year. At the beginning of the century many congregations depended on church bands to accompany congregational singing, but in the course of the century they were replaced by instruments such as harmoniums or organs.[7]

In the early decades of the nineteenth century, the relationship between ordinary Anglicans and their bishop was often a distant one. Vernon Harcourt, Archbishop of York for forty years, was accustomed to administering confirmation by "extending his hands over the congregation and pronouncing the words of Confirmation once." On the other hand, one Cambridge confirmation service in 1833 lasted from 10:30 in the morning until four in the afternoon. The rector of Long Stanton complained that the crowd was so great that his "gown was rent and [his] coat so torn, that [he] was unable to go home with it in that state." The parishes of Wolverhampton went seven years without a visit from their bishop; when he did arrive, he found three thousand people waiting to receive Confirmation. Recalling his own confirmation in Grantham Church with seven to eight thousand others, Dr. Corrie, Master of Jesus College, Cambridge wrote of "a sense of indescribable confusion, oranges being sold in the Church and the public-houses being ready for them before they came out."[8]

When the nineteenth century began, most students of Oxford and Cambridge Universities were candidates for ordination; indeed, the only other formal training for the ordained ministry available in Britain at the time was a one-year course offered by the Welsh diocese of St. David's, where the Seminary of Ystrad Meorig trained clergy whose circumstances did not allow them to attend university. Whatever their training, potential clergy were expected to demonstrate knowledge of the Bible, Greek, and the Thirty-Nine Articles. Throughout the early decades of the century, a number of voices expressed concern at the need for more thorough preparation for ordained ministry, and gradually other options for study were established: St. David's College in Wales, St. Bee's College in Cumberland, and in London, King's College and the Church Missionary Society's training institution, University College.[9] As late as 1832, Oxford University required only some knowledge of the "evidences of our holy religion," ability to read the gospels in their original Greek, the Acts and Old Testament of the English Bible, the Articles of Religion, and one course of twelve lectures. Edward Pusey, soon to gain notoriety as one of the leaders of the Oxford Movement, marveled that "one fortnight comprises the beginning and the end of all the public instruction which any candidate for Holy Orders is required to attend."[10] By 1839, students at the newly established Chichester Theological College were required to refrain from "all such amusements as are forbidden to the clergy by the canons . . ." In particular they were to avoid cards and dice, and other games of chance, and betting; attendance at public billiard rooms, races, theatres, also tandem-driving and hunting, and other boisterous sports. "It is also expected," the College decreed, "that students shall not take part in the amusement of dancing." Dinner or evening parties were permitted only twice a week, and never on Ember Days, Rogation Days, or during Lent, "or at least Wednesdays and Fridays").[11]

THE CHURCH OF ENGLAND AND SOCIAL REFORM

Most of the voices heard publicly in the Church of England viewed the growing sentiments for democratic reform among the rural and urban poor with considerable alarm; that alarm was answered by a sharp increase in criticism of, and disdain for, the clergy on the part of many. Nevertheless, many English people shared their leaders' fear that social unrest must inevitably lead to the excesses of the French Revolution, and they considered the Established Church to be one of the strongest defenses against such unimaginable chaos.

The early stages of the Industrial Revolution had already provoked anxiety among many who noted the unruly children who spent Sunday, the only day when they were not employed in the new factories, in alarming mischief. As early as 1780, Robert Raikes, a committed layman and publisher of a newspaper in Gloucester, established a Sunday school for poor boys, intended to teach literacy, the Bible, the Catechism, and provide Sunday afternoon worship. Over the next decades, societies in other British cities were established to provide Sunday schools, and by 1787, a quarter of a million children were enrolled in similar establishments. Despite their commitment to the spiritual and moral education of poor children, the Sunday schools by no means challenged the basic class assumptions of both church and society: In the words of one society founder, "There is no intention of raising them [the children] above their common level, for in that case how would our manufactories be carried on, our houses erected and our tables furnished?"[12]

It was frequently the Anglican Evangelicals who were most committed to improving the conditions of the poor and providing ministry for those on the margins of society. In Ireland, the Port of Dublin Society, "for promoting religious instruction of Seamen, agreeable to the constitution of the Established Church," organized by "a few Naval Officers and other Gentlemen" and with the support of the Archbishop of Dublin, was founded in 1822; the first Anglican seamen's chapel began its ministry the following year.[13] In England, prominent laypeople like Anthony Ashley Cooper, Earl of Shaftesbury not only worked for change in areas such as reform of the prison system and the Poor Laws, but also education for poor children and factory workers. In 1825, Lord Ashley also turned his attention to establishing a ministry with the thousands of seamen working as ships' crews under appalling conditions. (Before Parliament outlawed the slave trade in 1807, "the mortality rate among seamen engaged in this barbarous traffic in human flesh was even higher than that of their captive cargo. On an average voyage via West Africa and the West Indies, fully one-fifth of the sailors themselves would perish, of sickness, suicide and brutalization, and even more would desert or be discharged before the ship returned home.")[14]

The London Episcopal Floating Church Society hired a chaplain who used a boat, provided by the British Admiralty and fitted as a church, to visit ships docked at London. Similar ministries were soon organized in other English port cities, including Liverpool, Plymouth, Hull and Bristol. Chaplains were called upon not only to conduct services and provide pastoral care, but also to intervene in situations where seamen were kidnapped ("shanghaied") and taken to sea. In time this special ministry would spread beyond England to ports throughout the British Empire.[15] Although nurtured by Anglican Evangelicals, its growth beyond their ranks was painfully slow, highlighting what one historian calls "the Anglican dilemma":

> Should they remain passive, pending the organization of specifically Anglican seafarers' missions, hopefully some time in the future? Or, should they in the

meantime support existing nondenominational societies, as far as Anglican Church order would allow?

> ... [M]ost Evangelical clergy chose the latter ... As one Evangelical clergyman expressed it: "The question is not whether our Sailors shall be Churchmen [sic] or Dissenters ... it is whether they shall be Christians or heathens."[16]

In 1828, Parliament took the first of a series of actions that had significantly changed the way British people were governed. In that year the Corporation Act, put in place following the restoration of the monarchy and which limited public office and entrance into the universities to communicants of the Church of England, was repealed. This was followed a year later by the Catholic Relief Act, repealing the Test Act of 1673, which required office holders to affirm their specific rejection of the doctrine of transubstantiation.

In 1832, Parliament, which now included members from a broad religious spectrum, considered the first Reform Bill designed to address the corruption and favoritism which plagued British politics and which was one of the primary complaints among those seeking change. But the Bill was defeated on its first reading in the House of Lords because of the opposition of most of the bishops. The English church historian Owen Chadwick describes the response: "Whigs and radical newspapers pilloried [the bishops] as allies of boroughmongers, maintainers of graft and corruption and bribery, enemies of liberty and the civil rights of Englishmen." The Archbishop of Canterbury was heckled in public, the carriage of the Bishop of Bath and Wells was stoned, and in Carlisle, a crowd of eight thousand people burned the bishop in effigy. Bishops' palaces were guarded by troops. When the final vote was taken on the Reform Bill, none of the bishops in the House of Lords opposed it.[17]

Another reform of vital significance not only in England but throughout the Empire was the abolition of slavery, accomplished by Act of Parliament in 1833. The slave trade itself had been abolished twenty-five years earlier, due in large part to the support of Evangelicals like William Wilberforce, who shepherded the legislation through Parliament. Wilberforce and others then turned their attention to the total suppression of the institution of slavery; their campaign came to its fruition with Parliament's actions. The British government paid twenty million pounds in compensation to the owners of enslaved persons; recipients included highly placed clergy in the Church of England. "The Archbishop of Canterbury, for example, received an award of just under £9,000 (equivalent to approximately £500,000 in modern currency) in recompense for 411 [enslaved persons], and the Bishop of Exeter fared still better; along with three colleagues, he gained nearly £13,000. . . . "[18]

The anger unleashed at the Church's leadership in response to its opposition to many reform measures revealed passionate concern over its failings in response to current social crises. For many members of the Church of England, their rector was an unknown, often absent figure. In 1827, less than half the clergy who held livings were actually resident in their parishes. In Owen Chadwick's words, "The Church was of the land, its parochial system adapted to ministry in villages, its clergy gentlemen, its legal framework inflexible and unable to meet new circumstances. There was beginning to be a demand, because there was beginning to be a crying need, for pastoral and resident clergymen."[19]

This state of affairs was addressed by Parliament through a series of reform measures beginning in 1836, in the last years of the reign of George IV, and continuing into the early years of the young Queen Victoria. The initial reforms included abolishing livings traditionally held by bishops; equalizing bishops' stipends; and establishing a permanent Ecclesiastical Commission to oversee the Church's ministry. They were followed by stringent restrictions on clergy placement: incumbents could now hold only two benefices, which must be separated by a distance of no more than ten miles, neither of which could have a population of more than three thousand or a joint income of more than £1,000. Clergy were forbidden to augment their income through carrying on trade, and bishops were given the authority to require that each parish have two Sunday services, including a morning sermon and an afternoon lecture. Finally, the bloated cathedral staffs which accounted for enormous expenditures on a small number of clergy were drastically reduced; the eventual saving was estimated at £360,000 yearly, which was now made available to the Ecclesiastical Commission to augment the income of underpaid clergy and establish new parishes in the rapidly growing urban areas.[20]

THE CALL FOR ECCLESIASTICAL INDEPENDENCE: THE OXFORD MOVEMENT

The reforms approved by Parliament which directly affected the life and work of the Church of England were received with varying responses; many clergy were grateful for the improvement in their own circumstances, but others wondered whether it was appropriate for a legislative body now comprised of people of various religious affiliations (or none) to have such a strong hand in the administration of the national Church. Some voices even dared to criticize what they perceived as meddling in the Church's affairs by a Parliament no longer uniformly Anglican in its membership. They expressed concern that the well-being of the Church's internal life was compromised by its dependence on a State and wondered if the Reformers had not erred in creating a national Church "by law established."

Indeed, Parliament's action in reducing the number of dioceses in Ireland as a means of curtailing expenses in a setting where the overwhelming majority of the population was Roman Catholic caused an uproar among several clergy associated with Oxford University and gave birth to a movement which had far-reaching influence not only in England but throughout the Anglican world. Generally considered to have begun with Edward Pusey's 1833 sermon preached at the annual corporate worship of the judicial community, the so-called Oxford Movement was carried forward by a series of increasingly inflammatory pamphlets, published as "Tracts for the Times." Other parliamentary reforms were judged to undermine still further the Church's authority as the unique official expression of the faith of the English nation. In 1836, marriages in Dissenting chapels and civil ceremonies before registrars were permitted. Five years later, the British and Prussian governments approved a project establishing a Protestant bishopric in Jerusalem as a first step towards evangelistic activity in Palestine. While all bishops holding the position were to be consecrated by the Church of England, candidates were to be nominated alternatively by the British and Prussian governments and Parliament approved the consecration of bishops overseas with spiritual jurisdiction over both Anglicans and other Protestant communities who wished to receive their ministry. Prussian Lutheran bishops, even if consecrated by the Church of England, seemed to some a dangerous innovation that called into question the very foundation of the structure of Anglican ministry.

In spite of the reforms made to the Church and its ordained ministry, at least on the official level the Church continued to occupy an uncritical role in the ideology that shaped British assumptions for much of the century. From 1817 to 1828, the Archbishop of Canterbury's son was in fact Speaker of the House of Commons.[21] Aware that a reforming Parliament had made a number of concessions to improve the lot of England's poor, clerical voices of the period often warned their hearers that tampering with the divinely instituted laws undergirding *laissez-faire* capitalism ran the risk of violating God's plan for an ordered society and withheld from the poor the spiritual advantage they held by not being troubled with worldly affairs, what John Keble called their "calm tranquility, that godliness of life, that perfect resignation to God's providential love." Indeed, Keble believed that poor people are most equipped to perceive the fullness of Christian faith, and should "bless their state, since, compared with the rich, they have very few temptations. . . . Poverty is spiritually uplifting, for it is . . . a kind of fasting." Furthermore, the rich need the poor in order to exercise God's demand of charity.[22]

The Oxford Movement did not always speak with one voice when it addressed the relationship between church and state. Keble and Pusey did not object to the Royal Supremacy; Keble saw the monarch's oversight as a means of maintaining the spiritual independence of the Church, while Keble's young disciple R. H. Froude emphatically believed it was a mistake, and that the Church should rather exercise oversight over the state as it did in the medieval period. John Henry Newman's perspective considered that the Church's entire mission was to save souls and create saints; improvements to society were a by-product of faith, not its purpose. In its current state, he observed, the Church of England was "but the religion of a class," while a truly Catholic understanding of the church would include "specimens of every class among her children."[23]

Questions about the appropriate relationship between church and state inevitably led to the opening of conflicts thought settled since the time of the Reformation, or at least the Restoration. The *Tracts for the Times* caused enormous turmoil among English Anglicans, especially since suggestions for the recovery of a pre-Reformation polity also called into question the other reforms authored by Cranmer and his colleagues. The course of the Oxford Movement can be analyzed in relation to the broader Romantic movement that shaped the art, literature, music and even politics of the period: John Keble affirmed that the function of poetry was "moral and religious," but that "the poetic Church was being stifled by the increasingly encroaching policies of the State."[24] Years before he became famous for his 1833 sermon on "National Apostasy," Keble had published a volume of poems on the themes of each Sunday and holy day of the liturgical year, a focus on the liturgical and sacramental aspects of Anglican Christianity that sharply differentiated him from the prevailing mood of the Church of England and, at least in the minds of many, skirted dangerously close to Roman Catholic spirituality. Perhaps one of the best examples of his piety can be seen in his poem for the Feast of the Annunciation of the Blessed Virgin Mary (March 25).

> Ave Maria! Mother blest,
>   To whom caressing and caress'd,
> Clings the Eternal Child;
> Favoured beyond Archangels' dream,
> When first on thee with tenderest gleam
>   Thy new-born Saviour smil'd:
> Ave Maria! Thou whose name
> All but adoring love may claim,
>   Yet may we reach thy shrine;
> For He, thy Son and Saviour, vows
> To crown all lowly lofty brows
>   With love and joy like thine.[25]

The aesthetic dimension of spirituality espoused by the Oxford Movement was greatly advanced by the work of the Cambridge Camden Society, formed by a group of undergraduates at Cambridge University for the purpose of restoring the medieval vision of the Church of England to what they considered its appropriate glory. Their emphasis was not overtly theological but architectural; they sought to abolish the habit of renting pews and to restore not only the separate altar areas, or chancels, but all the symbolic aspects of medieval English Catholicism. The Society's scholars were at pains to document whatever traces of pre-Reformation architecture remained and to urge the restoration of elements eliminated in the time of the Tudors. Even the stone chantry altars, relics of a time when medieval Roman Catholic parishes had facilities for several priests to celebrate mass simultaneously, were commended.[26] The Society also advocated the restoration of traditional elements of worship associated with medieval church architecture such as processions, vested choirs, and the chanting of psalms.[27]

The combined influence of the Oxford Movement and the Cambridge Camden Society affected the practice of ministry throughout the Anglican Communion as increasing numbers of both clergy and laypeople were drawn to what came to be known as *Anglo-Catholicism*. Customs which had disappeared or been marginalized since the time of the Reformation were resurrected, provoking a variety of responses, both positive and negative. These included more frequent celebrations of the Eucharist, the use of traditional Eucharistic vestments, gestures such as facing the altar for the recitation of the Creed, genuflection and making the sign of the cross, invocation of saints, devotions directed to Christ present in the Blessed Sacrament, and the restoration of private confession. Bryan King, rector of the parish of St. George in the East, located in London's East End, was one of the earliest parish clergy to institute what came to be known as "Ritualist" practices. King was forced to rely on a group of "several dozen High Church gentlemen from outside the parish" as bodyguards, after what began as "shouting, stamping of feet, slamming of doors, whistling and striking of lucifer matches" degenerated into a situation in which, the rector reported, "walnut shells, orange peels . . . were thrown at me, and a row of boys . . . shot peas at my face with pea-shooters . . . Prayer books were thrown, windows were smashed, carpets were torn up and burnt in the stove, drugged dogs were turned loose." At one point, as many as fifty uniformed police were on hand during Sunday services in an attempt to maintain order.[28]

The *Societas Sanctae Crucis* (Society of the Holy Cross), a group of young clergy established to further evangelism in cities, was committed to fostering the spirituality and pastoral skills they considered essential to such a ministry. It was this group that introduced the practice of "preached retreats" now common throughout the Anglican Communion but initially borrowed from the

Jesuits, who had developed the format in the seventeenth century in order to make the spiritual exercises designed by their founder, St. Ignatius, available to a wider audience. Like so many of the practices of the Ritualist movement, it created deep mistrust and hostility not only from voices in the Church of England but from the popular press as well.[29]

Few elements of the Ritualist movement sparked more controversy than the revival of the practice of private confession to a priest. Confession created a situation in which women spoke, often in secrecy, of the most intimate details of their lives to their confessor, who might well ask what critics considered "improper," "corrupting" or "indelicate" questions. Perhaps passions generated by the Oxford Movement emerged not only from deep fear and mistrust of Roman Catholicism but from the implicit challenge to the traditional Victorian ideology of the family, in which women lived their entire lives subordinated either to their father or their husband.[30]

ANGLICAN MINISTRY AT MID-CENTURY

By the middle of the nineteenth century, the Church of England was deeply divided about its own identity in relation to the nation itself. That division had profound effects on the Church's practice of ministry, both by its ordained leaders and by those who continued to identify themselves as its communicants. But English society itself had become increasingly fractured under the pressure of the rapid social changes of urbanization and industrialization, accompanied by a sense of ever-growing secularization as traditional values and assumptions were undermined not only by change but also by ever-burgeoning scientific discoveries.

In 1847, a campaign to restore the Convocation of the Church of England as a forum for the Church's decision-making was initiated. The Convocation had not met formally since 1717, and the archbishops, half the clergy and nearly all the laity were initially opposed. However, the Convocation met in 1855, restoring to the representatives of the clergy, as Owen Chadwick observed, "the right to utter a voice."[31] On the other hand, in many ways the traditional clerical role was being redefined or limited; while clergy had traditionally held responsibility for village schools, from the 1840s that absolute authority passed from their hands to local school committees of management.

Chadwick's history of the church in the age of Queen Victoria shares a view commonly held by church historians that the first half of the nineteenth century was a period in which the urban working class was lost to the Church of England. E. C. Wickham's classic study of the phenomenon, *Church and People in an Industrial City,* argued that "from the emergence of the industrial towns in the eighteenth century, the working class, the labouring poor, the common people, as a class, substantially, as adults, have been outside the churches. The industrial working class culture has evolved lacking a tradition of the practice of religion."[32]

Historians have generally relied on data from the census of 1851, which included questions about religious affiliation, to describe the situation of the Church and its ministry at the century's mid-point. Projecting from the data, the educator Horace Mann considered that of a population just under 18 million, slightly more than five million people in England and Wales identified themselves as members of the Established Church, while the principal Dissenting churches counted four and a half million adherents. In urban areas, Dissent was stronger still; in the industrial town of Leeds, only fifteen percent of the population was Anglican, while thirty-one percent attended Dissenting chapels. Mann argued that on any given Sunday, more than five million people who could have attended church in fact did not, that there was space in urban churches for only a million and a half worshippers on any given Sunday, and that two thousand new churches and chapels were urgently needed. While his statistics have been questioned, it is certainly true that the Victorian period was a time of extensive construction of new churches, especially in the rapidly growing cities. But alongside the impetus it gave to the development of new ministries in the Church of England, the census of 1851 revealed, as Chadwick commented, that it was no longer possible for the Established Church to continue to claim that "it was the church of the immense majority of the country."[33] Gladstone, who had written strongly in support of Establishment, now not only gave up his allegiance to the Conservative Party in favor of the Liberal Party's more flexible attitude; as Prime Minister in the 1860s he led the fight to disestablish the (Anglican) Church of Ireland and create "a free church in a free state."[34]

Of the 13,000 clergy in the Church of England, Evangelicals numbered perhaps three thousand. The response of the Evangelical party to the events at mid-century was to continue to emphasize the necessity of individual conversion and a lifestyle immune to what they considered a decline in Christian values and principles.[35] Other Anglicans, however, took much more dramatic and consequential steps to respond to the contemporary context as they interpreted it, none better known than the theologian Frederick Denison Maurice.

FREDERICK DENISON MAURICE AND CHRISTIAN SOCIALISM

Maurice was deeply troubled by the often-violent social upheavals which had shaken England and all of Europe in the first half of the nineteenth century. With his friend J. M. Ludlow, Maurice formed a group to study the

Bible with the goal of identifying Christian principles around which society might be organized in ways that would avoid the conflict which he saw as directly opposed to the will of God. Maurice was convinced that Christian faith revealed a God of order, and that the two social institutions, family and nation, are established by God for the well-being of society. Indeed, he considered them as "schools" for educating people how to live in community, which he believed is the natural state of human existence. But the community *par excellence* is the church, holding up as it does a vision of the final unity of all humankind in relationship with God. The Church, he insisted, is by no means a human construction; far from being helpful, theological "systems" inevitably lead to partisan strife. Church history, he believed, is full of examples where human beings have attempted to substitute their own structures of belief and practice for the truly unified body which is God's intention. The only way to arrive at such unity is to "dig," by which he meant the disciplined study of scriptures in order to discover God's own purposes. Such digging would bring us to the encounter with God's passionate love for humankind and for the entire creation, revealed above all in the incarnation of Christ which makes possible the ultimate fulfillment of the whole creation in union with God.

> My business, because I am a theologian, and have no vocation except for theology, is not to build, but to dig, to show that economy and politics . . . must have a ground beneath themselves, that society is not to be made anew by arrangements of ours, but is to be regenerated by finding the law and ground of its order and harmony, the only secret of its existence, in God. . . . [T]o me it is the only [method] which makes action possible. . . . The Kingdom of Heaven is to me the great practical existing reality which is to renew the earth and make it a habitation for blessed spirits instead of for demons.[36]

The reflections undertaken by Maurice and his associates occurred against the background of another wave of social upheaval which was shaking both England and the rest of Europe at mid-century. Much of the turmoil in England was generated by the Chartist movement, which demanded "a new electoral law to include universal manhood suffrage, a secret ballot, salaries and no property qualification for members of Parliament, thereby making it possible for the workers to be represented in the House of Commons for the first time."[37] In the spring of 1848, the Chartists organized a mass demonstration in support of their program of "peaceful revolution," but it was dispersed by a massive show of military force. Now joined by Charles Kingsley, a country parson deeply moved by the plight of England's poor and fearful of the potential for violence implicit in continued confrontations, Maurice and Ludlow began what they called a movement for "Christian Socialism." A short-lived series of weekly newspapers, *Politics for the People,* served as an initial vehicle for an approach to social ills based on the doctrine of the incarnation and Maurice's firm belief that a only a society based on scriptural values and God-given order would achieve the justice taught by the Bible.

Like other programs designed to right the wrongs of English society, the Christian Socialist movement brought together well-intentioned but often naive clergy and laypeople of the upper and middle classes whose experience and knowledge of the reality of working-class life in England was minimal. Ludlow later wrote that the group were "the victims themselves of those fearful class-estrangements which they had come together to break down, they knew not a single working-man, of the thinking and reading class."[38] Indeed, it was not until the following year that the Christian Socialists began meeting with Chartists and other labor leaders.

Unlike Kingsley and Ludlow, Maurice did not support most of the Chartists' demands. He insisted that Christian justice did not imply either social or political equality, but rather a model in which classes worked together cooperatively on behalf of the common good. Such cooperation could not occur, however, without the commitment of the professional and upper classes to put the welfare of society above their own greed, as well as the education of the poor to understand their role in creating a just society. For his part, Kingsley confessed the role of the Church of England's clergy in supporting the circumstances of social polarization by identifying with the more prosperous elements of British society:

> We have used the Bible as if it were a special constable's handbook—an opium-dose for keeping beasts of burden patient while they were being overloaded—a mere book to keep the poor in order. . . . We have told you that the Bible preached the rights of property and the duties of labor, when God knows, for [every time] it does that, it preaches ten times over the *duties of property* and the *rights of labour.* We have found plenty of texts to rebuke the sins of the poor, and very few to rebuke the sins of the rich.[39]

While always acting as a cautious brake on the more progressive ideas of his colleagues, Maurice shared their awareness of, and sympathy for, the plight of the poor. His vision of the cooperative society led him and his associates to propose an alternative to the free-market capitalism of nineteenth century England, which they considered to be founded on sinful motives such as greed and competition. "Christian Socialism," they believed, could be put into practice and its benefits clearly revealed through the formation of a number of cooperative societies for the production and distribution of goods as well as the provision of services. In the years immediately following, a large number of such societies were established, including cooperatives for tailors, shoemakers, builders, piano-makers, printers, bakers, blacksmiths and needleworkers. But Maurice always insisted that ultimate leadership of the societies should rest with him and his associates, and he steadfastly refused to support any concerted action by workers to organize and take action in support of their demands. Maurice considered unions to be "class-war organizations sundering 'the Universal Brotherhood' that should unite workers and employers." "Every successful strike," he wrote, "tends to give the workmen a very undue and dangerous sense of their own power, and a very alarming contempt for their employer, and . . . every unsuccessful strike drives them to desperate and wild courses."[40]

After the perhaps inevitable collapse of the cooperative societies, Maurice dedicated himself to the establishment of a Working Men's College with the purpose of educating the poor to appreciate a more cooperative vision of the well-being of society as a whole and to act according to such values rather than individual or class interests. Maurice's lifelong interest in schooling, especially for those least likely to have access to it, reflects what the contemporary ethicist Ellen Wondra notes as his doubt that the "conversion of individuals and the transformation of cultures for which one longs—as Maurice undoubtedly did—can be brought about through other than essentially educational endeavors."[41] But underlying his work as an educator was his passion for unity, a longing and a commitment that had momentous effects on the practice of ministry among Anglicans in the years that followed. Indeed, one scholar argues that beyond his influence on Anglican Christianity, "Maurice stumbled across the very principle which has made the ecumenical movement possible—the recognition that somehow all Christians are already united to Christ and members of his Church."[42]

SCIENCE, FAITH AND MINISTRY

While the social conflicts that shook the Church of England and its ministry at mid-century were indeed dramatic, there were other traumatic movements and events that further challenged the Church's order. Some Anglican clergy had always been deeply interested in the implications of scientific discovery for Christian faith and practice; far from being opposed to the sense of wonder and adventure that marks the spirit of much early science, many of the names associated with the Enlightenment were in fact members of the clerical order who saw in the constant unfolding of empirically based scientific truth the possibility of a rational underpinning for Christian faith. Nevertheless, by the nineteenth century, science was developing in ways that challenged rather than confirmed what Christians had always believed.

"Rational" questioning of the literal truth of the scriptures was not unknown, especially among European thinkers and philosophers, and the Deists and Anglican Latitudinarians of the eighteenth century often urged that faith be interpreted in the crucible of common sense and secular learning. But it was not until the nineteenth century that scholars, especially in Germany, began the daring task of using "scientific" criteria to evaluate, not only the content of scripture, but the reliability of its texts. This new field of biblical criticism used the technique of textual analysis to call into question such previously unquestioned aspects of the scripture as whether Moses was the sole author of the first five books of the Hebrew Scriptures known by his name. Various scholars claimed to have discovered multiple texts within a single book—none more stringently evaluated than Genesis; even the authorship of the four gospels was called into question by various hypotheses postulating lengthy periods of oral transmission followed by the work of editing which made it impossible to consider the traditional authorship of the primary Christian texts as historically credible.

Meanwhile, archeological digs in a number of biblical locations and rapid advances in the science of geology were threatening both the cosmic and historical information recorded in the scriptural accounts. As Owen Chadwick remarked, "Genesis and geology went to war."[43]

Both Evangelicals and the Tractarian followers of the Oxford Movement lamented what they considered to be a tragic process of secularization that challenged not only the stability of the nation but its very soul. By mid-century, educated British readers had access to publications like the *Westminster Review* which were making available translations and commentaries on modern German biblical scholarship as well as writing by a daring group of English thinkers who identified themselves as "radicals" or "free-thinkers." Typical of them was Anthony Froude, whose older brother had been a disciple of the Oxford Movement. In 1849, Froude published a semi-autobiographical novel, *The Nemesis of Faith,* which tells the story of a young Anglican cleric who finds himself unable to continue in his vocation. The historian Rosemary Ashton describes it as

> the thinly veiled cry of distress from a tormented soul. The novel catches the intellectual atmosphere of the mid-century at a particularly sensitive moment, at the same time landing some blows, half-reluctantly, against religious orthodoxy. Though a product of the hothouse atmosphere of Oxford, its interest extends . . . far beyond the dreaming spires into the intellectual, cultural, and spiritual life of thinking men and women in London and the provinces, in Great Britain as a whole, and in the United States too. The excited response to *The Nemesis of Faith* made it one of the publishing sensations of the century.[44]

In 1859, Charles Darwin published his controversial work, *On the Origin of Species,* based on his discoveries in the course of a lengthy journey of exploration around the world. His account of the theory of natural selection, a process by which the evolution of life—including that of humans—can be explained without reference to God, made the most powerful attack on the literal authenticity of the Bible to which the Church had ever been called to make a response.

A few months later, a group of seven academics in the Church of England, all but one of them clergy and including a future Archbishop of Canterbury, published *Essays and Reviews,* a collection of articles which took seriously the scholarly questioning of traditional and literal readings of the scriptures and attempted to take account of those doubts in re-interpreting the nature of Christian faith. Benjamin Jowett, the renowned Oxford classicist, argued in his essay for a concept of *continuing* revelation and the necessity of constantly re-interpreting the scriptures in the light of the knowledge and experience of our own time. Others questioned the validity of the concept of hell as eternal punishment and traditional understandings of the inspiration of scripture.

The outpouring of opposition to *Essays and Reviews* can perhaps be explained by the fact that while similar attacks on conventional Christian belief had been made by voices from outside the Church, these authors occupied distinguished positions as clergy and academics and claimed to be working from a perspective of faith. Samuel Wilberforce, Bishop of Oxford and son of the Evangelical member of Parliament honored for his work against the slave trade, led the negative response to the book. Two of the authors were dismissed from their posts and indicted for heresy, though they were exonerated by the Judiciary Committee of the Privy Council (over the objections of the Archbishops of Canterbury and York). 137,000 laypeople signed a statement thanking the Archbishops for their stand; a declaration of opposition drafted at Oxford eventually garnered the support of 11,000 clergy. The Archbishop of Canterbury engineered a condemnation of the book by the Synod of Westminster.

Essays and Reviews had the effect of adding another dimension to the conflicts already shaking the Church. Many preachers felt called upon to defend the historical elements of the scriptures. Evangelicals and Anglo-Catholics, whose understanding of Anglican Christianity differed in so many ways, found themselves unlikely allies in protesting what seemed to them a flagrant attack on the authority of scripture in the name of secular learning and assumptions. Ordinary Anglicans were led by clergy who sometimes seemed to spend as much time and energy attacking their ordained opponents as fulfilling their pastoral roles. It was difficult if not impossible for the Church's ministry to be carried out without reference to, and identification with, one of the schools of thought—Evangelical, Anglo-Catholic, and Liberal or "broad church"—that were struggling for dominance in the Church of England.

ANGLICAN MINISTRY IN IRELAND

Anglicanism in Ireland is often assumed to be directly related to the Church of England, and it is true that the Reformation coincided with the lengthy struggle of the Tudor and Stewart monarchs to subdue and conquer the Irish people. Henry VIII succeeded in asserting his claim to be King of Ireland in 1541, but his immediate authority waned beyond the immediate environs of the city of Dublin. The emergence of a Reformed Church of Ireland in communion with the English Church was a complicated process, and the majority of the Irish people, including much of its nobility, never budged from their allegiance to Roman Catholicism. The Irish historian F. R. Bolton insists that "from the Reformation, [the Church of Ireland] had moved on parallel, though not identical, lines with the Church of England." This was particularly evident, he claims, during the seventeenth century, when its leaders "insisted that she was a 'free national Church.'"[45] The first Irish-language New Testament was published in 1602, followed by a translation of the *Book of Common Prayer* four years later. The entire Bible was not published in Irish until 1680, and an Irish version of the Church of England's 1662 Prayer Book took fifty years to make its appearance.

In the aftermath of the reign of James II and the "Glorious Revolution" which replaced him with William and Mary, "strong efforts [were] made to ensure that Roman Catholics (and Dissenters) were excluded from political life in Ireland, and what has come to be known as the period of Protestant (Anglican) Ascendancy began. It was to endure, in on form or another, for the best part of a century and a half."[46]

The status of the Church of Ireland changed dramatically when the Parliaments of both Great Britain and Ireland, which had previously been united only through a common monarch, approved the Acts of Union which took effect in 1801. The immediate effect of the Acts was to unite the Church of Ireland with the Church of England and to confer upon it the same Established status as that enjoyed by the English Church. While many in the Church of Ireland opposed the union, only two of the Irish bishops stood in opposition, the majority considering that it provided the only hope of a "Protestant ascendancy" in Ireland.[47]

In the aftermath of the union with the Church of England, the Evangelical movement played an important part in the Church's ministry in Ireland. The movement demonstrated the same priorities as in England, emphasizing particularly the importance of the Bible. A number of unofficial groups such as the Scripture-Reader's Society came into being; one of them, the Irish Society, was concerned "to teach Irish-speaking peasantry to read the Scripture in Irish to other people." Many of the bishops actively opposed the groups because they were inter-denominational in character, but they enjoyed great popularity; one Anglican priest in Kilkenny imported nine thousand copies of the Irish-language Bible from England each year for distribution.[48]

But perhaps inevitably, the specific realities of the context also added an especially strong anti-Roman flavor to the Evangelical movement in Ireland. The decades of the 1820s and 1830s were marked by what came to be known as the "Roman Controversy," in which the Church of Ireland made concerted efforts to convert Roman Catholics to Anglican Christianity. One community in the diocese of Limerick reported 470 conversions, and in a few months the diocese received over 1300 people from the Roman church, a phenomenon described by the bishop as "providential." "Controversial sermons were the rule, and crowds flocked to hear them, while the Romanist clergy replied with equally vigorous polemic." By the end of the 1830s, the dramatic controversies had declined, but the Church entered what one Irish historian calls a "more systematic stage"; in 1844, it established a "Priests' Protection Society" which helped protect Roman Catholic clergy and seminarians who were making the transition to Anglicanism.[49]

In the first half of the nineteenth century, the Church of Ireland nourished a sense of identity and ministry that took seriously its opposition to the Roman Catholic religion of the majority of the Irish people, a dimension of its life that continues even today. But its short-lived hope of a "Protestant Ascendancy" failed. (In 1871, the Irish Church Act would restore the complete autonomy of the Church of Ireland.) The historian C. A. Webster attributes its failure to win over a majority of the Irish people to its intimate connection with a state that many considered to be oppressive. And, he notes, Establishment also took a toll on the Church itself: it required that every parish be given a "full Church organization," resulting in "highly paid clergy with little or nothing to do, and very small flocks with a pastor for each of them."[50]

NOTES

1. Peter Virgin, *The Church in An Age of Negligence: Ecclesiastical Structure and Problems of Church Reform 1700–1840* (Cambridge: James Clarke, 1989), 54.

2. Virgin, *The Church in an Age of Negligence,* 109–111.

3. Peter C. Hammond, *The Parson and the Victorian Parish* (London, Hodder and Stoughton, 1977), 45–54.

4. Virgin, *The Church In An Age of Negligence,* 105.

5. Hammond, *The Parson and the Victorian Parish,* 58, 61.

6. Hammond, *The Parson and the Victorian Parish*, 63–66.
7. Hammond, *The Parson and the Victorian Parish*, 75, 86–89.
8. S. C. Carpenter, *Church and People, 1789–1889: A History of the Church of England from William Wilberforce to "Lux Mundi,"* London: SPCK, 1933, 252–253.
9. F. W. B. Bullock, *A History of Training for the Ministry of the Church of England in England and Wales* (St. Leonard's-on-Sea: Budd and Gillatt, 1955), 27–32.
10. Quoted in Bullock, *History of Training*, 49–50.
11. Bullock, *History of Training*, 59.
12. J. Parker Jameson, "The Sunday School in the National Period," in *Historical Magazine of the Protestant Episcopal Church*, Vol. LI (June 1982), 185–186.
13. Roald Kverndal, *Seamen's Missions: Their Origin and Early Growth* (Pasadena, CA: William Carey Library, 1986), 286.
14. Kverndal, *Seamen's Missions*, 3.
15. L. A. G. Strong, *Flying Angel: The Story of the Missions to Seamen*, London, Methuen and Co., Ltd., 1956, 14–15, 18. See also Kverndal, *Seamen's Missions*, 287–291.
16. Roald Kverndal, *The Way of the Sea: The Changing Shape of Mission in the Seafaring World* (Pasadena, CA: William Carey Library, 2008), 37. "The first successful national organization to represent the Church of England" was the Missions to Seamen, established in 1856. It struggled with opposition from some Anglo-Catholics to both the broad participation of laypeople in its ministry and its lack of a clear connection to a parish. 38–39.
17. Owen Chadwick, *The Victorian Church: An Ecclesiastical History of England, Vol. I* (London: Adam and Charles Black, 1966), 25, 27, 32.
18. Natalie Zacek, "West Indian echoes: Dodington House, the Codrington family and the Caribbean heritage," in Madge Dresser, ed., *Slavery and the British Country House* (London: English Heritage, 2013), 110.
19. Chadwick, *The Victorian Church*, I, 34.
20. Chadwick, *The Victorian Church*, I, 136–138.
21. J. H. L. Rowlands, *Church, State and Society: The Attitudes of John Keble, Richard Hurrell Froude and John Henry Newman, 1827–1845* (Worthing, UK: Churchman Publishing Ltd., 1989), 6.
22. Rowlands, *Church, State and Society*, 29, 37, 43.
23. Rowlands, *Church, State and Society*, 159, 195, 229.
24. Rowlands, *Church, State and Society*, 2–13.
25. John Keble, "82. The Annunciation of the Blessed Virgin Mary," *The Christian Year: Thoughts in verse for the Sundays and holydays through the year* (London: Frederick Stakes and Co., 1827), 124.
26. Matthew Bloxam, "On Chantry Altars," *Transactions of the Cambridge Camden Society: A Selection from the Papers Read at the Ordinary Meetings in 1839–1841* (Cambridge: T. Stevenson, 1841), 9.
27. John Sheldon Reid, *Glorious Battle: The Cultural Politics of Victorian Anglo-Catholicism* (Nashville: Vanderbilt University Press, 1996), 30.
28. Reid, *Glorious Battle*, 57–58.

29. John Tyers, "Not a Papal Conspiracy but a Spiritual Principle: Three Early Anglican Apologists for the Practice of Retreat," *Journal of Anglican Studies*, 8, 2 (November 2010), 165–183.

30. Reid, *Glorious Battle*, 48–49, 193.

31. Chadwick, *The Victorian Church*, I, 324.

32. E. R. Wickham, *Church and People in an Industrial City* (London: Lutterworth Press, 1957), 14.

33. Chadwick, *The Victorian Church*, I, 363–369.

34. Richard Shannon, *Gladstone: Volume II, 1865–1898* (London: Penguin, 1999), 65.

35. Chadwick, *The Victorian Church*, I, 440–446.

36. Frederick Maurice, ed., *The Life of Frederick Denison Maurice, chiefly told in his own letters* (London: Macmillan and Co., 1884), I, 136–137.

37. John C. Cort, *Christian Socialism: An Informal History* (Maryknoll, NY: Orbis Books, 1988), 140.

38. Cort, *Christian Socialism*, 145.

39. Quoted in Cort, *Christian Socialism*, 144.

40. Quoted in Cort, *Christian Socialism*, 144.

41. Cort, *Christian Socialism*, 148.

42. Ellen K. Wondra, ed., "Introduction," in F. D. Maurice, *Reconstructing Christian Ethics: Selected Writings* (Louisville: Westminster John Knox Press, 1995), xxix.

43. William J. Wolf, ed., "Frederick Denison Maurice," in *The Spirit of Anglicanism: Hooker, Maurice, Temple* (Wilton, CY: Morehouse-Barlow Co., Inc., 1979), 92.

44. Chadwick, *The Victorian Church*, I, 559.

45. Rosemary Ashton, *142 Strand: A Radical Address in Victorian London* (London: Vintage Books, 2008), 53.

46. F. R. Bolton, *The Caroline Tradition of the Church of Ireland: With Particular Reference to Bishop Jeremy Taylor* (London, SPCK, 1958), xiii, 2.

47. Kenneth Milne, "A History of the Church of Ireland," in Claude Costecolde and Brian Walker, eds., *The Church of Ireland: An Illustrated History* (Booklink, 2013), 37.

48. N. D. Emerson, "The Last Phase of the Establishment," in Walter A. Phillips, ed., *History of the Church of Ireland from the Earliest Times to the Present Day* (Oxford: Oxford University Press, 1933), III, 287.

49. N. D. Emerson, "Church Life in the Nineteenth Century," in Phillips, *History of the Church of Ireland*, 335.

50. C. A. Webster, "The Reconstruction of the Church," in Phillips, *History of the Church of Ireland*, 360–361.

Chapter Seven

Pioneers

Mission and Ministry in North America, 1800–1860

In the early years of the nineteenth century the fledgling Episcopal Church continued to reflect its English heritage but also demonstrated how its own context called for a unique style of ministry. In 1803, the Louisiana Purchase doubled the territory of the United States and extended its western boundary to the Rocky Mountains. Like other American churches, the Episcopal Church struggled to find ways of carrying out its mission in frontier conditions far from the relatively settled parishes of the eastern seaboard.

From the beginning, American Episcopalians approached the Church's mission from a distinctive standpoint. In general, Protestant churches depended on denominational or ecumenical missionary societies like the American Bible Society to carry on such work, and the Episcopal Church experimented briefly with a similar approach. But in spite of the debt they owed to the SPG and the SPCK, American Episcopalians understood mission primarily as the calling of the Church itself rather than of a particular agency or organization. As early as 1792, the General Convention had accepted a proposal "for supporting missionaries to preach the Gospel on the frontiers," including a special annual offering to finance their ministries. But most of the earliest efforts at expanding the Church's presence into the western frontier were undertaken at the diocesan level.[1]

HOBART AND MEADE

Leaders like John Henry Hobart, bishop of New York from 1816 to 1830, played key roles in the Episcopal Church's growth in its early decades. Hobart's energies were legendary. As bishop, he served as rector of Trinity

Church in New York City while traveling throughout the wilderness of New York State—thousands of miles each year—to establish and nurture fledgling congregations. When he became bishop, there were fifty parishes in all of New York, while at his death, there were nearly 170; in the same period, the number of clergy had grown from twenty-six to 133. In 1817, the General Convention established the General Theological Seminary in New York City, to prepare American candidates for ordination; Hobart was instrumental in its founding and also served as its president. He identified himself as a "high churchman," considering that the Episcopal Church had a unique identity and therefore a special mission in the young nation. Convinced of the necessity of the episcopate, he mistrusted the theology of pan-Protestant ventures such as the American Bible Society. When it began recruiting supporters among New York Episcopalians, he encouraged them to support the New York Bible and Prayer Book Society instead. His aggressive missionary activity on behalf of the Episcopal Church sometimes led him to strong—and public—disputes with other churches, whose ministries he considered defective and dangerously erroneous.

But the Episcopal Church as Hobart and other "high church" advocates understood it was far different from the church in the south, where commitment to the Prayer Book and acceptance of the episcopate co-existed with sentiments inherited from the Evangelical Movement and a theology often closer to that of John Calvin than that of Bishop Hobart. The diocese of Virginia occupied a significant place in nurturing this alternative understanding of the Church and its ministry.

Like the church in other parts of the country, the Episcopal Church in Virginia had been slow to recover from the shock and loss associated with the Revolutionary War. In 1818, a small group formed "The Society for the Education of Pious Young Men for the Ministry of the Episcopal Church in Maryland and Virginia," and just five years after the opening of the General Theological Seminary in New York, their work came to fruition in what became the Protestant Episcopal Seminary in Virginia, which began its work with one full-time and one half-time professor and fourteen students.[2]

If Bishop Hobart dominated much of the Episcopal Church's history in the first decades of the nineteenth century, Bishop William Meade played an equally significant role in its next generation. His missionary efforts in the rugged frontier areas of Virginia and the territories to the west, now Kentucky and Tennessee, are reminiscent of those Hobart undertook in the thinly populated regions of upstate New York. But Meade's episcopate, with ten years as Assistant Bishop and twenty as diocesan, lasted twice as long as that of Hobart, and began just as Hobart's was coming to its end.

Meade had a deep interest in the development of the seminary at Alexandria, which he foresaw as a center for the Evangelical wing of the

Episcopal Church. Relying especially on the scriptures, the Prayer Book, the Thirty-Nine Articles, and Hooker's *Laws of Ecclesiastical Polity,* he spent part of each year in residence at the seminary, where he taught pastoral care and preaching to the graduating class.[3]

In 1849, Meade published "Lectures on the Pastoral Office," which offer a glimpse of his distinctively Evangelical approach. His theology

> was akin to that of all Evangelicals in its stress on man's [sic] hopeless condition, the salvation offered in Christ, the sanctifying and guiding power of the Holy Spirit, the Bible as the sole foundation and rule of faith. . . . He believed that the fundamental teachings of the Gospel should be given the first place in preaching rather than the particular customs and doctrines of the Episcopal Church. He believed that preaching was the primary means by which [people] were won to Christ and built up in the faith . . . He refused to deny the validity of non-episcopal orders, holding to the episcopate as of very ancient origin and as the mode of government in the Anglican Church, but not as absolutely essential to the being of the Church. For example, he supported the interdenominational Bible Society from which the high churchmen abstained. He repudiated the doctrines of transubstantiation and of the sacrifice of the mass as unscriptural and untrue. To him membership in the Church was both a privilege and an obligation laid down by Christ. The Church was composed of "the great body of those who profess and call themselves Christians and who hold the substance of the truth as it is in Jesus." Its chief function was to teach the Bible, to witness to Christ, to engage in works of mercy. Its sacraments are of great help to the believer. But though Church and sacraments are essential, they are secondary, for they are both means, not ends.[4]

In 1841, Bishop Meade became one of the first American bishops to visit the Church of England, where he was received warmly by English Evangelicals and invited to preach in Trinity Church, Cambridge.[5]

By that time, the Oxford Movement had crossed the Atlantic and begun to affect the life of the Episcopal Church. The older high-church position espoused by Bishop Hobart was identified with the General Theological Seminary in New York which he had promoted, and many of the Oxford Movement's early American followers were connected to it. The Virginia Theological Seminary, on the other hand, staunchly defended the education advocated by Meade. In 1849, Eugene Augustus Hoffman, then a student at General where he would later become one of its most distinguished deans, visited the Virginia Seminary and considered that its students were "mostly rank Calvinists." He considered that his three days at Virginia "had a tendency to make me, if anything, a Higher Churchman than I have been." On the other hand, in the early 1850s Clinton Locke wrote that when he "told my Rector in Virginia that I was going to the New York Seminary as soon as my school engagement there was over, he rose to his feet and said solemnly, 'Young man, I consider that you are placing your immortal soul in peril.'"[6]

The historian Robert Bruce Mullin considers that "the theological crisis between high church and evangelical Episcopalians threatened the ecclesiastical unity more than any other crisis the church had yet faced." Writing in 1853, Calvin Colton blamed the crisis on "the willingness of certain Episcopalians to abandon the historic role of their church in favor of the new Tractarian ideas." Hobart, he asserted, had defended episcopacy as a divine institution but always celebrated its American form as "republican and popular" while American Tractarians had "seriously weakened the constitutional fiber of the church." Colton believed that they had the potential to separate the Episcopal Church from American society and culture.[7]

A similar concern led a group of clergy led by William A. Muhlenberg to present a Memorial to the House of Bishops in 1853. The Memorialists considered that the Episcopal Church's catholicity should be shared with the wider American society, increasingly unchurched, and argued for increased liturgical flexibility and the offer of episcopal ordination to clergy of other denominations as a first step towards creating a genuinely American "united Evangelical Catholicism." Like Colton, Muhlenberg and his colleagues believed that the Episcopal Church had a special vocation in the American context, and that the extreme separatism of the Oxford movement and its followers ran the danger of making that vocation impossible.[8] But while the Memorial can be seen as a first step towards an ecumenical consciousness, its hope of forging a clearly articulated stance for American Episcopalians which would overcome the animosity between Anglo-Catholics and Evangelicals was unsuccessful; that conflict would continue to affect the Episcopal Church's ministry throughout the century and beyond.

THE AMERICAN CHURCH: AN ENGLISH PERSPECTIVE

British Anglicans were sometimes fascinated by their encounters with the Episcopal Church. While by no means blind to what they considered its shortcomings, they were often particularly intrigued with the possibility of a church free of all links to the state. One close observer of the Episcopal Church and its ministry was Henry Caswall, an English cleric who spent ten years in the United States, serving as rector of Christ Church in Madison, Indiana, and also as a professor in the fledgling Theological Seminary of the diocese of Kentucky.

Caswall considered the American system of government to be appropriate for the circumstances, and also admired the "popular constitution of the American Church" as "a beautiful scheme, by which, on the one hand, the proper influence of the three orders in the ministry is maintained, while, on the other hand, the voice of the people not only receives due respect, but exerts as much authority as the most democratic Christian could desire." But as well suited to the American culture as the system might be, he was convinced that "a large proportion of the peculiarities of the system are exclusively American, and would be exotics in any other portion of Christendom."[9]

Caswall went to the United States in response to an appeal by the missionary bishop Philander Chase, who requested support from the English Church for a theological college to be built in Ohio, "in order that young men might be educated on the spot, and trained up for the sacred ministry with a full knowledge of the feelings and habits of western people."[10] Bishop Chase was one of many of the Episcopal Church's missionaries to the west who realized that the population among whom they would be working lacked the education which much of Church life and worship seemed to require, and that traditional styles of ministry inherited from the Church of England or the more settled societies of the eastern seaboard would need to be "translated" if the Episcopal Church were to exercise its ministry on the frontier.

Caswall's first exposure to American Anglicanism was at Grace Church in New York City. In 1828, he found the appearance of the congregation to be

> highly respectable; indeed, it appeared to contain none of the lower classes of society.... The service is almost identical with that of England; but the Litany is somewhat retrenched, the Nicene Creed is omitted in the Communion Service, the Lord's Prayer is not frequently repeated ... and the President is prayed for instead of the King.... I observed no clerk; and the responses were made by the whole congregation. The singing and chaunting [sic] were good.... The discourse ... reminded me of some of the best sermons I had heard in England.[11]

Caswall discovered other similarities between the two churches: "The ordinary clerical costume is much the same as in England, consisting of a suit of black, and a white neckcloth. The usual dress of a bishop is in no respect different from that of any other clergyman." When officiating, clergy wore a "surplice, with a black silk scarf, a pair of bands, a gown of black silk, and sometimes a cassock and a sash." Urban congregations offered Morning and Evening Prayer with sermons, and sometimes added a third service on Sunday night and a weekly lecture. Holy Communion was generally celebrated monthly. And, he noted, congregations

> are generally composed of highly-intelligent and respectable people, many of whom have received an excellent education. Hence, intelligent sermons are held in great esteem, and elegant composition is duly appreciated. Common-place discourses are disregarded, and old or borrowed ones are never tolerated. Some oratorical genius is always necessary to clerical success in republican America.

Yet it frequently happens that ordinary sentiments are dressed in a florid and figurative style, approaching to the nature of bombast.[12]

Upon arrival in Ohio, Caswall found that "westerners" universally spoke English, "with far more purity and clearness than in the rural districts of England," though he missed the "elegance of expression and melody of tone which characterize the well-educated Englishman." He considered that people in general appeared unhealthy: "a sallow complexion predominates." He was also concerned by the nearly total lack of knowledge of scripture or interest in religion among most of the population, but impressed that the students with whom he worked in Ohio had in many cases withstood family opposition in order to present themselves for theological study.[13]

Caswall included his own sketch of "the Episcopal Log-Church (in the woods) near Gambier [Ohio]" and recalled that "the admirable prayers of our liturgy are no less sublime in the forests of Ohio than in the consecrated and time-honoured minsters of York or Canterbury." Yet he realized that for a number of reasons, the Episcopal Church "has little influence on the population at large. Although many of the first families in the United States are enrolled among its members and friends, its field of usefulness is generally limited to the cities and towns."[14]

While Caswall valued his own experience of ministry in the western United States, he considered that clergy who enjoyed "a moderate degree of success in England" should probably not be tempted to follow him. It was, he noted, "the work of several years to acquire that familiarity with the habits and ideas prevalent in a new country, which is essential to a proper influence" among people who, "how ever kind and hospitable, still differ from you in many points of sentiment and taste." This is especially true, he believed, for married clergy:

> The difficulty of securing and retaining servants on this side of the Atlantic is inconceivable by all but those who have experienced it. Not infrequently a female delicately brought up is obliged, by stern necessity, even in the midst of wealth, to perform the lowest drudgery of sweeping, cooking and washing. . . . [M]any English ladies suffer exceedingly from the mere want of congeniality of those around them, and pine away. . . .[15]

For clergy who found it expedient to leave Britain, Caswall suggested that Upper Canada (now Ontario) might be more congenial; on the other hand, he recognized that some English clergy might dread the Canadian climate and be attracted by American prosperity and a rapidly growing church. He noted that many English clergy in fact served the American Church, and "by divesting yourself of prejudices, and by judiciously accommodating yourself to circumstance," it was possible to have a fruitful ministry. But he warned them that Americans "regard [clergy] as one of themselves"; hence, it was important to "lay aside the Englishman as much as possible, consistent with a good conscience." Concretely, this meant avoiding talk about England, especially "invidious comparisons," and above all avoiding mention of monarchy and "the union of Church and State." He cautioned that "the mass of the people have strong feelings on these subjects, and although topics like [these] may be freely discussed in highly refined circles, you must be cautious as to the persons with whom you discuss them."[16]

THE EPISCOPAL CHURCH MOVES OUTWARD

The Episcopal Church in the United States found itself confronted with a constantly expanding population in need of ministry, as well as gradually increasing interest in participating in the evangelization of other parts of the world. In 1820, the Domestic and Foreign Missionary Society was established along the lines of English groups as well as the missionary arms of other American churches and began its work of raising support among the clergy and laypeople of the Episcopal Church.

In 1835 the General Convention made constitutional changes so that the Domestic and Foreign Missionary Society would no longer be an agency of the Church, but "comprehending all persons who are members of this Church"—that is, the Episcopal Church and the Missionary Society were to be "one and the same: . . . To be an Episcopalian is to be involved in mission. The church is mission." Furthermore, while continuing to distinguish administratively between foreign and home missions, "the missionary field," the Convention declared, "is always to be regarded as one, THE WORLD—the terms domestic and foreign being understood as terms of locality adopted for convenience."[17] At the same time the Convention approved the election of missionary bishops who would have oversight of the northwest and the southwest regions of the expanding nation. As one bishop explained the concept, a missionary bishop is to be "sent forth by the Church, not sought for of the Church; going before to organize the Church, not waiting till the Church has partially been organized; a leader, not a follower."[18]

One early and significant arm of mission in the Episcopal Church in the early decades of the nineteenth century was the Sunday School, which grew out of the efforts of Bishop William White and others to organize a "First Day Society" in Philadelphia, "to provide an education to the poor and indigent children in the city, as a safeguard to society." Societies to support such schools soon sprang up in other American cities; while they depended on church members, they were non-denominational. The first Episcopal

Sunday School was established by Jackson Kemper and James Milnor at Christ Church, Philadelphia in 1814. By 1820, the non-denominational First Day Societies had either attached themselves to particular churches or been replaced.[19]

The establishment of Sunday Schools in Episcopal parishes was part of the Church's effort to strengthen its denominational identity over against other American churches. In 1826, the General Protestant Episcopal Sunday School Union was established to coordinate parish Sunday Schools, and by 1835 counted more than half the Episcopal Sunday Schools in the United States as members. As an unofficial and lay-controlled body, the Sunday School Union raised anxiety among some clergy; Bishop George Doane of New Jersey complained that the Church's Catechism was not sufficiently emphasized, and reminded clergy that they should not abdicate their responsibility for Christian education.[20]

In the early years of the Episcopal Sunday School movement, the curriculum in fact included not only the Prayer Book Catechism, but also "Bible teaching, memorization of verses, recitations on moral and Biblical topics, and services for children . . ." Classes

> were taught by unpaid teachers, many of whom had received what training they had in the Sunday-schools. Teacher training was rare. Classes usually met for an hour or two in the morning and returned for an equal length of time in the afternoon. Discipline equaled education. In addition, the Sunday-school Unions published a number of pious books and magazines specifically for children. Childhood prodigies of sainthood abounded, the lazy or naughty always got their just desserts.[21]

By 1835, efforts were being made to achieve official recognition for the Sunday School movement, although the General Convention failed to endorse it. Indeed, subsequent Conventions affirmed the central place of the Bible and Prayer Book in Episcopal education, the authority of the clergy over all educational enterprises, the parish and its liturgy as the appropriate forum for Christian education, and the relegation of the Sunday School to instruction of the unchurched. While the Union accepted this shift in emphasis, Bishop Meade of Virginia and other Evangelicals responded by condemning the high-church tendencies they perceived in the Union's current stance and founding a rival organization, the Protestant Episcopal Society for the Promotion of Evangelical Knowledge. As the importance of the Union declined, the new "Evangelical Knowledge Society" became the primary support for lay-organized and run Sunday Schools among Episcopal congregations.[22]

AFRICAN AMERICAN MINISTRY IN THE EPISCOPAL CHURCH

One early and abiding aspect of the Episcopal Church's mission and ministry in the first half of the nineteenth century was its support for freed slaves in the newly established African territory of Liberia. That interest was only one facet of the complex relationship between the Black population of the United States, both enslaved and free, and the now independent Episcopal Church.

As early as 1787, a previously enslaved person named Absalom Jones responded to racist mistreatment in a Methodist Church in Philadelphia by helping to lead the establishment of the Free African Society, a "benevolent and reform society" with the stated purpose of addressing "the 'irreligious and uncivilized state'" of some African Americans and "to support one another in sickness, and for the benefit of the widows and fatherless children." It was this Society that led, four years later, to the organization of St. Thomas' African Episcopal Church, with Absalom Jones as pastor. With support from Jones, a majority of the congregation voted to unite with the still-young Episcopal diocese of Pennsylvania. The reasons for this decision are not entirely clear, although one scholar proposes that it reflects the educational work among people of African descent carried out by the SPG before American independence. (It is interesting that in 1791 the congregation's decision was described as approving union with "the Church of England.")[23]

The agreement reached with Pennsylvania's first bishop, William White, reflected what the diocese called the "peculiar circumstances" of the congregation—no doubt a reference to its all-Black congregation and leadership and to the autonomy demanded by Jones, which included his own ordination as deacon and priest. Jones' ordination required a waiver from competency in the Biblical languages from both the bishop and the Diocesan Convention, and he served for nine years as a deacon before being ordained to the priesthood. The price of this remarkable union was that St. Thomas' Church had no vote in the diocesan Convention—a state of affairs which would not be altered until halfway through the Civil War.[24]

The ministry of Absalom Jones provides something of a template for understanding the particular challenges of ministry in a church afflicted with both prejudice and institutionalized racism. He worked tirelessly for the welfare of African Americans, both those of his own community and also those still suffering under slavery. He preached the importance of "virtuous and industrious living" in improving both the condition and status of the community in the eyes of the society as a whole; in a Thanksgiving sermon preached in 1808, he commended prayers for the conversion of the peoples of Africa, conduct that would provide no "cause of regret to the deliverers of our nation," gratitude to benefactors who had contributed to the cause of abolition, and thanks to God for the abolition of the slave trade. He had a lifelong passion for the education of Black Americans; like many of the white supporters of the Liberian mission, Jones suggested that slavery might be God's instrument for the conversion of Africa.[25]

The first half of the nineteenth century saw the establishment of several African American congregations in American cities: St. Philip's Church in New York, St. James' Church in Baltimore, St. Luke's Church in New Haven and St. Matthew's Church in Detroit. (St. James' was the only self-governing Black congregation established in a state that permitted slavery prior to the Civil War.) Although the membership of each of these congregations tended to include the most distinguished members of the local African American community, at the diocesan level none enjoyed the rights to which white parishes were entitled.

The ministries of these congregations demonstrate the wide spectrum of attitudes towards slavery and race which marked the Episcopal Church prior to the Civil War. All enjoyed the leadership of African American clergy, some of whom shared Absalom Jones' belief that while slavery was a great evil and must be abolished, the practice of Christian faith in general and Anglican Christianity in particular could provide a means for winning the support and approval of white Americans. Like other Americans who advocated the abolition of slavery, they were divided on the question of whether the freed slaves should remain in the United States, return to Africa, or settle in Haiti (the only republic in the world governed by Blacks).[26] James T. Holly, described by the historian Harold Lewis as "an avid emigrationist," was ordained at St. Matthew's Church in Detroit, a parish which had served as a destination on the Underground Railroad. After a brief ministry in New Haven, he led a group of about forty to establish a colony in Haiti, where he later served as its first missionary bishop.[27]

Actions undertaken by Black congregations which were aimed at improving the lot of free Blacks in the North and securing the abolition of slavery often met resistance from the Church's white leadership. The bishop of New York considered that Peter Williams, Jr., first rector of St. Philip's Church, "added to sincere and enlightened piety and a grade of talent of and theological requirements quite above mediocrity, great soundness of judgment, and prudence in actions and the just appreciation the sincere love and a consistent adoption of sound church principles." Nevertheless, in an effort to keep the Episcopal Church from being forced to state clearly its position on slavery, which might well have divided the Church, Williams was ordered to "preach merely the Gospel *without interfering with the political affairs of the time.*"[28]

In the South, African American churches were organized under the authority of white clergy and trustees. Where no separate congregations existed, slave galleries were provided in the rear of the church in order to maintain separation between enslaved persons and slaveowners. Prior to the Civil War large numbers of slaves became Episcopalians; by 1860 nearly half the members of the diocese of South Carolina were Black, and were the majority in many congregations. In 1824, the rector of Trinity Parish in Charles County, Maryland, reported the baptism of one white member and of twenty-six Blacks. Harold Lewis believes that the large numbers of Black Episcopalians in the slave states reflects "a virtually unbridled enthusiasm on the part of antebellum planters to bring blacks into the Episcopal fold." But he also notes that for the enslaved themselves, the Church of their owners could hardly be distinguished from the complex of institutions and structures that contributed to their oppression.[29]

NATIVE AMERICANS AND THE EPISCOPAL CHURCH

An inevitable aspect of the westward migration of white Americans was the encounter, nearly always problematic and often violent, with the Native peoples whom they were displacing and whose lands they were invading. Jackson Kemper, the first missionary bishop to be chosen and assigned to an area now comprising six states, considered evangelization and ministry with the Native people to be part of his mandate. He was an honored guest of the Oneida tribe, for whom he dedicated the first permanent church in what is now the state of Wisconsin, and early in his ministry he ordained two priests whose contribution to the work of the Church in what was then the western edge of the United States included not only dedicated work among Native peoples but the founding of Nashotah House, a theological seminary for the region.

From the beginning of his missionary work, Bishop Kemper realized that if the Episcopal Church was to make any impact at all on the western region of the United States, it would have to provide the opportunity for its leaders to be educated without having to travel to the east. Besides the seminaries in New York and Virginia, the Church already had three colleges: Hobart College in upstate New York, Trinity College in Hartford, Connecticut, and Kenyon College in Gambier, Ohio. Kemper envisioned a similar institution for the west, and in 1838, Kemper College opened in St. Louis, Missouri. (The bishop had no part in its naming.) By 1843, its president could report that

> The institution presents at this moment one of the most beautiful scenes of industry, cheerfulness, good order, and religious as well as mental improvement that you ever beheld. Thus, while forsaken by the church, it has pleased the Lord to visit us with great and unmerited favours . . . It should never be forgotten

that it is one of the objects of this establishment to send the gospel to various Indian tribes beyond the present boundaries of the Western States. To my mind, this is an object of such deep interest and importance, that I should rejoice to be counted worthy to go in person, and proclaim salvation to the poor and friendless sons of the soil beyond.[30]

Unfortunately, the College and its mission were short-lived, but another experiment in education for ministry inspired by Kemper did in fact take root and prosper. In 1841, several graduates of the General Theological Seminary responded to an appeal from Bishop Kemper for clergy willing to serve in the west. Their hope, in the words of James Lloyd Breck, was to "place ourselves under Bishop Kemper, all at one point, and there educate and preach; to live under one roof, constituted into a *Religious House,* under a Superior." This little community was among the first Anglican attempts to form a religious community since the monasteries were abolished by Henry VIII. While its monastic nature was short-lived (and widely criticized by most Episcopalians as dangerous "Romanizing"), Nashotah House in southern Wisconsin survived to become a center of both missionary activity and theological education. Both clergy and students kept a rigorous discipline beginning with Matins at 6 a.m. and including four hours of manual labor. Breck himself led field expeditions lasting several weeks in order to reach settlers in isolated areas and also to help students accustom themselves to the rigors of missionary life.[31]

The Episcopal Church's early interest in evangelizing the Native peoples of the West did not fade. Its campaigns were undertaken against the backdrop of what was perhaps one of the most tragic and shameful episodes in all the history of the relationship between the American government and Native peoples. The so-called Trail of Tears was the lengthy process carried out in the decade of the 1830s by which the so-called "Five Civilized Tribes" were forcibly removed from their ancestral homelands in the American southeastern states to "Indian Territory," now part of the state of Oklahoma. These tribes—the Cherokee, Chickasaw, Choctaw, Creek and Seminole—were described by white Americans as "civilized" because to varying degrees they had acquiesced to pressure from the federal government and adopted many aspects of the dominant white culture: farming on private farms, living in European-style houses, valuing western-style education, accepting Christianity, intermarrying in some cases with white Americans, adopting the use of English and even owning Black enslaved persons. These gestures of cultural acquiescence turned out to be useless in the face of the greed and hostility of the growing white population in the southern states, and thousands of Native people died during the transfer west.

Only a few years later, the Episcopal Church's Board of Missions sent the Bishop of Tennessee, James Otey, and its General Secretary, Sayre Harris, to investigate opportunities for mission in Indian Territory—or, in the words of the Board of Missions, to "elevate a portion of our red brethren from the manifold evils of their lot."[32] Shortly after their arrival in Indian Territory, they baptized the infant daughter of a family whose background was Episcopalian, prompting Harris to comment on the importance of ministry with Native women: He considered that only when Native women also adapted to the dominant culture would educated Native men no longer be in danger of reverting to their earlier customs. "[E]ducate the squaw, and you form the sister, the wife, the mother, who will change as if by magic their homes." Many of the sites visited by the observers were headquarters of American troops charged with maintaining order and recently founded schools for both girls and boys. Harris challenged one doctor he encountered who was working on a Choctaw translation of the scriptures in his spare time, wondering aloud whether "his labours tended to perpetuate the language, and make more remote the very desirable period when the English alone would be the sole medium of communication between themselves and other tribes, thus hastening their civilization." Otey and Harris reported to the Board of Missions their opinion that "there is abundant room for more labourers" in Indian Territory, and proposed the appointment of a bishop as well as the development of Episcopal schools.[33]

Their strong advocacy of ministry with Native people can be considered as a primary impetus for the development of an ever-increasing commitment to Native ministry which continued throughout the period of the settlement of the West by white Americans. Unfortunately, as Harris' remarks make clear, that ministry was understood not only to convert Native people to Christianity and the Episcopal Church but to destroy effectively the culture of the people with whom they ministered and to replace it with the "Christian" culture of white America.

THE EXPANSION OF ANGLICAN MINISTRY IN CANADA

Meanwhile, to the north of the United States, Anglicans in Canada were led by bishops committed to evangelizing the rapidly expanding numbers of settlers moving into the middle-and far-western regions, as well as the many Native peoples whose lands they were invading. Unlike the Episcopal Church, which had to rely on its own resources for its expansion and missionary activity, Canadian Anglicans began their work dependent on support from both the British government and the SPG. Indeed, Bishop Jacob Mountain, whose ministry as first bishop of Quebec began in the late eighteenth century, never really accepted the idea that Canadians were fit to serve the Church's ordained ministry. His mighty struggle to maintain the Church of England as an established church over against the large Roman Catholic majority of Quebec led him to active engagement in political affairs. His attitude towards the local members of the Church is clearly demonstrated in a letter to the Home Secretary written as the nineteenth century was dawning.

> Of the persons born in the country, I need not inform your Grace that few indeed have been so educated as to give them any decent pretension to instruct others, and among the persons who come to settle here, there is less possibility of finding proper subjects. Your Grace, I am sure, would be far from recommending it to me to open the Sacred Profession for the reception of such adventurers, as disappointed speculations may have disposed to enter it.[34]

John Strachan, first bishop of Upper Canada (now southern Ontario), was just as committed to the established character of the Church of England as Mountain was. But he also understood the need for a different kind of ministry in the frontier conditions of the Canadian wilderness, with clergy nurtured and trained in Canada rather than in England. He was instrumental in the founding of McGill University in Montreal, and both King's College and Trinity University in Toronto. Writing of Bishop Mountain's ministry, he wrote,

> It cannot . . . be concealed that his habits and manners were calculated rather for an English Bishop than the Missionary Bishop of Canada. We want a primitive Bishop who will go around the Country & preach the Gospel to the people, stir up a religious spirit among them, gradually bring them into order, and abstain in all matters of indifference from hurting even their unreasonable prejudices.[35]

Bishop Strachan understood early in his episcopate that the Church of England in Canada would not survive as an established church, and by the 1830s he began annual meetings with the clergy of Upper Canada. He himself understood those gatherings to point towards a time when each diocese would have its own synod and lead to "the ultimate union of all the British North American Bishoprics, to convene at stated times in General Synods or Convocations." His vision—and his actions—sometimes preceded the legislation that permitted them; the first legally constituted synod after permission was given by the Canadian Legislature did not meet until 1857.[36]

The British government suspended financing of the SPG's work in Canada in 1835, a step which required Anglicans to become self-supporting. The Canadian church historian Henry Roper considers that "the transition from a church supported by the state to one in which support came from below was one of the most important changes which has occurred in Canadian Anglicanism."[37] In the early years, Canadian Anglicans worshipped in "barns, roadside inns, and schools." Laypeople often resisted supporting the ministries which had historically been funded from abroad, and even the task of building churches in new and growing communities was challenging. In Peterborough, Ontario, ministry began in 1826, with the arrival of an SPG missionary. Funding for a building was sufficiently difficult that the last payment on the debt was made forty years after the beginning of the project. In Newmarket, Anglicans worshipped in a

> frame church, facing south, [which] was 56 feet by 36 feet, with a tower covered in tin. Transepts and galleries were added later, but the original church was a box with the chancel laid out at one end and a high pulpit on the north wall, reached by steps on the right. The holy table was in front of the pulpit, and a sanctuary was created by the line of the communion rail. The "horse box" pews allowed seating on all sides, and there was a table in the middle of each pew.[38]

The rapid expansion of Anglicanism in Canada seems to have profited from its increasing autonomy; at any rate, the pioneering bishops and clergy leaders were followed by episcopal leadership drawn from both Evangelical and Anglo-Catholic backgrounds, the addition of a number of new dioceses as the population began to move westward, and the increasing participation of laypeople in the Church's governance. The first bishop to be elected by a diocesan synod illuminated the growing democratic sentiment among Canadian Anglicans: the followers of the two candidates fought their battles in the public press and the eventual winner was elected by an enormous (and noisy) majority of laypeople and the bare minimum of clergy votes. Canadian Anglicanism became even more oriented towards missionary expansion and evangelism as the vast expanses of the north and west were gradually settled. The first visit by a bishop to the Red River Valley (now the province of Manitoba) occurred in 1844, where a missionary priest was encountered who had been preparing Native children for confirmation by teaching them the Catechism and the Thirty-Nine Articles; the bishop wondered at the appropriateness of the curriculum but was satisfied that it was not without value.[39]

The extreme conditions under which ministry took place in the vast regions of the Canadian north required a willingness to live and work in isolation and at times deprivation of many of the necessities of life. As late as 1865, the first bishop of Rupert's Land was a two-week journey from the nearest railroad; one Canadian bishop observed that anyone ministering in the Red River area "ought to have an iron constitution, a loud voice, and be able to row, swim, and do all sorts of mechanical work. An unhandy scholar would never do. Where is to be found Paul the tent maker?"[40]

While the ministry of the Anglican Church in Canada was making its way from the eastern seaboard into the vast mid-section of British North America, settlers were leapfrogging to the Pacific coast, where England and the United States were engaged in often heated conflicts over the American northwest. At mid-century, the two colonies of Vancouver Island and British Columbia were established to assert firm British control over the region; the Church soon followed, with energetic missionary activity and church building among both settlers and Native peoples overseen by the first bishop of British Columbia, George Hills. By the middle of the nineteenth century, Anglicans in Canada had developed their own unique style of ministry, shaped by the often-harsh conditions imposed by nature and gradually taking on the characteristics of a people whose culture was increasingly distinct from that of the country from which it, and they, had come.

It was in the Pacific Northwest that a unique Anglican mission straddling what would eventually become the boundary between Canada and the United States affected the religious history of the area. The bishop's visit to the Red River Valley followed by more than twenty years the establishment of the first Anglican chaplaincy at Fort Garry (now Winnipeg, Manitoba) and what the Church Missionary Society termed its Northwest America Mission. The first two priests at Fort Garry decided to bring young Native men to the fort for an education so that they could be returned as evangelists to their own people. In the late 1820s Spokan Garry and Kootenay Pelly, whose names reflected their tribes and also that of the director of the Hudson's Bay Company, spent four years learning English, agriculture, and receiving religious instruction from the Bible and the Prayer Book. In 1829 they returned to their respective tribes (who occupied territory in the valley of the Columbia River, now in the United States).[41]

The response of tribes in the Northwest to the two Native evangelists was remarkable, and within a few years reports of the widespread practice of a religion obviously based on Christianity, though incorporating Native elements as well, began to be received from multiple sources. Five other young men attended the school in Fort Garry, and the first Protestant missionary to visit Oregon Territory reported a visit to a band of the Nez Perce people:

> About eleven o'clock . . . I found them all assembled, men, women and children, between four and five hundred, in what I would call a sanctuary of God, constructed with their lodges, nearly one hundred feet long and twenty wide; and all arranged in rows, through the length of the building upon their knees, with a narrow space in the middle. . . . I could not have believed they had the means or could have known how, to erect so convenient and so decent a place of worship. . . . They all continued in a kneeling position during the singing

and praying, and when I closed prayer with an Amen, they all said what was equivalent in their language.

Two other missionaries from the American Board of Missions made a similar report:

> Were greatly affected at night, at witnessing the Nez Perces at prayer. They were assembled in a circle, on their knees, with an old man, to all appearances very earnest in prayer. I learned through an interpreter something of the prayer. It appears to be the Lord's Prayer, with perhaps some additions. I inquired of myself, Is it possible that some of these beknighted heathen are even now numbered in the sheepfold of Christ? And while waiting for the dilatory motions of the Christian Church may have been led by an unseen hand to the Lamb of God?[42]

Unfortunately, the highly evangelical and Calvinist missionaries of the American Board of Missions who made these observations considered that the Native believers had not been sufficiently instilled with the doctrine of the total depravity of humankind. For their part, the Indians rejected their teaching and not a single convert was made during their initial work. They were joined in the area by Roman Catholic missionaries, who were impressed by the widespread indigenous form of Christian belief they encountered, and who took it as a foundation on which to build rather than an erroneous faith to be condemned.

The subsequent history of the encroachment of white settlers into the tribal areas of the Northwest and the division of traditional Native homelands between the United States and Canada reveals an all too familiar story of violence, treachery and deceit directed against the Native people, and the inevitable—and futile—armed resistance by the tribes. Spokan Garry, who had argued against war, led the negotiations which finally ended the revolt. Garry had spent his life trying to maintain the faith of his own people in the face of aggressive missionary activity by both Calvinists and Roman Catholics, but the first Episcopal bishops of Oregon were utterly uninterested in work with the Native people, preferring to direct their ministry instead to the newly arrived white settlers. The competition among churches with different theologies and styles of worship, the disdain with which most Christians viewed the Native people and their religious faith, and the indifference of the Episcopal Church to the context in which it had come to minister resulted in the disappearance of what had once been a promising and enculturated Anglican ministry among the peoples of the Pacific Northwest. Spokan Garry died many years later, his *Book of Common Prayer* beside him, his farm occupied, and his crops stolen by a group of white men, reduced to living in a tepee pitched on a borrowed campsite, ignored and forgotten by those who shared his own tradition. He is honored today with a stained-glass window in the Episcopal Cathedral of St. John the Evangelist in the city of Spokane, Washington, which carries on the name of his tribe. But at the time of his death, there was no Episcopal priest to bury him; his funeral was conducted by a Presbyterian minister.[43]

NOTES

1. Ian T. Douglas, *Fling Out the Banner: The National Church Ideal and the Foreign Mission of the Episcopal Church* (New York: Church Hymnal Corp., 1996), 25.

2. Joseph M. Consant, *No Turning Back: The Black Presence at Virginia Theological Seminary* (Brainerd, MN: Evergreen Press, 2009), 16–17.

3. Allan Yuill, "William Meade, 1789–1862: Third Bishop of Virginia, the 'Beloved Diocesan,'" *The Churchman*, 77 (Fall 1963), 6.

4. Yull, "Meade," 6.

5. Yull, "Meade," 8.

6. Powel Mills Dawley, *The Story of The General Theological Seminary* (New York: Oxford University Press, 1969), 134–135.

7. Robert Bruce Mullin, *Episcopal Vision/American Reality: High Church Theology and Social Thought in Evangelical America* (New Haven: Yale University Press, 1986), 179–180.

8. See Mullin, *Episcopal Vision/American Reality*, 181–183.

9. Henry Caswall, *America and the American Church* (London: J. G. and F. Rivington, 1839), vi–vii.

10. Caswall, *America*, 22, 25–26.

11. Caswall, *America*, 19.

12. Caswall, *America*, 294, 296.

13. Caswall, *America*, 32–34.

14. Caswall, *America*, 44, 46.

15. Caswall, *America*, 345–346.

16. "Constitution of the Domestic and Foreign Missionary Society," in *Journal of the Proceedings of the Bishops, Clergy and Laity of the Protestant Episcopal Church in the United States of America* (New York: Protestant Episcopal Press, 1835), 129.

17. Walter H. Stone, "A Turning Point: The General Convention of 1835," in *Historical Magazine of the Episcopal Church*, Vol. 4 (September 1935), 171

18. Caswell, *America*, 347, 353.

19. J. Parker Jameson, "The Sunday School in the National Period," *Historical Magazine of the Protestant Episcopal Church*, LI (April 1982), 286–287.

20. Jameson, "Sunday School," 288

21. Jameson, "Sunday School," 288.

22. Jameson, "Sunday School," 289.

23. Anne C. Lammers, "The Rev. Absalom Jones and the Episcopal Church: Christian Theology and Black Consciousness in a New Alliance," *Historical Magazine of the Protestant Episcopal Church*, 51 (June 1982), 164, 168–170, 172, 174.

24. Lammers, "Absalom Jones," 176–177.

25. Lammers, "Absalom Jones," 180–182.

26. See Harold T. Lewis, *Yet With A Steady Beat: The African American Struggle for Recognition in the Episcopal Church* (Valley Forge, PA: Trinity Press International, 1996), 25–38.

27. Lewis, *Yet With A Steady Beat*, 33–34.

28. Lewis, *Yet With A Steady Beat*, 31.

29. Lewis, *Yet With A Steady Beat*, 33–38.

30. Harriet E. Davidson, "The Rise and Fall of Kemper College," *The Historiographer* XLVII, 2 (September 2009), 1, 5.

31. Thomas C. Reeves, "James Lloyd Breck and the Founding of Nashotah House," *Anglican and Episcopal History* LXV (March 1996), 54, 70–81.

32. Kenny A. Franks, "Missionaries in the West: An Expedition of the Protestant Episcopal Church In 1844," *Historical Magazine of the Protestant Episcopal Church*, XLIV (September 1975), 319.

33. Franks, "Missionaries," 320, 321.

34. Henry Roper, "The Anglican Episcopate in Canada: An Historical Perspective," in *Frontiers Then and Now: The Canadian Anglican Episcopate 1787–1987* (Toronto: Anglican Book Centre, 1989), 4–5.

35. Roper. "Anglican Episcopate," 5–6.

36. Roper, "Anglican Episcopate," 6–7.

37. Roper, "Anglican Episcopate," 7.

38. Elwood Jones, "Reaching Out for Two Hundred Years: Church Growth and Church Extension 1780–1989," in Alan l. Hayes, ed., *By Grace Co-Workers: Building the Anglican Diocese of Toronto 1780–1989*, 144–145.

39. Roper, "Anglican Episcopate," 8–11.

40. Roper, "Anglican Episcopate," 11.

41 Thomas E. Jessett, "Anglican Indians In the Pacific Northwest Before the Coming of White Missionaries," *Anglican and Episcopal History* XLV (December 1976), 401–402.

42 Jessett, "Anglican Indians," 405–406.

43 Jessett. "Anglican Indians," 406–412.

Chapter Eight

Missions

Global Anglican Ministry in the Early Nineteenth Century

The ministry of the Church of England in the nineteenth century was not only subject to repeated challenges arising from the dramatic social and political changes of the first half of the century. Such changes were also reflected in Anglican ministry wherever it was undertaken. This is the time when English-speaking Anglicans believed themselves to be called to share their expression of faith with peoples in other parts of the world whose cultures were far removed from the assumptions that had shaped Anglican ministry in times past. In doing so, they helped affirm the judgment of Stephen Neill's classic study that "the active participation of Christendom as a whole in the work of the Christian mission belongs to the nineteenth century."[1] The astonishing spread of Anglican Christianity in the second half of the nineteenth century could not have occurred without widespread support from the English-speaking churches of the British Isles and North America. The many societies that sent missionaries around the world were supported by faithful laypeople inspired by the prospect of contributing to the salvation of people who otherwise, they believed, would be doomed to eternal punishment; and also by the vision of a world transformed by Anglo-Saxon civilization to embrace its customs, values and civilization. Anglican hymn-writers joined their colleagues of other denominations in producing a corpus of mission-oriented hymns, stressing the challenge and joy of evangelizing those still untouched by the Christian gospel. Typical of them and perhaps one of the best-known is "From Greenland's Icy Mountains," written by Reginald Heber, later Bishop of Calcutta.

> From Greenland's icy mountains, from India's coral strand;
> where Afric's sunny fountains roll down their golden sand:

From many an ancient river, from many a palmy plain,
they call us to deliver their land from error's chain.

What though the spicy breezes blow soft o'er Java's isle;
though every prospect pleases, and only man is vile?
In vain with lavish kindness the gifts of God are strown;
the heathen in his blindness bows down to wood and stone!
Waft, waft, ye winds, his story, and you, ye waters, roll
till, like a sea of glory, it spreads from pole to pole:
till o'er our ransomed nature the Lamb for sinners slain,
Redeemer, King, Creator, in bliss returns to reign.[2]

THE CHURCH MISSIONARY SOCIETY

One of the most significant instruments by which the Church of England responded to those challenges as the new century was beginning was a newly established missionary society which from its founding sharply differentiated itself from the hundred-year-old Society for the Propagation of the Gospel. At the dawn of the century, a group of Evangelical clergy and laypeople led by John Venn, Rector of Clapham Parish at their head, founded the Society for Missions to Africa and the East, soon to be known as the Church Missionary Society (CMS). One popular history of the Society describes it as founded on "the Church-principle, but not the high-Church principle"—that is, while stressing loyalty to the Prayer Book and the importance of bishops, it also emphasized the role of laypeople in the Church's mission and ministry, and demonstrated a willingness to work with like-minded Christians of other traditions.[3]

The Society for the Promotion of Christian Knowledge had supported the work of Danish and German Lutheran missionaries in India since the early eighteenth century. One historian described this curious situation as "unique as . . . a missionary undertaking run by an Anglican society for about a hundred years with the help of Lutheran missionaries" who used Lutheran liturgy, music and catechism and who never received episcopal ordination.[4] As it looked towards the future of ministry in India from the vantage point of the late eighteenth century, SPCK proposed giving "the natives a Church of their own, independent of our support; we ought to have sufficient Bishops in the country, who might ordain Deacons and Priests, and secure regular succession of truly apostolical Pastors, even if all communications with their parent Church should be annihilated."[5] A similar vision would soon be articulated by the burgeoning CMS.

The first two CMS missionaries were also German Lutherans. They were assigned to the West African colony of Sierra Leone, which had been established as a haven for formerly enslaved persons of African ancestry who had been freed and repatriated. The first English lay missionary sponsored by CMS was sent to New Zealand in 1809; the first English clergy were sent out six years later. In 1824, the Church Missionary Institution was established in Islington to train its German missionaries in both the English language and Anglicanism, and to provide orientation for its English missionaries. By that time CMS had already assigned a hundred missionaries, of whom more than fifty continued in active ministry: about one third were English laypeople, another third English clergy, and a third German. Sierra Leone's governor welcomed CMS missionaries as suitable candidates for serving as the "head teacher, pastor, and civil administrator" of the colony's villages.[6]

But the rapid growth of the CMS had not been accomplished without fostering considerable controversy among English Anglicans. Much of the support for CMS came from local chapters which served not only to generate income but also to further the Evangelical agenda in the Church of England. More conservative Anglicans were troubled by what they perceived as behavior more suited to Dissenters and even radicals with dangerous ideas about changes to the class system on which they assumed British stability to depend.

When supporters of the CMS attempted to establish a new chapter in the city of Bath, Josiah Thomas, the Archdeacon of Bath interrupted the meeting to deliver a strong condemnation of what he considered to be a threat to the very order of society.[7] In Thomas' view, the CMS was guilty of intruding on the work of the SPCK and the SPG, already well established (and respectable) missionary arms of the Church of England. He was also troubled by the policy of the CMS to raise money from "servants, schoolboys and apprentices," which implied that members of the working class might consider themselves eligible for full participation in an organization of the Church of England. In a series of pamphlets from supporters and opponents of the Bath chapter, arguments for and against the inclusion of poor Anglicans in such an enterprise generated considerable passion. Encouraging "egalitarian principles," one clergyman argued, was a "dangerous folly," while others feared "among the lower orders prejudice against the Church" and a "great ascendency" in church and society on the part of Evangelicals.[8]

In response, supporters of the CMS argued that far from being a threat to social order, involving the poor in ventures such as the Church's mission made them "more content by familiarizing them with the 'habits of arrangement and economy'"; furthermore, it "ennobles their minds . . . and helps to wean them from that selfishness which their condition in life might make them liable to contract."[9] In spite of the negative voices of clergy like

Archdeacon Thomas, the Society continued to grow and in fact played a significant role in the increasing strength of the Evangelical movement among English Anglicans.

The CMS continued to be interested in the possibility of ministry in India as ever larger portions of South Asia came under British control. It cherished strong hopes for the evangelization of Muslims, but since conditions made such an undertaking impossible, it began working with Orthodox churches in places such as Malta, Egypt, Turkey, Ethiopia and South India as a means to gain access to their Muslim neighbors. Opposed to active proselytization of Orthodox Christians, the CMS hoped that they would reform themselves once the scriptures were made readily available to them. But a twenty-year relationship with the Syrian Orthodox Church in South India ended after some of its missionaries denounced what they called "Syrian errors."[10]

The importance placed by the CMS on the work of laypeople as Christian missionaries broadened the Church's understanding of ministry, and by 1820 the Society listed two "Female Missionaries." As the CMS increased its presence in India, the number of women missionaries grew, since cultural restraints in that setting made it impossible for male evangelists to speak directly with women. The women listed as missionaries were often either wives of clergy or were married to clergy once they arrived in the mission field; but in many cases when their husbands died, as widows they remained to continue their own ministry.

The figure of Henry Venn, clerical secretary of CMS for thirty years, looms over its history at mid-century. The son of the Society's founder, Venn never visited any of its missions, but his influence on its strategy was enormous. Venn's attitude towards what he called an "indigenous church" was spelled out in the CMS's "official paper on "Native Church Organization." Its goal was the "development of Native Churches with a view to their ultimate settlement, upon a self-supporting, self-governing, and self-extending system. When this settlement has been effected, the Mission will have attained its *euthanasia*, and the Missionary and all Missionary agency can be transferred to the regions beyond."[11] He distinguished sharply between the work of the *missionary*, who is responsible for evangelization of new converts to Christianity, and that of the *pastor*, "who teaches the young Christians." He envisioned "Christian Companies" under the direction of a "Christian Headman," ultimately looking towards a Native episcopate and local catechists and teachers whose support would come from the local church.[12] "It has always been a recognized principle," he wrote, ". . . that Native Converts should be habituated to the idea that the support of a Native Ministry must eventually fall upon themselves." And, he warned, "the Native Pastor should never be trained up in habits and expectations too far removed from his countrymen. . . . In mission fields, in which the Native population is accustomed to look up to their European Rulers as the doers of everything, the Converts are too apt to expect that they shall be supported and kept in leading strings by their Missionaries."[13]

In some ways, Venn's attitude to the practice of mission reflects the assumptions of British superiority that shaped much of the ideology of empire: "It has been only lately discovered in the science of Missions, that when the Missionary is of another and superior race than his converts, he must not attempt to be their pastor," or they will never form "a vigorous native Church."[14] Eugene Stock, the CMS's own Editorial Secretary, recognized the challenge represented by Venn's vision of an independent Native Church to other, earlier ways of engaging in mission. Looking back from the vantage point of the end of the nineteenth century, he wrote:

> In early days the paternal system prevailed in Missions. . . . Evangelistic work was transformed into pastoral work, and the evangelist became the pastor. Now, pastoral care of the converts was of course indispensable; but not at the cost of the evangelization of the Heathen. . . . The result was that agencies and money designed to evangelize the Heathen were used to make provision for the worship and instruction of Christians. . . . There was much that was attractive in the system to the outward eye. A mission village, with a kindly German missionary in the central bungalow—the Germans were ideal for this work—pleased every visitor. But such a mission could never have its *euthanasia* in a self-governing, self-supporting, and self-extending Church.[15]

The CMS realized that in places such as Canada, Australia and New Zealand, where English settlers quickly outnumbered the population of Native peoples, the Church of England must provide ministry to its own through a "colonial church organization" before embarking on the organization of a native church, and that the latter would ultimately be incorporated into the established Church of England. The SPG had always accepted responsibility for both forms of ministry; the CMS, on the other hand, had no interest in the organization of the colonial churches, and as the century progressed, its practical relationships with those churches at times were conflicted.[16]

Venn's leadership of CMS coincided with the rapid growth of mission in West Africa, as formerly enslaved persons from other regions of Africa were resettled in Sierra Leone and then made their way to their own homelands. The first Sierra Leonian priest, Samuel Adjai Crowther, was a member of the Yoruba tribe whose original homeland was in the Niger delta; he would later be consecrated in Westminster Abbey as the first Africa-born Anglican bishop. The expansion of the work of CMS in Africa inevitably brought it into contact with cultures whose family structure was based on polygamy. Henry Venn considered the custom to be inherently sinful, condemned by scripture and the evidence of nature, which has determined the "providential equality of the number of men and women in every land, at all times." He insisted that baptism "carries with it a public profession of submission to the law of Christ, which the polygamist ultimately violates . . ." and therefore polygamous male converts must separate from all but their "true wife." At the same time, he charged missionaries with the duty to insist that the converted husband provide for the welfare of the wives and children to be abandoned, "and in every other lawful way [repair] the injury which a separation may occasion to the woman." Difficulties, he acknowledged, will arise, "as in every transition from a wrong to a right course of action," but he considered that only a small number of families would be affected, since he believed that only the wealthiest of husbands could afford more than one wife.[17]

Venn's understanding of the appropriate process for establishing Christian missions in new contexts sometimes brought him into conflict with other perspectives. Venn considered that the process of establishing what he called a "Native Church" should precede the appointment of a bishop, which he understood as the "crown of mission." Bishop Wilberforce of Oxford strongly opposed him, arguing that the presence of a bishop is not the crown but the "keystone" of mission.[18] Such conflicts helped to underline the identity of the CMS as an active advocate for Evangelical principles in a Church that was increasingly riven by partisan conflict.

MISSION IN INDIA

The lengthy history of Britain's subjugation of the Indian subcontinent which reached its zenith in the nineteenth century, is also the story of the Church of England's complex encounter with that multi-faithed, multilingual, multicultural region. While the East India Company discouraged evangelization among the native peoples lest it cause inter-religious conflict, the presence of Evangelical missionaries from the CMS soon led to a campaign to allow mission to proceed, particularly in the light of English horror at the various consequences of a caste system which shaped and ordered Indian society in ways the first missionaries found abhorrent.

A new charter for the East India Company early in the century allowed for missionary activity as long as religious freedom was not curtailed, and shortly after, in 1814, Thomas Middleton was consecrated as the first Bishop of Calcutta. Twenty years later, Madras and Bombay also received bishops from the Church of England.

In 1832, Daniel Thomas Wilson was consecrated as bishop of Calcutta and Metropolitan of India. A staunch Evangelical, he asserted the superiority of

Christianity not only for its spiritual truth but for its civilizing effects, and considered the Church of England uniquely qualified for its mission.

> The christian [sic] nations are the only highly civilized and powerful ones; the only nations raised by their religion to degrees of prosperity and happiness previously unknown; the only nations encircled by the Heathen and Mohammedan people, the objects of their admiration and love. And among the nations our own is distinguished, both by the purity of her religion, and the prodigious empire entrusted to her hands by Almighty God, among the teeming population of East Asia.[19]

Wilson had no time for Westerners who urged that missionaries keep their distance out of respect for the religious traditions of India, which he considered corrupt and contemptible; indeed, he characterized such a position, which accepted that "Hindooism [sic] is as good for Hindoos, and Islamism [sic] for Mohammedans, as Christianity is for Christians" as "semi-infidel," leaving the world to "perish in idolatry, imposture, sensuality and misery."[20] In 1839 he began construction of a new cathedral, which he envisioned with

> a beautiful spire, rising up two hundred and twenty feet, the fine deeply-buttressed gothic nave, chancel and transepts, marking the massive grandeur of the Christian religion, the magnificent organ sounding out "Thou Art the King of Glory O Christ," my native presbyters, in their snow-white vestures, walking down the aisle, the Christian neophytes responding in the choir, and Jesus acknowledged as the Lord of all.[21]

It was Bishop Wilson who insisted that the congregations of southern India ruthlessly eliminate every trace of the caste system, some aspects of which had continued to survive.[22] Early Indian converts in the south objected to Wilson's policy of intolerance, not only towards caste but also towards the incorporation of elements from traditional culture such as the liturgical use of flowers and Tamil music and poetry. In spite of the advice of Christian David, the first ordained Tamil Christian, under Wilson's leadership and in the years that followed the missionaries refused to consider permitting any remnants of the caste system to survive; indeed, the baptismal liturgy used in India incorporated a renunciation of caste.[23] Wilson's policy was shared by Bishop Daniel Corrie, the first bishop of Madras, who blamed the catechists and German Lutheran missionaries who had initiated evangelical efforts in south India, for "ministering among the people without reproving their errors."[24]

The missionaries at work in India hoped that an upper class educated in the English language and in western Christian values would eventually help to change those aspects of Indian society that were judged to be erroneous or destructive, even if most never actually became Christian.[25] This hope resulted in the establishment of an ambitious network of schools, which has been described by one contemporary Indian critic as "a secular project to transform Indians into deracinated replicas of Englishmen even while they remained affiliated to their own religious culture."[26]

The early attempt to use schools as instruments of evangelization was sometimes counterproductive; at the Telugu Mission in southern India, the conversion of three students in the early 1850s nearly emptied the school of students, who returned only gradually, and "the public excitement was now beyond control. An infuriated crowd pulled down the railings of [the missionary's] compound, and attacked his home"; only the arrival of the police prevented further damage. Of the first five converts at Telugu, four were ultimately ordained in the Church of England.[27]

On the other hand, the ministry associated with the Tirunelveli region of southern India demonstrated remarkable success. When the Bishop of Madras visited the area in 1851, he confirmed over 2,600 people in ten CMS stations and five SPG stations, and also ordained two new priests and five Tamil catechists as deacons. By 1855, there were 375 village congregations, numbering some 27,000 Christians, two thirds of whom were baptized, and nearly four thousand communicants. In 1856, the bishop returned to the area and confirmed nearly four thousand. At another service, which lasted four hours, drew a congregation of eighteen hundred and included two sermons (one in Tamil and one in English), he ordained several Tamil deacons.[28]

On the following day, one of the new deacons preached at an early service. Paul Daniel had been baptized a quarter of a century before, and worked as a catechist for many years before his ordination. He spoke no English and had no formal theological training, but was a gifted preacher. An older Tamil colleague remarked, "He has got what you call eloquence, Sir. He expresses his ideas in rich, suitable words. . . . His exposition of the doctrine of the Cross, and the work of the Spirit, was beautiful." In the words of one English missionary,

> He was mighty in the Scriptures, and quoted, [from memory], verse after verse, throughout his sermon, from every part of the sacred volume with perfect ease, without ever once referring to his Bible. He never took so much as a scrap of paper to the pulpit in the form of notes, and yet he always rigidly adhered to his text. His imagination was fertile, his resources in illustration inexhaustible; his language clear, copious, appropriate, and euphonious in the highest degree, and abounding in alliteration, which is considered a great beauty in Tamil. One of the Native Christians, when referring to his preaching after his death, remarked to me that his words passed out of his mouth like pearls upon a string; referring, I doubt not, to the beauty and regularity with which they followed one another.

This remarkable Tamil Anglican served only four years in ordained ministry; his life was cut short by cholera, which he contracted after visiting a woman who was suffering from the disease.[29]

Kevin Ward's account of the history of Indian Anglicanism notes that in the course of the nineteenth century, a number of members of India's elite did become Anglicans, and represented their church's point of view in the religious disputations that were an important medium for dialogue among the multiple traditions struggling for allegiance in India. He also underlines the importance of the mission's encounter with Hindu customs that were considered to degrade the status of women, especially child marriage, the practice of *sati* whereby widows were encouraged to commit ritual suicide upon the death of their husbands, and the circumstances in which many surviving widows were forced to live.[30]

While the Church of England in India would eventually turn its attention to the poorer strata of Indian society, that shift in emphasis would occur only after it became clear that most elite Indians would never respond positively to evangelization. Although Bishop Corrie insisted on the elimination of caste-related practices only in the context of the church and chose not to address the issue in the wider Indian society, even that limited challenge often had dramatic consequences. On one occasion, when a lower-caste catechist attempted to preside at the funeral of an upper-caste woman, he was threatened by the crowd of mourners.[31]

A recent major study of Christianity in India emphasizes that while the ecclesiastical and educational institutions established by the missionaries fostered a strong sense of identification with them, all Indian Christians in fact experienced a "dual identity." Indian Christians, "whether high caste or low caste or aboriginal/tribal . . . in origin, tended never to shed their distinctive identities based on 'birth' . . . This meant that virtually all Christians tended to identify themselves as much by birth, caste, and community, as by church, denomination, or theological outlook."[32]

MINISTRY IN THE SOUTH PACIFIC

As the nineteenth century was beginning, Richard Johnson, the first Anglican chaplain in Australia, was succeeded by Samuel Marsden. Unlike Johnson, he understood the Church's task to include the establishment of Christian institutions, and with financial support raised by his patron, William Wilberforce, Marsden established churches, orphanages and schools, and recruited teachers and clergy.[33]

Kevin Ward observes that the religiously pluralistic population tended to view the ministry overseen by Marsden as "an arm of officialdom, a repressive 'moral constabulary.'" As increasing numbers of English settlers intruded on the lands occupied for tens of thousands of years by the Aboriginal population, violence ensued, and while the colonial government attempted to control the situation, outraging the settlers by hanging those who were convicted of murdering Aboriginals, the Church remained silent. Marsden, himself a wealthy large landowner, believed that given the unwillingness of the Aboriginal population to adopt English "civilization," efforts at evangelization were probably useless. "Whether anything can be done with these degraded Tribes I have my doubts. It is our duty to try what we can do. The time may come when they feel more wants than they do at present. They seem to have all they wish for, Idleness and Independence."[34]

In the early decades of the nineteenth century, the Anglican church was the arm of a government that provided financial backing and practical support. Twelve chaplains arrived on the mainland before 1821, and two in Van Dieman's Land. All received land for their own use, enabling them to attain a standard of living appropriate to their social status. Land was also made available for churches, schoolrooms and parsonages. Convict labour and other assistance was offered to help construct necessary buildings, and stipends were paid from the British exchequer. The clergy were essentially members of the civil establishment and the terms of their appointment subjected them to the jurisdiction of governors.[35]

Brian Fletcher observes that "much of the clergy's time was spent preaching to the convicts, conducting rites of passage, engaging in pastoral work and, to a lesser extent, attending executions." Congregations, he notes, were "far from responsive," many of them Irish Roman Catholics and others with no previous experience of Anglican Christianity. The clergy, none of whom had ever exercised ministry under such conditions, were "identified with the employing class and the regime that had wrenched them from their homeland and subjected them to harsh treatment."[36]

As time went on, both the number of penal colonies and free settlers from England continued to grow; in New South Wales, large numbers of English sheep farmers assembled enormous tracts of land, transforming the landscape and introducing new complexity into Australian society. As in Upper Canada, one seventh of all Crown lands were set aside for the support of Anglican clergy and church schools; the colony's educational system was controlled by the Church and by 1829, the Church of England ran twenty-five local primary schools, two schools for orphans and a number of Sunday schools. Shortly afterward, it added two "King's Schools," secondary schools which "offered the sons of affluent parents, regardless of creed, a classical, scientific and religious education imparted by Anglican teachers." Growing numbers of prosperous Anglican laypeople attended Sunday services, formed close relationships with the clergy and provided money and sometimes land for the construction of churches and schoolrooms. Membership of a church linked to the English establishment was a sign of gentility and a badge of respectability. Moreover the church provided a means of countering the taint of convictions, thereby making the colony more suitable as a home for settlers and their families.[37]

The important role played in government by the Anglican clergy, the financial support it received from the government and the Church's monopoly on education inevitably raised the question of the Church of England's legal status as an "established" church, and even contemporary historians are divided on the issue. There is no doubt that in the first decades of English settlement, Australian Anglicans enjoyed a privileged position within colonial society.[38]

While the earliest clergy associated with the Anglican presence in Australia were from the Church's evangelical wing, Archdeacon William G. Broughton, who arrived in the colony in 1829, was more sympathetic to the high-church party and the SPG. Though the clergy increasingly reflected the theological diversity that marked Anglicanism in other parts of the world, Fletcher notes that there was little effect on church life:

> The forms of worship did not vary greatly and church interiors were plain, normally with the traditional three-decked pulpit located centrally. Galleries were constructed for the convicts who stood under guard. At ground level were the high-backed pews rented by the wealthier colonists, and benches for those who could not afford pews. Mattins and Evensong were conducted as prescribed in the 1662 *Book of Common Prayer,* as was the Holy Communion service although it was rarely conducted by Evangelical clergy. Services were lengthy and the congregations were more observers than active participants. The officiating clergyman read the prayers and delivered the sermon. The parish clerk, from his niche at the base of the pulpit, led the people through the verses and responses, and announced the hymns. Choirs and eventually organs provided musical accompaniments in the better appointed and more fashionable churches . . .[39]

The influx of both prisoners and free settlers of other religious persuasions and a governmental policy favorable to moderating the traditional privileges of the Church of England contributed to rapid changes in the religious landscape. Anglican laity, many of whom identified with the Church's Evangelical wing, had a variety of opportunities to support the Church's social ministry through campaigns to distribute Bibles, address the abuse of alcohol, minister to the elderly and the ill, and support evangelistic work among the Aboriginal population. Many of the organizations which supported these causes were ecumenical and presaged changes which would dramatically alter the Church of England's position in the Australian colonies.

In 1836, William Broughton was consecrated as Bishop of Australia. That same year, the colonial government introduced a "Church Act" which made governmental financing available to all the denominations present in the colony in proportion to their numbers and the amount of local support they enjoyed. In subsequent years, several new dioceses were established to respond to the growing colonial population in Tasmania, South and West Australia; the absence of any ecclesiastical infrastructure beyond the level of the congregation meant that bishops enjoyed almost total control over their dioceses. Ironically, it was governmental financial support that enabled the rapid growth of Australian Anglicanism. That support began to wane by mid-century (though it was not abolished in Western Australia until 1895). Nevertheless, the historian Patricia Curthoys observes that by 1861,

> the Australian church—its clergy and laity and, most significantly, its bishops—had come to accept that it was just one of several religious denominations with equal status under law. It had no special privileges or prerogatives as far as the state was concerned. However, it remained enthusiastic about taking advantage of the provisions of the legislation making available substantial sums of money for the employment of clergy and the construction of church buildings. Although it would have to compete with every other religious tradition, the Anglican church was the principal beneficiary of a system that essentially rewarded the denomination with the largest number of affiliated members regardless of their involvement in church life.[40]

Life in each of the Australian colonies reflected both social and institutional idiosyncrasies, which had the effect of creating not only significant discrepancies in the life of the church but also profound uncertainty about how best to provide for the future of Anglicanism in what remained a sparsely settled continent. An 1850 conference of bishops agreed on the desirability of some form of self-government by synod, but initial controversy surrounded just how large a role laypeople should be given in church affairs. A request to the British government for legal action to establish self-rule went unanswered, and as a result, each diocese chose its own avenue to achieve the goal, contributing to the intense regionalism which marked this period in the Church's history.

In New Zealand, the Church Missionary Society had a long and complex relationship with the original Māori inhabitants. It was Samuel Marsden who challenged the CMS to work with the Māori, but warned that like the Australian Aborigines, they must first be "civilized"; hence, the first English missionaries were "Christian artisans or lay-settlers." The first Māori baptism did not take place until 1825. Fifteen years later, the Māori chiefs ceded sovereignty to Queen Victoria in the Treaty of Waitangi, and in 1841 George Selwyn was appointed as New Zealand's first bishop.[41]

Marion Grau's study of mission with the Māori from a postcolonial perspective notes the reciprocal nature of early exchanges between the two communities: "Māori received access to goods and technologies, the missionaries made inroads both in 'civilizing' and in spreading the various forms of the gospel." This exchange, she observes, was facilitated by the Māori attraction to the Bible as a power-laden artifact, carrying more authority than oral tradition, an attraction used to positive effect by both Māori preachers and missionaries.[42]

The ministry of George Selwyn, New Zealand's first bishop. was funded in part by the CMS although he was a high-churchman. Like his missionary colleagues, he was an ardent advocate of the rights of the Māori people, especially with regard to the arrival of English settlers and their frequent incursions on Māori land. The CMS hope for a Māori church seemed on the way to being met; by 1845, an estimated 43,000 Māori were attending services.[43] But Selwyn's concern for the clergy's educational standards, and his criticism of the quality of the training the CMS missionaries had provided, meant that the first Māori deacon was not ordained until twelve years after Selwyn's arrival. Meanwhile, the Māori population declined, especially in relation to the English settlers who continued to arrive in constantly increasing numbers. Violent struggles over land often pitted the bishop and clergy, who attempted to protect the Māori people's rights, against the settlers. In 1857, Bishop Selwyn succeeded in providing the Church in New Zealand with a constitution guaranteeing its autonomy.[44]

That constitution was the culmination of a lengthy process of creating a church for New Zealand that would be independent of control by either the English church or state, and also free from financial dependence on the colonial legislature. Much of Selwyn's episcopate was spent in devising ways to extricate the Church in New Zealand from the multiple legal and canonical regulations by which the Church of England controlled overseas churches.[45]

An informal synod of clergy in 1844 to discuss practical concerns such as baptismal sponsors and the reception of polygamous households was "the first experiment of its kind in the Anglican Church." When a second synod was convened three years later, the CMS missionaries were uncertain about the consequences of breaking their ties with the "Home Church," but the Constitution, influenced in part by that of the Episcopal Church in the United States, accomplished its goal of an Anglican church for New Zealand which was effectively free of foreign control.[46] The document, which bore the approval of church and state authorities in Britain, was finally signed in 1857. It represented the culmination not only of Selwyn's hopes but those of a great many clergy and laypeople, large numbers of whom had expressed their hope for "some system of Church government which, by assigning to each order of the Church the appropriate duties, might call forth the energies of all, and thus enable the whole body of the Church most efficiently to perform its functions."[47] Selwyn's "determined pioneering of provincial autonomy for colonial churches, based on elected synods comprising elected representatives of clergy and laity as well as bishops, and the election of bishops" is credited with playing a significant part in the emergence of what came to be known as the Anglican Communion.[48]

Unfortunately, the ministry of the Anglican Church in some parts of New Zealand was profoundly affected by the ongoing conflicts between the English settlers and the Māori people. Western culture took its toll with "drunkenness, disease and death," and the settlers repeatedly attempted to buy or seize traditional Māori lands which were held by tribes rather than individuals. In the years between 1860 and 1865, sporadic warfare erupted, and some mission stations were destroyed. "Archdeacon Maunsell and his family had to flee from his ruined home and take refuge in the forest." Most Māori did not join in the fighting, and those who did "prayed and read the Scriptures before fighting, and regularly kept their Sunday services." In the aftermath of the violence, a fanatical cult created a wave of apostasy among some Māori Christians and two missionaries were murdered. It is estimated that about one quarter of the 35,000 Māori who remained on the islands were disaffected from the Church.

Contemporary Māori scholarship notes the ambiguous role played by the English missionaries in their relationships with the Māori people. As early as the 1820s, some missionaries had turned to gun trading to finance other projects. Literacy "quickly undermined the precepts of the Māori oral tradition," and with it the role of the *tohunga* and *maumatua* (elders) in preserving tribal wisdom and values. On the other hand, the missionaries sometimes served as mediators and peacemakers in tribal disputes.[49] The Treaty of Waitangi had been supported by the missionaries as the best hope of maintaining some Māori rights in the face of the rapidly increasing—and aggressive—British settlement. But the colonial government's interpretation of its prerogatives soon demonstrated that the trust of Māori and missionaries alike had been misplaced, when the government "put into place a series of laws and practices that took away the very rights of Māori guaranteed in the Treaty. From 1840 to 1852 fifty-five million acres of Māori land had moved to government control . . ."[50]

The missionaries themselves often contributed to the disillusion experienced among many Māori Christians; Marion Grau notes that "the class relations the Europeans knew at home were rebuilt into hierarchical race relations in numerous missionary contexts. Missionaries often created households separate and boundaried from indigenous peoples, thereby replicating and foreshadowing colonial racial relations and discrimination."[51]

In his study of the relationship between the Church of England and British imperialism, Rowan Strong argues that the experience of the Church in Australia and New Zealand at mid-century contributed to a significant change in the nature of Anglican identity. In their search for an *autonomous* sense of identity (a search in which Canadian Anglicans also shared), they helped redefine Anglicanism as a "World Church" in which "episcopacy was now to be the basis for a global Anglicanism. Bishops would now be indispensable, . . . and not just for British colonies, but wherever a significant number of Anglicans were to be found."[52] Ironically, a model of Anglican identity freed from its ties to the state did not surrender its commitment to British imperialism; rather, he insists, "the new autonomous paradigm . . . was one that also retained its continuities with the past in terms of much of its discourse of empire"—specifically in the importance of struggling against "heathenism" and its affirmation that the British Empire has a God-given mission. What was new about the paradigm was its "self-understanding, its relationship to the state, and its polity in the colonies."[53]

THE EPISCOPAL CHURCH: THE BEGINNING OF OVERSEAS MISSION

In 1826, the Domestic and Foreign Missionary Society, founded only six years earlier, reminded the Episcopal Church's General Convention that "for the reputation and interest of the Protestant Episcopal Church in the United States of America and in justice to the benevolent intentions of the General Convention . . . missionaries should without delay be sent to foreign lands."[54]

The first overseas missionaries, a party consisting of a printer, two clergy and their wives, were assigned to Greece four years later. Shortly afterward they were joined by Elizabeth Milligan, sister of one of the women already in Greece and the first unmarried woman appointed for overseas ministry. Greece was chosen as a primary destination because it had recently captivated the imaginations of the West by gaining its independence from the Ottoman Empire but was considered by American Episcopalians to be "without the Holy Scriptures and destitute of education," as well as belonging to "a corrupt form of Christianity" or devoid of Christian faith altogether.[55]

The decade of the 1830s marked a turning point for the Episcopal Church and its own missionary activity. It resolved to send twenty new missionaries for work in the American mission field, and also to appoint two missionaries for service in Liberia.

Many Episcopalians were especially interested in the evangelization of Liberia, because that newly established outpost of American presence on the west coast of Africa had been conceived and established as a homeland for formerly enslaved persons, whose continued presence in the United States was feared by many white Americans, even those who supported abolition, to lead inevitably to civil strife. Not only could Liberia provide a place for the descendants of enslaved Africans to return to the continent of their origin; it was seen too as a base and instrument for "civilizing" and evangelizing Africa. There was also early interest in the possibility of a mission to China, where American representatives of other churches were already establishing their presence. By 1835 two clergy had been appointed to begin the Episcopal Church's mission to China, and James Thompson, an Englishman of African descent and his wife, who had formerly been enslaved, were assigned to Liberia.[56] In 1851, the House of Bishops elected John Payne as the first Missionary Bishop of Liberia, where he served for twenty years and was responsible for the translation of the Bible into Grebo, one of the principal Liberian languages.[57]

LATIN AMERICA: THE BEGINNING OF ANGLICAN MISSION AND MINISTRY

Latin America would seem to be an unlikely setting for Anglican missionary activity, given the fact that (whatever the reality) it was universally assumed that the entire region, from Mexico to the tip of South America, was firmly Roman Catholic. Most nineteenth-century Anglicans had a strong aversion to Roman Catholicism. Nevertheless, both political realities and the sense that, however erroneous the Church of Rome might be, in a world of finite missionary resources it was better to concentrate on the conversion of the "heathen," meant that Anglicanism in Latin America was a tenuous presence throughout the century.

Small British outposts along the Caribbean coast in what are today Belize, Nicaragua and Honduras were established in the eighteenth century but survived almost without clergy for several hundred years.[58] The influx of Anglicans depended upon the changed relationship with England in the aftermath of the struggle of most Latin American countries for independence from Spain in the early decades of the nineteenth century. That struggle was primarily the work of the *criollo* bourgeoisie, descendants of the original Spanish colonists who had been excluded for centuries from any real power in the colonies. The newly independent states saw in Great Britain a possible ally in distancing themselves from Spain, while England saw Latin America as an enormous region of untapped economic potential. Furthermore, many of the new ruling groups were enamored of the Enlightenment and believed that the progress of their countries depended on loosening the grip of the Roman Catholic Church and its perennial alliance with the most conservative elements of Spanish society. They also realized that if Europeans were to be welcomed in their countries, they would have to be permitted some freedom of religion. In many cases, laws were passed allowing non–Roman Catholic ministries to be established, provided that no attempt was made to convert the local population. Nor were British officials eager to carry out evangelization among the local population, preferring to maintain good relations with the local government.

In 1810 the British government secured a trade agreement with Portugal which guaranteed religious freedom for British subjects. The treaty, however, provided that "the British should not proselytize among the Portuguese population and should abstain from all acts of public demonstration of their religion." In 1819, taking advantage of this agreement, the first Anglican church in South America was established in Rio de Janeiro, Brazil (at that time still a colony of Portugal).[59] Even the Roman Catholic bishop of Rio de Janeiro did not object to the Anglican presence in his city: "The English really have no religion at all," he wrote, "but they are a proud and obstinate race. If we oppose their wish in this matter, they will not only persist in it more and more, but will make it a matter of infinite importance. But if, on the other hand, we give way to them, they will build their chapels, and no one will ever go there." Anglicans were allowed to build a chapel in Valparaiso, Chile, "only if the building was behind a high board fence and without a steeple or bell."[60] Other Anglican chaplaincies were established in Argentina in 1820, Venezuela in 1834, Uruguay in 1840, Costa Rica in 1848, and in Peru a year later.[61]

The first evangelizing activity among Indigenous South Americans occurred in connection with several expeditions of the H.M.S. *Beagle* in the waters around Tierra del Fuego, at the tip of South America. In 1829 its captain, Robert Fitzroy, captured a boy, two young men and a young woman from the native tribal people who inhabited the region, and returned with them to England, where they were taught the English language, English "civilization" and English Christianity.

Two years later, the *Beagle* made a return voyage to Tierra del Fuego (this time with Charles Darwin on board), and the three surviving Fuegians were returned to their own people with the hope that they would serve as evangelists among them. Within a short time all three had reverted to their tribal customs. But the situation of the Fuegian Indians continued to interest Evangelical Anglicans in England, and in 1833 Richard Matthews unsuccessfully attempted to establish a missionary presence there. Captain Allen Gardiner was a remarkable former sea captain who experienced an awakening of faith which led him to take his family to South America in order to evangelize the native peoples. In 1842 his efforts with a community of Fuegians were rebuffed but he was able to establish contact with a tribe in Patagonia, in the extreme south of the continent. Gardiner immediately returned to England and in 1844 he established the Patagonia Missionary Society to fund ministry in that part of the world. Gardiner made three trips to South America, and while he was able to distribute religious books in Uruguay and Argentina, his efforts to establish a mission among the Fuegians and Patagonians were unsuccessful. On his last trip, in 1850, he was accompanied by a surgeon and five others, but following the loss of their boats and most of their supplies, and unable to obtain assistance from the native peoples, the entire party died.[62]

By mid-century, Anglicanism was more firmly rooted in other parts of Latin America, although its presence was still limited to chaplaincies for English expatriates and the Afro-Caribbean descendants of British and Spanish enslaved persons. On the Atlantic coast of Nicaragua, where a Canadian missionary began work in about 1848, "deep church roots were established and traditional Anglicanism grew and developed. Formal liturgy with vestments, British hymns and music, English clergy and the use of English in church, school and home were hallmarks of Anglicanism in southeast Nicaragua." The first Anglican church building was not, however, built until nearly fifty years later.[63]

The beginnings of Anglican ministry in Panama are the direct result of the California gold rush, and the desire of American fortune-hunters to cross the isthmus in order to reach ships that could carry them to the gold fields of the Pacific coast. William A. Aspenwall, an American businessman, initiated the construction of a railroad to convey travelers quickly from the Atlantic to the Pacific coast. Panama's small population made it necessary to seek workers from beyond the isthmus, and "Aspinwall arranged for thousands of immigrants from the West Indies to come to Panama. Thus began the immigration of residents of Jamaica, Barbados, Trinidad, and many other islands, most of them British colonies. Many of these workers who came to Panama were Anglicans, members of the Church of England in the West Indies."[64]

In 1852, the Episcopal Church's Board of Missions indicated its desire to send a missionary to serve the burgeoning community of West Indian workers and American overseers. In the following decade, four clergy exercised a brief ministry before succumbing to yellow fever and other illnesses then endemic to the isthmus. Services were held in the Railroad Company's buildings, and at least one of the clergy was described in the local press as "the resident Minister of the Railroad Company" and "chaplain to the Panama Railroad Company." When the first church was constructed some ten years later in the town of Aspinwall (now Colón), the Company provided the bulk of the funds. The church was consecrated in 1865 by Bishop Alonso Potter, Bishop of Pennsylvania, during a journey from the east coast to California. It proved to be his last official act; by the time his ship arrived in California, the bishop was dying of what was then known as "Panama fever."[65]

CHINA: THE BEGINNING OF ANGLICAN MISSIONS

Nineteenth century Europeans and North Americans shared a common fascination with China; perhaps its ancient culture was especially alluring because of the imperial reticence to allow any significant importation of western ideas into what its own people called the "Middle Kingdom"—that is, the nation at the center of the world. Several European powers, notably Great Britain, France and Germany, struggled to achieve access to the raw materials, the products and the vast market controlled by China. The First Opium War, fought by Britain over its right to import opium into the Chinese market, and concluded in 1842, is still remembered as a dark period in Chinese history.

Forced to allow European "concessions" for import and export in several coastal port cities and to cede the island of Hong Kong to the British, China also soon found itself the target of western missionaries representing various strains of Christianity. Even Anglicans arrived in what Kevin Ward calls "a particularly fragmented form, in a variety of church traditions and national identities, American, English and Canadian." William James Boone, who had been working as a missionary in China since 1840, was consecrated as Bishop of the American Mission in China in 1844. While the first CMS missionary for China was appointed as early as 1836, the first two clergy to work on behalf of CMS after the opening of the ports arrived in Shanghai in 1843. (A much smaller SPG presence did not appear in northern China until twenty years later.) In 1849, Hong Kong was established as the "diocese of Victoria," although its ministry to Chinese residents did not begin until more than a decade later.[66] The shed-like hall in which the first Anglican services were held was replaced in 1849 by a Gothic cathedral, three times as costly as a comparable church built in England. Its early congregation was drawn from the few thousand expatriates and the garrison of the British armed forces, for whom more than a third of the cathedral's seats were reserved. As one author comments, its "rather exclusive social composition mirrored the sharp divisions of race and class which characterized the early colonial period in Hong Kong." While an English reporter of the period considered it "an unsightly pile, quite disturbing the oriental appearance of the place," it was in fact built at the heart of the English colonial presence, "standing just below the Governor's residence and just above the other great institutions of

Victorian Hong Kong—the Hong Kong Bank headquarters, the High Court and the Hong Kong Club."[67]

From its beginnings, Anglican ministry in China, like that in India, engaged both expatriate Christians from the English-speaking countries and converts from the local population. As early as 1850, the Church Missionary Society established what later became Hong Kong's St. Paul's College as a training school for Chinese clergy and catechists.[68] While St. John's Cathedral served English-speaking Anglicans, St. Stephen's Church, founded in 1865, was the center for ministry with Chinese converts.[69]

SOUTH AFRICAN ANGLICANISM AND THE BISHOP COLENSO AFFAIR

Anglican ministry in southern Africa was a function of both increased shipping traffic between Europe and Asia and the complexities of European politics. As early as 1652, the Dutch East India Company had established a presence at Cape Town in order to service ships making the lengthy voyage around the southern tip of Africa. Its European population, the Afrikaners, most of whom were staunch Calvinists, included not only Dutch but also German, Scandinavians, and French Huguenot settlers. This population gradually began pushing north and east and also introduced slavery into the region, where it had been previously unknown. As a result of the Napoleonic Wars at the end of the eighteenth and the beginning of the nineteenth century, the Cape Colony passed into British hands. Anglican chaplaincies soon followed, along with missionaries from other English denominations and the (ecumenical) London Missionary Society. In 1820, British settlers began occupying land to the east traditionally held by the Xhosa people. A year later, the SPG sent its first missionary to the Cape Colony, while the CMS sent a missionary to begin the evangelization of the Zulu people.

The relationship between the British colonists and the Afrikaner (Boer) population which had preceded them was never close, and when slavery was outlawed throughout the British Empire in 1834, thousands of Afrikaners moved eastward into Natal and northward in what came to be known as the "Great Trek," where they established two Boer republics. The great Zulu king Shaka mounted bloody resistance to the incursions of white colonists into his people's territory, but in 1843 the British annexed Natal and immediately opened it to English sugar cane plantations. By mid-century, white settlers had penetrated most of southern Africa. Although the British colonial government had abolished slavery, it by no means created a color-blind society; stringent racial segregation continued to be the norm in the southern African colonies.

Southern Africa's first diocese was established at Cape Town in 1847; Bishop Robert Gray arrived the following year. In 1853, two additional dioceses, Natal and Grahamstown, were formed.

Bishop Gray played a crucial role in the history of southern African Anglicanism.[70] He argued persuasively that the Anglican understanding of the Church and its ministry required that important decisions affecting its life should not be made by the bishop alone; arguing for the creation of a diocesan synod, he wrote to his diocese in 1851 that "the Presbyters, the Deacons, and the Laity of the Church have each their separate functions, responsibilities, privileges, which at present are in much danger of being overlooked." A significant aspect of his insistence on the importance of a locally established synod was his equally firm belief that Anglicans in Cape Town should enjoy self-government, free of control by both English Church and State.[71]

But whatever the importance of Gray's role, he is probably best remembered for his part in the saga of John William Colenso, first Bishop of Natal. As a missionary bishop, Colenso believed passionately that his responsibility was not only to the growing population of English settlers but also to the Zulu tribe whom the British were struggling to control and whose lands were being colonized. He helped publish the first Zulu grammar and the first English-Zulu dictionary, and translated part of the New Testament into Zulu. Colenso incurred the anger of both the government and many British settlers by protesting against what he considered to be unnecessarily harsh and repressive colonial policies. Many in the Church, including the Bishop of Cape Town, were offended by his willingness to call into question aspects of the Christian faith which he considered to be hostile to authentic ministry with the Zulu people. That behavior not only brought him into conflict with his peers and immediate superiors but placed him at the center of a storm that profoundly affected Anglicans around the world and led to developments that continue to shape the practice of ministry even today.

Bishop Colenso was one of the first Anglican missionary leaders who understood the profound implications for ministry when faith takes shape in contexts radically different from those in which Anglican Christianity had first been formed. In 1855, he published *Remarks on the Proper Treatment of Polygamy,* in which he challenged the notion that conversion to Christianity must inevitably entail the breakup of polygamous households. Six years later, in a study of the epistle to the Romans, he called into question the doctrine of eternal punishment and the necessity of the sacraments for salvation, which he considered to imply the pastorally offensive condemnation of all previous generations of Zulus.

Colenso's understanding of the implications of mission and ministry for the native peoples of Africa contrasted sharply with that of Gray and most of the other English missionaries, almost all of whom considered the extension of British rule and that of Anglican Christianity as intimately related.

> In 1848, when Robert Gray was introduced to [three tribal leaders] by the military governor of the Cape, ... the Bishop saw no incongruity in the strains of God Save the Queen which opened the meeting, no impropriety in the governor's bombastic and paternalistic address to the three chiefs, and he regarded the whole episode as a most auspicious opening for mission work. ... To Gray and to the Anglican missionaries who came from the established Church of England to work in the future diocese of Grahamstown, British government was synonymous with Christianity and benevolence.

Bishop Cotterill, second bishop of Grahamstown, considered "any clergyman who ignored the rightful authority of the Civil Government as 'unfitted, whatever might be his other qualifications, for the office of a missionary.'" Mandy Goedhals, a contemporary South African historian, calls the relationship between the Church and the British colonial authorities a "Constantinian compromise" which clearly "interfered with the church's spiritual independence."[72]

Goedhals notes that with the exception of Colenso, early Anglican ministry

> assumed that African culture and religion had no value, that English Christianity embodied the gospel, and was therefore the form in which its good news ought to be presented. Anglican converts among the Xhosa were taught to recite the Psalms, the Ten Commandments and the Creed. Services on mission stations took on an Anglo-Catholic character, and apart from translation of the scriptures and the liturgy into the vernacular, there was little attempt at indigenization ... Moreover, the structure of the church which developed in southern Africa was not characterised by a free and equal brotherhood, but distorted by hierarchical inequalities and by the prejudices of white colonists.[73]

In 1863, the bishops of the South African Church, led by Bishop Gray of Cape Town, deposed Colenso. But he refused to accept their decision and appealed to the Privy Council on the grounds that his appointment had been made by the Church of England, not South Africa, and that therefore only the British government had the authority to remove him from office. The crisis caused enormous concern in the Church of England; the high church party, always staunch advocates of the power of bishops, defended the authority of Bishop Gray, while the more liberal broad-church party tended to support Colenso. Evangelicals opposed both.[74]

The Privy Council ruled in favor of Colenso, and he continued to receive his episcopal salary and maintained control of the diocesan cathedral. However, Bishop Gray declared him excommunicated and proceeded to consecrate another bishop with the same territorial jurisdiction, and the English missionary societies withdrew their support for Colenso's ministry. In 1865, he published another controversial work, *The Pentateuch and the Book of Joshua Critically Examined*, in which he expressed the doubt he shared with many European scholars with regard to the historical authenticity of the first books of the Hebrew scriptures. Much of his remaining ministry was dedicated to defending the Zulu people in a series of confrontations with the colonial authorities.

The effect of Colenso's challenges to both colonial and ecclesiastical authority, along with other similar challenges from other voices, had an effect on Anglican history far beyond the borders of South Africa. In 1865, the Synod of the Church of England in Canada sent an urgent letter to the Archbishop of Canterbury, in which they expressed their feelings of isolation and confusion in the face of controversy on a number of issues and requesting that he call a gathering of all the bishops in communion with the Church of England, in order to strengthen their sense of unity and to achieve some clarity on the great debates shaking the churches. In response, the Archbishop, John Thomas Longley, sent messages to the 114 bishops in communion with Canterbury, inviting them to meet with him at his official residence, Lambeth Palace, for four days of consultation, beginning on September 24, 1867.[75] That meeting would prove to have permanent consequences, not only for the 76 bishops who accepted the invitation, but for the sense of identity—and the practice of ministry—of Anglicans around the world.

NOTES

1. Stephen Neill, *A History of Christian Missions* (London: Penguin Books, 1964, 1986), 179.

2. Hymn 254, *The Hymnal of the Protestant Episcopal Church in the United States of America 1940* (New York: The Church Pension Fund, 1940).

3. Jocelyn Murray, *Proclaim the Good News: A Short History of the Church Missionary Society* (London: Hodder and Stoughton, 1985), 1.

4. Hans Cuattingius, *Bishops and Societies: A Study of Anglican Colonial and Missionary Expansion 1698–1850* (London: SPCK, 1952), 29, 41.

5. SPCK Report, 1791, quoted in Cuattingius, *Bishops and Societies*, 52.

6. Murray, *Proclaim the Good News*, 10–20.

7. See William C. Barnhart, "Anglican Volunteerism, Ecclesiastical Politics, and the Bath Church Missionary Association Controversy, 1817–1818," *Anglican and Episcopal History* 77 (March 2008), 1–21.

8. Barnhart, "Volunteerism," 10–11.

9. Barnhart, "Volunteerism," 19.

10. Murray, *Proclaim the Good News*, 32–34.

11. Eugene Stock, *The History of the Church Missionary Society: Its Environment, Its Men and Its Work* (London: Church Missionary Society, 1899), II, 83.

12. Murray, *Proclaim the Good News*, 42, 49.

13. Max Warren, ed., *To Apply the Gospel: Selections from the Writings of Henry Venn* (Grand Rapids: William B. Eerdmans Publishing Co., 1971), 60.

14. Warren, *To Apply the Gospel*, 62–63, 78.

15. Stock, *Church Missionary Society*, II, 413.

16. Stock, *Church Missionary Society*, II, 84.

17. Warren, *To Apply the Gospel*, 79–80.

18. Murray, *Proclaim the Good News*, 41.

19. Daniel Wilson, *Sermons Delivered in India during the Course of the Primary Visitation* (London: J. Hatchard and Son, 1838), 16.

20. Wilson, "Sermons," 76.

21. Cecil John Grimes, *Towards an Indian Church: Two Centuries of the Growth of the Church in India in Constitution and Life* (London: SPCK, 1946), 81.

22. Sidney Lee, ed., *Dictionary of National Biography*, LXII (London: Smith, Elder, 1900), 88.

23. Kevin Ward, *A History of Global Anglicanism* (Cambridge: Cambridge University Press, 2001), 220.

24. Theodore Rajalakshmi, *Anglicanism in Madras* (Madras: CLS, 2006), 64–65.

25. Ward, *A History of Global Anglicanism*, 222.

26. Gauri Viswanathan, *Outside the Fold*, 5; quoted in Ward, *A History of Global Anglicanism*, 223.

27. Stock, *Church Missionary Society*, II, 177, 179.

28. Stock, *Church Missionary Society*, II, 182–183.

29. Stock, *Church Missionary Society*, II, 182–183.

30. Ward, *A History of Global Anglicanism*, 222–228.

31. Rajalakshmi, *Anglicanism in Madras*, 258–259.

32. Robert Eric Frykenberg, *Christianity in India: From Beginnings to the Present* (London, Oxford University Press, 2008), 263–264.

33. William L. Sachs, *The Transformation of Anglicanism: From state Church to global communion* (Cambridge: Cambridge University Press, 1993), 55.

34. Ward, *A History of Global Anglicanism*, 276.

35. Brian Fletcher, "The Anglican Ascendancy 1788–1835," in Bruce Kaye, ed., *Anglicanism in Australia: A History* (Carleton, Victoria: Melbourne University Press, 2002), 9.

36. Fletcher, "Anglican Ascendancy," 11.

37. Fletcher, "Anglican Ascendancy," 18–20.

38. Fletcher, "Anglican Ascendancy," 15–16.

39. Fletcher, "Anglican Ascendancy," 22.

40. Patricia Curthoys, "State Support for Churches," in Kaye, ed., *Anglicanism in Australia: A History*, 50.

41. Murray, *Proclaim the Good News*, 22–24.

42. Marion Grau, *Rethinking Mission in the Postcolony: Salvation, Society and Subversion* (New York: T. and T. Clark, 2011), 221.

43. Robert Glen, ed., *Mission and Moko: Aspects of the Work of the Church Missionary Society in New Zealand 1814–1832* (Christchurch, NZ: Latimer Fellowship, 1992), 12.
44. Ward, *A History of Global Anglicanism,* 288–289.
45. See W. M. Jacob, "George Augustus Selwyn, First Bishop of New Zealand and the Origins of the Anglican Communion," *Journal of Anglican Studies,* 9 (May 2011), 38–55.
46. Stock, *The History of the Church Missionary Society,* II, 86–88, 90.
47. John H. Evans, "The Constitution of The Church of the Province of New Zealand," *Anglican and Episcopal History* LVI (June 1987), 154.
48. Jacob, "George Augustus Selwyn," 55.
49. Moeawa Callaghan, *Theology in the Context of Aoteoroa New Zealand* (unpublished thesis, Graduate Theological Union, Berkeley, CA, 1999), 7–8.
50. Callaghan, *Theology,* 13.
51. Grau, *Rethinking Mission in the Postcolony,* 221–222.
52. Strong, *Anglicanism and the British Empire,* 217–219.
53. Strong, *Anglicanism and the British Empire,* 280–282.
54. Julia C. Emery, *A Century of Endeavor 1821 – 1921: A Record of the First Hundred Years of the Domestic and Foreign Missionary Society* (New York: Department of Missions, 1921), 48.
55. Emery, *A Century of Endeavor,* 50, 56–57.
56. Emery, *A Century of Endeavor,* 58–61.
57. Constant, *No Turning Back,* 27.
58. See Robert W. Renouf, "Anglicanism in Nicaragua 1745–1985," *Anglican and Episcopal History,* LVII (December 1988), 382–396, and Ennis Duffis, "Capellanía en Centroamérica," in Ashton Jacinto Brooks, ed., *Eclesiología: presencia anglicana en la Región Central de América,* (San José, Costa Rica: DEI, 1990), 35–45.
59. Guillermo Cavieses, *¡ANGLICANOS! Latin American Anglicanism: A Study of the Ecclesiology and Identity of the Anglican Churches of Latin America* (unpublished thesis, Uppsala University, 2010), 28.
60. Ward, *A History of Global Anglicanism,* 103.
61. Justo l. González and Ondina E. González, *Christianity in Latin America* (Cambridge: Cambridge University Press, 2008), 190–191.
62. For an analysis of the mission to the Fuegian people, see Larry Douglas Smith, "FitzRoy and the Fuegians: A Clash of Cultures," *Anglican and Episcopal History* LIX (September 1990), 386–403.
63. Renouf, "Anglicanism in Nicaragua," 383–384.
64. John L. Kater, "The Beginnings of the Episcopal Church in Panama, 1852–1904," *Anglican and Episcopal History* LVII (June 1988), 149.
65. Kater, "Episcopal Church in Panama," 149–151.
66. Ward, *A History of Global Anglicanism,* 246.
67. Stephen Vines, *The Story of St. John's Cathedral* (Hong Kong: FormAsia, undated), 4–5, 8, 12–14.
68. Kenneth Scott Latourette, *A History of Christian Missions in China* (New York: Russell and Russell, 1929, 1967), 267.

69. Patricia P. K. Chiu, "Female Education and the Early Development of St. Stephen's Church, Hong Kong," in Philip L Wickeri, ed., *Christian Encounters with Chinese Culture: Essays on Anglican and Episcopal History in China* (Hong Kong: Hong Kong University Press, 2015), 47–64.

70. "There can be little doubt that the CPSA [Church in the Province of Southern Africa] owes its greatest debt in terms of its constitutional shape, its missionary endeavors, and even its spirituality, to Robert Gray, the first Bishop of Cape Town." Frank England, "Tracing Southern African Anglicanism," in Frank England and Torquil Paterson, eds., *Bounty in Bondage: The Anglican Church in Southern Africa* (Johannesburg: Ravan Press, 1989), 20.

71. England, *Tracing Southern African Anglicanism,* 21–22.

72. Mandy Goedhals, "From Paternalism to Partnership," in Frank England and Torquin Paterson, eds., *Bounty in Bondage: The Anglican Church in Southern Africa* (Johannesburg: Ravan Press, 1989), 106–107.

73. Goedhals, "From Paternalism to Partnership," 107–108.

74. Stock, *The History of the Church Missionary Society,* II, 362.

75. Owen Chadwick, "The Lambeth Conference: An Historical Perspective," *Anglican and Episcopal History* LVIII, 3 (September 1989), 261.

Chapter Nine

Tremblings

Ministry in the Church of England, 1860–1900

As dramatic as the social conflicts that shook Anglican ministry at mid-century were, there were other traumatic movements and events that further challenged the Church's ministry, both in England and among Anglicans around the world. The second half of the nineteenth century is the missionary epoch *par excellence*; the constant and growing work of missionaries on every inhabited continent assured that as the British Empire continued to expand, the Church of England participated in that expansion.

SHAKING THE FOUNDATIONS

Some of the most authentic accounts of ministry in the Anglican tradition have in fact been penned by novelists whose engagement with the fabric of English society inevitably leads them to include both clergy and the people with whom they come in contact. Early in the nineteenth century the novels of Jane Austen and the Brontë sisters introduced readers to an intimate portrait of "typical" clergy in a variety of contexts.

The party strife which caused such concern to many at mid-century was masterfully portrayed in a series of novels by Anthony Trollope, set in a fictional cathedral town and its environs which are modeled on the city of Winchester. Beginning in 1855, the Barchester novels depicted the ministries of a whole spectrum of characters whose portraits are shaped by the Church of the day and which in turn shaped how readers conceived of the clergy who daily crossed their paths. Trollope created devoted and well-meaning but often ineffectual clergy, long-suffering rural parsons, upwardly mobile and ambitious ecclesiastical bureaucrats, bishops whose approach to their calling reflected the quieter certainties of times now past and others who were eager to enter energetically into the important issues and conflicts of the day. He placed them in constant interaction with other church dignitaries, harassed clergy wives and uncomprehending rectory children, young clerics fascinated by the innovations of the Oxford Movement and others determined to hold fast to a more Evangelical point of view—and always, the laypeople who received (or suffered) their ministries and who applauded their faithfulness, often overlooked their failings, and sometimes scorned their faults.

This novelist's vision of an English Church shaken by conflict and change is confirmed both by his contemporaries within the Church and by later historians. Owen Chadwick's monumental two-volume study of *The Victorian Church* documents many of the ways in which the practice of ministry responded to and was shaped by broader events and movements. The stresses and anxieties awakened by critical biblical scholarship at mid-century were only deepened as Charles Darwin's theories of evolution became more widely popular in the course of the next decades. In 1860, Thomas Huxley and the Bishop of Oxford clashed over the subject of evolution at a meeting of the British Association. By the end of the century, Frederick Temple, Archbishop of Canterbury, had publicly accepted Darwin's theory of evolution as both "permissible and respectable," indicating, in Chadwick's view, "the final reception of the doctrine . . . among the divines, clergy and leading laity of the established Church" of a point of view that had already been accepted by a constantly growing number of educated Christians.[1]

The conflict represented by the challenges to traditional belief represented by science and history reflect in part the increasing gap between the industrial cities and the more traditional countryside and the rift between classes in both. Chadwick notes that the country parish, once the meeting place for the entire population, lost much of its role as an agent of unity; even though some clergy supported agricultural unions, as farm laborers became more politically aware of their situation, many became alienated from all religious institutions.[2]

The growing gap between secular knowledge and religious practice led many to question whether the universities, traditionally the primary source of theological training, provided adequate preparation for ordained ministry. In 1854, the Bishop of Oxford established Cuddesdon College for university graduates to provide "an habituation to religious practices and thoughts, in short, spiritual training." In 1861, the Convocation of Canterbury requested "more special and distinctive training of candidates for Holy Orders."[3] Several years later, the same Convocation specified that even minimal preparation for ordination should include theological, practical and liturgical competence: Acquaintance with the scriptures and the study of the New Testament in Greek; the Prayer Book, the Thirty-Nine Articles, sermon preparation, church music, children's religious education, school administration, parish visiting, and "the habit of audible and distinct reading and speaking in the congregation." A more thorough preparation would include critical study of the New Testament and enough Hebrew for "devotional study," Church history, the Fathers of the early Church, dogmatic theology, the English theological tradition, with "special reference to the evidences of Christianity," as well as "ritual, ecclesiastical law," and the ethical and philosophical dimensions of theology.[4]

In the later decades of Victoria's rule, the challenge to traditional faith represented by science and historical studies was often seen as a process that would inevitably weaken the practice of religion, a threat not only to faith but to the social order built on traditional Christianity. Doubt and scepticism became increasingly significant pastoral issues, affecting as they did not only laypeople but the clergy to whom they turned for reassurance. Chadwick considers that by the end of the nineteenth century, "religion had abandoned, or was abandoning, an ancient claim to give truths about the physical world."[5]

The Church of England struggled especially to meet the religious needs of the burgeoning cities in the face of a shortage of both church buildings and clergy. In Chadwick's view, the practice of ministry in the two widely differing settings reveals that they substantially influenced each other. Lay readers, who first appeared in response to the clergy shortage in London parishes in the 1860s and whose ministry was originally restricted to preaching and leading worship under special circumstances, gradually began to be seen as a useful arm of ministry in rural dioceses as well. In the course of the next few decades, their role broadened to include the conduct of regularly scheduled worship in parish churches. On the other hand, the Mother's Union, which provided congregational recognition for women married in the Church of England and encouraged a stable and patriarchal model of the family in the face of the rapid social changes which were challenging it, began in 1876 in a rural setting but spread to city congregations.[6]

In the last decades of Victoria's long rule, the Church of England remained a significant institution within society, though in many ways the role of its ministry became more ambiguous. In 1851, England's population was divided more or less evenly between cities and countryside. When Victoria died in 1901, three quarters of its people lived in urban areas, with the middle class increasingly moving to the suburbs. In 1887, two million of its children attended Church of England schools, and three quarters of all children in England and Wales attended Sunday school. The number of baptisms rose throughout the century. Interestingly, given the many challenges to the Church, so too did the number of clergy; in 1881, the Church counted 21,663 persons in holy orders; in 1901, the number was 25,235.[7]

But the Church faced changes in how English families lived. As one contemporary scholar comments,

> The house, once a workplace as well as a home, had become a self-contained, private, exclusively domestic space. In the eighteenth century "family" had meant "kin," those related by blood; now its primary meaning was the inhabitants of a household, barring the servants—that is, the nuclear family. . . . Privacy had become the essential atrtibute of the middle-class Victorian family.[8]

In the words of a French observer of the period, "Every Englishman . . . imagines a 'home,' with the woman of his desire, the pair of them alone with their children. That is his own little universe, closed to the world."[9]

In the face of the rapid changes in English society during Victoria's reign, some voices in the Church struggled to affirm the continuing significance of the role and character of the English clergy. In an 1872 publication, John Henry Blunt argued that due to the general rise in education among all social classes, clergy must keep themselves up to date with regard to current affairs while remaining "servant[s] of Christ, separated from among His ordinary servants and endowed with special grace to do His work." Blunt's vision of the role of the clergy demands of them loyalty to both Church and State, personal holiness, and a clear sense of vocation to both rich and poor.[10]

Even as many struggled to maintain the traditional role of clergy in Church and society, their role in the Church's ministry was being augmented by the participation of large numbers of laypeople. Vestries assumed more responsibilities for congregational life and in 1897 all clergy were requested to provide for the election of a parochial church council. While membership was to be limited to "male communicants," women also assumed more active ministries at the congregational level: the diocese of Salisbury reported two women churchwardens and in the parish of Great Staughton in Huntingtonshire, both wardens were women.[11]

LAY WOMEN AND THE CHURCH'S MINISTRY

It was the Mother's Union that provided the most visible and accessible opportunity for women to participate in the Church's ministry. Its founder, Mary Sumner, was both the product and the instrument of the Evangelical movement: born into a devout and prosperous Anglican family and married to a country parson who was a bishop's son, she became a strong voice on behalf of what has been called the "Victorian cult of maternalism," based on a "dualistic vision of society consisting of the Christian hearth presided over by the virtuous woman and the fallen world which men negotiated at some risk to their soul."[12]

Mary Sumner had an active role in the Girls' Friendly Society, which was founded in 1875 to promote "purity of life and friendship" among young girls and women; but she worried that it failed to emphasize the unique and crucial role of *motherhood* as a vocation essential to the well-being of both the family and society.

The Mothers' Union reflected Sumner's opinion that women needed training in order to fulfill their special vocation. It proved to be popular with both Anglo-Catholics and Evangelicals, and women of all classes. (On the other hand, the organization helped maintain class distinctions by creating two forms of membership: one for "cottage mothers" who participated in "branch meetings" and another for "subscribing members," who paid at least one shilling annually and met in "drawing room meetings" where papers were read and discussed. This distinction was supported by two different publications: one for the members in general and another for "the educated classes."[13]

The startlingly rapid growth of the Mothers' Union demonstrates the attractiveness of its program for Anglican women, not only in the British Isles but throughout the Empire. Within just over a decade, it had branches in eighteen dioceses, with fifty-seven in the diocese of Winchester alone, and had begun to play an active role not only in the Church but by addressing social issues: It stood vehemently against Parliament's efforts to make divorce more accessible and was opposed to women "who engaged in paid employment outside the home, especially in factories," which it considered to weaken interest and opportunity to practice the specifically feminine vocation of motherhood. The Mothers' Union had no interest in the fledgling women's suffrage movement, arguing that women's influence was more important than their rights and that, like outside employment, direct participation in politics would lead to the loss of "their womanly nature and domestic influence." Like most Evangelicals, Sumner and her colleagues believed that the social problems they saw around them would be solved not by politics but by conversion; hence, the Union's strong support for religious education in the schools.[14]

The Mothers' Union grew rapidly throughout the British Isles and also wherever the Church of England had been established. While this growth happened initially among expatriate women in places such as Australia, India, and other British settlements and colonies, many of whom were the wives of clergy or British soldiers, the organization soon came to understand itself as having an "imperial vocation." Its ideological support was a commitment to "divine patriotism" composed of a sense of Christian duty along with a belief in the "inherent rightness of British identity as an imperial power." Indeed, the Empire was understood to be God's providential purpose for the "English-speaking race," understood as "bringing all people under good and godly rule." The primary sign of the superiority on which its strength depended was a "home infused with the values of Christian motherhood," along with "belief in the universality of Christian motherhood and its responsibilities." Hence by the end of the century branches for "'native' indigenous women" were being established in Hong Kong, India, and Swaziland. Contemporary observers may be troubled by the unexamined assumptions underlying the Mother's Union but there is no doubt that, in the words of one contemporary historian, it offered Anglican women in widely diverse circumstances "a sense of belonging to an organization which valued the reality of their lives."[15]

RURAL MINISTRY IN THE CHURCH OF ENGLAND

If the focus of the Church of England's attention had turned to the critical need for enlightened and committed ministry in the cities, the small country parishes that had once provided ministry to a rural majority found both their numbers and their importance considerably reduced. By the end of Victoria's reign the gentlemen clergy of an earlier age had mostly been replaced by clergy with a "narrower, more specialized outlook than [their] old-style predecessor." Brenda Collins' study of rural clergy attributes the change to the fact that most rural clergy had prepared for ordination not at the great universities but in the more restrictive environment of a theological college, while the role of the churches in the countryside was itself greatly reduced. But the figures associated with country churches at the end of the nineteenth century were often deeply dedicated to their work: The Rev. William Kingsley was "still a working parson on his hundredth birthday."[16]

A 1901 study of the religious situation in England summed up the effects of the last century on the life of the churches in England. Most poor and working-class men, it found, did not go to church; "tradesmen and the middle class of the poorer boroughs" were active but more likely to attend Baptist or other non-conformist churches than the Church of England; and the strength of all the churches lay with the burgeoning population of the suburbs. Chadwick observes that in the last decades of the century many people noted and wondered that substantially more women than men participated in the Church.[17]

RELIGIOUS ORDERS IN VICTORIAN ENGLAND

The Oxford Movement, which had begun in 1833, continued to shape the ministry of the Church of England throughout Victoria's reign and beyond. As an increasing number of clergy sought to practice their ministry with regard not only to the medieval past but to the continuing example of the Roman Catholic and Eastern Orthodox traditions, it was perhaps inevitable that proposals for a structured ascetic life in community, abolished by Henry VIII, should reappear. By 1850, the notion had become popular enough that it was ridiculed in the British humor magazine *Punch*.[18]

The initial movement towards restoring the religious life for women was motivated in part by the example of the social ministry undertaken by the Roman Catholic Sisters of Mercy. As early as 1845, the Sisterhood of the Holy Cross had been established in the Church of England, with a rule devised by the Oxford Movement's leader Edward Pusey. The sisters worked with orphans and established a school for poor children. Their presence in a city parish, its rector wrote, initially caused alarm: The parishioners "do not know what to make of the Sisters, suspect them of being disguised Roman Catholics. . . . The result is that the usefulness of the Sisterhood is greatly threatened; the poor are regarding them with suspicion instead of love and veneration."[19]

A similar community, the "Church of England Sisterhood of Mercy of Devonport and Plymouth," was established in the diocese of Exeter three years later. Its first Superior, whom Pusey called "the restorer after three centuries of the religious life in the English Church," was a remarkable woman named Priscilla Lydia Sellon. Working in the most densely populated area in England, with 130,000 people to the square mile, and in which the only place of worship was a room over a beer shop, Lydia Sellon and her companions established schools for poor boys and girls in the face of vicious opposition from Evangelical clergy and laity. A public inquiry chaired by the Bishop of Exeter followed, in which the community was completely vindicated.[20] The sisters gained considerable recognition for their ministry during a cholera epidemic which swept through the poor neighborhoods of the Devon ports. One priest who accompanied them wrote in the aftermath, "[N]ever have I witnessed anything that surpassed or even equaled the self-abandonment of these humble Sisters. It was not merely the nursing and tending the sick. . . . There was a halo of sanctity around the persons of these calm Sisters which inspire hope . . ."[21]

In 1854, eight sisters from the two orders accompanied Florence Nightingale to work as nurses during the Crimean War. The two orders were joined in 1856; some years later, Mother Lydia herself accompanied a team of sisters who went to work in Hawaii in response to an invitation from Queen Emma, who became an associate of the Society.[22] The order ultimately declined, but a third order dating from the decade of the 1840s, the Community of St. Mary the Virgin, not only survived but flourished, ultimately participating in missions to India and South Africa.[23]

In 1863, Joseph Lyne, who took the religious name "Father Ignatius," undertook the establishment of a Benedictine community at Claydon Rectory, Suffolk—"the first Benedictine monastery in communion with Canterbury since the Reformation." While applauding the community's youthful energy, Bishop Wilberforce of Oxford found much to criticize: "You are sacrificing yourself," he wrote, "to the puerile imitation of a past phase of service which is just as impossible for you to revive in England as it would be to resuscitate an Egyptian mummy and set it upon the throne of the pharaohs." Though Lyne became a figure of public controversy, his community never had more than six members and he ultimately left the Church of England.[24]

Two years after Lyne's initial efforts, S. W. O'Neill, curate at Wantage, Oxfordshire, proposed a community for men which would serve "the perfection of our church and her success in propagating the gospel." Its spirit, he suggested, "must be the same as that which of old inspired the rules of so many great orders, but its form must be adapted to the present time." O'Neill proposed that the Bishop of Oxford approve the establishment of a community which would have a permanent presence in London to be dedicated to mission and address "the dangers of the fashions and scepticism of the present day," as well as a house in Oxford where scholars would live under a religious rule, with a special commitment to provide religious retreats and also to participate in the overseas mission of the Church. Bishop Wilberforce responded positively to the proposal and the following year the Society of Saint John the Evangelist established its Mission House at Cowley, Oxford. In 1870, two of its members traveled to the United States to establish a branch of the "Cowley Fathers." The Society eventually undertook mission work in India, South Africa and Canada.[25]

The early years of the Cowley Fathers are most associated with its Father Founder, Richard M. Benson. Father Benson worked tirelessly to strengthen the presence of religious communities both in England and in the United States. One Cowley priest who wrote about Father Benson many years later observed that his career was "in the strictest sense a continuation and a spiritual application of the deepest life-energy of the [Oxford] Movement."[26]

Benson considered that the vocation to the religious life was a special call to personal sanctification and to the life of the community, alongside that call to faithfulness which every Christian receives. He understood it to be "subordinated to the life of the Church." On the other hand, he believed that for those who accepted them, the vows of poverty, chastity and obedience are not merely "counsels of moral improvement" but the "revelation of divine grace." Hence, "things which are trifles in the laity are enormities in priests," and still more in the case of religious because they represent violations not only against their calling to the Church but their own sanctification. Like his medieval predecessors, Benson believed that the religious life represented a "higher calling" which benefits not only those who receive and accept it but those members of the Body of Christ who live in the secular world.[27]

While most churches of the Anglican Communion have long been accustomed to the ministry of religious orders, their reappearance in the Church of England provoked fierce controversy which lasted for many years. The conflict even affected public opinion about a famous murder case, in which a young woman suspected of killing her half-sister confessed to the crime after an extended stay with the sisters of the Community of St. Mary. The Rev. James Davies wrote that it was life with the sisters which had inspired her to confess: "The devoted lives, the self-denying discipline which she saw around her, and the very atmosphere which she breathed within the holy retreat, subdued, or melted—moulded her as a preparation." Others, however, had a very different opinion. Many Anglicans would have agreed with the Congregational minister who "cast doubt on the substitute religious families to which a young woman might 'submit herself' without her natural family's assent"; indeed, one of the strongest criticisms against the new orders as they seemed to be challenging or eroding the highly structured (and patriarchal) authority of the Victorian family.[28]

URBAN MINISTRY IN THE LATE NINETEENTH CENTURY: ENGLAND

The grim conditions which had piqued the consciences of Maurice, Kingsley and others at mid-century did not significantly improve during Victoria's reign. Believing that Christians could not continue to acquiesce in the misery that surrounded them, both Anglicans and members of other denominations initiated a number of Church-oriented responses. Perhaps one of the best-known was the Salvation Army, a lay organization organized on military lines by its founder, William Booth, in 1865. Its street rallies, bands and clarion calls for conversion made a dramatic impact in the poor neighborhoods of London. Some Anglicans responded negatively to what they considered the "vulgarization" of religion but others noted the success of its approach. In 1882, William Carlile, a curate in north London, organized the Church Army on similar lines but with the added goal of bringing the poor back into the Church of England. Three years later, the bishops of the Convocation of Canterbury gave the Church Army their unanimous approval, a training house was opened and within less than twenty years more than a thousand workers had been prepared for ministry.[29]

Growing awareness of the special challenges of urban ministry provided the impetus for a call for the development of new pastoral skills on the part of city clergy. In 1887 John Gott, the Dean of Worcester Cathedral (and future

Bishop of Truro), warned Cambridge University students preparing for ordination that their congregations were better educated and demanded awareness and wisdom from their clergy. Urban life, he observed, "is more intense"; "a city day has more time than a village day."[30] Gott believed that city clergy required organizational as well as communication skills, and should hold their congregations to high standards; he recommended communicant classes for both regular attenders and "backsliders" and twice-weekly Confirmation classes for two months.[31]

Gott was aware not only of the priest's traditional responsibility for the entire population of the parish but of the enormous challenge such a charge represented for urban clergy. He understood the danger of clergy burn-out and analyzed its many possible causes: a shallow spiritual life, what might be called spiritual fatigue, the press of overwork, the conflicts within the Church, "forgetfulness of God's presence" and "self-indulgence." In the face of such pitfalls, he urged his students to pay special attention to their own spiritual disciplines and to be careful to renew their baptismal and ordination vows yearly.[32]

Gott may be taken as an example of the Anglican priest who worked hard at developing a broad sense of the style of ministry called for in the complexity of an industrial city. He spoke from the vantage point of his experience not only as a cathedral dean but as Vicar of Leeds, one of the early centers of English industrial development. (Perhaps his attentive perspective to the duties of that charge was influenced by the fact that his grandfather had been responsible for introducing the factory system so characteristic of the Industrial Revolution into that city's woolen trade.)[33]

The remarkable figure of one of England's longest-reigning monarchs loomed over and above the complex history of the Church of England as it struggled to deal with the realities of the late nineteenth century. Victoria took her role as "supreme governor" of the Church of England seriously, and while the choice of bishops rested with the Prime Minister, she was accustomed to propose names and occasionally to veto his choices. She abhorred extremists of any persuasion, a characterization she used for both Evangelicals and Anglo-Catholics. Like her royal predecessors, Victoria seems to have assumed that the rigid social distinctions of English society were part of the "natural order" established by God for the well-being of creation, an assumption that extended to her unquestioning support for England's right to govern many of the other peoples of the world, not only for the well-being of her own English subjects but for their own. Chadwick notes her preference for "learned men" whom she "expected to be liberal." Her attitude towards those who addressed the needs of the poor was uniformly negative: the Queen, it was reported, "can't understand why the clergy should go fussing about the poor and servants. . . ."[34]

But both clergy and committed laypeople did in fact continue to "fuss" about the poor throughout her reign. The shape of their ministries was determined in part by their understanding of the nature of the Church and its mission, but also by the unspeakable misery in which so many English people were forced to live and work.

The social historian Bill Bryson noted the frequency with which the British press at mid-century published revelations of the conditions in which both slum-dwellers and the poor forced to live in public Workhouses were housed. Such publicity created what he calls a "new breed of benefactors" who

> began to found an extraordinary range of organizations—a Committee for Promoting the Establishment of Baths and Wash Houses for the Labouring Classes, a Society for the Suppression of Juvenile Vagrancy, a Society for Promoting Window Gardening Amongst the Working Classes of Westminster, even a Society for the Rescue of Boys Not Yet Convicted of Any Criminal Offense—nearly always with the hope of helping the poor to remain or become sober, Christian, industrious, hygienic, law-abiding, parentally responsible, or otherwise virtuous. Still others strived to improve housing conditions for the poor.[35]

The remarkable Ritualist ministry of St. George-in-the-East at mid-century served as a model for a number of zealous Anglo-Catholic clergy during the next decades. Throughout the East End of London and in other metropolitan centers, Anglican clergy set about elaborating rules of life for clergy staff that mimicked the monastic rules being developed in religious communities. The Daily Offices and Eucharist formed the heart of their spiritual discipline; the Eucharist was customarily celebrated with liturgical elements drawn from pre-Reformation English Catholicism and the contemporary Roman Catholic Church. Increasing numbers of churches restored devotion to the Virgin Mary and other saints, as well as to Christ present in the reserved Sacrament. (The "Confraternity of the Blessed Sacrament" was established in 1862 to encourage Anglicans to reverence the Sacrament and to make reparation for the many ways in which they believed the Sacrament was denigrated by others.)[36] The clergy responsible for urban ministry with Anglo-Catholic trappings argued that their parishioners lived uniformly drab and venal lives of misery. They could, it was claimed, profit most from worship that provided a clear sense of the intimate presence of Christ through the Eucharist, a transcendent awareness of community through the Communion of Saints, a heightened moral sense through the rigorous practice of regular Confession, and an experience of the "beauty of holiness" through the elaborate drama of a Solemn High Mass.

One of the figures most closely identified with the Ritualism which grew out of the Oxford movement was Alexander Heriot Machonochie. After a brief period as curate at Wantage, he was assigned to St. George-in-the-East during the rector's absence. Like his predecessor Bryan King, Machonochie soon found himself at the center of a situation spinning out of control: "Last Sunday afternoon," he reported, "the curate fell down in a fit in the middle of the service . . . followed by a most horrible row and at last fighting." For several weeks the parish was wracked by rioting, while Machonochie's requests for police protection went unanswered.[37]

Machonochie's ministry at St. George's was followed by a number of years at St. Alban's, Holborn, which was designed as a "free church," "built especially for the sake of the poor." Its immediate neighborhood was described as an area of "dark courts and high tenement buildings"; one space of 1500 by 600 feet housed eight thousand people. The church was built by two philanthropists and Machonochie was given free rein to establish a clergy house staffed with five priests. The clergy were expected to keep a semi-monastic rule, to engage in constant visits to the homes of their poor neighbors, and to maintain open hours at the Clergy House every evening.[38]

By 1863, ritualism was spreading rapidly, especially in the parishes of East London and other urban slum areas. Opposition from both Evangelicals and liberal Broad-Church advocates increased, and St. Alban's Holborn continued to be the focus of attention and concern. In response to a suit, the Court of Arches decreed that many of the liturgical changes popular in Ritualist parishes, such as elevating the elements of Communion, the use of incense and mixing the Communion wine with water were illegal. Machonochie found himself forced to defend his liturgical practices in court in four consecutive years, once suffering suspension for three months.[39] But while the controversial ministry of Machonochie and his team of clergy was battered by opponents beyond the parish, the poor of Holborn responded with loyalty and devotion. Two thousand communicants signed a petition to the Bishop of London in support of their ministry. In a meeting with the bishop, a committee of working men from the congregation warned him, "This is a working man's question, and when the working classes in this country become aware of the way in which their heritage in Church matters is attacked, they will rise up, and the Church of England, as an Established Church, will fall."[40]

The historian Bernard Markwell considers that in the generation following the work of F. D. Maurice and the Christian Socialists at mid-century, it was the religious orders and the Ritualist Anglo-Catholics who kept alive the urgency about ministry in the urban slums.[41] Edward Pusey, one of the original pillars of the Oxford Movement, did much to encourage Anglo-Catholics to take ministry with the poor with appropriate seriousness, both by inspiring young people and nurturing the earliest religious communities and their work.

He took every opportunity to draw the connection between sacrificial ministry and a rich sacramental life. "If we would see [Christ] in His sacraments," he wrote, "We must also see Him wherever He has declared himself to be, and especially in his poor . . . The poor are the Church's special treasure, as the Gospel is their special property." Stressing the *holiness* of the poor, Pusey imagined "organized bodies of clergy," living among the poor, would form "the vanguard of this revolution. . . ." The task, he argued, "is to grapple with our manufacturing system as the Apostles did with the slave system of the ancient world."[42]

While they garnered less attention in their own time and in subsequent generations, Evangelicals also made their presence known in the London slums, none better known than John Edwin Watts-Ditchfield. At the age of eight he had been a worker in a cotton mill, and is described as "a determined social reformer," a stance rooted in his incarnational theology. Christ's life, he wrote, "was largely concerned with the material and physical improvement of man [sic]. His words as judge . . . take cognisance only of what today be called 'social work,' and strangely enough, omit all reference to what we are accustomed to regard as purely spiritual needs of men." From the beginning of his ministry, Watts-Ditchfield was a tireless visitor in the homes of the poor and conducted special Sunday afternoon services for the men of the parish. From an initial attendance of 120, soon 800 men were participating in a service which he described as intending "to lead men through Christ to a higher, purer, and nobler life in God, and to prove that Christianity is not a failure, but the one thing that can make a true man—a gentleman, indeed, in the highest sense . . . To accomplish this, the character of the service is distinctly a religious one, while at the same time it is one in which all can join, and which all can thoroughly enjoy." When he took the idea of the Men's Service with him to the parish of Bethnal Green, in East London,

> An hour and a half before the service, the Vicar assembled a brass band and toured a portion of the parish, handing out printed invitations, stopping at every important street corner and before each of the public houses for the Vicar to give a short address. . . . The Men's Service itself followed a very simple format. Neither the Book of Common Prayer nor an Anglican hymnal was used. Rather, a small orchestra supported the singing of hymns from Sankey's book [of gospel songs]. Watts-Ditchfield preached extemporaneously for about thirty minutes, and the service concluded with simple prayers and a blessing.[43]

The figure of Stewart Headlam is often associated with the urban ministry undertaken in England in the later decades of the nineteenth century, combining as he did insights from both an earlier generation of Christian Socialists and the sacramental emphasis of the Anglo-Catholics. Headlam also served at

St. Matthew's Church in the Bethnal Green area of East London, and though he rejected aspects of the theology associated with the Ritualists, his respect for their pastoral ministry led him to adopt much of their liturgical and pastoral style. Like Maurice before him, Headlam believed that baptism reveals the true nature of all humankind as children of God; this belief led him to assert the fundamental equality of all, and equality that is not only spiritual, as Maurice would have had it, but is material as well: Every time the clergy baptize the "labourer's little baby, [they are] bearing witness to the truths of equality in a more far-reaching way than any French Revolution."[44]

Headlam's theology, built as it was on an understanding of the Incarnation that affirmed the goodness and beauty of creation, led him to some radically unpopular behavior in the course of his long ministry. "All joy, mirth, beauty are sanctified" by the Eucharist, he asserted. It was this belief that impelled him to establish the "Church and Stage Guild," through which he proposed to extend ministry to those engaged in show business, and especially the music halls that lit up the lives of countless poor English workers but were conspicuously ignored or condemned by a Church that continued to identify itself with the most respectable classes of English society.[45]

Headlam also founded and directed the Guild of St. Matthew, which is generally understood to have carried on the Christian Socialist principles outlined by Maurice a generation earlier. Headlam was one of the earliest voices among the English clergy willing to call into question the fundamental capitalist principles on which the British economy was based and which had been generally assumed to reflect the natural law of a supremely orderly God. His understanding of socialism was not dependent on Marxism, which he considered inevitably oppressive, nor did he support the nascent Independent Labour Party, on the grounds that its agenda was too narrowly focused on the participation of the working class. No secular party, he argued, could adequately further a vision of society which was ultimately based on a vision of the reign of God.[46]

No aspect of the ministry undertaken by Headlam was more problematic than his embrace of music hall culture, which led to his dismissal as curate at St. Matthew's and later to the bishop of London's refusal to license him to preach. As the historian John Richard Orens observes, "In the beauty of the dance . . . Headlam saw a sign of the Kingdom of God. To watch the human body, the temple of the Holy Spirit, in motion was to witness a sacrament: the presence of God in flesh. The same Lord worshipped in the Mass was present on the stage of the Alhambra." While aware of Headlam's mistakes and shortcomings, Orens considers him to be "a powerful and prophetic voice who helped awaken the Church to its social mission, and socialists to the danger of collectivist tyranny."[47] Indeed, the full impact of his work on the future of ministry in the Church of England would only become clear in the generations that followed him. His was one of the strongest voices articulating the reality of the Incarnation as the foundation of all the Church's social ministry.

NOTES

1. Owen Chadwick, *The Victorian Church,* II (London: Adam and Charles Black, 1966), 10, 13.

2. Chadwick, *The Victorian Church,* 154–157.

3. F. W. B. Bullock, *A History of Training for the Ministry of the Church of England in England and Wales* (St. Leonard's-on-Sea, UK: Budd and Gillatt, 1955), 95, 129.

4. Bullock, *History of Training,* 131.

5. Chadwick, *The Victorian Church,* II, 24, 35.

6. Chadwick, *The Victorian Church,* II, 163–164, 192.

7. Chadwick, *The Victorian Church* II, 189, 218, 221, 244, 256.

8. Kate Summerscale, *The Suspicions of Mr. Whicher or The Murders at Road Hill House* (London: Bloomsbury, 2008), 109.

9. Hippolyte Taine, quoted in Summerscale, *Suspicions,* 109.

10. John Henry Blunt, *Directorium Pastorale: The Principles and Practice of Pastoral Work in the Church of England* (London: Rivingtons, 1872), v, 5, 80–87.

11. Chadwick, *The Victorian Church,* II, 200.

12. Cordelia Moyse, *A History of the Mothers' Union: Women, Anglicanism and Globalization 1876–2008* (Woodbridge, Suffolk: Boydell Press, 2009), 18–22.

13. Moyse, *Mothers' Union,* 22, 26–27, 32–34, 38.

14. Moyse, *Mothers' Union,* 28, 65–66, 68–69.

15. Moyse, *Mothers' Union,* 78–83, 90–91.

16. Brenda Collins, *Victorian Country Parsons* (London: Book Club Associates, 1977), 31, 34.

17. Chadwick, *The Victorian Church,* II, 222, 235.

18. Peter F. Hanson, revised and edited by A. W. Campbell, *The Call of the Cloister: Religious Communities and Kindred Bodies in the Anglican Communion* (London: SPCK, 1964), 47.

19. Charles H. Harrison, *The Religious Orders of the Anglican Communion,* unpublished dissertation, Divinity School, University of Chicago, 1932, 8.

20. Thomas Jay Williams, *Priscilla Lydia Sellon: The Restorer After Three Centuries of the Religious Life in the English Church* (London: SPCK, 1950), xxi, 35–36, 38–39, 43, 58.

21. Williams, *Sellon,* 75.

22. Wiliams, *Sellon,* 183, 223, 236.

23. Hanson, *The Call of the Cloister,* 228–229, 232–233, 239, 241, 242ff.

24. Hanson, *The Call of the Cloister,* 53, 58–59, 68.

25. Hanson, *The Call of the Cloister,* 74–75, 77–78. 81, 84ff.

26. Lucius Cary, SSJE, in Richard M. Benson, *The Religious Vocation* (London: A. R. Mowbray & Co., 1939), 6.

27. *The Religious Vocation,* 48, 56, 92–93, 145, 151.
28. Kate Summerscale, *The Suspicions of Mr. Whicher,* 240.
29. Chadwick, *The Victorian Church,* II, 293–298.
30. John Gott, *The Parish Priest of the Town: Lectures Delivered in the Divinity School Cambridge* (London: SPCK, 1887), 6–7.
31. Gott, *The Parish Priest,* 102ff, 115.
32. Gott, *The Parish Priest,* 178, 195, 197–200.
33. Sidney Lee, ed., *The Dictionary of National Biography [Supplement January 1901 – December 1911]* (Oxford: Oxford University Press, 1912), 141.
34. Chadwick, *The Victorian Church,* II, 328–339.
35. Bill Bryson, *At Home: A Short History of Private Life* (New York: Doubleday, 2010), 421.
36. Hanson, *The Call of the Cloister,* 429.
37. Edward Francis Russell, ed., *Alexander Heriot Mackonochie: A Memoir* (New York: E. & J. B. Young & Co., 1890), 47, 55–61.
38. Russell, *Mackonochie,* 68–69, 81, 86.
39. Reed, *Glorious Battle* (Nashville: Vanderbilt University Press, 1996), 138, 148–157.
40. Reed, *Glorious Battle,* 161; Markwell, *The Anglican Left: Radical Social Reformers in the Church of England and the Protestant Episcopal Church, 1846–1954* (Brooklyn: Carlson Publishing, Inc., 1991), 42.
41. Markwell, *The Anglican Left,* 41.
42. Markwell, *The Anglican Left,* 32–36.
43. David B. McIlhiney, *A Gentleman in Every Slum: Church of England Missions in East London 1837 – 1914* (Allison Park, PA: Pickwick Publications, 1988), 77–78, 80, 82–83.
44. John Richard Orens, "Christ, Communism and Chorus Girls: A Reassessment of Stewart Headlam," in *Historical Magazine of the Protestant Episcopal Church,* Vol. 49 (September 1980), 238.
45. McIlhiney, *A Gentleman in Every Slum,* 238–239.
46. McIlhiney, *A Gentleman in Every Slum,* 244–245.
47. McIlhiney, *A Gentleman in Every Slum,* 246–247.

Chapter Ten

Britannia

Ministry in the British Empire, 1850–1900

The nineteenth century was undoubtedly a time when Anglican ministry was shaken by differences and conflicts. It was also, however, a century in which the Anglo-Saxon peoples on both sides of the Atlantic rested comfortably on the assumptions that whatever their differences, their culture and institutions were manifestly superior to those of the rest of the world. Perhaps no one spelled out those assumptions more clearly than Cecil Rhodes, who served as Britain's governor of Cape Colony in the late nineteenth century and was responsible for extending British control over what are today Botswana, Zambia and Zimbabwe. He wrote,

> I contend that we are the first race in the world, and that the more of the world we inhabit the better it is for the human race . . . [G]od is manifestly fashioning the English speaking race as the chosen instrument by which he [sic] will bring in a state of society based upon Justice, Liberty and Peace . . . I think what he would like me to do is to paint as much of the map of Africa British red as possible.[1]

MINISTRY IN WEST AFRICA

By the time Rhodes became a major figure in colonial Africa, Anglican missions already stretched across the continent's mid-section. A historian of the Church Missionary Society noted that from the point of view of the CMS, western Africa represented "a clean slate," "free of complications" represented by bishops, the Company, chaplains or ancient Christian churches. One of the principal goals of the CMS presence in west Africa was to bring to an end the practice of slavery. The mission to the Yoruba people, which had already begun in 1846, was followed by the development of the Niger Mission, culminating in the 1864 consecration of Samuel Adjai Crowther in Westminster Abbey to be its head. Crowther was the first person of African ancestry to be consecrated a bishop in the Church of England.[2]

Crowther had already proved to be an extremely effective missionary, negotiating with village chieftains to permit the establishment of Church missions and especially of schools, which he considered the cornerstone of evangelization in Africa. Crowther's own teaching style was simple and straightforward, and he personally oversaw the translations of both scriptures and educational materials into several languages of the Nigerian Delta. He believed that "as far as possible principles and insights with which the hearers were familiar were to be used in preaching the Gospel." Unlike some missionaries, who feared to introduce Africans to Biblical references to sacrifices for fear that they would equate them with their own tribal practices, he argued that "the widespread practice of animal sacrifice provided a useful basis for teaching about the efficacy of the blood of Jesus Christ."[3]

Crowther's consecration focused a serious conflict within the CMS on the policy of local leadership, a cornerstone of Venn's understanding of missionary methods. Crowther had been ordained to the priesthood in 1843, and Venn oversaw the ordination of two more African clergy in 1854 and another three in 1857. In Sierra Leone, native pastors were placed in charge of the colony's congregations. Venn's program was vigorously opposed by an outspoken CMS missionary working in the Niger region named Henry Townsend, who argued strongly against Crowther's consecration. Crowther, he argued, was seen by other Africans as "the white man's inferior. . . . This state of things is not the result of the white men's teaching but has existed for ages past. The superiority of the white over the black man, the Negro has been forward to acknowledge. The correctness of this belief no white man can deny."[4]

The response of the CMS leadership in London was ambiguous, affirming Crowther's episcopal ministry but ultimately ruling that he would have no authority over those Nigerian towns where white missionaries were located. This state of affairs continued until 1879, when the new secretary of CMS removed Crowther from authority over the African workers in the Niger Mission. This was followed by the drafting of a secret report critical of Crowther's administration in 1880, and the dismissal of twelve out of fifteen African clergy in 1890 by the secretary of a commission assigned to investigate the administration of the Niger Mission. Shocked at this challenge to his authority, Crowther objected and was reprimanded and dismissed from the commission.

Crowther's son, Dandeson Crowther, played an important and controversial role in the development of Anglican ministry in Nigeria both during and after his father's ministry. In 1871, he assumed responsibility for two thriving mission stations, and succeeded in making significant inroads both in persuading converts to give up their traditional religious practices and also in ending the traditional custom of destroying twins at birth. In 1874, Dandeson Crowther was appointed Archdeacon of the Lower Niger. Like others of his generation, he

> evinced the drive and social aspirations of their parents but not their subservient piety. . . . Independent, confident, and considerably less in awe of political and ecclesiastical authority than their parents, . . . to European eyes they often appeared arrogant and pretentious, in part because they were prone to challenge the ethnocentrism and dominance that was so much a part of European missionary enterprise. . . .[5]

While the mission in the Niger Delta enjoyed remarkable success, it did not escape persecution. In 1875, Joshua Hart, a Native convert, was killed for refusing to eat meat that had been sacrificed to idols. A major persecution that followed came to an end when the chief responsible accepted Christianity and oversaw the dumping of two boatloads of tribal deities into a nearby river. Within a short time, a nearby church regularly welcomed a thousand worshippers to its services.[6]

But the actions of the CMS investigative committee in disciplining Bishop Crowther and limiting his authority were followed by the Society's decision to establish English authority over the entire Niger Mission, which had been organized as a "Native Church" for more than a decade. Their actions provoked a strong reaction from Crowther's son and many other African clergy.

> The archdeacon embarked on a tour of West Africa, during which he addressed congregations and church committees in the native pastorates of both Lagos and Sierra Leone. As one of the most respected leaders in the Niger Mission, and one who had only recently suffered from European domination of the Niger, what he had to say had great impact. The press made the most of it. His own personal grievances aside, he was resolved then that a mission like the delta, which had thrived so well without European involvement and was partly self-supporting, could well survive independently of foreign assistance. He had found the attitudes and actions of the European missionaries most objectionable and was convinced that the issue of race was at the bottom of the crisis. Wherever he went he asserted that "on the Niger the African was simply a victim of white racial prejudice." This belief fired him with a determination to prove that Africans were capable of running their own affairs without European intervention.

The following year, the CMS issued a report "deplor[ing] the low moral and spiritual condition of the Niger congregations" and announcing its intention to impose English leadership, including a bishop, on the Delta Ministry. With the support of clergy throughout the Delta and especially from Sierra Leone, in 1892 Dandeson Crowther declared the independence of the Niger Delta Native Pastorate, which comprised five mission stations.[7]

While Crowther and his colleagues argued that they were simply following the principles established by Henry Venn in establishing a "Native Church," in fact none of the clergy was native to the area and all had to learn the local language in order to perform their ministry. On the other hand, the concept was "used in its broadest sense to mean any African (particularly West Africans) who happened to be working in the Niger at the time, as opposed to Europeans. After all, the issue at stake (as these protagonists perceived it) was not ethnic identity but racial integrity." (The term "native" was later dropped from the name of the ministry.)[8]

The Niger Delta Pastorate continued independently of the CMS for twenty years; the CMS eventually came to appreciate its effectiveness sufficiently to turn control of one of its own mission stations over to the Pastorate. Ultimately its ministry grew to over 120 mission stations and encompassed an area that extended fifty miles into new territory. The Church of England refused, however, to give the Pastorate its own bishop, and it was perennially short of both financial and clerical resources. Dandeson Crowther always insisted that the Pastorate was an Anglican body, and after two decades, it surrendered its independent identity and submitted to the authority of the Church of England and its bishops.[9]

THE UNIVERSITIES MISSION TO CENTRAL AFRICA

The return in 1856 of the British medical missionary and explorer David Livingstone to England after fifteen years in Africa electrified the British public. Dedicated to "commerce and Christianity," the spread of British "civilization" and an end to the slave trade still rampant in the Portuguese colonies, he appealed especially to the communities of Oxford and Cambridge to carry on the work to which he had dedicated his life. In response, the Oxford and Cambridge Mission to Central Africa was established in 1859. Durham and Dublin Universities soon joined in what became the "Universities Mission to Central Africa" (UMCA), dedicated to "the establishment of one or more Stations in Southern Central Africa, which may serve as centres of commerce and Christianity, for the promotion of the spread of true religion, agriculture, and lawful commerce, and the ultimate extirpation of the slave trade." Pusey and Keble, the venerable leaders of the Oxford Movement, lent their support and the UMCA emphasized the importance of a missionary bishop who would reflect the Movement's "insistence on ecclesiastical order."[10]

In 1861, Robert Gray, Bishop of Cape Town, consecrated Charles Mackenzie, a young priest serving as an archdeacon in the British colony of Natal, as the Church of England's first missionary bishop. He began his work accompanied by a team consisting of two clergy, a lay "superintendent," a carpenter and an agricultural laborer, and traveled with Livingstone and his party into the region of the Zambezi River. Even before they reached the site of their proposed mission station, they met a slave party, and intervened to set eighty-four newly captured enslaved persons free, "giving the Universities Mission an instant flock."[11] The party soon found itself in the position of defending the freed slaves' tribe from a marauding tribe that captured slaves for Arab traders. At the request of the chief, the missionaries agreed to participate in a raid on their enemies' village, with the stipulation that no prisoners be taken. The ensuing battle, "aimed," as the bishop wrote, at "striking a death-blow to the slave trade," resulted in the death of five members of the enemy tribe; Bishop Mackenzie had himself led the attack and participated in the fighting.[12]

Mackenzie and his team attempted to establish a mission reflecting the principles of the Oxford Movement: daily Morning and Evening Prayer, the Eucharist on Sundays and holy days, and Sunday Bible reading with any who were willing to participate. But tribal conflicts continued to plague the settlement, and Mackenzie himself died of tropical illness early in 1862.

The news of the mission's involvement in tribal warfare and the death of the first missionary bishop caused consternation among many in England, including the supporters of the UMCA. But the organization survived, and Mackenzie was succeeded by another missionary bishop, William Tozer. Bishop Tozer relocated the UMCA mission to the island of Zanzibar, where a mission school was established and extensive ministry with children rescued from slavery was undertaken.[13] Bishop Tozer's successor led the UMCA back to Central Africa, and successfully established a chain of mission stations around the area of Lake Malawi, which effectively established a permanent Anglican ministry in Central Africa. (One site was reportedly chosen by a group of freed slaves who accompanied the missionaries, who considered it to be similar to the birthplace for which they were searching.)[14]

EAST AFRICA

The East Africa Mission was established by CMS in the 1840s but entered a lengthy period of dormancy. At mid-century, Arab traders continued to engage in the slave trade along the continent's eastern coast, and British ships were occasionally able to intercept them, remove the Africans who had been taken prisoner, and take them to India. An "African Asylum" established in

India, funded by the British government, eventually provided housing and some practical education to some two hundred formerly enslaved people. Six were eventually sent back to Africa as missionaries; two of the men later became the first Native clergy in the Eastern Equatorial Africa Mission.[15]

CMS's mission was revitalized in 1874. Work in what is today Uganda began in 1876, but it was not until six years later that the first Ugandan converts were baptized. James Hannington, first bishop of Eastern Equatorial Africa, was an English country parson who was moved to volunteer for service in Africa by the murders of two earlier missionaries and the publication of a letter from the explorer David Stanley in which he challenged "Christendom to send missionaries to Uganda."[16] In 1882, he made a five-year commitment to the Church Missionary Society, and after a brief visit cut short by illness, he returned with a team of missionaries to begin the establishment of an Anglican presence in central Africa. The team consisted of twelve clergy, eleven laymen, and the wives of four of the team's members.

Hannington decided to search for an overland route from Kenya, and set out in 1885 with several companions and a caravan of porters from Free Town, on the coast of the Indian Ocean. Hannington seems to have embraced his role as missionary bishop with enthusiasm. His party were greeted warmly as they made their way from one mission station to the next; at one stop they were able to rescue enslaved persons from Somalian traders, while at another, "the natives welcomed him with a four-hours' carnival of gun-firing, shouting and dancing," in which the bishop joined. In return, Hannington offered a feast for six hundred guests. During the feast, he discovered that two of his porters were guilty of petty theft; he responded by having them "tied up to posts in sight of the guests." On another occasion, he chased and killed an elephant to provide meat for his party.[17]

Hannington's approach to Uganda brought him into the territory controlled by the Kabaka (king) Mwanga II of Buganda, the largest and most powerful among the Ugandan tribal groupings. Mwanga was fearful that the Christian missionaries represented a threat to Bugandan independence, and ordered a subordinate tribe to stop and imprison Hannington and his party. Some of the members of his caravan escaped, but many were speared to death. After a lengthy and painful imprisonment, Hannington himself was murdered. The following year a group of thirty-two Anglican and Roman Catholic men and boys, most of them pages in Mwanga's court, refused his sexual advances and were also executed. Hannington and these other victims of the Bugandan king are known and commemorated throughout the Anglican Communion as "the martyrs of Uganda."[18]

In the years following, Anglican ministry in East Africa grew and was also shaped by forces over which it had little control. Germany and Great Britain were jockeying for political control over the entire eastern part of the continent, a dispute that was settled in 1890 by a treaty ceding coastal East Africa to Britain. A. R. Tucker, the first Bishop of Uganda, took up his duties in 1891. Describing his arrival, he wrote:

> No words can describe the emotion which filled my heart as . . . I stood up to speak to fully 1000 men and women who crowded the church of Buganda. It was a wonderful sight! There close beside me, was the Katikiro—the second man in the kingdom [of Buganda]. There, on every hand, were chiefs of various degrees, all Christian men, and all in their demeanor devout and earnest to degree.

Bishop Tucker ordained two of the missionaries who had accompanied him from England, confirmed seventy new Anglicans and commissioned six native lay evangelists, three of whom had refused chieftainships for the sake of full-time ministry.[19]

Tucker had been an artist before embracing his clerical vocation, and his reports to CMS headquarters regularly included sketches of the African landscape and especially of the people and places associated with his ministry. Like most ministries associated with the spread of Anglicanism under the aegis of the Empire, Bishop Tucker's work reveals deep ambiguities. He eagerly embraced British control of East Africa and the model of authoritarian leadership identified with the Empire, and one contemporary historian points out that his sketches enabled CMS personnel in England to make decisions about its East African ministry without any first-hand knowledge of the reality of its mission field. Joan Plubell Mattia categorizes them as "part of the process of abstraction, which helped to contribute to the presence and operation of the Victorian Empire in East Africa, making East African knowledge a subset of European knowledge."[20]

On the other hand, Tucker embraced the idea of developing a "native church" under African leadership, and throughout his episcopate he lived in a reed and mud house even when other CMS missionaries were given European-style houses. "The objects at which we aim (or rather ought to aim)," he wrote, "is so to carry on our work so that gradually one European missionary after another, as the native church becomes stronger, may be withdrawn until at last she stands alone, strong in the Lord and in the power of his might." Furthermore, he opposed the colonial government, particularly with regard to its policy of forcing Africans to work on Uganda's cotton plantations, which brought suffering to the workers and also impeded the development of an economy in African hands. He ordained forty-seven Africans during his ministry, and the Constitution he wrote for the Church in Uganda integrated missionaries and African priests.[21]

The last years of the nineteenth century were difficult ones for Anglican ministry in East Africa. Conflicts, sometimes violent, between Roman Catholics and Anglicans and between Christians and Muslims marred the mission. Tribal allegiances often undercut church identity, and the unpredictability of Mwanga made ministry uncertain. Yet the Anglican ministry grew. In 1893, the first six Native clergy were ordained as deacons, two of whom were important chiefs who governed whole provinces. A Native Church Council supervised construction of a church building with five hundred trees as pillars, paid for with a contribution of one shell from each of the nearly four thousand people who attended it. The Council also arranged for Bible classes and "in 1892 they appointed six female 'elders,' 'to help in teaching the girls and women, and to look into the private life of the women who came for baptism.'"[22]

In 1893, some of the English missionaries, troubled by what they perceived as what they considered the "low level" of their converts' spiritual life, began a season of personal renewal including prayer, confession and consecration. "They then held special services, . . . telling [their congregation] plainly that they themselves had received a fresh baptism of the Holy Spirit, and inviting them to come to the Lord and claim the same blessing. The result overwhelmed them." Hundreds of people experienced a remarkable renewal of their faith and accepted new responsibilities within the church community. "In the following year twenty-three [Bible] classes were being held simultaneously, *every day,* before the early daily service; and after the service about the same number of classes for candidates for baptism."[23] This remarkable experience can be seen as a foretaste of the great East African Revival of the 1930s, which had such a powerful effect on Anglican mission and ministry in the Africa of the twentieth century.

SOUTH ASIA

In India, an unexpected and bloody outbreak of violence against the British presence, begun in 1857 among Indian soldiers of the Bengal Army, spread and continued into the following year. While its causes are many, undoubtedly the increasing activity of Christian missionaries was perceived by many Indians as a threat to their traditional religious identity and culture. In 1858, the charter of the East India Company was revoked and India passed under direct colonial rule in the form of the British "Raj."

As part of the British establishment, a role it occupied throughout the nineteenth century and well beyond, the Victorian Church in India was concerned to minister to the increasingly numerous English residents as well as in the evangelization of the Indian population.

The presence of SPG missionaries in various parts of India provided an alternative style of Anglican ministry to that of the CMS, with the result that the nature of Indian Anglicanism demonstrated significant diversity almost from its beginnings. By the middle of the nineteenth century, even though their numbers were small compared with the total population of the subcontinent Indian Anglicans outnumbered English expatriates.

> Recent studies of the results of missionary ministry in British India emphasize the social implications of large-scale conversion, especially among lower-caste women. Insistence on monogamy and dress judged more "decent" by Victorian standards had the effect of mimicking the behavior of upper-caste Indian women; Christian faith could therefore be seen as an avenue to higher social status, but at the expense of taking on some of the rigid restrictions that isolated and bound Brahmin women.[24]

The issue of caste which had complicated the practice of Anglican ministry in India from the beginning remained an issue throughout the nineteenth century. In the 1860s and 1870s, large number of Dalit, traditionally known as "untouchables," became Christians, usually through the decision of caste elders rather than by individual conversion. The education associated with Christian missions opened social and economic opportunities to a caste whose status had condemned them to inevitable misery.[25] Some Indian Christians considered the missionaries' attack on caste as "an aggressive attack on Indian social structure," and reminded them that caste was "the only basis on which they could maintain contact with their Hindu neighbors."[26]

In the southern region of Bengal, Anglican missionaries from the Oxford Mission and monks and nuns from England relied on schools and hostels for students as an important arm of evangelization in urban areas, but also attempted to penetrate into the villages far from the cities. They struggled with the practical issues related to their educational work: Should village children be sent on to high schools in the cities, or encouraged to remain at home?[27] By the end of the century, they were confronting incipient Indian nationalism and a revival of Hinduism.

In retrospect, many Indian Christians criticized the nature of the "church organizations imposed on them by the missions," and one missionary even came to believe that "the ways of the Anglican Church are not at all suitable for an Indian church." The problem, he asserted, was that "our Church *as a whole* has learnt ... to be patient of a great diversity of ways ... But the same cannot be said of Missionary Societies."[28] Perhaps he had in mind what was known at the time as the "Great Ceylon Controversy" which erupted in 1876 between the new Bishop of Ceylon, R. S. Copleston and the CMS.

The context of the controversy was a familiar one, in which missionaries of the CMS were working alongside English chaplains assigned to the pastoral care of the English planters; as the CMS Editorial Secretary observed, the difficulties experienced in new movements are "greatly complicated when evangelism among the Heathen, and the pastoral guidance of infant Native Churches, are going on side by side with ordinary ministrations for British settlers or British troops." The Bishop of Madras had asked for permission to allow laypersons to be licensed to officiate at services, and proposed two lay orders, readers and subdeacons, the first to read the service and preach, while the second would administer the chalice at Holy Communion, prepare candidates for baptism, and when necessary baptize and officiate at funerals. But such permission was not forthcoming. However, in the diocese of Ceylon, Native laymen were appointed by the bishop as "pastoral catechists," in some cases "virtually in charge of small congregations."[29]

In many places, the planters participated in an ecumenical group, the "Tamil Coolie Mission," which hired and supported CMS missionaries to work with their workers, or "coolies." The newly arrived bishop of Ceylon determined that the chaplains, many of whom spoke only English, should function much like an English parish rector, with authority over the missionaries in their area. The missionaries complained, not only because the chaplains did not speak Sinhalese or Tamil, but also because many of the chaplains were partisans of the Oxford Movement, while the Ceylonese Christians, used to services held in coffee-stores or schoolrooms, were opposed to "crosses, and flowers, and painted windows with figures in them." When the chaplains insisted on constructing chapels and decorating them, the CMS told its missionaries to officiate only in buildings owned by the Society or the planters. The bishop objected, and when the CMS missionaries refused to back down, he withdrew their licenses and took over the Coolie Mission. The Metropolitan of India restored all the licenses except that of the senior missionary, and the matter actually became part of the agenda for discussions at the 1978 Lambeth Conference. Tensions continued when the missionaries objected to participating in the Eucharist as celebrated by the bishop because of his introduction of what they considered unacceptable high-church ceremonial. Only arbitration by a committee which included the Archbishops of Canterbury and York succeeded in achieving a compromise: the bishop would give the missionaries general licenses to minister in a wide area, and have authority over lay missionaries only when they were basically "doing a clergyman's work." For their part, CMS agreed that the missionaries would not boycott services presided by the bishop.[30]

Anglicans in Canada, Australia, New Zealand and South Africa had achieved a considerable measure of self-government by the 1860s, but the process was slower and more problematic in the Indian context. Cecil John

Grimes, Archdeacon of Calcutta in the early twentieth century, argued that during Victoria's reign it came to be widely understood that Anglicans in other parts of the world were "not merely transplanted fragments of the Church of England, but infant or, in some cases, adolescent churches," which needed the freedom to take responsibility for their own life.

> Merely to reproduce a passive, inarticulate imitation of the Church of England, tied and bound by its practice and formularies, and more particularly by the peculiar relationship to the state which the mere accidents of history had wrought, could never satisfy the needs, develop the religious genius, or build up among the peoples of other races a truly indigenous Church.[31]

In 1883, the Anglican bishops of South Asia issued a pastoral letter addressed "to all people of whatever race and religion in India and Ceylon." While insisting that they had no intention of "imposing upon an Indian Church any thing which is distinctively English or even European," they nevertheless affirmed that the Scriptures, the sacraments and the ministry of bishops were "unchangeable," and hence were as relevant to Indians in the nineteenth century as to Christians of any other time and place. "But in regards to the conditions under which these are presented, the Church adapts herself, and we desire to see herself adapt herself more and more, to the circumstances and to the tempers of every race of men." It was the mission of the Church of England, they believed, to "give to India that pure Truth, and that divinely appointed Order, in possession of which India shall work out her own spiritual life, bear spiritual fruit of her own, continue her own spiritual gifts to the wealth of the universal Church of God."[32]

Henry Stanley Newman, an English visitor to the Anglican missions of South Asia in the same period, expressed gratitude for the positive effects of the English presence and satisfaction that a substantial degree of local control was already in evidence, particularly in South India, where people were "more settled and contented, more thoroughly in acceptance of the English Government . . . and realize the advantage it is to them." In the region of Tirunelveli (which the British called Tinnevelly), in the extreme south of India, he found the Anglican presence to be "self-supporting and indigenous," entirely governed by the "Native Church Council, . . . without a single European being present at its deliberations." Eighty-four Tamil clergy were accompanied by only four European missionaries. A Sunday service in Palamcotta drew a congregation of over a thousand; Newman noted that no musical instruments were used, and that men and women sat on opposite sides of the church.[33] He was intrigued that at a Sunday afternoon service, the sermon was preached in a question-and-answer format.

Kevin Ward assessed Indian Anglicanism of the colonial era as "an establishment like no other: that of the ruling power in India, but definitely not of, or for, the indigenous population." Probably those who were committed to its mission would have vehemently contradicted Ward's judgment, but it is supported by the observation of the first Bishop of Lahore, writing late in the nineteenth century, that "there were two churches (native and European) . . . united under one bishop."[34]

MINISTRY IN AUSTRALIA AND NEW ZEALAND

The Anglican ministry which began in the unpromising context of a prison colony and in proximity to an Aboriginal population disparaged by the constantly growing number of English immigrants had by mid-century burgeoned into a church to which some forty percent of the population belonged, "the largest, most inclusive and most influential denomination in Australia," in spite of its frequent identification with "the landed gentry and the urban middle class." It was, wrote the Australian historian Brian Fletcher, "above all the faith of the dominant members of society" but without the direct links to the state which marked the Church of England. Indeed, it was sometimes criticized for ignoring the working class, and likely to "carry the employers' point of view into its pastoral work."[35]

The story of ministry in Australia reflects the nation's peculiar history. The Church's original structure had created a collection of independent dioceses, each governed by a bishop and a synod composed of clergy and laity. A broad spectrum of Anglo-Catholic, Evangelical and Broad Church perspectives was present from the beginning, and the Evangelicals insisted on autonomous dioceses: Sydney was always determined to keep its Evangelical identity. A General Synod on the national level was not established until 1872, and then only because the British government believed it lacked the power to appoint bishops for Australia. That date marks the time when Australian Anglicans began to think nationally. One of its best-known nineteenth-century leaders, Bishop Henry Montgomery, analyzed the particular Australian character as the result of the interaction between the environment and "imported culture": "an Englishman whose character had been modified by exposure to [local] conditions. . . . " Many Anglicans continued to identify with England, supported the British Empire, and felt a link to the monarchy through the Church of England.[36] (Indeed, the tension between the local and the universal, the diocese and the national church continued to be an issue for Anglican reflection in Australia in the twentieth century.)[37] Bruce Kaye reckons that a number of elements have provided Australian Anglicans with the means to form a common sense of identity: he cites the language of the *Book of Common Prayer* and a common liturgy; the relationship with the Church of England—and rivalry with the Roman Catholic Church; the social composition of Anglican parishes; and the episcopacy. Ultimately however, Kaye relates Anglican identity to "the general issue of Australian regionalism."[38]

Eugene Stock, who wrote the history of the Church Missionary Society from its founding to the end of the nineteenth century, was strongly committed to Henry Venn's vision of "Native Churches." But when he turned his attention to the Church in New Zealand, he concluded, with more than a touch of sadness, that "New Zealand was not like India or Africa or China. There could never be a really independent Native Church for a small minority of the population. The Māori Christians must always continue, what they already are, members of the Colonial Church; the Colonial Church should take care of them."[39]

In 1883 the Society initiated a new policy towards its work on the islands. It created a local Board, made up of three bishops, three CMS missionaries, and three English colonists, to oversee the ministry with the Māori people, and began transferring financial support from CMS to the local Church. The local administration of the Māori congregations was in the hands of their own Church Boards. But Stock betrayed the prejudices or his own perspective and perhaps of many of his contemporaries as well when he wrote that the Māori "are easily influenced by new superstitions. The Mormons have found them an easy prey, and like all uncivilized races, they are prone to believe in witchcraft . . . Their partial but unintelligent adoption of English habits and dress has made them victims of disease." On the other hand, "they are not so bad as they are often painted." The abuse of alcohol, he noted, had greatly declined; and he reminded his readers that there were also "peaceful and thriving communities that are supporting their own churches and clergy."[40] It is a poignant, and painful, observation with which to summarize the victimization of a proud people—a process in which prejudice all too often trumped good intentions.

MINISTRY IN CANADA

Like Anglicans in Australia, New Zealand and South Africa, by mid-century Canadian Anglicans were aware of the value and significance of synodical government that would include the voices of laypeople as well as bishops and clergy. The first diocesan synod in Canada was held in the diocese of Toronto in 1853, "the first synod with lay delegates in the British colonies. . . . When synods became a reality the lay representatives, together with the clergy, were expected to advise and assist in the temporal affairs of the church, to be concerned with matters of discipline, and to share in the election of bishops." John Baycroft notes that while the participation of laypeople in spiritual matters has evolved to a considerable extent, such concerns were originally conceived to be restricted to the clergy and the role of laypeople was left undefined.[41]

In 1867 three British colonies—Canada, now divided into Quebec and Ontario, New Brunswick and Nova Scotia, were combined into a confederation and became a self-governing dominion of the British Empire. For Anglicans, this action meant that the "Church of England in Canada" was now an autonomous member of the incipient Anglican Communion and responsible for its own mission and ministry. The confederation was enlarged in 1870 by the addition of Manitoba, the following year by British Columbia and in 1873 by Prince Edward Island. (Alberta and Saskatchewan remained part of the vast Northwest Territories until early in the twentieth century.)

Extending over an even wider area than its neighbor to the south but with a much smaller population, the issues shaking Anglicans on both sides of the Atlantic were felt differently in the more urban east and the frontier west. In western Canada, two remarkable bishops played an important part in the spread of Anglicanism from the more settled east. Robert Machray, Bishop of Rupert's Land for thirty-nine years, was an evangelical whose mission was "to spread the gospel where it had not been before, among peoples who had no knowledge of Christianity." Machray saw education as one of the primary tools for evangelism and revived St. John's College as well as serving as headmaster and warden of the College School and College. The first bishop of British Columbia, George Hills, was an Anglo-Catholic who considered liturgy as an integral part of the Church's evangelization but who also "encouraged missionary activity among native peoples, as well as the construction of new churches in the growing settlements of the colony."[42]

The Canadian historian Henry Roper notes that "throughout the latter part of the Victorian era, the church was torn by conflict between evangelicals and high churchmen," but points out that while education and philanthropy were considered appropriate by both parties, they "did not question the foundations of society or engage in political activity. Both evangelicals and their opponents agreed that the church must be a missionary church, bringing the gospel to the converted and the unconverted."[43]

In the more urban centers of the eastern provinces, Anglican ministry was focused on the parish; the conflict between Evangelicals and Anglo-Catholics often pitted clergy against their congregations, and annual congregational meetings could be tumultuous. As diocesan structures became more complex, parishes often mounted campaigns of "passive resistance", causing the bishop of Toronto to threaten to suspend clergy who failed to follow diocesan directives. Home visits to parish families were widely considered to be the primary daily activity of parish clergy and assumed to assure the financial well-being of the congregation. One of the practical issues raised by a conflicted polity was the role of women in congregational governance. While The Church Temporalities Act had defined the Parish Vestry as "all-pew-holders," it required a judgment by the Chancery to affirm that women's votes were valid. When new churches began offering free pews, a canon approved in 1884 required Vestries of all future "free churches" to be restricted to male parishioners only.[44]

If, as Roper affirms, "by 1867 the Church of England in Canada was on the way to becoming a Canadian church, contributing to and being shaped by the evolution of a country in the new world, whose population, constitution, social structure, and economy were in constant flux,"[45] that evolution continued beyond the end of the nineteenth century, but was given significant impetus when its first General Synod was finally held in 1893.

One important aspect of Anglican ministry with Native (First Nations) people in Canada was its network of residential schools for Native children, modeled on those in the United States, which removed children from Native homes in order to facilitate their assimilation into the dominant white culture. A legal process for hastening assimilation was created by the "Gradual Civilization Act" of 1867. Two years later, the Canadian government abolished the Native self-government promised in earlier treaties, and by the mid-1870s residential schools operated by the Anglican and other churches had become a key instrument in the state's policy of eroding the identity of Native peoples. The Canadian theologian Wendy Fletcher described the policy and its effects: The government, she writes, believed that "'Aboriginal people were sunk in ignorance and superstitious blindness,' and that only children at an early enough age can be liberated from the depravity of their natural state."[46]

First Nations descendants affirm the painful consequences of the policy:

> In effect, students were made to feel ashamed of their ancestry, while teachers and other authority figures constantly sought to reinforce the innate superiority of "white" society and values. On the one hand, this indoctrination involved the devaluing of parents and all aspects of Aboriginal culture. On the other hand, schools attempted to disconnect children from their background by prohibiting communication in an Aboriginal language.[47]

The residential schools formed a significant dimension of ministry with First Nations people in Canada throughout the nineteenth and well into the twentieth centuries.[48] In our own time, revelations about physical and sexual abuse on the part of staff, which was a part of the endemic reality of the schools throughout Canada, have called forth profound apologies from the Anglican

Church and broad attempts at reparation funded jointly by religious and governmental organizations.

LAMBETH ANGLICANISM

The decision of the Archbishop of Canterbury to call together the bishops in communion with the Church of England in the fall of 1867 marked the beginning of a gradually evolving understanding of the global nature of Anglican Christianity. Responding to a request from the Canadian Church for a broad forum to discuss the issues raised by the "Colenso Affair" in South Africa, The Archbishop of Canterbury determined to invite "the attendance, not only of our Home and Colonial bishops, but of all who are avowedly in communion with our Church," 144 in number, to gather at Lambeth Palace for a four-day consultation.[49]

Archbishop Langley was concerned to emphasize that "at this meeting no declaration of faith shall be made, and no decision come to what shall affect generally the interests of the Church, but that we shall meet together for brotherly counsel and encouragement . . . I should refuse to convene any assembly which pretended to enact any canons, or affected to make any decisions binding on the Church." Rather, it was Langley's hope that the Conference would "bind the Colonial Church, which is certainly in a most unsatisfactory state, more closely to the Mother Church."[50]

Of the 144 bishops who received an invitation to the Lambeth Conference, slightly more than half attended: eighteen English bishops, five Irish, six Scottish, twenty-four from "the Colonial Church" and nineteen from the United States. Some bishops found the travel required beyond their financial means or physical condition; many others, including the Archbishop of York and five English diocesan bishops, declined the invitation because they believed that it would complicate the authority structure of the Church of England. Their concern would seem to have been merited, since the bishops adopted a resolution to the effect that "in the opinion of this Conference, unity of faith and discipline among the several branches of the Anglican Communion will be best maintained by due and canonical subordination of the synods of the several branches to the higher authority of the synod or synods above them."[51] (No action was ever taken on this proposal for a "higher authority" above the national synods of the autonomous churches of the Communion, and in fact the bishops who gathered at future conferences seem to have worked hard to avoid any institutional framework at the level of the Communion itself which might compromise the independence of the member churches.)

Ironically, Bishop G. A. Selwyn, already well known for his efforts towards introducing representative government by synod (including the laity) into the Church in New Zealand and for influencing the structure of other churches now claiming their own independence to varying degrees, now turned his attention to the structures he considered necessary to hold the churches of the Communion together. Selwyn's travels through Canada and the United States after the 1867 Lambeth Conference made him an obvious choice to convey the concerns of many overseas Anglicans for a second Conference. Now returned from New Zealand and serving as bishop of Lichfield, he was concerned that the loosening ties among increasingly autonomous churches would weaken their sense of communion with other Anglican churches. In his petition to the bishops of the Canterbury Convocation, he pointed out that overseas bishops no longer received royal letters patent and were no longer consecrated in England, and hence took no oath of allegiance to the Archbishop of Canterbury. He emphasized the importance of clarity with regard to the nature of the relationship among the different overseas "branches" of the Church of England and asked, "What is the best mode by which all the churches of the Anglican Communion shall be confederate together?" He recommended that the Archbishop of Canterbury should occupy the position of "head" to whom "all the colonial churches must be united, not by law, but by voluntary compact," and that he should be designated as "Patriarch."

He also urged the Archbishop, in consultation with the Communion, to devise a structure which would

> regulate all those points currently unregulated, and that the authority and the nature of the constituent assembly by which this would be done would need to be identified and recognized. . . . He claimed that the colonial churches' greatest concern was that they would diverge from the Church of England. . . . He also urged that a process was required to deal with heterodox bishops.[52]

The response of Archbishop Tait and the Canterbury Convocation was measured; while approving the idea of a conference in principle, they stipulated that it not address matters of faith, affirmed that the authority of such a gathering would be purely dependent on the voluntary assent of those attending, and that the idea of a "patriarch" be dropped. Archbishop Tait was adamant that there could be no "discussion of doctrine, or about the administration of ecclesiastical law in any diocese, and that the independence of every church must be respected." Even so, the American House of Deputies barely approved the concept. A resolution affirming that "all exchange of friendly greetings, all evidences of the existence of the unity of the spirit in the bond of peace between the Church of England and the Protestant Episcopal Church in America, whether by bishops in conference, or otherwise are especially welcome to the Church" passed only by a margin of 108 to 96.[53]

The second Lambeth Conference, held in 1878, was attended by one hundred bishops, slightly more than two-thirds of the total number of Anglican bishops in the Communion. In the Conference proceedings, only the American bishops were considered to fall outside the definition of "Home" or "Colonial" bishops.[54] Bishop Selwyn's concern for a Communion of churches exercising their mission and ministry with oversight and, when necessary, discipline by some sort of international synod under the leadership of a patriarch, was clearly not the vision of Communion shared by most Anglicans, wherever their home.

It is surely the third Conference, held in 1888, that had the most impact on the future of Anglican ministry. In both England and the United States, some Anglicans had expressed concern about the impact of the fragmentation of Reformed Christianity on the Church's ministry and mission. At mid-century, Frederick Denison Maurice had been a strong English voice stressing the importance of unity among Christians. In 1870, William Reed Huntington, a distinguished parish priest in Worcester, Massachusetts, published *The Church-Idea: An Essay Toward Unity*, in which he argued that the Church is comprised of all baptized people, and that Anglicanism could provide the principles by which a "Church of the Reconciliation" could take shape. He identified those principles as "the Holy Scriptures as the Word of God," the "Primitive Creeds as the Rule of Faith," the "Two Sacraments ordained by Christ Himself" and "the Episcopate as the key-stone of Governmental Unity"; together they constituted what he called "the Quadrilateral of Pure Anglicanism."[55]

Huntington's book sparked considerable interest among Episcopalians and in 1886, meeting in Chicago, the House of Bishops adopted a resolution proposing his four principles as a basis for uniting Christians. The bishops affirmed that the Episcopal Church "does not seek to absorb other Communions" but rather, by cooperating with other churches, to "discountenance schism, to heal the wounds of the Body of Christ, and to promote [Christian] charity." In the service of these goals, they declared the Church ready "in the spirit of love and humility to forego all preferences of her own" with regard to "all things of human ordering or human choice, relating to modes of worship and discipline, or to traditional customs." But they also insisted that unity could only be restored by returning to those principles which "we believe to be the substantial deposit of Christian Faith and Order committed by Christ and his Apostles to the Church unto the end of the world." On those principles, they asserted, no compromise is possible.[56]

The principles articulated by the American bishops were those identified by Huntington sixteen years earlier, though with some significant amendments. The Holy Scriptures were now defined as "the revealed Word of God"; only the Nicene Creed was required, as "the sufficient statement of the Christian Faith"; "Baptism and the Supper of the Lord" were required to be "ministered with unfailing use of Christ's words of institution and of the elements ordained by Him"; and the "Historic Episcopate" is permitted to be "locally adapted in the methods of its administration to the varying needs of the nations and peoples called of God into the unity of His Church."[57]

Though approved by the bishops, the House of Deputies failed to vote on this "Chicago Quadrilateral." However, two years later, the Lambeth Conference of 1888 adopted a resolution reiterating the principles as adopted by the American House of Bishops, although with some significant changes. The Lambeth resolution stated that the principles involved provided "a basis on which approach may be made by God's blessing towards Home reunion." While the resolution itself does not make clear to what exactly "Home reunion" refers, the records of preliminary discussions indicate that the bishops did not take seriously the possibility of reunion with the Roman Catholic Church, and that they had in mind primarily the churches of "the English-speaking races."[58] Gillian Evans also points out that the resolution reflected the context of the British Empire and the "practical need to hold together Anglican churches in widely differing conditions all over the world." Evans notes too that the Quadrilateral was intended to spell out "the irreducible minimum, the heart of Christian truth on which all Christians could meet in agreement."[59]

In the form in which they were adopted by the bishops at Lambeth, the principles define the Scriptures as "containing all things necessary to salvation" and "the rule and ultimate standard of faith." The Apostles' Creed is "the Baptismal Symbol" while the Nicene Creed is "the sufficient statement of the Christian faith." The third and fourth articles were stated in the form in which the American bishops had spelled them out.[60]

One of the effects of the Chicago-Lambeth Quadrilateral was to emphasize the ministry of bishops as an integral aspect of Anglican Christianity. Both the High-Church Anglicans of the eighteenth century and the Oxford Movement had argued that the episcopate is a defining characteristic of Catholic, as opposed to Protestant, Christianity and that its preservation in Anglican churches was essential to its catholicity. While it might appear that the Quadrilateral reinforced this perspective, most of its interpreters disagree. Robert Wright quotes Boyd Vincent, Assistant Bishop of Southern Ohio in the late nineteenth century, who affirmed that in the minds of the bishops who participated in the discussions at Lambeth, the wording of the resolution made no reference to "a Scriptural origin or a doctrinal nature in the institution" of the episcopate, and that it was "deliberately chosen as declaring not a doctrine but a fact." The English historian Henry Chadwick agrees, observing that the ministry of bishops "presupposed an evaluation not so much of history as of the living tradition of the Church."

The Lambeth Resolution of 1888 did not respond to any specific opportunities for immediate cooperation or reunion with other churches; its significance lay in the principles which it spelled out. While addressing the relationship between Anglicans and those of other churches, it also had the effect of defining the core identity of Anglican Christians and the tenets on which relationships between and among the churches of the Anglican Communion were to be based in future. Indeed, the dialogue leading to the approval of the Quadrilateral by bishops in both the Episcopal Church and the Lambeth Conference demonstrates how thoroughly the concept of a "family" of churches bound *in communion* had become the primary sense of Anglicanism as a concept and a distinctive way of expressing Christian faith.

But the Quadrilateral could also be said to incorporate the irony or ambiguity at the heart of those relationships. On one hand, it accepts that bishops in distinct parts of the Communion will exercise their ministry in various ways, depending on the exigencies of their particular context. On the other, it requires that the Eucharist be celebrated with bread and wine (presumably made from grapes) in spite of the fact that those elements themselves belong to Western culture and are completely foreign to Anglicans in many parts of the world. The language of "Home reunion" also demonstrates that at a time when the Empire seemed to be advancing not only Anglican Christianity but British "civilization," most of the bishops continued to view the Church of England as occupying a central and dominant place in the life of the Communion.

NOTES

1. W. T. Steed, ed., *The Last Will and Testament of C. J. Rhodes,* 1902; quoted in Klaus Koschorke, Frieder Ludwig, Mariani Delgado, eds., *A History of Christianity in Asia, Africa and Latin America, 1450–1990: A Documentary Sourcebook* (Grand Rapids: William B. Eerdmans Publishing Company, 2007), 208–209.

2. Jocelyn Murray, *Proclaim the Good News: A Short History of the Church Missionary Society* (London: Hodder and Stoughton, 1985), 53–58.

3. Jehu J. Hanciles, "Bishop Crowther and Archdeacon Crowther: Inter-Generational Challenge and Opportunity in the African Christian Encounter," in Chima J. Korieh and G. Ugo Nwokeji, eds., *Religion, History and Politics in Nigeria: Essays in Honor of Ogbu U. Kalu* (Kanham, MD: University Press of America, 2005), 58.

4. Lamin Sanneh, "The CMS and the African Transformation," in Kevin Ward and Brian Stanley, eds., *The Church Mission Society and World Christianity, 1799 – 1999* (Grand Rapids, MI: William B. Eerdmans Publishing Co., 2000), 189–190.

5. Hanciles, "Bishop Crowther and Archdeacon Crowther," 66–67.

6. Stock, *The History of the Church Missionary Society*, II, 462.
7. Jehu J. Hanciles, "Dandeson Coates Crowther and the Niger Delta Pastorate: Blazing Torch or Flickering Flame?" *International Bulletin of Missionary Research* 18 (October 1994), 167.
8. Hanciles, "Dandeson Coates Crowther," 170.
9. Hanciles, "Dandeson Coates Crowther," 170–171.
10. Brad Faught, "Tractarianism on the Zambezi: Bishop Mackenzie and the Beginnings of the Universities Mission to Central Africa," *Anglican and Episcopal History*, LXVI, 3 (September 1997), 304–307.
11. Faught, "Tractarianism on the Zambezi," 312, 315.
12. Faught, "Tractarianism on the Zambezi," 317.
13. Faught, "Tractarianism on the Zambezi," 327; Robert Keable, *Darkness or Light: Studies in the History of the Universities' Mission to Central Africa* (London: UMCA, 1914), 91, 104.
14. George Herbert Wilson, *History of the Universities' Mission to Central Africa* (New York: New World Book Manufacturing Co., 1936, 1971), 35–42.
15. Stock, *The History of the Church Missionary Society*, II, 431.
16. Charles D. Michael, *James Hannington, Bishop and Martyr: The Story of a Noble Life* (London: S. W. Partridge and Co., 1886), 68.
17. Michael, *James Hannington*, 116–118, 142.
18. Michael, *James Hannington*, 145–146, 158.
19. Stock, *The History of the Church Missionary Society*, III, 436–437.
20. Joan Plubell Mattia, "Walking the Rift: The Missionary Art of Bishop Alfred Robert Tucker," *Anglican and Episcopal History*, 80 (September 2011), 251.
21. Mattia, "Walking the Rift," 245, 251, 261.
22. Mattia, "Walking the Rift," 449.
23. Mattia, "Walking the Rift," 451–452.
24. See, e.g., Eliza F. Kent, *Converting Women: Gender and Protestant Christianity in Colonial South India* (New York: Oxford University Press, 2004).
25. Duncan B. Forrester, *Caste and Christianity: Attitude sand Policies on Caste of Anglo-Saxon Protestant Missions in India* (London: Curzon Press, 1980), 69, 75.
26. Forrester, *Caste and Christianity*, 119, 124.
27. Brethren of the Epiphany, *A Hundred Years in Bengal: A History of the Oxford Mission 1880–1980* (Delhi: SPCK, 1979), 32, 35, 58.
28. Brethren of the Epiphany, *A Hundred Years in Bengal*, 21, 53–54.
29. Stock, *The History of the Church Missionary Society*, III, 198–202.
30. Stock, *The History of the Church Missionary Society*, III, 203–212.
31. Cecil John Grimes, *Towards An Indian Church: The Growth of the Church of India in Constitution and Life* (London: SPCK, 1946), 96–98.
32. Grimes, *Towards An Indian Church*, 107.
33. Henry Stanley Newman, *Days of Grace in India: A Record of Visits to Indian Missions* (London: G. W. Partridge and Co., 1880), 149, 179–188.
34. Ward, *A History of Global Anglicanism*, 215.
35. Brian H. Fletcher, *The Place of Anglicanism in Australia: Church, Society and Nation* (Mulgrave, Australia: Broughton Publishing, 2008), v, 6–7, 33.

36. Fletcher, *The Place of Anglicanism,* 1–2, 7–8, 10, 25, 40, 42–43.

37. Tom Frame, "Local Differences, Social and National Identity 1930–1966," in Bruce Kaye ed., *Anglicanism in Australia: A History* (Victoria: Melbourne University Press, 2002), 100.

38. Bruce Kaye, "The Emergence and Character of Australian Anglican Identity," in *Anglicanism in Australia: A History,* 173.

39. Stock, *The History of the Church Missionary Society,* III, 535.

40. Stock, *The History of the Church Missionary Society,* III, 555.

41. John A. Baycroft, "Episcopacy in Relation to Synods," in *Frontiers Then and Now: The Canadian Episcopate 1787–1987* (The Archbishop Owen Memorial Lectures 1987) (Toronto: Anglican Bok Centre, 1989), 34–35.

42. Henry Roper, "The Anglican Episcopate in Canada: An Historical Perspective," in *Frontiers Then and Now*, 32–33.

43. Roper, "The Anglican Episcopate in Canada," 13.

44. Richard E. Ruggle, "The Saints in the Land, 1867–1939", in Alan L. Hayes, ed., *By Grace Co-Workers: Building the Anglican Diocese of Toronto 1780–1989,* 190–193.

45. Roper, *The Anglican Episcopate in Canada,* 10.

46. Quoted in Daryl Balia and Kirsteen Kim, eds., *Edinburgh 2010, II: Witnessing to Christ Today* (Oxford: Regnum Books International, 2010), 89.

47. Balia and Kim, Edinburgh 2010, II, 91–92.

48. *Witnessing to Christ Today* notes that "the exact dating of school closures varies depending on what is used for the benchmark. 1998 is the date on which the last facility, originally constructed as a residential school, closed." 114, n. 21.

49. Randall T. Davidson, ed., *Origin and History of the Lambeth Conferences of 1867 and 1878, With the Official Reports and Resolutions* (London: SPCK, 1888), 6–7.

50. Davidson, ed., *Origin and History of the Lambeth Conferences of 1867 and 1878,* 8.

51. Davidson, ed., *Origin and History of the Lambeth Conferences of 1867 and 1878,* 9, 12, 15–16.

52. W. M. Jacob, "George Augustus Selwyn, First Bishop of New Zealand and the Origins of the Anglican Communion," *Journal of Anglican Studies*, 9 (May 2011), 53–53.

53. Jacob, "George Augustus Selwyn," 54.

54. Davidson, ed., *Origin and History of the Lambeth Conferences of 1867 and 1878,* 30.

55. William Reed Huntington, *The Church-Idea: An Essay toward Unity* (New York: E. P. Dutton and Co., 1870), 157.

56. *The Book of Common Prayer* (New York: The Seabury Press, 1979), 877.

57. *The Book of Common Prayer,* 877.

58. J. Robert Wright, "Heritage and Vision: The Chicago-Lambeth Quadrilateral," in J. R. Wright, ed., *Quadrilateral at One Hundred: Essays on the Centenary of the Chicago-Lambeth Quadrilateral 1886–88 – 1986–88* (Oxford: A. R. Mowbray and Co., 1988), 15.

59. Gillian R. Evans, "Permanence in the Revealed Truth and Continuous Exploration of Its Meaning," in Wright, ed., *Quadrilateral at One Hundred,* 111–112.
60. *The Book of Common Prayer*, 877.

Chapter Eleven

Evangelism
Global Anglican Ministry, 1850–1900

ANGLICAN MISSION IN EAST ASIA

The conditions under which Anglican Christianity reached China, Korea and Japan were distinct from most of the expansion representative of the nineteenth century. Like India, these three imperial states valued highly developed cultures reaching back to antiquity; but unlike India, their political independence was not at issue.

All three countries had experienced evangelism earlier in their history. An East Syrian church flourished in China as early as the seventh century, and was active in the thirteenth century; Franciscans were also active in the twelfth and thirteenth centuries. In the sixteenth century energetic Jesuit missions had made significant inroads in both China and Japan and Roman Catholic influence had also been felt in Korea, but those missions ultimately ended in persecution and Christianity survived only as a clandestine faith.

While the western powers never seriously considered the conquest of the East Asian empires, they did yearn for economic domination and struggled for opportunities to develop trade with East Asia, efforts strongly resisted by all three countries. Britain fought two wars with China in the nineteenth century after China attempted to stop the importation of opium. In the aftermath, China was forced to allow foreign interests to establish a presence in a number of port cities, and the island of Hong Kong actually became a British colony in 1843. At first its bishop, consecrated for the "Diocese of Victoria" in 1849, also had general oversight of all British ministry in both China and Japan. The opening of Japan to foreign interests was accomplished by a show of American military force under the command of Commodore Matthew C. Perry in 1854. Korea agreed to allow missionaries into its territory as part of negotiations with the United States undertaken in the 1880s in response to increased threats from Japan (which culminated in the Japanese annexation of Korea in 1910).

ANGLICAN MINISTRY IN CHINA

China occupied a special interest for the Episcopal Church in the United States even before mid-century. William Jones Boone, based in Shanghai, was appointed bishop of the Episcopal Church Mission in China in 1844. Huang Kuang-tsai, the first Chinese deacon, was ordained in Shanghai in 1851; he was ordained to the priesthood twelve years later. CMS missionaries arrived in Shanghai in 1843; SPG began its work somewhat later in Beijing, with responsibility for the diocese of North China when it was established in 1872. The Anglican presence in China was further fragmented by the work of a group of English Evangelicals under the direction of the China Inland Mission. However, Kevin Ward notes that in spite of its complex diversity, "there were many contacts between the different areas, including an active interchange of Chinese catechists and evangelists." Ward considers the CMS mission in southern China and the American mission in the Shanghai area to have been the most successful of the Anglican ministries in the nineteenth century.[1]

In the southeastern province of Fujian, the Anglican ministry overseen by the CMS grew more quickly than that of any other church in the region, with a total of 113 mission stations and over 3,500 converts (including candidates for baptism) by 1880. The bulk of the leadership of the congregations was in the hands of a group of ninety-three Chinese catechists; only seven clergy were working in the area, which meant that the sacraments were available to most Anglicans only sporadically. The CMS did not hesitate to use the power granted to the missionaries under the treaties signed by China: when a mob destroyed mission property in 1878 and the provincial government offered what the missionaries considered to be inadequate compensation, they took the case to the consular court. (The court, however, sided with the government.)

While the Bishop of Hong Kong continued to hold nominal authority over the Anglicans in the province, in 1883 the CMS divided the churches in Fujian into "a system of pastoral districts overseen by a Provincial Church Council made up of missionaries, Chinese clergy, catechists, mission school teachers, and lay delegates," chaired by the senior missionary. But when tensions arose between senior Chinese clergy and younger missionaries, the CMS in London ruled that the Council had no "legislative" or "executive" powers, and that in the absence of the chair, the nest senior missionary rather than the Chinese vice-chair would preside over the Council. On the other hand, the historian Ryan Dunch notes that

> the Chinese preachers [of whatever denomination] were in a position of leadership and honor relative to their congregations. They were literate, educated men, playing the role of teacher to those under their care. The titles by which they were addressed—*mushi* (literally "shepherd-teacher," a neologism used to translate "pastor" or "Reverend" and reserved for ordained men) and the classical Chinese term *xiansheng* ("sir" or "master," applied to . . . CMS catechists) both carried connotations of the respect due to teachers. Moreover, there is evidence that the Protestant pastors sought to behave as men of status in local society, or were expected by others to do so—and that this was one of the major causes of the perennial conflicts between Protestants and their neighbors.[2]

In many cases these Chinese Anglican leaders played important roles as mediators in conflicts between Christians and others, sometimes—to the disapproval of CMS authorities in England and to most missionaries—even representing their parishioners in litigation before civil magistrates, a role to which they were not legally entitled. They were expected to attend all Anglican weddings and funerals, each occasion calling for a significant gift of cash. While the Chinese clergy and catechists' salaries were at least the equivalent of that of a village school teacher, they had more expenses and may have sometimes "regarded themselves as occupying a higher social station than that allotted them under Chinese social norms and thus sought a lifestyle higher than their salary would sustain," which burdened them with unsustainable debts.[3]

Ward describes Samuel Joseph Isaac Schereschewsky as "the most remarkable of all the Anglican missionaries in China." Born a Jew, trained as a rabbi, and converted by Baptists, he eventually became an Episcopalian and spent his entire ministry in Asia. He is best remembered for establishing St. John's University in Shanghai, for his magisterial work in translating the Bible into Mandarin Chinese, and (in collaboration with the British missionary J. S. Burden), completing the work of translating the *Book of Common Prayer*, incorporating elements from both the English and American rites, into Chinese.[4] (Burden, who became bishop of Victoria in 1874, was a controversial figure, "not popular among British residents in Hong Kong." Along with Schereschewsky, he was identified with the conflict among Christian missionaries over the appropriate Chinese term to translate the English word "God" as well as arguments over whether women missionaries should adopt Chinese dress, and he advocated the use of rice and tea in Chinese celebrations of the Eucharist.)[5]

The early Anglican presence in Shanghai was affected by the Taiping Rebellion, a revolt against the Qing dynasty led by a quasi-Christian sect which, while ultimately unsuccessful, was responsible for the death of as many as twenty million Chinese. Two battles were fought for control of Shanghai in 1860–1862; in the second battle, British and French troops joined in and repulsed the rebel army. The American Civil War also disrupted the ministry of the American Church Mission, significantly reducing the number of personnel. The situation was further troubled by ongoing tension caused by the Americans' displeasure that British missionaries in Shanghai were not subject to the authority of the local (American) bishop. Nevertheless, the American mission flourished in the second half of the century. By 1870 there were 150 communicants and 261 pupils in American-sponsored schools. More Chinese clergy were ordained, including Yen Yűn-ching, one of the outstanding Chinese leaders of nineteenth century Anglicanism. (Yen spent much of his ministry on the staff of St. John's University and prepared several scientific textbooks. In 1894 he toured Britain on behalf of the Anti-Opium Society, and visited the Episcopal Church in the United States in support of ministry in China.)[6]

Much of the work of Anglican ministry in China was effected through its commitment to education. As in India, making western-style education available to local students was considered to be the most effective way of impacting not only the religious dimension of the local culture but the culture as a whole. There were many aspects of Chinese culture that western missionaries found troubling: the ancient legal and governmental structures and the classical education that supported them, the position of women in society, and particularly the widespread custom of foot binding which made it difficult for women who had undergone the process to walk. The corps of Christian missionaries in China was nurtured by thousands of young American volunteers, both men and women, who were recruited through the Student Volunteer Movement for Foreign Missions (SVM). The program was founded in 1886, growing out of the work of both the Young Men's and Young Women's Christian Associations.[7]

The missionary community approached the task of education with diverse goals. Programs directed at training Chinese assistants to work in the early congregations and as primary evangelists tended to emphasize Biblical knowledge and Christian faith. Other missionaries emphasized the importance of training Chinese in "Christian values" to play leadership roles in what they anticipated would be a "new China"; the institutions they founded preserved significant training in the Chinese classics without which no candidate could hope to be active in civic affairs. Finally, other institutions preferred to emphasize western-style learning, especially in law and science, in the service of a vision of a China renewed by the importation of the knowledge associated with European and American culture.⁸

When Schereschewsky became bishop in 1877, he immediately began pressing for a school, a college and a theological seminary.⁹ St. John's University began in 1879 as "a training school for native evangelists" drawn from the two Episcopal schools already in Shanghai; students were generally from poor families and the Church paid their expenses. The issue of what language of instruction to emphasize preoccupied the school's administrators early in its history; Yen, the College's Chinese deputy head joined a group of Chinese merchants in pressuring the College to opt for English-language instruction, a point of view enthusiastically endorsed by Hawks Pott, the headmaster who assumed the direction of the University in 1887.

> In addition to practical reasons such as attracting "a better class" of students, providing those in the ministry with "means of livelihood," and even self-support of the college, Pott and his colleagues at St. John's valued English for its role in broadening the students' "mental horizon" and developing their "analytical power." . . . Some even went so far as to regard English as a kind of "moral language," believing that Western civilization could offer "a better spiritual, moral, intellectual, social and physical environment for helping to produce strong character than the civilization of the East." . . . By August 1882, after only a year, the number of students in [the English] department had increased from six to forty-nine.¹⁰

The result, in the opinion of a contemporary Chinese scholar, Edward Li-Hua Xu, is that "at St. John's the English-language world dominated the Chinese-language world; in addition, the hybrid campus student culture was strongly Westernized."¹¹ "The students of St. John's were known for their fluency in English," he comments, but their inadequacy in their own language became a cause for reproach . . . Actually, in an educational environment like this it was not uncommon for some students to know more about the history and culture of Western countries than of their own. (Xu notes that the nineteenth century missionaries at the college were also eager for students to be proficient in Chinese, since it was important for both professional success and service as an evangelist.)¹²

Xu adds that

> adding English to the curriculum significantly enhanced the reputation of St. John's giving it an image of a school for the rich and powerful. The use of English as the medium of instruction further raised the academic standard of St. John's. With such a bilingual background, St. John's was able to implement, without much difficulty and certainly without the language obstacle, educational systems from the West. It was only natural for St. John's to become the first

institution in China to give courses in sociology, civil engineering, and business administration, while its strongest programs remained those of liberal arts. It was largely because of this advantage in the English language that St. John's had become . . . the doyen of missionary educational institutions in China.

Ironically, he considers that "though the integration of Chinese and Western cultures had always been one of its major goals, . . . in St. John's case, due both to its all-English policy and to the salient presence of so many American influences on student life, the campus culture was weighed heavily toward the Western end of the scale."[13]

Education for clergy and laypeople called to ministry is always a challenge for Christian communities, but never more so than when new churches are being established and those responsible for them hope to see leadership pass from foreign hands to Christians who "belong" to the new context. In his recent study of Anglican theological education in China, Philip Wickeri identified five issues which must be addressed: the *standards* to which new leaders are to be educated; the *language* of education; the *relationship between denominational and ecumenical training*, especially given the Anglican insistence on the importance of "spiritual and ecclesial formation" as well as academic and practical education for its proposed leaders; *financial resources* for undertaking such training; and the issue of the *contextualization* of the inherited tradition.[14]

In China, formal theological education

> began slowly among [American] Episcopalians in China, and more slowly still among Anglicans. In both cases, the training of clergy up until the early twentieth century was informal and even haphazard, making use of a mentoring or apprenticeship method, by both English and American missionaries. Chinese converts first became evangelists and catechists, with limited but important functions. They preached, made pastoral visits, and provided basic Christian education, especially in rural areas. Only a few went on to become priests.[15]

Some attempts were made to establish more formal sites for theological training. St. Paul's College in Hong Kong may have been intended originally as a training school for clergy, and it attempted briefly to educate CMS missionaries, but in fact it became a boys' school, where the earliest Chinese clergy received their secondary education. By 1880, there were four Anglican sites for theological study: Ningpo Theological Training College, St. Paul's Divinity School in Hankow, the diocesan school that became Foochow Theological Seminary in 1883, and the most important, the Theological School at St. John's University in Shanghai. Wickeri comments that the standards of most of these schools were not very high and most students, both urban and rural, came with little more than a primary school education. They studied for three or at most four years, after which they became catechists or evangelists, and perhaps priests. In a very few instances, the most promising students were sent abroad for study.[16]

A significant aspect of the Church's ministry in China was the introduction of western medicine to a society that already had a tradition of medical care dating back thousands of years. The Church Missionary Society had a large hospital in Hangchow and a hospital for victims of Hansen's disease in Pakhoi, while the American Episcopal mission maintained a hospital in Shanghai.[17]

Another particular emphasis of the Anglican presence in China was ministry with the large numbers of seamen whose ships docked in Hong Kong or the five "Treaty Ports" established on the Chinese mainland to accommodate foreign business interests and to provide restricted residential areas for foreigners. While the Church of England's mission to seamen had begun early in the nineteenth century, it was not until 1885 that the Rev. A. G. Goldsmith was assigned to Hong Kong. By that time, some 140,000 British seamen visited the port yearly. Goldsmith began what became a rapidly expanding ministry, which provided a reading room, offered evening classes in reading, writing and simple arithmetic, and occasionally rescuing apprentice seamen from trouble with their superiors, either aboard ship on while they were ashore.[18]

Anglican missionaries were also deeply committed to the education of Chinese girls and women. "By the late nineteenth century, Chinese and Western missionary educators were in agreement that women needed to be trained in order to create better homes. These better homes, with children taught by more educated mothers, would strengthen China's capabilities for nation building."[19]

In Hong Kong, it was the wife of the first bishop of Victoria who requested funding from the Society for Promoting Female Education in the East to begin the work of educating young women. Writing in 1857, she pointed to "the growing necessity of educating the females as Christians, that our young men may not have the drawback of heathen wives." By 1863, the Diocesan Native Female Training School was formally established and housed in its own building, and reported that

> the course of education has embraced instruction in Chinese and English reading, writing, plain needlework, geography, and Bible history, and more especially a training in the religious truths and moral habits of the Christian faith. The object aimed at has been to prepare the girls for taking hereafter a position of usefulness in native society as the future wives and mothers of the rising generation of Chinese inhabitants in the colony.[20]

The Hong Kong Chinese educator Patricia Pok-Kwan Chiu points out that Anglican education for women in Hong Kong, like that of other mission schools in the colony, reflected the attitude articulated in an 1841 essay published in a collection of writings by women missionaries, that "Christianity is the only remedy for the sufferings of women in heathen and Mohammedan (sic) countries; and Christian education can be imparted on no large or efficient plan, but through the interposition of their own sex . . ." Chiu argues that while the education provided to Chinese women accepted the subservient role presumed by both Chinese and Victorian Christian social norms, it ironically also empowered the women who served as missionary educators to transcend traditional limitations imposed on women by their own societies.[21]

Chiu also documents the ambivalent results of Christian missionary education for women. Students at the Diocesan Native Female Training School, she observes, received an education similar to that of an English boarding school, rising

> early in the morning, arrange bedroom, prepare Chinese lessons before breakfast, first hour after breakfast devoted to family prayer, Scripture lesson (Mimpriss), and repetition of hymns. Followed by English reading with questioning both on meaning of the words and on the subject of the lesson, writing, simple arithmetic or object lesson, concluded with singing, geography, or the elements of grammar; an hour in middle of day lunch, each girl have ten cash, half a penny, given her. Assu (interpreter) teaches Chinese and at the same time explains the lesson from Mimpriss read in the morning, and the children are examined and instructed upon it. Needlework occupies the remainder of the afternoon. Four thirty dinner; eight o'clock to bed.[22]

The question of the appropriateness of the education offered by the School was raised early in its history. The first of its students to pass through the School fulfilled expectations by marrying a catechist from Foochow and became a teacher in the CMS school there. But unlike male graduates of English-language schools whose language skills assured them of elite status, almost all the women educated in English became the mistresses of European colonists. In response to this unforeseen outcome, the Diocesan Native Female Training School became an orphanage for boys and girls, and the focus of missionary education for girls "shifted from a high-profile English school for middle-class girls to vernacular schools for the poor, orphaned, rescued and marginalized" which would provide an "elementary Chinese education taught in the Chinese language, to prepare the girls for their humble yet useful sphere of life as Christian wives and mothers."[23]

Mainland schools for women sometimes had similar ambivalent histories. The Jane Bohlen School for Girls was founded in Wuchang in 1875 as the result of a bequest from a Philadelphia family to the American Episcopal Missionary Board. Its proposed function was "to produce a Chinese women's vanguard that would, in a militaristic analogy typical of the day, help 'conquer' China for Christ. . . . [T]hey would represent the idealized version of the good Christian wife, mother, and helper. In this way they would offer a positive role model for China's women."[24]

Within a few years, scandals involving student pregnancies and the death of an unmarried teacher in childbirth led the local population to believe it was a brothel. For a period of eleven years no missionary teachers could be recruited, and it was only at the end of the century that the school received a new lease on life as an expanded boarding school for middle-school-aged girls and a new name, St. Hilda's School for Girls. Its students were to be "the children of missionaries and/or the fiancées of the boys at the adjoining Boone School, Central China's training school for Episcopalian ministers."[25]

In her study of Chinese women in the early years of missionary activity, Kwok Pui-Lan notes the significant obstacles to evangelism among women: wealthy families would have been horrified if female members joined a foreign religion, and "decent women were not supposed to appear in public, let alone worship together with men in a church." Widely distributed anti-missionary propaganda spread outrageous rumors about the behavior of Christians, who were accused of "gouging out the eyes of dead people to make medicine or kidnapping children, . . . participating in adulterous relations during Christian gatherings . . . [and putting] poison into wells . . ." Furthermore, equality before God was perceived as undermining the hierarchical structures hallowed by Confucian teaching, "threatening the fabric of the traditional order."[26]

The relative success of ministry among women in China depended much on the arrival of single female missionaries in the later years of the nineteenth century. Women working in urban areas tended to be focused on activities for women offered by the local church, while rural missionaries practiced a more itinerant ministry. And throughout China, "Bible women"—locally trained lay evangelists—came to occupy an important place in the Church's missionary activities. Kwok notes that they

> assumed important teaching roles in the women's communities, serving as instructors in Sunday schools, women's prayer groups, and [missionary] station classes. . . . In bigger stations, where there was a dispensary or a hospital for women, the Bible woman would preach the Gospel to the women patients while they were waiting for consultation or for medicine. She would also visit in-patients, teaching them the Christian Primer, the Ten Commandments, the Lord's Prayer, Christian hymns, and prayers. In some cases, where there were no male preachers, the Bible woman would even take charge of the church,

discharging the duties of a pastor except for some special rites. On the other hand, the struggle for recognition of the importance of Chinese women in the Church's ministry was a lengthy one. At an ecumenical conference of women missionaries held in 1890, only one Chinese woman was present.[27]

As the influence of western thought—education, science, technology, medicine—began to make inroads on traditional Chinese culture, it was natural that the religion associated with these "advances" seemed attractive to some. In 1899, the missionary pastor of St. Peter's Church in Shanghai wrote,

> The number of our enquirers keeps steadily increasing. We now have about sixty people under instruction. . . . The majority are respectable middle people, and as far as we can see, they come to seek for admission into the Christian Church, because they think that in some way this elevates them, though the full nature of this elevation, though the full extent of this *elevation* they cannot at first be expected to understand.[28]

Yet the obvious "successes" of Christianity in China also evoked strong patriotic resistance, which would grow stronger as the new twentieth century dawned. Kevin Ward describes this "deep ambivalence": On one hand it was the "Christian powers" who had weakened the Chinese government; but "on the other hand, Christianity, and especially its educational institutions, was regarded as a source of regeneration for China, pointing to ways of overcoming China's chronic weakness."[29]

As the nineteenth century drew to a close, Chinese resentment at the presence of the foreign missionary community exploded. In 1895, a carefully planned attack by a group of Chinese nationalist rebels at Huashan, a hill-station near the city of Kucheng, in Fujian province, resulted in the massacre of an Irish missionary family from the Church Missionary Society, including both parents, two children and their nurse, as well as six women (one Irish, one English and four Australian) who were missionaries of the Church of England Zenana Missionary Society. Three children, one left permanently disabled, and three missionaries, one of them badly disfigured, survived the attack.[30]

The Kucheng Massacre turned out to be only a bloody forerunner to a much broader movement known as the Boxer Rebellion, a complex popular uprising that targeted the foreign missionary community and in which the imperial Chinese government ultimately participated. In Taiyuan, the capital of Shanxi province, scores of Protestant and Catholic missionaries and their families, hundreds of Eastern Orthodox and Chinese Protestants and many thousands of Roman Catholics were executed, and the foreign legation quarter of Beijing was under siege for fifty-five days, ending only when an international force of twenty-thousand soldiers defeated the Chinese Imperial Army.

The experience of one of the many missionaries who served the Church in China during that time has come to be an important, if critical, window into the nature of Anglican ministry of the period and its interaction with Chinese society. Roland Allen was only twenty-seven years old when he went to Beijing in 1895 under the auspices of the Church of England Mission to North China, a group associated with the SPG. Allen was assigned to open a training school for preparing boys as catechists; he soon took on the direction of a day school, the operation of a printing press and also served as a chaplain at the British Legation. He returned to England at the time of the Boxer Rebellion but went back to China two years later; after only nine months, he was forced by illness to return again to England, and never revisited China. He wrote: "At present the Chinese commonly look upon the missionary as a political agent, sent out to buy the hearts of people, and so to prepare the way for a foreign dominion, and this suspicion has been greatly strengthened by the fact that western nations have ... used outrages upon missionaries as a pretext for territorial aggression."[31] Even Roland Allen would surely have been astonished at the changes that would come to China—and Chinese Christianity—in the course of the turbulent twentieth century.

ANGLICAN MINISTRY IN JAPAN

Anglican ministry in Japan is generally said to have arrived in 1859 with two missionaries from the Episcopal Church. But as early as 1846, a remarkable Church of England medical missionary was already living and working—against Japanese government policy—on the island of Okinawa. Bernard John Bettelheim, of Hungarian Jewish background, became a Christian through the ministry of two Anglican priests with whom he studied Arabic in Turkey—one of the twenty-five languages he mastered. He and his family were able to live on Okinawa for eight years, "dispensing western medicine, and preaching the gospel," as well as translating portions of the scriptures into both Japanese and Okinawan.[32]

The stress of the incursion of Western influence contributed to internal conflicts which in 1868 led to the overthrow of the traditional feudal order in which the samurai (warrior) class had played a dominant role, and the restoration of the Japanese imperial house. In the aftermath, some samurai lost faith in the religious traditions that had undergirded their place in society and found Christianity, especially in its rigorous and even ascetic forms, to be an attractive alternative.[33]

The first Anglican clergy in Japan after the government grudgingly allowed foreigners into the country were John Liggins and Channing Moore Williams, both graduates of the Virginia Theological Seminary and missionaries of the Episcopal Church in the United States. Since missionaries were not allowed to evangelize freely until 1873, prior to that date Liggins and Moore dedicated themselves to "'civilizing' activities of schools and hospitals, rather than any direct evangelistic outreach."[34]

Early attempts at evangelization encountered great difficulties. Channing Moore Williams secretly baptized his first Japanese convert only in 1866, more than ten years after his arrival in the country.[35] Years later, G. F. Verbeck, one of the first missionaries of the Reformed Church, wrote that "we found the natives not at all accessible touching religious matters. When such a subject was mooted in the presence of a Japanese, his hand would, almost involuntarily, be applied to his throat, to indicate the extreme perilousness of such a topic . . ." Dr. Verbeck attributed this attitude to "the abominable system of secret espionage, which we found in full swing when we first arrived and, indeed, for several years after . . ." A twentieth century American bishop who served the diocese of Kyoto considered that "the hostility was due not so much to religious prejudice as to the traditional belief that Christianity was detrimental to the national welfare and independence."[36]

Like the mission to China, the Anglican presence in Japan was also marked by the participation of missionaries from England and Canada; the CMS sent its first missionaries in 1869, the SPG began its work four years later, and in 1888 Canadian Anglican missionaries arrived in Japan.

The story of Anglicanism in Japan demonstrates a flexibility and awareness of issues of context that are not always evident among nineteenth century missionaries. At the SPG school-church which was established in Kobe, in 1879 four new Christians were permitted to receive Holy Communion without confirmation, since the Church of England had no bishop in the islands, a situation which an early historian of the Japanese missions described as similar to "an army without a general."[37] (Channing Moore Williams had been consecrated as the Episcopal Church's Bishop of China and Japan in 1866 and had already performed the first Confirmations of Japanese converts in 1875; as in China, the distinct jurisdictions of English and American missionaries required a certain amount of ecclesiastical diplomacy to establish "spheres of influence," mutual cooperation, and ultimately one united Japanese Anglican church.)[38]

Like most other Anglican missionaries of the nineteenth century, Bishop Williams considered that in a society such as Japan, where there was little support for Christianity, schools and medical facilities provided the best hope of changing minds. Assisted by two missionary deacons recently trained at Nashotah House, he established the Rikkyo School in Yedo (now Tokyo), which ultimately grew into the prestigious St. Paul's University. Another school was soon founded in Osaka. Given the limited assistance provided by the Episcopal Church, all the schools were required to be financially self-supporting. In 1883, the Rev. C. T. Blanchet, director of the American Episcopal boys' school in Tokyo, argued that missionary education should seek to "bring the youths of the country under Christian influence, with the hope of their ultimate conversion"; to provide training for Japanese teachers, evangelists, and pastors; and to help "develop and establish a self-supporting and self-propagating native Church." Girls' schools, one of which grew into the highly respected St. Margaret's School and included a college for women, became an important part of Anglican ministry in the latter decades of the nineteenth century. In the port city of Yokohama, the Church also established a school for mixed-race children who were habitually shunned by their birth-families.[39]

Meanwhile, Dr. Henry Laning, an American medical missionary, initiated the establishment of St. Barnabas Hospital in Osaka, which Bishop Williams credited with the evangelization of half of all those baptized in that city. The work of an English lay missionary, Miss Riddell, in establishing a hospital for victims of Hansen's Disease in Kumamoto is credited with moving the imperial government to establish a network of institutions devoted to the same illness.[40]

The Episcopal Church and the English missionaries of the SPG agreed to form a joint theological seminary and in 1878 Trinity Divinity School reported thirteen Japanese students preparing for ordination.[41] In general, Japanese graduates were required to work for several years as catechists under the supervision of a foreign missionary before being ordained as deacons and priests. Later a further condition of ordination was added: "Before a catechist could be ordained the congregation which he was to serve as pastor was required to pay at least one-third of his salary."[42]

A.C. Shaw, one of the first clergy sent to Japan by the SPG, had a remarkable and lengthy ministry. Unlike many of his colleagues, he "had no great faith in opening mission schools as a method of evangelization. . . . [He] considered his time better spent in preaching and catechizing." In his first four years in Tokyo, he had baptized 150 new Christians, holding services at first in a Buddhist temple, later in a shop and back room, and at last in the new St. Andrew's Church, a "tiny brick building, holding about 120 persons, with lancet windows, a decent chancel apse, and wooden seats." Shaw held services in both Japanese and English, "preachings to non-Christians, devotional meetings, daily offices for clergy and catechists." When the building was destroyed in the earthquake of 1891, it was replaced by a church with double the capacity, served by three Japanese clergy, which served as the center of SPG's ministry.[43]

Shaw's detailed description of his work as an evangelist in rural Japan provides an important window into ministry in the Japanese context towards the end of the nineteenth century. Describing a visit to a fishing village where an aged catechist maintained a tiny congregation, he noted that while a few of the catechist's neighbors were willing to give Shaw a hearing as he explained "the chief truths of Christianity," he was challenged by two hearers. The first raised the problem of evil and questioned the practicality of Christianity. Shaw responded by describing the effect of trouble and trial as a disciplining of the character and by pointing out the similarity of Christian ethics to the Japanese value of respect and reverence for the ties and obligations of family life. The second, more difficult challenge, came from a fisherman who would have willingly been baptized but whose brother reminded him that Christians are forever cut off from the rituals by which families maintain ties with their ancestors. "Such," Shaw writes, "are the conditions and circumstances of life under which it is necessary for the convert to break away from the ancient faith; and to realize them is to realize the difficulty of embracing Christianity in a country like Japan."[44]

Throughout the imperial period, Christians in general found their place in society to be problematic. The figure of the emperor as the divine embodiment of Japanese identity challenged the religious allegiance of new Japanese Christians, who experienced significant discrimination in the early decades. Even among those who welcomed the incursion of western science, education and technology, Christianity was considered to be a "danger from the point of view of the national welfare."[45]

It was in response to their problematic position within Japanese society that led Japanese Anglicans to see the importance of their own autonomous church. Edward Bickersteth, who had been appointed as the Church of England's Missionary Bishop for Japan, was one of the staunchest supporters of a Japanese church. The synod of representatives from the British and American missions, "a freely elected body in which Europeans and Americans were greatly outnumbered by Japanese," responsible for its establishment unanimously approved the proposed plan; and in 1887 the Nippon Sei Ko Kai (Holy Catholic Church of Japan) was formed by combining the two jurisdictions. It was the first autonomous church in communion with Canterbury in which British settlers were not the majority, and anticipated the concerns of the 1888 Lambeth Conference in adopting a constitution "on the basis of the Holy Scriptures, the Nicene Creed, the Sacraments and the Three Orders [of ministry]" and in resolving to "place on record the desire for the establishment in Japan of a Christian Church which, by imposing no non-essential conditions of communion, shall include as many as possible of the Christians of this country."[46] Remarkably, though the church numbered only three thousand members and the first Japanese bishops were not consecrated until well into the twentieth century, nineteenth century Anglicans nourished the hope that one day Christianity might come to serve as the national religion.[47]

Throughout the nineteenth century and well into the twentieth, the Nippon Sei Ko Kai wrestled with the appropriate stance to take with regard to the increasing national emphasis on devotion to the figure of the emperor. In 1890, the imperial government ordered that all schools teach the official Shinto-based devotion to the emperor. Like most Japanese Protestants, Anglicans—including the first Japanese priest, Imai Judo—accepted the compatibility of the imperial cult and Christian belief, considering that "the spirit of Japan (*yamato damashii*) would be perfected, rather than erased, by Christianity."[48]

The experience of ministry in Japan was shaped—and challenged—by what has been described as a sharp distinction between public and private realms (*ooyake* and *watakushi*), a dichotomy that goes back to the earliest stage of the development of Japanese national identity. "Obedience in the public, official arena was a matter of the ooyake, but the private side was maintained in the watakushi.... The ooyama structure in Japan is a hierarchy: the family is a private matter in relationship to the greater ooyake, but within the family itself the father is the ooyake." This distinction, writes Bishop John Takeda, lay behind the fact that "most Christians tacitly accepted the imperial ooyake teaching.... Indeed, the teaching of the emperor's divine nature had been increasingly taken for granted by the majority of Japanese Christians, an ambiguous fact given the conflict with the essential nature of Christian faith." Bishop Takeda also attributes the tendency to consider Christian faith a matter of private rather than public life which has prevailed in Japanese Anglicanism to the same distinction between the *ooyake* and *watakushi* realms.[49]

In his history of the first few decades of Japanese Anglicanism, written at the beginning of the twentieth century, Herbert Moore identified a number of significant questions that the new church must face beyond the pressing ones of its relationship to the imperial state. Some voices had already been raised asking whether the three orders of ministry affirmed by Anglican tradition were appropriate, whether traditional Anglican vestments belonged in Japanese services of worship, and what was the proper place of the Thirty-Nine Articles in Japanese Anglicanism. While the Articles were translated into Japanese and printed with the Prayer Book, unlike English and Canadian clergy those ordained in the Nippon Sei Ko Kai were not required to give assent to the Articles at the time of their ordination. Moore notes that white is the traditional Japanese color of mourning, exactly the opposite of its usage in traditional Anglican liturgies; How free, he asked, are Japanese Anglicans to alter such traditions to fit their own context? Must the Nippon Sei Ko Kai follow the western tradition of separating baptism and confirmation, or as an eastern form of Christianity might it adopt the Orthodox custom and administer baptism and chrismation in one rite? And yet another question with regard to the relationship between church and imperial state: Japanese law permitted the remarriage of divorced persons, and a man was allowed to marry his deceased brother's wife; what are the implications for the Church's own teaching and practice of Holy Matrimony? No doubt Moore would have been surprised if he knew that such questions, far from being resolved in the short term, continue to trouble Anglicans more than a century later and in a Communion far more diverse than he could have ever imagined. The difficulties to confront the Nippon Sei Ko Kai in the twentieth century would have been equally unimaginable to its members as the new century dawned.

ANGLICAN MINISTRY IN KOREA

Unlike the Anglican presence in both China and Japan, the ministry begun in Korea was entirely the product of the Church of England's missionary activity. In 1889, Charles Corfe, a former British naval officer, was consecrated to be the missionary bishop of Korea, and went accompanied by two lay missionary doctors. By the end of 1891, he had been joined by two priests, two deacons and two ordinands (none of whom spoke Korean).

Bishop Corfe was supported by the SPG and represented an uncompromising Anglo-Catholic understanding of Anglicanism and its ministry. He was clear about the uniqueness of the venture, which he conceived as "rearing, in a country almost entirely heathen, a Branch of the true Church of God, at once Catholic and Apostolic; a Church, moreover, which being outside the British Dominions, would have to be free from the limitations imposed by a Church in union with the State." He considered that the development of a Korean Anglicanism required a strong authoritarian hand and a liturgy directly drawn from the English *Book of Common Prayer,* which, he believed, "(taken in its entirety) to be as adequate an instrument of the grace of God in Corea (sic) and in every part of the heathen world as it is in her Colonies . . ."[50]

On the other hand, Corfe was determined to prohibit the "wide diversities of ritual and practice which within the four corners of the Prayer Book, as found in England, either as matters of indifference to the future Church in Corea or as worthy of being imitated by those who might easily fall" into division. In conjunction with his clergy, Bishop Corfe accordingly devised a single eucharistic rite that would, he assumed, save "that mission from that 'strife of tongues' which so greatly impedes the Church as the Evangelizer of the heathen at home and in the Colonies." With an imposed uniform rite, he asserted, "on the side of the native Christians the effect of the Use has been to produce, from the first, an orderliness and intelligence in Divine Worship, and, moreover, a service . . . resembling so closely its English prototype . . ." In the first rite, introduced in 1897, the use of incense was mandated, discussion of which was actually part of the agenda of the 1897 Lambeth Conference.[51]

Bishop Corfe believed that in a missionary setting such as Korea, the Church could and must emphasize a level of discipline that would have been unacceptable to Christians in England. He was aware that such discipline—fasting, almsgiving, and the faithful observance of Sunday worship—could not be imposed on English Christians but he invited those few British Anglicans living in Korea to "identify [themselves] with our native brethren and take your great part in building up a national Church in Corea." Such discipline, he believed, was absolutely essential for the new Korean converts, and would be "absolutely new to them, and so much opposed to the self-indulgent habits of the Corean people."[52]

By the end of the nineteenth century, the incipient Anglican mission in Korea had four stations, each with its own permanent structure, in Seoul, Chemulpo, and Kongwa Island as well as in Manchuria. It was responsible for English-and Japanese-language ministry as well as its work with Korean converts. Expenses connected with the buildings and the clergy salaries were paid by the SPG, while sources in England provided the funding for hospitals, medical work, an orphanage, and a printing operation.[53]

Bishop Corfe and his missionary companions believed that their evangelistic work must not be rushed, and the first baptism was performed only in 1897. Translation of the Prayer Book depended on their mastery of the Korean language; in the Eucharistic liturgy, the "State Prayers" for the Queen and royal family were replaced by Collects for the Emperor and the conversion of the Korean people.[54]

Corfe decided to incorporate customs derived from the early Church in order to guarantee strong discipline. Potential converts were admitted first as catechumens, and dismissed from the Eucharist before the recitation of the Nicene Creed; Corfe was particularly concerned that the Lord's Prayer not be used when catechumens were present. "Notorious offenders" were to be excommunicated until they had made a public confession to the congregation after the dismissal of the catechumens. In the case of "impenitent sinners," a category designed to apply especially to those "whose failure (for whatever inexcusable cause) to attend the Church Services at the appointed times has become a scandal, or therefore a source of injury to the other members of the Church, as instituting a breach of unity," the bishop issued a document forbidding them both access to the sacraments and to the church itself. In practice, this document was issued primarily to those who had "lapsed into heathenism" and withdrawn from association with Christians.[55] The end of the century saw a church still in its infancy, but with a vigorous missionary presence conscious of the challenge—and the opportunity—to develop

Korean Anglicanism free of the conflicts that had troubled it in other places. Sadly, their efforts could not prevent the conflict that would visit the Korean Church in the twentieth century through no fault of its own.

THE GROWTH OF LATIN AMERICAN ANGLICANISM

The deaths in 1850 of the first missionaries at the southern tip of South America did not mean the end of the project which had cost them their life. Renamed the South American Missionary Society (SAMS), the organization Gardiner had founded continued to send missionaries to the Native peoples of the southern tip of the continent, and in 1872 the first natives of Tierra del Fuego were baptized. Charles Darwin commented, "The success of the Tierra del Fuego Mission is most wonderful, and charms me, as I always prophesied utter failure. It is a grand success."[56]

SAMS considered its mandate to be the evangelization of non-Christian peoples, not to interfere with the Roman Catholicism of the majority population. Gardiner's son was instrumental in continuing the work of SAMS, strongly identified with the Evangelical party of the Church of England, with the Mapuche people of Araucania in southern Chile. In the 1880s W. Barbrooke Grubb, a Scottish missionary for SAMS, expanded its work among the several tribes of the Chaco people of Paraguay and northern Argentina. In both settings, SAMS promoted primary evangelism and also initiated health and education programs.[57]

In the 1890s a team of SAMS missionaries established a significant presence in Araucania which served as advocates of the Mapuche people in the face of substantial government corruption. In her history of the Anglican Church of Chile, Barbara Bazley describes their "missionary methodology" as "announcing the message of salvation and the necessity of a personal conversion to Christ" but buttressed by "practical ministries that would demonstrate that the missionaries did not intend to exploit them but to serve them." Those ministries were education, necessary because "in the Spanish-speaking world of the Frontier, there were unscrupulous people who would take advantage of their ignorance"; medical service, given the high rate of mortality from easily treatable diseases; and "offering the possibility of a life free of alcoholism to the youth."[58]

A recent study of the Mapuche missions described the missionary technique, or "model of intervention" identified with SAMS as "association with the existing chiefs and education of their offspring, translation into the local language and circulation of the [scriptures] in printed form, encouragement of a 'cultural nationalism' in an elite destined to be legitimated by the local representatives of the colonial government." By the end of the nineteenth century, the missionaries had introduced modernizing tools and stressed a "technological transformation" by teaching skills such as carpentry, apiculture, ironwork, shoemaking, horticulture. They were also careful to provide food and lodging to keep the Mapuche from leaving the mission during harvest time.[59]

In Panama, the Episcopal Church's ministry continued to be impeded by its inability to keep clergy in the post: during the first twenty years of its presence, nine clergy attempted to serve the Church but either died or beat a fairly hasty retreat. Under new management, the railroad company which had helped support the ministry suspended its collaboration, and pastoral duties were often left to the British and American consuls. With the initiation of a French attempt to build a canal across the isthmus in 1882, and the influx of large numbers of West Indians to provide the labor, the bishop of the West Indies was moved to request the Archbishop of Canterbury's help in securing Anglican ministry for them. A response came from the South American Missionary Society, which sent two clergy, and the oversight of the Episcopal Church's ministry was transferred to the bishop of Jamaica. For the rest of the century, Anglican ministry was the responsibility of the Church of England.[60]

In Central America, the Anglican presence established among West Indians and English-speaking expatriates continued to grow throughout the second half of the nineteenth century. In some cases, it was laypeople who organized services and sought the support of clergy from overseas. In Costa Rica, a group of English and German laypeople established an independent congregation which was non-denominational until the end of the nineteenth century, when the Bishop of British Honduras (Belize) was asked to send an Anglican pastor. This congregation appears to have had no interest in the evangelization of Costa Ricans or Native peoples, but rather served as a chaplaincy or "social club" for the foreigners who had made Costa Rica their home. Even after the diocese of British Honduras agreed to provide clergy, "the church was run in a congregational style. It was the congregation who decided the clergy's fate and the services were conducted on a congregational model, although the Book of Common Prayer was used. . . . Any innovation proposed by the bishops was ignored completely."[61]

Similar experiences were part of the history of Anglican ministry throughout Central and South America, wherever numbers permitted the establishment of English-speaking enclaves among the majority-Spanish-speaking population.

On Costa Rica's Atlantic coast, a different situation prevailed. Following the failure of the French efforts at building a canal across Panama, thousands of West Indian laborers migrated to Costa Rica in search of work on the banana plantations and in the construction of the North Atlantic Railroad that connected San José with the city of Limón. Limón became the center of English-speaking West Indian life and culture in Costa Rica. The community grew towards the end of the century with the arrival of large numbers of immigrants from Jamaica, some of them teachers and other professionals.

Among them were those who could perform the role of religious leaders in the community, and thus were able to consolidate the presence of the Anglican church in the province of Limón. It was not until 1898 that a church building was constructed, under the authority of the diocese of British Honduras.[62]

If Anglican ministry in Latin America generally limited itself to English-speaking chaplaincies and mission to Native peoples, the most notable exception in the nineteenth century was the establishment of a missionary presence in the predominantly Roman Catholic setting of southern Brazil. Once religious freedom was permitted and the Roman Catholic Church disestablished in 1889, two recent graduates of the Virginia Theological Seminary, Lucien Lee Kinsolving and James Watson Morris embarked for the city of Porto Alegre with the purpose of establishing an Episcopal presence. The Brazilian theologian Carlos Calvani describes the assumptions that shaped their undertaking:

> Theology influenced by Protestant individualism, fruit of the spiritual revivals, predominated. The influence of the doctrine of "Manifest Destiny," according to which God chose the Anglo-Saxon peoples (particularly the North Americans) to expand God's reign on earth, was strong. The ways selected would be the propagation of the pure gospel and the education of the people, through emphases on universal sin, the love of God and in expiation through faith in Christ. This "package" included the condemnation of the Roman Catholic Church as an apostate institution, combat against non-Christian religions and the effort to save all the pagans from eternal condemnation. That was basically the nucleus of the preaching of all the Protestant North American missionaries who arrived in Brazil in the second half of the nineteenth century.[63]

Calvani points out that while the first missionaries to Brazil shared a theology with other missionary churches, their understanding of the Church was different, and displayed a more catholic understanding of the nature of the Christian community. Shortly after the turn of the twentieth century Kinsolving, already a bishop, emphasized that its gatherings "are not a congregational organization. The church does not exist as an aggregate of separated and independent congregations. The council is an expression of our ecclesiastical life, an organic part of the church."

The Roman Catholic Church manifested considerable hostility towards the establishment of the new Church, and its leaders experienced persecution and even physical threats.[64] Its displeasure at the incursion of the Episcopal missionaries was not misplaced, since their intent was to establish an alternative to what they considered a corrupt form of Christianity by offering the Episcopal Church as a distinct and different option The first issue of the Church's journal described its approach:

> Leaving aside invented traditions and seeking to listen only and simply to the voice of Christ, we hoist the flag of all religious progress, and are already beginning the struggle against falsehood and superstition. We will continue in the modest development of that great work in the following order: explanations of biblical passages, so that our readers are instructed and exhorted by the words of inspiration themselves, and so be equipped to respond to anyone who seeks explanations of the faith they hold (1 Peter 3:15); translations of selections chosen from well-known authors of the Christian world, in order to offer material to feed devout spirits, and religious news carefully selected and coordinated to emphasize the influence and progress of the gospel in the world.[65]

The ministry developed under Kinsolving and Morris's direction sought to provide a worship "devoid of formalism and pomp with which Romanism lulled and distracted us for centuries." In its early years worship was mostly limited to Morning Prayer, "without liturgical adornment" and with the clergy dressed in suits and clerical collars without vestments. The missionaries worked for a year in Pelotas before celebrating the Eucharist. Calvani describes a method frequently employed in the early years of Brazilian Anglicanism: the "week of evangelization" or "week of mission," evening sessions held from Wednesday to Sunday with "hymns sung by choirs or quartets, testimonies of conversion and an evangelistic sermon," usually preached by one of the Episcopal missionaries but sometimes by a Methodist or Baptist pastor.[66] Kevin Ward observes that the early success of the Episcopal mission was especially pronounced among "professional people and city dwellers, attracted to the liturgical order and intellectual freedom of Anglicanism."[67]

ANGLICAN MINISTRY AND THE BEGINNINGS OF AMERICAN EMPIRE

In the early years of the nineteenth century, the newly independent United States had doubled its size with the Louisiana Purchase, which extended its western boundary to the Rocky Mountains. At mid-century, military action against Mexico resulted in the annexation of Texas and what is now the American Southwest. Conflict over the Pacific Northwest, initially shaken by both American and British claims, was settled peacefully by extending the border between the United States and Canada all the way to the Pacific. By mid-century the popular American belief that its "manifest destiny" was to stretch from the Atlantic to the Pacific had been fulfilled, and was further augmented with the purchase of Alaska from Russia in 1867.

But while its steady growth across the continent enjoyed wide support, it was only in the last decade of the nineteenth century that the United States acted upon more global ambitions. The Spanish-American War, fought in 1898, resulted in Spain's withdrawal from Cuba and Puerto Rico, its last colonial outposts in the New World, and cessation of its attempts to suppress an independence movement in the Philippines. At war's end, the United States occupied both Cuba and Puerto Rico (though Cuba was given its independence a few years into the twentieth century), and took over the struggle to prevent the independence of the Philippine Islands. That war of conquest, which is largely unknown outside the Philippines, may have cost half a million lives.

Five Episcopal chaplains accompanied the first American troops into the Philippines. One study of the chaplains' role in the late nineteenth century describes their duties as "conducting Sunday services, visiting the sick and wounded, counseling the troubled and depressed, securing suitable reading material for the troops' entertainment, and providing facilities for decent recreational activities to help the men resist the moral evils of camp life." But chaplains were also called upon often to perform what the author calls "handyman" tasks; before the beginning of hostilities it was an Episcopal chaplain who was sent to the headquarters of the Filipino revolutionary army to collect intelligence, since it was rightly assumed that "the Filipinos would never suspect a chaplain of spying."[68]

Once hostilities broke out between the American and Filipino armies, the chaplains were joined by four representatives of the Brotherhood of St. Andrew, at the time a popular organization for men in the Episcopal Church. On behalf of the Domestic and Foreign Missionary Society, they were sent to "'spiritually assist' the chaplains in their work and to try to bring the teachings of the church to the people of the islands." The team was comprised of two clergy and two laymen; the clergy were commissioned as missionaries by the Presiding Bishop and "their presence in the islands was approved by President Roosevelt and the Secretary of War." The team of missionaries used a rented house in Manila as a headquarters and chapel, where Morning Prayer was said daily and the Eucharist was celebrated on Sundays in both English and Spanish. Services for English-speaking expatriates were also held at the home of an English businessman and his wife. While the missionaries were initially hesitant to exercise their ministry among Christian Filipinos who were Roman Catholics, their minds were changed by stories of the many abusive practices of the Spanish clergy who still dominated the islands. The first Filipino Episcopal congregation began services on Christmas Day, 1898.[69]

The mission, however, proved to be short-lived. The Brotherhood of St. Andrew withdrew its support a year later; conflicts between the remaining chaplains and the cumbersome bureaucracy of the Domestic and Foreign Missionary Society further weakened the mission; by 1901, the Filipino congregation had completely collapsed. Charles Henry Brent, the first bishop of the Philippines, appointed after the General Convention of 1901, steadfastly refused to sanction ministry among Filipino Christians; his policy of refusing to raise "altar against altar" limited the Episcopal Church's ministry to "settlement work," schools, clinics and hospitals. While he eventually relented and allowed the schools and hospitals to provide religious instruction and even permitted an Episcopal chapel, his basic policy was to "leave evangelism entirely up to Providence." As a result, Anglican ministry would eventually depend upon a new focus and new leadership in the twentieth century.[70]

THE BEGINNING OF ANGLICAN MINISTRY IN HAWAI'I

Christian missionaries had been present in Hawai'i under the patronage of members of the Royal Family since the early nineteenth century, but a visit by King Kamehameha III to England in 1849 established a relationship with Queen Victoria which resulted in a request for an Anglican missionary in the islands. The Hawaiian monarchy was the result of the successful rise to power of the Kamehameha dynasty over the other tribal chiefs who had traditionally shared the rule of the islands, and the king may well have seen a church on the model of the Church of England as a useful instrument for supporting a monarchical form of government. His successors, King Kamehameha IV and Queen Emma, succeeded in obtaining a missionary bishop from England. Kamehameha himself translated most of the *Book of Common Prayer* into the Hawaiian language. In 1862 Bishop Thomas Staley arrived and, taking advantage of the islands' political independence, immediately began to establish what he called the "Hawaiian Reformed Catholic Church," characterized by Kevin Ward as a "somewhat exotic creation." Queen Emma traveled abroad and braved considerable opposition from the mostly Congregationalist American business community settled in the islands when she obtained plans and "a boatload of stones" to begin building the Cathedral of St. Andrew. Queen Emma also established and supported St. Andrew's Priory School for Girls, originally staffed by a community of English nuns.[71]

The future of the independent Hawaiian Church was, however, compromised by the ever-increasing power of the American settlers who had begun arriving on the islands early in the nineteenth century. Preceded by British explorers who introduced diseases which reduced the population by 80%,

American business interests were first drawn to the islands by the sandalwood trade, but were soon joined by others who demanded the right to own land on which to establish giant sugar plantations.[72] The end of this process of de facto occupation came when Hawai'i's last reigning monarch, Queen Lili'uokalani, was overthrown in 1893 by a group of American businessmen supported by a party of Marines from the U.S.S. Boston. Declaring an "American Republic of Hawai'i," they placed the Queen under house arrest for almost a year. During her captivity she wrote the most well-beloved piece of music sung in Hawai'i churches, "The Queen's Prayer." During her time of imprisonment, Bishop Alfred Willis insisted he was the Queen's priest and demanded visitation rights, threatening the wrath of Almighty God on the good Christians who were now claiming to run the government.

Released from imprisonment, the Queen requested baptism and became an active member of St. Andrew's Cathedral. She watched helplessly as the Hawaiian Islands became an American protectorate in 1898 and the Reformed Catholic Church was transferred to the Episcopal Church in the United States. Queen Lili'uokalani's insistence on peace helped bring the Hawaiian people under American domination and rule without violence. Believing to the end of her life that the kingdom of Hawai'i had been "stolen," she firmly opposed violence and eventually acquiesced in the de facto American Territory of Hawai'i.[73]

A century later, the Native Hawaiian scholar Pualani Hopkins would declare, "Since the beginning of evangelism and mission in Hawai'i 173 years ago, becoming a Christian has involved the denial of our own heritage and the denigration of values basic to our culture." Looking towards the next century of ministry and mission, she wrote:

> For me, and for many others like me, the challenge of the future to the Christian Church . . . is to create a nurturing and accepting environment that allows me to belong to the church without having to check my cultural identity at the door of the cathedral before entering. The challenge is to create a place that people like me can call home.
>
>   Any discussion of mission and the challenge of the future can only be meaningful in the context of a critique of the present and a remembrance of the past . . .

And, she concluded,

> the church must make room for aspects of native spirituality that are consonant with Christianity. . . . Our traditional call to worship by blowing a shell is no less valid than a tolling bell, our drums no less authentic than a pipe organ, our poi and coconut water no less a meal than bread and wine. We are as God made

us; and God loves us as we are. Will the church do the same, so that going to church will be synonymous with going home?[74]

At the end of the nineteenth century, a relatively few Anglican Christians would have found Hopkins' question significant, and many would find it unintelligible. But it would take on new urgency in the twentieth century, as Anglican ministry and mission continued to spread (and contract) in dialogue with the great upheavals and movements of that century. In our own time, it has become more insistent still, as Anglicans of the third millennium, diverse beyond the most extravagant dreams of our ancestors, continue to seek to be faithful to the gospel in a way that will guide us to where we belong: a place called home.

NOTES

1. Ward, *A History of Global Anglicanism*, 246–247.
2. Ward, *A History of Global Anglicanism*, 23–24.
3. Ward, *A History of Global Anglicanism*, 28–30.
4. Ward, *A History of Global Anglicanism*, 247–248.
5. G. F. S. Gray, revised by Martha Lund Smalley, *Anglicans in China: A History of the Zhonghua Shenggong Hui (Chung Hua Sheng Kung Hui)* (Episcopal China Mission History Project, 1996), 14.
6. Gray, *Anglicans in China*, 10, 12–13, 16.
7. Terrill E. Lautz, "The SVM and Transformation of the Protestant Mission in China," in Daniel H. Bays and Ellen Widmer, eds., *China's Christian Colleges: Cross-Cultural Connections, 1900–1950* (Stanford, CA: Stanford University Press, 2009), 3.
8. Ryan Dunch, "Science, Religion, and the Classics in Christian Higher Education to 1920," in Bays and Widmer, eds., *China's Christian Colleges*, 61.
9. Gray, *Anglicans in China*, 7, 11.
10. Edward Yihua Xu, "Liberal Arts Education in English and Campus Culture at St. John's University," in Bays and Widmer, eds., *China's Christian Colleges*, 109–110.
11. Xu, "Liberal Arts Education," 108.
12. Xu, "Liberal Arts Education," 111, 114.
13. Xu, "Liberal Arts Education," 111, 124.
14. Philip Wickeri, "Clergy Training and Theological Education: The Anglican-Episcopal Experience in China," Conference Paper, Yale-Edinburgh, History of the Missionary Movement and World Christianity, June 30–July 2, 2011, 5–6.
15. Wickeri, "Clergy Training," 7.
16. Wickeri, "Clergy Training," 6–8.
17. Latourette, *A History of Christian Missions in China*, 455–457.
18. L. A. G. Strong, *Flying Angel: The Story of the Missions to Seamen*, 53–54.

19. Helen Schneider, "The Professionalization of Chinese Domesticity: Ava B. Milam and Home Economics at Yenching University," in Bays and Widmer, eds., *China's Christian Colleges,* 3.

20. Patricia Pok-Kwan Chiu, "'A Position of Usefulness': Gendering of Girls' Education in Colonial Hong Kong (1850s-1890s)," *History of Education,* 37 (November 2008), 789–780.

21. Chiu, "'A Position of Usefulness,'" 791–793.

22. *Female Missionary Intelligencer,* IV (November 1861), 200–203; quoted in "'A Position of Usefulness,'" 794–795.

23. Chiu, "'A Position of Usefulness,'" 801.

24. Judith Liu and Donald P. Kelly, "'An Oasis in a Heathen Land': St. Hilda's School for Girls, Wuchang, 1928–1936," in Daniel H. Bays, ed., *Christianity in China: From the Eighteenth Century to the Present* (Stanford: Stanford University Press, 1996), 229.

25. Liu and Kelly, "'An Oasis in a Heathen Land,'" 230.

26. Kwok Pui-Lan, *Chinese Women and Christianity 1860–1927* (Atlanta: Scholars Press, 1992), 11–13.

27. Kwok, *Chinese Women,* 81–82, 89.

28. *Shanghai Sheng Bide Tang ershi zhou zili jiniankan (Commemorative Volume on the Twentieth Anniversary of Independence of St. Peter's Church),* September 1933, 5; quoted in Philip Wickeri, *Reconstructing Christianity in China: K. H. Ting and the Chinese Church* (Maryknoll, NY: Orbis Books, 2007), 23–24.

29. Ward, *A History of Global Anglicanism,* 249.

30. Ian Welch, "Mission, Murder and Diplomacy in Late 19th Century China: A Case Study," unpublished paper, 2nd Annual ANU Missionary History Conference, 2006, 15, 18.

31. Quoted in Philip Wickeri, *Seeking Common Ground: Protestant Christianity, the Three-Self Movement and China's United Front* (Maryknoll: Orbis, 1988), 38.

32. CMS MissionUpdateOnline: http://mission.typepad.com/church_mission_society_cm/2009/08/index.html. Accessed on February 21, 2011.

33. John M. Takeda, "Public and Private Church: The Experience of Japanese Anglicans, Past and Future," *Anglican and Episcopal History,* LXV, 4 (December 1996), 417–418.

34. Troy D. Mendez, "A History of Mission: International Students and Virginia Theological Seminary," unpublished, 2008, 10; quoted in J. Barney Hawkins IV, "International Students at Virginia Seminary: A Long History with a Rich and Transformative Practice," in Richard J. Jones and J. Barney Hawkins IV, eds., *Staying One, Remaining Open: Educating Leaders for a Twenty-First Century Church* (Harrisburg, PA and New York: Morehouse Publishing, 2010), 33.

35. Beverley D. Tucker, "Channing Moore Williams (1829–1910): Apostle to Japan," *Anglican and Episcopal History,* LXVI, 3 (September 1997), 282.

36. Henry St. George Tucker, *The History of the Episcopal Church in Japan* (New York: Charles Scribner's Sons, 1938), 75–77.

37. Herbert Moore, *The Christian Faith in Japan* (London: SPG, 1904), 60–61.

38. Tucker, "Channing Moore Williams," 282–283, 295ff.

39. Tucker, "Channing Moore Williams," 288–290, 294–295; Henry St. George Tucker, *The History of the Episcopal Church in Japan*, 121–122.

40. Tucker, "Williams," 288; Henry St. George Tucker, "History," 143.

41. Tucker, "Williams," 292.

42. Henry St. George Tucker, "History," 135.

43. Moore, *The Christian Faith in Japan*, 63–65.

44. Moore, *The Christian Faith in Japan*, 96–100.

45. Henry St. George Tucker, *History*, 110.

46. Henry St. George Tucker, *History*, 137–139.

47. Ward, *A History of Global Anglicanism*, 261–262.

48. Ward, *A History of Global Anglicanism*, 262.

49. Takeda, "Public and Private Church," 415–416, 421–422.

50. Charles John Corfe, *The Anglican Church in Corea* (London: Rivington, 1906), xi, xiii.

51. Corfe, "The Anglican Church in Corea," xiii, xv, xvii.

52. Corfe, "To the Laity of the Church of England in Corea: A Pastoral Letter, June 25, 1899," in *The Anglican Church in Corea*, 1, 8; "To the Clergy and Laity of the Church of England in the Diocese of Corea: A Pastoral Letter, July 18, 1899," in *The Anglican Church in Corea*, 13.

53. Corfe, "To the Members of the Mission Staff. A Pastoral Letter, Advent 1900," in *The Anglican Church in Corea*, 21, 26–27.

54. Corfe, "The Book of Common Prayer and Liturgical Translation," in *The Anglican Church in Corea*, 108.

55. Corfe, "The Book of Common Prayer and Liturgical Translation," in *The Anglican Church in Corea*, 108, 109, 111; "Church Discipline," in *The Anglican Church in Corea*, 137–138.

56. Stephen Neill, *A History of Christian Missions*, 272.

57. Ward, *A History of Global Anglicanism*, 104–105.

58. Barbara Bazley, *Somos Anglicanos* (Imprenta Editorial Interamericana, 1995), 100–102. Tr. mine.

59. André Merrard and Jorge Pavez, *Mapuche y Anglicano: Vestigios fotográficos de la Misión Araucana de Kepe, 1896 – 1908* (Santiago: Ocho Libros Editores, 2007), 12–13, 18, 21. Tr. mine.

60. Kater, "The Beginnings of the Episcopal Church in Panama," 153, 155–156.

61. Julio E. Murray, "The Episcopal Church in Costa Rica: Its First Century," *Anglican and Episcopal History*, LX (September 1991), 346.

62. Murray, "The Episcopal Church in Costa Rica," 348–351.

63. Carlos Calvani, "Eclesiologia em mudança: Uma leitura da Igreja Episcopal Anglicana do Brasil," *Inclusividade*, IX (April 2010), 78–79. Tr. Mine.

64. Calvani, "Eclesiologia," 79–80.

65. Calvani, "Eclesiologia," 80.

66. Calvani, "Eclesiologia," 80–81.

67. Ward, *A History of Global Anglicanism*, 106.

68. Mark Douglas Norbeck, "False Start: The First Three Years of Episcopal Missionary Endeavor in the Philippine Islands, 1898–1901," *Anglican and Episcopal History* LXII, 2 (June 1993), 215–216.

69. Norbeck, "False Start," 218–221.

70. Norbeck, "False Start," 224–225; 229–236.

71. Kevin Ward, *A History of Global Anglicanism*, 291; Willis H. A. Moore, "'Ehā ali'i wahine: Four royal women," *The Historiographer*, XLIII, 1 (Lent 2005), 7–9.

72. Haunani-Kay Trask, "The Taking of Hawaiian Sovereignty: Manifest Destiny and Sugar-Planter Capitalism," in *Hawaiian Sovereignty: Myth and Reality* (Mānoa: Center for Hawaiian Studies, University of Hawai'i at Mānoa, undated).

73. Ward, *A History of Global Anglicanism*, 291.

74. Alberta Pualani Hopkins, "The Challenge of the Future; Creating a Place Called Home," in John L. Kater, ed., *The Challenges of the Past, The Challenges of the Future: Essays on Mission in the Light of Five Hundred Years of Evangelization in the Americas* (Berkeley, CA: Church Divinity School of the Pacific, 1994), 73, 79.

Chapter Twelve

Tensions

Anglican Ministry in the United States of America, 1860–1900

THE EPISCOPAL CHURCH AND CIVIL WAR

While most of the mainstream Protestant churches in the United States divided over the issue of slavery, the Episcopal Church maintained an official neutrality that preserved its unity even in the face of strong passions on both sides. However, following the secession by eleven southern states to form an independent "Confederate States of America," the bishops of Louisiana and Georgia called for a convention of bishops, clergy and lay delegates "to consider their relations to the Protestant Episcopal Church of the United States, of which they have so long been the equal and happy members." The bishops affirmed that

> this necessity does not arise out of any dissension which has occurred within the Church itself, nor out of any dissatisfaction with either the doctrine or discipline of the Church . . . We are still one in Faith, in purpose and in Hope; but political changes, forced upon us by a stern necessity, have occurred, which have placed our Dioceses in a position requiring consultation as to our future ecclesiastical relations. It is better that these relations should be arranged by the common consent of all the Dioceses within the Confederate States than by the independent action of each Diocese.[1]

Only one southern bishop, James H. Otey of Tennessee, disagreed; shortly before secession, he wrote that whatever happened to the American union, "our Church organization will remain firm and unbroken, amidst all the storms and convulsions which sweep over the political world." Bishop Otey made it clear that he participated in the Confederate Church "with a reservation respecting the principle which he felt was involved."[2]

By late 1861, a Constitution based on that of the Episcopal Church in the United States had been adopted and sent to the dioceses for approval. In November 1862, the Episcopal Church in the Confederate States of America held its only "national" synod and approved the preparation of a *Book of Common Prayer* appropriate for its use. The most significant change from the American book was the substitution of the term "Confederate States of America" wherever the phrase "United States of America" occurred; a Pastoral Letter from the House of Bishops assured its readers that except for changes related to the political situation, the Confederate Prayer Book preserved the American Church's book, "with whose doctrines, discipline and worship we are in entire harmony."[3]

The bishops underlined the urgent need for mission, especially in a time of war:

> Many of the States of this Confederacy are Missionary ground. The population is sparse and scattered; the children of the Church are few and far between; the Priests of the Lord can reach them only after great labor and privation. . . . Unless we take care that the Gospel is sent to these isolated children of the Church, who will heed their cry? They have no Church to cry to, but the Church which we now represent, and they cast themselves upon us in full faith that we will do our whole duty towards them. They are one with us in faith, and care, and suffering; they are bearing like evils with those which disturb us, and they have no worship to cheer and support them, no Gospel to preach to them patience and long-suffering. For Christ's sake they pray that they may be given at least a Mother's bosom to die upon. . . . And now it only remains for us to bid you, one and all, an affectionate farewell. . . . May God's gracious Providence guide you in safety to your homes, and preserve them from the desolations of war. And should we not be permitted to battle together any more for Christ in the Church Militant, may we be deemed worthy to be members of the Church Triumphant, where with prophets, apostles, martyrs, saints, and angels, we may ascribe honor and glory, dominion and praise, to Him that sitteth upon the Throne, and to the Lamb, forever.[4]

The impact of the Civil War on Episcopalians in the South was especially difficult because most of the war was fought there. A large number of Episcopal clergy volunteered as chaplains, and Leonidas Polk, bishop of Louisiana, resigned his office and accepted a commission as a general in the Confederate Army. Writing half a century later, Joseph Cheshire, Bishop of North Carolina, was at pains to emphasize the strong pastoral ministry undertaken by many southern clergy on behalf of the physical and especially the spiritual welfare of enslaved people. He considered that while there was strong sentiment against slavery as an institution among many white southerners at the time of the war, the widespread sense of loyalty to their own states and culture, and support for states' rights to leave the Union, made it impossible for the Church to raise the possibility of emancipation at a time when most white southerners believed themselves to be engaged in a war in defense of their liberty and their way of life.[5] Perhaps many white Episcopalians in the South would have agreed with the House of Deputies of the Confederate Church when it resolved that "this Church desires specially to recognize its obligation to provide for the spiritual wants of that class of our brethren, who in the providence of God have been committed to our sympathy and care in the national institution of slavery."[6]

On the congregational level, parishes in the parts of the South where fighting was most severe found themselves called to ministries that most would have found inconceivable before the outbreak of war. The diaries of civilians struggling under fire and military occupation provide vivid descriptions of how the war changed congregational life. In Winchester, Virginia, only a few miles from the border between North and South, Mary Greenhow Lee vividly portrayed a congregation and community that was occupied by Union troops for much of the war. "The idea," she wrote, "that by this time to-morrow night we may be in their hands, is too terrible for my mind to grasp." Shortly after, she noted, "All is over and we are prisoners in our own houses."[7]

Christ Church, Winchester was used briefly by the Union Army as a jail for Confederate soldiers. Its rector joined the Confederate Army, first as a member of the Virginia Cavalry and later as its chaplain. A local layman was ordained deacon and also served as mayor during most of the war. As both mayor and deacon, he tended to seek ways of accommodating the church to the demands of an occupying army—much to the outrage of parishioners more zealous for the southern cause. Throughout the most difficult days of occupation, Mrs. Lee hosted weekly prayer meetings in her home.

On one occasion, Mrs. Lee unsuccessfully urged the deacon to use the resources provided by the Confederate Church's Prayer Book, outlawed by the Union authorities. When the Wardens refused to observe a Day of Prayer announced by the President of the Confederate States, Mrs. Lee took matters into her own hands, called a gathering at her own home, and

> to my surprise there were more than thirty persons present. . . . I conducted the services, but confined myself to the [Confederate] prayer book prayers. I was very gratified at the success of our little effort; all enjoyed it, & there was certainly much real feeling. You cannot imagine how strange it feels, to know we are having services in our own homes, that we would not dare to have in public.[8]

During the last occupation of Winchester, Christ Church's parishioners became accustomed, if not reconciled, to the presence of large numbers of Union soldiers at worship. Mrs. Lee described her reaction:

> I found our pew filled up with Yankees; it was very impertinent, as they have never ventured up so high before; I took pleasure in making room for Dr. Cromwell by me when he came in, that the Yankees might see that a Confederate could get in where they could not. The communion was administered; only one Yankee communed & he was a poor mild-looking private; I rather respected him for coming forward for himself.

She found herself wondering at her own lack of hospitality: "One not accustomed to these scenes will think them very unChristian, but I cannot even in Church feel charitably to the enemies not only of my country, my friends, but also of my God, for they respect neither God nor man."[9]

One of the gruesome aspects of ministry throughout the American South during the War was the task of ministering to the wounded and dying on both sides. Like many of her friends, Mary Lee made regular visits to the makeshift hospitals that occupied some of the town's public buildings whenever battles were fought in the vicinity.

> Our own men and the Yankees, all mixed up together in the same rooms; Nettie and I staied (sic) til dark, doing what we could for them; there were numbers of ladies there, & our enemies, as well as our friends, received our attentions; you remember how I always said, I would not go to their Hospitals, but I never thought of our own men in them, not (sic) could I give to one sufferer, & pass another by in silence . . . I am so tired & it is wrong to be weary when I am trying to do good, even to our enemies; but it is a wearisome life.[10]

The townspeople of Winchester, as of communities throughout the affected states, understood providing food to the wounded as a taxing but essential ministry. "In my peculiar vocation (that of feeding people)," Mrs. Lee wrote, "the necessity for exertion comes three times a day, Sunday not excepted." They also attempted to address spiritual needs: "Went to the Hospital and while there, found Dr. Boyd had arranged to preach to the men. Mrs. O. Brown, Miss Mary Brooks & I formed the choir; it was so ludicrous that I could scarcely retain a grave countenance." Nor were these often opinionated but compassionate laypeople unaware of the novelty of their roles: "I propose," Mary Lee wrote, "that we shall declare ourselves a separate & independent sovereignty, & elect a Queen to reign over us, the women having proved themselves more valiant than the men."[11]

The aftermath of the War had far-reaching effects on the ministry of the Episcopal Church. The reconciliation between the Episcopal Church in the

Union and the dioceses which had formed the Church in the Confederate States raised several issues which the General Convention of 1865 had to address. Because of their highly visible role in the South, many lay leaders were not included in the general amnesty decreed by the American government; their arrival at Convention could have precipitated their arrest. The Church in the Confederate States had approved the election of a new bishop for Alabama and had organized the diocese of Arkansas; neither action had been approved by the Episcopal Church. Nevertheless, two southern bishops and delegates from three dioceses made the daring step of attending the 1865 General Convention. The warm welcome they received, and the speed with which the Convention approved the bishops of Alabama and the "missionary bishop of the Southwest" (who had been named by the Confederate Church as bishop of Arkansas) indicated that for most of the Episcopal Church's leadership, re-integrating the southern dioceses into its ranks was more important than other principles or issues. By spring of the following year, all the dioceses which had absented themselves from the 1865 General Convention had reunited with the Episcopal Church.[12]

POST-WAR MINISTRY IN THE EPISCOPAL CHURCH

The years immediately following the Civil War were exceedingly difficult for the Episcopal Church in the defeated South. As Harold Lewis commented, "While some black Episcopalians remained in the Church, both in white and black congregations, most black Episcopalians sought spiritual nurture and religious instruction elsewhere." He cites the example of the diocese of South Carolina, in which African Americans comprised nearly half its membership before the War, and in which only 395 black communicants remained in 1868; only two Black congregations remained in all of Alabama. The response of the post-war Episcopal Church was, in Lewis' words, "a new missionary strategy that it deemed to be more in keeping with the times . . . [B]lacks were seen as a group to be 'worked among.'" Within three years, the Freedman's Commission, placed under the Board of Missions immediately after the War, had opened thirty parochial and industrial schools in which it supported 65 teachers and 5,000 students.[13]

Many of the post-war leaders in the Episcopal Church believed that the work of education was a necessary but secondary aspect of the Church's evangelistic mission among the formerly enslaved people in the South. It was widely recognized that Black leadership would be more effective, and the training of both African American teachers and clergy was encouraged. Nevertheless, of the twenty Black clergy ordained in the decade following the war, only six became priests, while the others remained in the diaconate. No Black priest was ordained in South Carolina until 1895.[14]

Although the Civil War had ended slavery in the United States, the decades following demonstrated amply that racism shaped American churches as profoundly as it did the other institutions of American society. Almost no white voices within the Episcopal Church, in the north or south, considered the possibility that African Americans could or should participate fully in its life on the basis of equality with its white members. Throughout the United States, segregated churches remained the norm, and an overwhelming attitude of paternalism and racial superiority determined the nature of the Church's ministry.

The work of the Freedmen's Commission, soon renamed the Commission of Home Missions to Colored People, was considered an integral part of the Church's domestic missionary efforts. Harold Lewis points out that

> The commission's first report suggests that the Episcopal Church, which for two and a half centuries had don little to contribute to the uplift of blacks, and indeed in many places had used religion to further subjugate them, goes to great lengths to exculpate itself from any responsibility for the condition of blacks prior to their emancipation. Indeed, the committee, speaking on behalf of a church that had been conspicuous by its silence on the question of slavery out of deference to the vast number of its communicants who were slaveholders, seems to ignore this history and to seek instead the higher ground; of a *noblesse oblige*.[15]

The work of the commission was replaced by the Church Commission for Work Among Colored People, established in 1884.[16] During the period of Reconstruction, segregated church institutions became the norm: St. Stephen's Mission and School in Petersburg, Virginia eventually grew to include the Bishop Payne Divinity School, which provided theological education for most of the Church's Black clergy.[17] In 1888, the diocese of South Carolina established a separate archdeaconry for Black congregations.[18]

In the Church's network of schools, scattered across the south, white and African American educators worked under extremely difficult conditions to teach their Black students the skills with which they could find a place within the separate and decidedly unequal society in which it was assumed they would continue to live. While the defeat of the Civil War affirmed what many white Episcopalians already believed—that slavery itself was wrong—it did little or nothing to shake the belief they had inherited from their ancestors that the distinct strata by which society is organized hierarchically are ordained by God and that to presume to eliminate them violates the very God-given order of creation.

The remaining decades of the nineteenth century were marked by the erosion of African American civil liberties at the same time that the Episcopal Church was wrestling with how to structure ministry with the Black Episcopalians who remained in the Church's southern dioceses: "[D]uring the same period in which southern states enacted Jim Crow laws, white Episcopalians in the South circumscribed the freedom of African Americans in the ecclesiastical sphere."[19] While plans for separate black jurisdictions were generally rejected, in 1889 two dioceses removed Black congregations from representation at their diocesan conventions.

> Leading black Episcopalians actually agreed with white paternalists about some of the reasons for bringing African Americans into the church: their denomination had the potential to become a stabilizing and uplifting presence within the black community. They disagreed with whites, however, about who should have the primary responsibility for ministering to the black population in the South.[20]

Serious attempts to address the issue of white paternalism that disenfranchised Black leadership in the Episcopal Church would not appear until well into the twentieth century and the civil rights movement that challenged the Church's institutional and structural racism that had shaped its life in the aftermath of the Civil War.

MINISTRY WITH TRIBAL PEOPLES

In the United States, the second half of the nineteenth century consolidated the effects of the doctrine of "manifest destiny" that had shaped the nation's relentless push to the Pacific and its bloody encounters with the Native tribal peoples. Those encounters, which had already taken such a dreadful toll on Indigenous peoples and their cultures, formed the inevitable backdrop to the Episcopal Church's expansion and mission on the American frontier. The westward movement of white settlers that so affected the Native peoples of North America continued throughout the nineteenth century. The Episcopal Church and its missionaries played an important part in the reorganization of tribal society that was the inevitable result of the clash between Natives and pioneers. The treaties that established the system of reservations which assigned fixed boundaries to Indian land—treaties repeatedly broken by American settlers and their governments—assumed that the Native peoples of the American West would gradually accept settlement and adopt American religion and culture. In order to minimize competition among churches, the various denominations were assigned particular tribes and reservations for their missionary work.

The history of the Church's mission among tribal peoples in the Midwest was greatly influenced by the remarkable ministry of Henry B. Whipple, who became bishop of Minnesota in 1859 and whose first encounter with the Native members of his diocese came at the invitation of John Johnson Enmegabowh, a Native deacon who served as pastor of a mission comprised of Ojibwe Episcopalians. Whipple's early experience with the misery of the Native population of Minnesota determined his commitment to become their advocate at a time when the Dakota Indians of the northern Plains were responding to their desperate situation with increased violence.[21]

Whipple was convinced that the violence was the result of their mistreatment by American government agents and representatives, who had ignored the treaties that promised money, goods and services in return for their ancestral hunting grounds. Indeed, the behavior of the Bureau of Indian Affairs had reached scandalous, even shocking proportions.

War between the Dakota and the American occupying army lasted only thirty-seven days, and in the inevitable aftermath over three hundred Dakota warriors were condemned to death. Whipple determined to plead their cause before the President, and on September 16, 1862, he met with Abraham Lincoln to outline the situation faced by the Plains peoples. Lincoln, Whipple later wrote, was "deeply moved"; Lincoln himself commented, "Bishop Whipple . . . talked with me about the rascality of this Indian business until I felt it down to my boots. If we get through this war, and I live, this Indian system shall be reformed!" While Lincoln's good intentions were never to be fulfilled, he did in fact order the review of each of the Dakota warriors' trials and reduced the sentences of 264 of the 303 Dakota warriors originally condemned to death. Whipple's biographer comments that he "emerged from this tragedy into the nation's consciousness as a leading advocate of justice for Native Americans. It was the first step along a path that would define his life."[22] It also served as a reminder to him and to the Church that the role he had assumed was not an easy one: "Diatribes against Whipple appeared in the newspapers, accusing him of finding excuses for a race of bloodthirsty savages." When he confirmed forty-seven Dakota in 1863, the headline in the local press read, "Holiest Rites of Religion Given to Murderers!"[23]

Owanah Anderson, a historian of Choctaw ancestry, has cataloged the history of the relationship between Native Americans and the ministry of the Episcopal Church. She describes the effect of the imprisonment of the Santee Sioux in 1865: "Since a near mass conversion to Christianity in their traumatic period in stockades and prisons back in Minnesota, the Santee had undergone a radical transformation. In effect, they abandoned their own cultural identity, societal order and process for leadership selection. The chieftain traditionally chosen by heredity, was now chosen by popular election."[24]

Settled in their new reservation in the Dakota Territory, and accompanied by three missionaries, the Rev. Samuel Hinman, his wife Mary, and Emily West, the Native people of the Santee reservation became the center for mission to other bands of Sioux. A school was opened, several churches were built, and Hinman began translating the *Book of Common Prayer* into the Santee dialect and training candidates for ordination—all without support from the Episcopal Church's Mission Board. The strength with which the Santee Episcopal community was established meant that the future evangelization of the Sioux people was conducted primarily by catechists and clergy who were themselves Sioux. From the beginnings on the Santee reservation, the Yankton Lakota and Dakota bands, among others, were drawn into the Episcopal Church. Anderson notes that forty-five clergy and the first Indian bishop of the Episcopal Church were all nurtured on the Santee Reservation.[25]

Bishop William Hobart Hare was responsible for developing Anglican ministry on the Sioux reservations. In 1872, the Episcopal Church took what one historian called "the unprecedented step of creating a missionary jurisdiction on the basis of race": the Missionary Jurisdiction of Niobrara, which included both the Dakota Territory and the northwestern part of Nebraska.[26] Hare believed that "the Church had responsibility not only to convert the Indians but to train them in practical ways for their future, whatever that might be." Hare was convinced that the process of evangelization was best accomplished by Native leadership, and he oversaw the ordination of dozens of Sioux clergy and the appointment of even more lay leaders as helpers and catechists.[27] Describing Hare's preparation of the Indian clergy, one Sioux priest recalled:

> Hare taught them the Bible and the Prayer Book and gave them a little booklet on how to run a parish. That's all! But the teachings of those early Indian ministers were simple. Sound, sincere, solid, stimulating and stabilizing! The teachings were effective; Hare had 10,000 souls settled in 100 chapels on the ten Sioux reservations ministered to by the Indian clergy and catechists, with only half dozen well-chosen white clergy. Some of the Indians were sent away to study, others were trained at home.[28]

Hare was also responsible for the establishment of boarding schools, which he considered central to the Church's ministry. The schools, he wrote,

> should be plain and practical and not calculated to engender fastidious tastes and habits, which would make the pupils unhappy in, and unfit for, the lowly and hard life to which their people are called; that, as the Indians have not been accustomed to labor, the school training should be such as would not only cultivate their intellect, but also develop their humble life, such as sawing, sweeping, etc., etc.; that in order to do this and also for the sake of economy, that the

scholars should take care of themselves . . . and that the scholars should have such training in the responses and music of the Services that they should form the nuclei of Christian congregations where they have not been gathered, and valuable auxiliaries where they are already in existence.[29]

The remaining decades of the nineteenth century marked the continuing growth of Episcopal ministry with Native people, even as the traditional hunting grounds were overrun by white American settlements, reservations were divided and reduced by Congressional action, and sometimes shaken by violent resistance on the part of Native people to what Anderson calls a "holocaust." Generations of missionaries—clergy, teachers, and nurses—settled on the reservations assigned to the Episcopal Church's oversight, not only in the American Midwest but in the desert southwest and the areas of the northwest.

The relationship between American government policy and the Episcopal Church's mission and ministry was often conflicted. When the Oneidas of New York requested that the General Convention of 1868 support their attempt to keep their traditional lands, the House of Bishops agreed, but the Deputies refused, "pronouncing it inexpedient and against the policy of the Convention and the interests of the Church that the Convention should interfere with policies confided to the control of the state." While still opposed to government funding for the support of the Church's work, by 1870 the Church was nominating government agencies to the reservations under the oversight of the Episcopal Church.[30] The General Convention of 1871 established an Indian Commission similar to the Freedmen's Commission to coordinate ministry among Native peoples. Fundamental to the Church's missionary strategy was the establishment not only of Native congregations but of hospitals and schools. While the hospitals addressed the physical needs of people who had often undergone terrible suffering as a result of the invasion of their lands and the poverty and misery that inevitably followed, the schools were designed to separate Indian children from the influence of family and traditional culture and assist in the process of Indian integration into the culture of white America. In 1887, the American government required that all Indian children be educated in boarding schools.

> The objective of the new educational policy was to establish schools hundreds of miles from reservations so that Indian children would be far removed from their parents and tribal affiliations. School discipline at the boarding schools was severe and rigid. Children were ridiculed for speaking their Native languages, their beliefs, and their manners, dress, and long hair. Runaways were whipped, and parents were sometimes denied the right to visit their children. In some cases, students were not allowed to return home for vacations.[31]

FRONTIER MINISTRY

The Episcopal Church and its leaders in the conflicted West were challenged to respond to the needs of the Native peoples whose lands were being overrun but also to provide pastoral care to the tens of thousands of white settlers who were pouring into the area. The discovery of gold in California in 1848 provoked a stampede of hopefuls that overran the territory, which had been part of Mexico until the Mexican War. Travel from the eastern half of the United States was accomplished either by land through hundreds of miles of Indian Territory, or by sea, which called for the risky crossing of the Isthmus of Panama, where yellow fever was pandemic, by mule train or railroad before continuing on to San Francisco by ship. Nevertheless, in spite of its isolation from the rest of the United States, California achieved a precipitous admission to the Union only two years after the discovery of gold. Conditions on the western frontier could hardly have been more daunting for mission and ministry: most of the institutions depended upon to provide a sense of social order were lacking. Schools were almost non-existent; the rule of law was a sometime thing, with "frontier justice" far more likely to be meted out by disgruntled individuals; crime and violence were widespread, medical care, sporadic, and what government existed was marked by an astonishing degree of corruption. Indeed, for much of the nineteenth century only a veneer of local government maintained a delicate protection from social chaos.

Against such a backdrop, Episcopalians in San Francisco set about to organize a diocese as early as 1850. Interestingly, the local clergy and laypeople who engineered its formation apparently had no intention of affiliating with the Episcopal Church in the United States, and even investigated the possibility of obtaining a bishop from the Greek Church. When this attempt failed, the Convention elected a priest who declined the invitation, and three years were to pass before the diocese requested admission to the General Convention. But since there had been no sign of assent to the Episcopal Church's institutional structures, the General Convention of 1853 ignored the request, refused to seat its lay delegates, and elected William Ingraham Kip as Missionary Bishop to organize a new Episcopal diocese.[32]

Kip's autobiography describes a horrendous journey by sea in the company of his surely bewildered wife and young son, as they endured travel by mule train across Panama, unspeakable lodgings on the way, an epidemic of yellow fever on board the ship to California which took the lives of a significant number of passengers, and culminating in a shipwreck off the coast of California.[33]

Once arrived in San Francisco, however, Kip found San Francisco to be something of a "boom town" in spite of the decrepit condition of many of the newly established Episcopal congregations. Indeed, "there were only three Episcopal clergy and two church buildings in all of California."[34] Beyond the city, conditions were primitive, and ministry was undertaken under conditions far different from those to which the aristocratic bishop had been used in the east.

In Stockton, he first preached in the courthouse

> where the judge's seat made a good pulpit and the jury room answered for a "vestry room" . . . Kip's offices, wherever he went, frequently were sought by dying church members, an experience that impressed him for the sadness of their being alone and without family, soon to lie "in nameless graves on the hill sides or river banks!" . . . On happier occasions, Kip performed marriage services at sites where there was no permanent rector, "the only way of keeping the church alive," he recognized.[35]

Frequently accompanied by his wife and son, Kip also travelled to the mining camps scattered through the California mountains, preaching with "an earnestness and interest in preaching, greater even than I have felt in some of the splendid churches at the East." Over the years, he visited the old Mexican towns where Spanish was still the language of choice, as well as the growing number of American Army bases being established to bring some semblance of order to the vast expanses of wilderness. He traveled (accompanied by armed guards) to southern California through bandit-infested regions of the state, and marveled at the culture of the Native peoples being rapidly displaced. "By 1890 he had seen the diocese divided once, the number of communicants grow to more than 8,000, the clergy to ninety-nine, parishes and missions to eighty-one, church buildings to sixty-one. In thirty-six years he had baptized nearly 19,000 people and confirmed more than 11,000."[36]

The expansion of the Episcopal Church in the American West is in part the story of remarkable episcopal leadership; during his long episcopate, Bishop Kip had many colleagues whose dedication and energy equaled his. Daniel S. Tuttle was elected in 1866 as Bishop of Montana with jurisdiction in Utah and Idaho, the fourteenth missionary bishop to be elected by the Episcopal Church.[37]

Bishop Tuttle's autobiography, written many years later and reprinted towards the end of the twentieth century, emphasizes some of the challenging dimensions of ministry on the frontier. In the first place, there was the physical danger and hardship of frontier life. On the occasion of her birthday which found his wife visiting in the east, he wrote her, "News comes that the Indians have attacked and burned two stage stations. Perhaps our mails will all be stopped. This town is filled with women and children in refuge from ranches. But General Howard is near Bannack, with six hundred men, and we will doubtless be protected. Do not worry." Responding to a request for an essay on his ministry, Tuttle wrote, "I cannot just now send what you wish. I am on my tour of visitation. I preach in log cabins. I sleep on blankets, sheets being unknown things. I am the guest of bachelors in their dirt-roofed mansion. I travel by stage, on horseback, afoot. I am moving about almost constantly. . . . I have gone about five hundred miles, and have twelve hundred more before me."[38]

Tuttle's understanding of his role as "pioneer-bishop" was shaped by his realization that most of the settlers with whom he came into contact were almost certainly strangers to the Episcopal Church, and indeed, many probably had little or no religious background of any kind. Like many Episcopalians of the nineteenth century, Tuttle understood that the Church had a calling to tend the spiritual well-being of the whole community (with the exception of Roman Catholics), which both broadened his sense of responsibility and altered his perspective with regard to denominational boundaries. Of the members of his first Vestry in Virginia City, Nevada

> one vestryman, high up in civil office, got into an altercation with a lawyer over some matters retailed by gossip, and would have shot him dead had not a friend near by struck up the pistol. One was a Unitarian. Another, the most godly of them all, and the one on whom I leaned for Christian and churchly earnestness, became involved in a dispute, and missed, by the smallest margin, the fighting of a duel. Still another was an appallingly steady drinker, though never mastered by drink. Another, a kind, good-hearted man, grew so mad from drink that one night his wife fled from him in terror. My heart was grieved and distressed at this. But I never hated the people, they were too kind and good to me for that.[39]

Tuttle was himself aware of his own need to change the perception of the bishop's calling in a missionary situation:

> He who has been rating himself as the Episcopalian minister or priest must recast his thought and take it into his heart that he is the ambassador of Christ, and is to be the messenger and minister of His all-embracing mercy and love. . . .
> Then the people who do not belong anywhere religiously, the unattached people the worldly people and the wicked people in the town, how about them? . . . I am the ambassador of Christ and must represent as fully as I can His mercy and love. These are His little ones, His wandering ones, His weak ones, His misguided and beguiled ones, His lame and defective and lost ones.[40]

Tuttle obviously sat loose to the subtleties which tended to divide Christians in more settled contexts, administering Communion to members of any church, licensing a Baptist as Lay Reader, teaching a Cumberland Presbyterian how to use the Prayer Book. In this way, he wrote, "The bishop of Montana, it is felt by all Montanans, belongs to them. They consult him, he influences them . . . And so the bishop of any territory, ringing all the door-bells of that territory, and making cordially the acquaintanceship of all people, by this and his annual visitations, gets to be regarded, in a remarkable degree, as the pastor of all." Indeed, Tuttle argued that

> the most wide-reaching and long-lasting results for good, the American clergyman wins as pastor. If children love him, and women respect him, and men have full confidence in him; if the happy are happier to welcome him among them, and the sorrowful lighter of heart, more hopeful of the future, and stronger for duty by his coming, if he is a prophet among them in the true sense of the word, that is, one speaking for God and the realities of the world invisible, then, it seems to me, the daily life and pastoral converse of such a man of God with his flock will contribute far more to their spiritual advancement than any special efforts he can make as priest of the Church or preacher of the Word.[41]

But while Tuttle, and many of those who shared his missionary ministry on the frontier, found that the institutional dimension of their previous work in the settled churches of the east faded in significance, they by no means ignored the work of establishing Church structures. Bishop Tuttle established a diocesan center in Salt Lake City, in the heart of Mormon country, and dedicated both time and financial resources to establishing a hospital and school—and a cathedral. Yet while valuing such institutions as essential for improving the quality of the communities they served and even serving as a form of "community evangelization," he insisted that they must be shaped not by past experience but by the new context. The Cathedral in Utah, he argued, "is to be developed along lines adapted to American ideas and adjusted to American habits. We cannot import any ready-made article for our service. Even the noble foundations of our mother Church in England must be object lessons for us to study, rather than patterns for us to imitate."[42]

The gradual establishment of an Episcopal presence throughout the territories and states of the American West was undoubtedly in part the product of leaders such as Kip and Tuttle, some of whom were called on to exercise their ministry in situations of hardship and danger and in circumstances for which they were totally unprepared by previous experience. But their work was complemented by equally heroic service from both priests and laypeople. Tuttle himself wrote of the work of one such lay missionary, Emily Pearsall, in Salt Lake City in the early 1870s:

> She taught singing and sewing in our St. Mark's school . . . Sunday afternoons she went into neglected neighborhoods on the outskirts of the city and held cottage meetings. She was the overseer of the homes of the "pensioners" of our Charity Fund. She was the judicious distributer of the contents of our "Clothing-Room,"

provided from the boxes and barrels kindly sent us from the East. . . . I find her memory most tenderly cherished in many homes, . . . because she was in them for sweet help when sickness was there.[43]

WOMEN IN MINISTRY

Like the restoration of religious orders in the Anglican Communion, a renewed interest in the order of the diaconate for both men and women was largely due to the Oxford Movement and the research it provoked on the nature of ministry in the early Christian Church. In 1862, the Dean of Chester Cathedral in England published a study of the diaconate in the New Testament which argued so convincingly that women were included in the order that the Bishop of London admitted Catherine Ferard as the first deaconess in the Church of England. A number of diocesan institutes for training women as deaconesses had soon been established. In the United States, the example of the Kaiserswerth deaconesses in the Lutheran Church in Germany provided models for groups of dedicated women in a number of dioceses.[44]

The path to the institutionalization of deaconesses was complex, owing mostly to the continued distrust of any form of ministry that might appear to be too "Roman" and what Mary Donovan calls "the problem of how to control the women."[45] It was only in 1889 that the Episcopal Church's General Convention approved a canon regularizing the order of deaconesses (while leaving unaddressed its relationship to the three orders of bishop, priest and deacon). Deaconesses were to be "set apart" by the bishop with the laying on of hands for Christian service, to remain unmarried, and to exercise their ministry under the bishop's control and supervision. Donovan observes that "the move was significant because it was the first official recognition of women's ministries in the Episcopal Church." Similar recognition of the order of deaconesses in England came at the Convocation of Canterbury in 1891.[46]

While only a small number of women were able to respond to the opportunities for ministry provided by the religious orders and the order of deaconess, the last half of the nineteenth century also called forth a number of women who offered themselves for work as missionaries, both overseas and in the American West. Mary Donovan documented the importance of women as missionaries in western jurisdictions of the Church in the second half of the nineteenth century:

> Lively, curious, adventurous, retiring, shy, self-effacing—the women who went westward as missionaries were a varied lot. Some taught and administered Episcopal schools; others served as nurses, physicians and hospital administrators. Many of the women ministered to Indian reservations or to isolated

communities too small to support resident clergymen. Though none of the women were ordained as clergy, they were the mainstay of the liturgical life of many communities—reading Morning Prayer, or even baptizing and burying when no clergyman was available.[47]

Under the remarkable leadership of three sisters—Mary Abbot Emery, Margaret Theresa Emery and Julia Chester Emery—over a period lasting for more than forty years, the newly formed Woman's Auxiliary to the Board of Missions, established in 1872, organized an extensive national network of support for missionaries which provided the resources for people like Emily Pearsall.[48] Its first General Secretary, Mary Abbot Emery, challenged the women of the Episcopal Church

> to think seriously whether she really cares anything for the Missionary work which is being done by the Church or whether she confines her sympathy and her labors to her own country, her own parish or her own family. What we want every member of the Association to do is to think and to read much about Missions, to keep herself constantly informed upon the subject, and to be ready to present it frequently to others in such a way as shall win their interest in the work and create a desire to share in it.[49]
>
> The heart of the Auxiliary's work took place at the level of its local chapters, where groups of women accepted the responsibility not only of fund-raising but of providing supplies for the Church's appointed missionaries. Missionaries made their needs known to the national office, which then invited local chapters to pack and ship needed supplies for the mission family—clothing, books, furniture—and equipment for the mission—hospital supplies, medicines, church-school materials, needles, fabric—whatever was necessary for the work. Generally the auxiliary from a church worked with the same missionary year after year, becoming acquainted with members of the mission family, the type of clothing needed in that particular climate, and the mission's work. . . . The monetary value of the fully stocked boxes increased dramatically: The total worth of boxes sent in 1875 was $61,000; ten years later it was $127,000; and in 1900, $191,000.[50]

The chapter of the Woman's Auxiliary organized in Westchester County, New York in 1880 developed a relationship lasting for half a century with the Episcopal Church's Navajo Mission. When George Wadleigh arrived as a missionary to the Navajo in 1892, it was to the Westchester County Auxiliary that he addressed his request for funds to provide a male worker "to control the boys outside the classroom" and a supply of "neckwear . . . something like a Windsor scarf, made of silk or any other neat fabric" to replace the "red bandanna handkerchief, which they tie around their necks, and the effect is villanous [sic]."[51] Far more significant was the Auxiliary's response to the bishop when he requested funding for a hospital in Navajoland. Their "munificent generosity and enthusiasm" supported the work of the first medical missionary, Eliza Thackara, and "thus it was that the women, carrying dispensary kits and school books, brought lasting Episcopal witness to Navajoland. With Eliza Thackara in the vanguard in the 1890s, a hardy throng of eastern women—medical missionaries and school teachers—left hearth and home in snug New England villages to toil in this distant and arid land."[52]

The 1889 General Convention gave the Woman's Auxiliary control over its own funds for the first time, through the establishment of the United Offering (later the United Thank Offering). Indeed, the last decades of the nineteenth century were marked by gradually broadening opportunities for women to participate in the life of the Church. The Girls' Friendly Society was established for young women working in the mills of Lowell, Massachusetts, but grew into an international organization providing pastoral care and social activities to young working women. The Daughters of the King offered a spiritual community organized under a simple rule of life which also supported the Church's mission.[53] By the end of the century, writes Mary Donovan,

> The Church had officially established a vocation for women—the deaconess—and deaconess training schools were graduating women trained in the religious and practical skills necessary for mission work. Many women were finding employment as teachers, nurses, physicians, and administrators in the growing number of Church-sponsored institutions in the United States and overseas. . . . [The first secretary of the Woman's Auxiliary] declared her faith that "the day is sure to come when man's work and woman's work in the Church will be clearly seen to be only co-ordinate parts of one great and glorious whole." Neither she nor her sisters lived to see that day, but their efforts had brought it within the realm of possibility.[54]

MISSION AND THE "HOME FRONT"

As the Episcopal Church expanded its ministry westward across the North American continent and in other parts of the world, it faced a perennial problem: How to generate interest and support among Episcopalians in the more settled regions of the Church, who could be assumed to have access to more resources, for the difficult and often costly work of mission in in newly developing ministries. The personal correspondence and appeals of persons actively engaged in those ministries was augmented by educational materials and other publications such as *The Spirit of Missions,* which was founded in 1836 and "for over a century would educate Episcopalians about their church's work at home and abroad."[55]

Two years after the Civil War, the Church's Office of Domestic Missions established the "Domestic Missionary Army of the Young Soldiers of Christ" in an effort to awaken both interest and support among Episcopal children. Karen Keely, its chronicler, notes that it was an early effort to join enthusiasm for mission with the growing interest in "systematizing" financial support for the Church through pledges and weekly offering envelopes. The project, she writes,

> was to organize young readers into an "army" of domestic missionaries—one hundred thousand "soldiers" was the goal—who would raise funds for a missionary diocese and correspond with a missionary in that diocese. Young volunteers paid twenty-five cents a year for the privilege of becoming a private in the Domestic Missionary Army, while a one-dollar annual "bounty" made the giver a captain if he was a boy or a color-bearer if she was a girl. The solders enlisted for five years' service in the Army and were assigned to a "regiment" of 1200 soldiers each . . . Membership dues for the 1200 members of each regiment amounted to three hundred dollars or more, which was used for direct support of a missionary.[56]

The enormous initial success of the Army—within a short time over twenty thousand children had enlisted—led to its own publication, *The Young Christian Soldier*, which, like *The Spirit of Missions*, "featured news of domestic missions, with letters from abroad and from domestic missionaries, and stories of settling into missionary homes and of missionary anecdotes." Keely notes that the rhetoric described the mission field as a "battlefield, with children enlisted on the side of God's forces against heathenism."[57]

Keely's study of *The Young Christian Soldier* relates it to the genre of children's literature which was popular among English-speaking Christians of all denominations in the latter nineteenth century, and which attempted not only to instruct but also to entertain children. (The magazine often included serialized novels for children and teenagers.) Its primary rhetoric was military, though it sometimes argued against war and violence; and Keely observes that while women's only role in the military was as nurses, in the Domestic Missionary Army girls were encouraged to assume active membership (although the rank of captain was reserved for boys).[58]

The Domestic Missionary Army proved to be a short-lived undertaking, lasting only five years before being replaced by the "mite boxes" which children were invited to fill with their own and others' donations to be forwarded for the support of missionaries at home and abroad.[59]

In the last decades of the nineteenth century, many Episcopalians, along with observers in other denominations, worried that two-thirds of the membership of Protestant churches were female; the percentage of active participants in church activities who were women was even higher. One evangelist on the staff of the YMCA argued that while "one of the marvels of the Christian religion is the beauty of its womanly virtues . . . Christianity is also essentially masculine, militant, warlike, and if these elements are not made manifest, men and boys will not be found in increasing numbers as participants in the life of the church." And a Baptist clergy-scholar argued that

> businessmen's failure to participate in church in large numbers, and their preference for the lodges that were so popular across the United States during this period, demonstrated that the social needs and spiritual aspirations of men were much better served by the lodge than by the church. . . . Church religion was too other-worldly and feminized; lodge religion was "practical" and fit "the religious needs of a man's religious nature." But "if the lodge satisfies men, . . . the church can do it. It can be a home of enjoyment, a means of fellowship and sociability, a place of activity, discussion, and responsibility, a satisfaction to the religious nature, far better than the lodge."[60]

This emphasis on what has been called "muscular" or "practical" Christianity led to the formation of "denominational brotherhoods" in most American denominations. Identified as "the first church's men's club to achieve national prominence," the Episcopal Church's Brotherhood of St. Andrew (BSA) grew in 1883 out of a Bible class for young men taught at St. James' Church in Chicago by James Houghteling, a wealthy businessman.

Houghteling convinced his Bible class to rename itself the BSA and to take a greater interest in the poor and homeless. He also asked his class to evangelize more young men and to reorganize along military lines. As a result, young men who arrived at St. James' were greeted by a BSA leader and directed to one of two aisles where the Brotherhood held pews. Each aisle had its BSA "lieutenant," who in turn had under him several "privates"—one or more to a pew. In addition, there was a BSA "quartermaster," who kept Brotherhood pews supplied with hymn-books and invitation cards. Once inducted, members agreed to a rule of life that included daily prayer "for the spread of Christ's Kingdom among young men," and to bring "at least one male friend per week to church or Bible study." Within three years, the BSA had spread to churches throughout Chicago and beyond, held a a national conference, adopted a constitution and begun publication of its own journal, *St. Andrew's Cross*. By 1891, the journal had a circulation of 7,000.[61]

The BSA continued to play a significant role in the ministry of the Episcopal Church throughout the remainder of the nineteenth century and beyond. It spread to other churches of the Anglican Communion and spawned similar organizations in other denominations. Its strong emphasis on the ministry of laymen in evangelism began with its original chapter at St. James' Church in Chicago:

> Sunday morning worship services at St. James saw nearly two hundred men coming from rooming houses and hotels at the invitation of the Brothers Andrew who, before and between services, would go into the streets actively seeking out men and inviting them to church. The brotherhood began putting Bibles in rooming houses and hotels around the church, nearly 25 years before the Gideons began their work in hotels.

Its Lay Readers Program, later adopted by the Episcopal Church, trained laymen to establish mission congregations in new suburbs where they led Morning and Evening Prayer and conducted programs of Christian Education for children and adults. At the end of the century, membership had reached 15,000, in a thousand chapters spread across seventeen countries. The Brotherhood's own brief account of its history states that from its beginnings and well into the twentieth century,

> the Brotherhood of St. Andrew was considered the evangelistic arm of the Church, and it was heavily involved in every aspect of lay ministry. Brothers Andrew traveled the US and overseas, mostly at their own expense, spreading this ministry-to-men. Where the Brotherhood was established, they encouraged chapters to become involved in starting hundreds of new Mission Churches through the Lay Reader Program.

The BSA also sent a team of four missionaries to assist in the establishment of an Episcopal presence in the Philippines during the American efforts to pacify and occupy the Islands after the Spanish-American War in 1898. Capturing and organizing some of the zeal generated by the optimism of the Social Gospel movement and the passion for sharing Christian faith with others that so marked American Christianity in the latter decades of the nineteenth century, the BSA claims its work as instrumental in doubling the number of Episcopalians and increasing the number of parishes by fifty percent.[62]

RELIGIOUS ORDERS IN THE UNITED STATES

In the United States, orders for women can be traced back to the middle of the century, when William Augustus Muhlenberg sought an innovative style of ministry at the Church of the Holy Communion in New York City. He took the order of Lutheran deaconesses established earlier in the century in Kaiserswerth, Germany, as his model. With great caution because of the widespread prejudice against tendencies considered "Romanizing," Anne

Ayres became the first American woman to respond to Muhlenberg's call and dedicate herself formally to a life of ministry in community. Over the next decade, several women joined her in what became an organized sisterhood in 1852.

Although Ayres herself assumed a number of administrative roles in the complex social ministry of the parish, the Sisterhood of the Holy Communion was primarily associated with an infirmary and clinic, and later with the new St. Luke's Hospital which was established in 1858. Mary Donovan notes that "though the sisters had no training as nurses, during their years of operating the infirmary they gained experience and established basic nursing procedures. In doing so, they were among the pioneers of the nursing profession in the United States." They also served as a vivid example of "the importance of such orders to the development of Church-sponsored institutions."[63]

Ayres was at pains to distinguish the Sisterhood of the Holy Communion from Roman Catholic religious orders, many aspects of which she criticized strongly.

> The sisterhood was to be a community of Christian women devoted to works of charity but held together only by unity of purpose. There were no lifetime vows, only a simple statement of commitment, usually to a three-year term, with the provision that, whenever she wanted, a woman might leave the sisterhood simply by making her intention known to the pastor. Sisters were clothed in a plain adaptation of "the ordinary attire of a gentlewoman." Community life revolved not around a schedule of religious devotions but around the sisters' charitable acts and services. Within the society, however, each sister was to work for "an advancement in personal holiness" through Bible reading, private prayer and corporate worship.[64]

Other religious orders for women were established in the decades following. Some were branches of English orders; others, like the Community of St. Mary, founded by several members of the Sisterhood of the Holy Communion who became dissatisfied with Sister Anne Ayres' leadership, were not. But unlike the Sisters of the Holy Communion, all required the traditional monastic vows of poverty, chastity and obedience, wore distinctive habits, and practiced a daily round of worship. As a result, they often found themselves under attack from Church authorities who mistrusted their faithfulness to Anglican Christianity.[65]

In 1879, the English Cowley Fathers established an American presence at the Church of St. John the Evangelist in Boston. The first American order for men was founded by James O. S. Huntington, son of a distinguished American bishop, who began his ministry as an urban priest among the poor immigrants of New York's Lower East Side. He was soon joined by two other priests, with whom he formed the Order of the Holy Cross in 1880. Its members developed a Rule which it considered more "American-democratic" than that of the highly authoritarian Cowley Fathers, and dedicated themselves to social service, especially with poor men and boys. In 1886, Huntington attracted considerable attention by campaigning vigorously for Henry George, a candidate for mayor of New York City. George, the author of a best-selling book titled *Progress and Poverty*, argued that the chief cause of poverty is the unequal ownership of land. He proposed substituting taxes on the profit made from the use of land for all other taxes, including those on labor. This "single-tax" theory appealed to many on both sides of the Atlantic who were concerned to improve the situation of the poor.[66]

In 1887, Huntington was instrumental in the formation of the Church Association for the Advancement of the Interests of Labor (C.A.I.L.) which was established to "work closely with labor unions for the elimination of social abuses, propagate social reform movements within the Protestant Episcopal Church, and to offer church mediation in strikes and other areas of labor-management conflict." Eager to experience for himself the life of typical working Americans, he spent part of 1889 as an agricultural worker. He later joined the Knights of Labor, an even more militant group that supported the burgeoning American labor movement. But in 1892, Huntington and the other members of the Order of the Holy Cross came to believe that American slum neighborhoods did not lend themselves to the kind of ministry that had so distinguished the Church of England. They withdrew from active ministry on the Lower East Side, moving first to a house in Westminster, Maryland, and later to the Order's Mother House in the tiny Hudson Valley village of West Park, New York.[67]

Over the next few decades, a number of attempts to establish religious orders for both men and women were undertaken in both England and the United States. Most failed to survive, and they were inevitably affected by the frequent conflict between Anglo-Catholics and Evangelicals in both countries. One historian of the period notes that there was considerable anti-Roman Catholic sentiment in England at mid-century, the result in part of the decision by the Vatican to restore the Roman episcopate in England, and influenced too by the number of high-profile defections to Rome by leading Anglo-Catholics such as John Henry Newman. In the heated atmosphere of the times, many saw the newly established religious orders and the Ritualist clergy as a kind of "fifth column" that would inevitably betray the Anglican tradition.[68] Bishops often found aspects of the rules, generally copied from Roman Catholic models, to be problematic for several reasons. Indeed, the concept of monastic vows, especially the vow of chastity, seemed to some to call into question the Reformation principle of the sanctity of the married state, while some also criticized the principle of submission to direction by a priest as a threat to the understanding of personal spiritual freedom enshrined in the Prayer Book. It was perhaps the secrecy surrounding life within monasteries and convents that most concerned critics.[69] While recognizing that the persons who sought membership in orders uniformly testified to a call from God, a study of the Anglican experience of religious orders written in 1932 and incorporating material from interviews with a number of superiors identified several more mundane motivations for the growth of the religious life among Anglicans: the desire for economic security, sublimation of affections, a desire to avoid the marriage relationship, and—perhaps most significant—a desire for service. At the same time, its author observed that these "natural" motivations can in fact contribute to a real vocation from God.[70]

By the end of the nineteenth century, religious orders had become a familiar aspect of ministry in both England and the United States. The 1897 Lambeth Conference took note of their development, recognizing "with thankfulness the revival alike of brotherhoods and sisterhoods and of the office of deaconess in our branch of the Church."[71] Their ministry was nowhere more visible, or significant, than in the urban areas where misery continued to define the life of the poor.

URBAN MINISTRY IN THE LATE NINETEENTH CENTURY

In the United States, the influence of both Christian Socialists and Anglo-Catholic Ritualists grew rapidly in the years after the Civil War. The "Social Christianity" or "Social Gospel" movement is generally understood to have had its earliest beginnings in the 1850s, when William Augustus Muhlenberg attempted to transform the Church of the Holy Communion in New York City through its liturgical life (daily Morning and Evening Prayer, a weekly Eucharist, and liturgical celebration of the Church Year) and through its social service, which included facilities for sending both adults and children to the country for holidays, an employment agency for women, nursery and schools and an infirmary which grew into St. Luke's Hospital. In 1853, the "Muhlenberg Memorial" which he presented to the Episcopal Church's General Convention suggested that the worship and ministry of the Episcopal Church were inadequate for reaching the urban poor, and proposed a radical reform of how the Church undertook its ministry. The Memorial suggested a relaxation of the canonical requirements for ordination, so that bishops could freely ordain candidates, both Episcopalians and others, who would be able to conduct more informal worship without being confined to the use of the *Book of Common Prayer.* At the heart of this proposal was a vision of a wider community of Christians who would share in the historic apostolic ministry through their ordination by Episcopal bishops. While Muhlenberg's proposals were not approved, his own ministry continued to be directed towards the poor. Shortly after the end of the Civil War he created a community, St. Johnland, on Long Island, the nucleus of a total Christian environment which was to include housing, institutions for children and the elderly, and at its center a community church—one of the few proposals for a utopian community ever to have emerged within Anglicanism.[72]

While the negative effects of the Industrial Revolution impacted American society later than in England, by mid-century many cities suffered from poverty as extreme as that of the English working class. Historians consider that it was the Episcopal Church Congress, an annual gathering of clergy and laity that began meeting in 1874, where "social issues first came to the semiofficial attention of a major American religious body."[73]

Several well-known clergy of the period distinguished themselves by drawing their congregations' attention to the conditions of the poor, and by preaching that Christian ethics are as applicable to commerce as to personal life. Meanwhile, the increasing militancy of the American labor movement was bringing class conflict to the consciousness of American Christians. In 1886 Henry Codman Potter, Bishop of New York, issued a Pastoral Letter in which he foresaw no end to the conflict between capital and labor until "Capitalists and employers of labor have forever dismissed the fallacy, which may be true enough in the domain of political economy, but is essentially false in the domain of religion, *that labor and the laborer are alike a commodity,* to be bought and sold, employed or dismissed, paid or underpaid as the market shall decree."[74] Potter's colleague, Frederick Dan Huntington, Bishop of Central New York, concurred, writing to urge "a Christian solution of labor problems" and stating that "a system in which men and women of the wage-earning class are subject to the control and caprice of their paymasters is not one that consistent Americans or intelligent Christians can contemplate with complacency."[75] Huntington was the author of a prayer "For the Emancipation of Workers," a shortened form of which was included in the Episcopal Church's 1928 revision of the *Book of Common Prayer.* The prayer articulates an implicit critique of capitalism, advocating "the Christian conception of work as a 'vocation,'" to be understood as God's call to serve one another, "not for selfish, material profit ('mammon'), but for the common good of all."[76]

In support of the Church's newly found concern for the situation of the working class, the Church Association for the Advancement of the Interests of Labor (C.A.I.L.) was founded in 1886 and within a few years forty-seven bishops had accepted positions as vice-presidents. The Constitution of C.A.I.L. spelled out its underlying principles:

The essence of Christ's teaching is the fatherhood of God and the brotherhood of man [sic]; God is the sole possessor of the bounty of the earth and man is his steward; labor, defined as "the exercise of body, mind and spirit in the broadening and elevating of human life," is the duty of every [person] and should be the standard of social worth; when all [people] are enabled so to labor, one great cause of present distress will disappear.[77]

The obligations accepted by C.A.I.L.'s membership demonstrate a perspective that unites concrete social actions and spirituality as a seamless whole which would mark Episcopalians' engagement with urban ministry for the next several decades. Members committed themselves to prayer and sermons "setting forth the teachings of the gospel as the guide to the solution of every question involved in the interests of labor"; "proper use" of printed publications, lectures, and "the encouragement by precept and example of a conscientious use of the ballot." "Special duties" were listed as reading "at least one journal devoted to the interests of labor" and the study of "the social questions of the day in the light of the Incarnation."[78]

The urgency with which some of the Episcopal Church's leaders addressed the issues of working-class misery was reflected in the development of what came to be known as "institutional parishes," congregations that undertook a broad spectrum of social services. In various settings, they responded to almost every conceivable social need: they provided schools, nurseries and day-care centers, employment services, hostels, medical services, study centers, lectures, public baths, soup kitchens, recreation and other services. At a time when private and government social agencies were practically non-existent, institutional churches began to remake their neighborhoods. The prototype of such parishes was St. George's Church in New York, whose rector, William Rainsford, oversaw "the abolition of pew rents, continuous weekday use of his plant, and the development of a program to meet the needs of the immediate neighborhood"—much of it funded by the parish's senior warden, J. Pierpont Morgan. In 1891, St. Bartholomew's Church, one of the most fashionable in the city, opened a parish hall designed with even more lavish and varied facilities for community ministry; the Vanderbilt family were the principal donors. In the next decade nearly eleven million dollars—an enormous sum at the end of the nineteenth century—was spent in maintaining its ministry.[79]

Other aspects of the Episcopal Church's ministry in response to the challenge of the cities deserve mention. One is the emergence of official Church-related agencies established to address specific social problems. The New York Protestant Episcopal City Mission, established by Bishop Potter in 1885, reflected his belief that as bishop, "the poor of a great city, the outcast and the stranger, the criminal and the pauper, should be preëminently his parishioners."[80]

Another significant feature of the Church's engagement with poverty was the establishment of a number of *unofficial* groups dedicated to social reform or change. The Society of the Companions of the Holy Cross was comprised of women, many of them teachers and college professors, who kept a common rule of life and also dedicated themselves to study and volunteer work in settlement houses and other similar institutions. Its founder, Emily Malbone Morgan, called on its members to "understand by our association together . . . our own vocation as that of women living in the world and having individual influence, social or otherwise, banded together to meet the serious religious, education, and social problems of our age, first by prayer, and then by battle."[81]

Companions also figured prominently in the radical left wing of the Episcopal Church, as did women who participated in the Christian Socialist League and the League for Industrial Democracy. "Many of these laywomen turned away from conventional marriages in favor of deeply prayerful vocations committed to 'building the kingdom of God on earth.' College women, both faculty and students, believed they were called to productive lives of sisterhood and social reconstruction . . . Throughout the settlement house movement, women were nurtured through regular worship and their relationships with other like-minded Christian women."[82]

The Society's house at Adelynrood, Massachusetts, became the scene of lengthy retreats and conferences where members could enjoy serious conversation on both spiritual and secular themes, and also the site for welcoming working women and their children for holidays in the country with an opportunity for both recreation and spiritual formation. Groups such as the Companions of the Society of the Holy Cross embodied some of the questions and tensions with which Episcopalians were wrestling at the end of the nineteenth century: What is the relationship between the *spiritual* dimension of Christian faith, epitomized by a disciplined life of worship, study, prayer and regular retreat from the world, and the more *activist* demands of the gospel to intervene directly on behalf of the suffering of the poor? While Emily Morgan, its founder, knew a great deal about factory conditions and was a convinced Socialist, she considered that "the Society lived in the world but was nevertheless removed from it and public action was incompatible with its objectives." Vida Scudder, one of its more radical members and a professor at Wellesley College, had encountered the Christian Socialists in England and returned to the United States determined to be engaged in the burgeoning settlement house movement which also attracted the attention of other members. Indeed, "several of the Settlements served as informal headquarters for the Society in their particular cities," and some members became active and vocal advocates of the growing labor unions.[83]

The Social Gospel movement in the Episcopal Church provided an opportunity for laypeople to exercise ministry in new ways. Educators used their classrooms to promote consciousness of the social demands of the gospel. Writers such as Richard Ely, whose 1889 book *The Social Aspects of Christianity* is considered "the first influential effort on the part of a prominent American to state 'the social side of the Church's mission,'"[84] offered convincing arguments in defense of strikes and against the conditions imposed on working people by industry. Committed laypeople joined progressive clergy in organizations such as the Christian Social Union, which not only produced numerous tracts urging the Church's attention to social ills but also attempted to articulate a mediating position between the contradictory interests of capital and labor.

American Episcopalians also carried on the more radical questioning of the fundamental economic and political structures of their society through organizations such as the Society of Christian Socialists, founded in 1889. Its prime mover was the Reverend William Bliss; its program was based on the belief that "the teachings of Jesus Christ lead directly to some form of Socialism; [and] that therefore the Church has a definite duty upon this matter and must, in simple obedience to Christ, apply itself to the realization of the social principles of Christianity." While the Society did not support revolution, it did advocate a gradual, evolutionary socialism, in which the capitalist system would be replaced by cooperative economics. The process would be hastened by "legislative measures [for] the nationalization of land, railroads, telegraph, telephone, and all resources; public ownership of local transit, light, and heat systems; woman suffrage, compulsory education, the eight-hour day; and prohibition."[85]

In 1890, Bliss left his parish to found the Mission of the Carpenter, a project sponsored by the diocese of Massachusetts, in order to provide a kind of parish laboratory for ministry based on Christian Socialist principles. But a twentieth century historian noted that in spite of Bliss's obvious passion and ability, the Society's "membership remained small" and

> its members . . . greatly overestimated the radicalism of American Protestants. The Society's demand for collective ownership was far too radical to draw any large following from the middle-class church public. Yet its idealism and its lack of emphasis on immediate problems prevented it from appealing successfully to discontented labor groups or from coalescing with the infant socialist movement outside the Church.[86]

One of the noteworthy aspects of the Episcopal Church's participation in urban ministry is the remarkable emphasis it placed on *education* as the primary instrument for raising the awareness of its members about issues of poverty and social alienation. Its engagement with social ministry itself reveals how deeply the sense of responsibility for the whole society—part of its heritage from its English parent—remained alive among American Episcopalians towards the end of the nineteenth century. As Henry May observed, "Episcopalianism had never lost touch completely with the medieval dream of society guided and led by the church."[87]

Episcopal involvement in social ministry reflects the growing acceptance among its more learned leaders of the *principle* of evolution, no longer limited to biology but also rapidly becoming a vehicle for new thinking in the social sciences and even theology itself. In the hands of American Christians of the late nineteenth century, such ideas bolstered a belief in progress as the inevitable outcome of God's purpose for the creation and of Christian faith, Even thinkers as socially acute as Richard Ely, an Episcopal priest generally credited with creating the discipline of sociology, assumed that all that was needed to accomplish the "Christianization" of the social order was for people to be shown, or taught, a more rational and humane way of life. Later scholars have noted the inherent difficulty in an approach to ministry that confuses love and justice, and results in a general air of unrealism and unwarranted optimism.[88]

But if the passionate optimism—and naïveté—of the progressive clergy and laypeople who advocated and participated in the Church's social ministry failed to change Church and society in the definitive ways they hoped, their work nevertheless permanently affected the Episcopal Church's understanding of its ministry. It set its mission in a social context, and sealed its identity as a church with a particular commitment to, and identification with, urban life and culture. And it answered in the affirmative, in ways that survived into future generations, the question of whether or not the gospel has a social dimension.

NOTES

1. Joseph Cheshire, *The Church in the Confederate States: A History of the Protestant Episcopal Church in the Confederate States* (New York: Longmans, Green and Co., 1912), 18.

2. Quoted in Paul G. Ashdown, "Commission from a Higher Source: Church and State in the Civil War," *Historical Magazine of the Protestant Episcopal Church*, XLVII, September 1979, 324.

3. Cheshire, *The Church in the Confederate States*, 63.

4. Cheshire, *The Church in the Confederate States*, 67–68.
5. Cheshire, *The Church in the Confederate States*, 106ff.
6. Cheshire, *The Church in the Confederate States*, 114.
7. Mary Greenhow Lee, *Diary*, unpublished manuscript, Archives Room, Handley Regional Library, Winchester, Virginia, 3–4. Used by permission.
8. Lee, *Diary*, 64, 100–101, 314.
9. Lee, *Diary*, 699, 731.
10. Lee, *Diary*, 34, 37.
11. Lee, *Diary*, 252, 347, 58.
12. See Cheshire, *The Church in the Confederate States*, 169ff.
13. Lewis, *Yet With A Steady Beat*, 40, 47.
14. Lewis, *Yet With A Steady Beat*, 50–51.
15. Lewis, *Yet With A Steady Beat*, 48.
16. W. D. Weatherford, *American Churches and the Negro* (Boston: The Christopher Publishing House, 1957), 47.
17. A. A. Taylor, *The Negro in the Reconstruction of Virginia* (Washington: Association for the Study of Negro Life and History, 1924), 177ff.
18. Weatherford, *American Churches and the Negro*, 46.
19. Gardiner H. Shattuck, Jr., *Episcopalians and Race: Civil War to Civil Rights* (Lexington, KY: The University Press of Kentucky, 2000), 15.
20. Shattuck, *Episcopalians and Race*, 17.
21. Anne Beiser Allen, *And the Wilderness Shall Blossom: Henry Benjamin Whipple, Churchman, Educator, Advocate for the Indians* (Afton MN: Afton Historical Society Press, 2008), 47–52.
22. Allen, *And the Wilderness Shall Blossom*, 11–15.
23. Allen, *And the Wilderness Shall Blossom*, 103, 104.
24. Owanah Anderson, *Four Hundred Years: Anglican/Episcopal Mission Among American Indians*, 84.
25. Anderson, *Four Hundred Years*, 84ff.
26. Edward S. Dunscombe, "The Northern Arapahoe Experience of Episcopal Mission Work and United States Policy, 1883–1925, Part L: Background," *Anglican and Episcopal History*, 56 (June 1997), 195.
27. Anderson, *Four Hundred Years*, 110–111.
28. Vine Deloria, quoted in Anderson, *Four Hundred Years*, 111.
29. Dunscombe, "The Northern Arapahoe Experience," 195–196.
30. Julia C. Emery, *A Century of Endeavor 1821 – 1921: A Record of the First Hundred Years of the Domestic and Foreign Missionary Society of the Protestant Episcopal Church in the United States of America* (New York: Department of Missions, 1921), 178–179.
31. William G. Robbins, "Against Indian Culture," Oregon Historical Society, Online Oregon History Project, http://www.ohs.org/the-oregon-history-project/narratives/this-land-oregon/political-economic-culture/against-indian-culture.cfm. Accessed October 20, 2010.
32. William Ingraham Kip, *The Early Days of My Episcopate* (New York: Thomas Whittaker, 1892), 124–126.

33. Kip, *The Early Days*, 24–55.

34. Mary Judith Robinson, *From Gold Rush to Millennium: 150 Years of the Episcopal Diocese of California 1849–2000* (San Francisco: Episcopal Diocese of California, 2001), 16–17.

35. Robinson, *From Gold Rush to Millennium*, 18.

36. Robinson, *From Gold Rush to Millennium*, 19–33.

37. Daniel Sylvester Tuttle, *Missionary to the Mountain West: Reminiscences of Bishop Daniel S. Tuttle 1866–1886* (Salt Lake City: University of Utah Press, 1987), 23.

38. Tuttle, *Missionary to the Mountain West*, 239, 447.

39. Tuttle, *Missionary to the Mountain West*, 173–174.

40. Tuttle, *Missionary to the Mountain West*, 464, 465.

41. Tuttle, *Missionary to the Mountain West*, 3, 408.

42. Tuttle, *Missionary to the Mountain West*, 382.

43. Mary S. Donovan, "Women Missionaries in Utah," *Anglican and Episcopal History* LXVI (June 1997), 154.

44. See Mary S. Donovan, *A Different Call: Women's Ministries in the Episcopal Church 1850 – 1920* (Wilton, CT: Morehouse-Barlow, 1986), 88–95. The movement of deaconesses which began in Kaiserwerth with a home for recently discharged female convicts developed into a large network of reformatories, hospitals and schools with affiliated houses in several European countries as well as in the Middle East and in America. See Lucy Rider Meyer, *Deaconesses, Biblical, Early Church, European, American: The Story of the Chicago Training School for City, Home and Foreign Missions, and The Chicago Deaconess House*, Chicago, The Message Publishing Co., 1889.

45. Donovan, *A Different Call*, 98.

46. Donovan, *A Different Call*, 92, 105.

47. Donovan, "Women Missionaries in Utah," 155–156.

48. Donovan, "Women Missionaries in Utah," 154, 158.

49. Donovan, *A Different Call*, 66.

50. Donovan, *A Different Call*, 70–71.

51. Anderson, *400 Years*, 179–180.

52. Anderson, *400 Years*, 181–182.

53. Donovan, *A Different Call*, 76–86.

54. Donovan, *A Different Call*, 86–87.

55. Karen A. Keely, "'Let the Children have their part': *The Young Christian Soldier* and the Domestic Missionary Army," *Anglican and Episcopal History*, 79 (September 2010), 200.

56. Keely, "'Let the Children have their part,'" 206–207.

57. Keely, "'Let the Children have their part,'" 207, 212.

58. Keely, "'Let the Children have their part,'" 213–227.

59. Keely, "'Let the Children have their part,'" 231–233.

60. Fred Smith, *A Man's Religion* (New York, 1913), Carl D. Case, *The Masculine in Religion* (Philadelphia, 1926), quoted in Clifford Putney, "Men and Religion:

Aspects of the Church Brotherhood Movement, 1880–1920," *Anglican and Episcopal History*, 63 (December 1994), 453–455.

61. Putney, "Men and Religion," 460–461.

62. The Brotherhood of St. Andrew, "A Brief History of the Brotherhood of St. Andrew," http://www.brotherhoodstandrew.org/aboutus2.html (accessed November 11, 2011).

63. Donovan, *A Different Call*, 34, 36–37.

64. Donovan, *A Different Call*, 33.

65. See Donovan, *A Different Call*, 37–43.

66. Bernard K. Markwell, *The Anglican Left: Radical Social Reformers in the Church of England and the Protestant Episcopal Church, 1846 – 1954* (Brooklyn: Carlson Publishing, Inc., 1991), 89–90, 96, 99.

67. Markwell, *The Anglican Left*, 103, 106.

68. Markwell, *The Anglican Left*, 41.

69. Hanson, *The Call of the Cloister*, 300–303; Harrison, *The Religious Orders of the Anglican Communion*, 96.

70. Harrison, *The Religious Orders of the Anglican Communion*, 12–14, 17.

71. Resolution 11, Lambeth Conference 1897, Lambeth Conference website, http://www.lambethconference.org/resolutions/1897/1897-11.cfm, accessed on July 7, 2010.

72. James Thayer Addison, *The Episcopal Church in the United States, 1789–1931* (New York: Charles Scribner's Sons, 1951), 167–186.

73. Charles H. Hopkins, *The Rise of the Social Gospel in American Protestantism 1865 – 1915* (New Haven: Yale University Press, 1940), 38.

74. Hopkins, *The Rise of the Social Gospel*, 93.

75. Manross, *The Episcopal Church in the United States*, 286.

76. Massey Hamilton Shepherd, Jr., *The Oxford American Prayer Book Commentary* (New York: Oxford University Press, 1963), 45.

77. Hopkins, *The Rise of the Social Gospel*, 51.

78. Spencer Miller, Jr., and Joseph F. Fletcher, *The Church and Industry* (New York: Longmans Green and Co., 1930), 55–56.

79. Hopkins, *The Rise of the Social Gospel*, 154.

80. Aaron I. Abell, *The Urban Impact on American Protestantism 1865 - 1900* (Cambridge: Harvard University Press, 1943), 183.

81. Quoted in Sheryl A. Kujawa-Holbrook, *Freedom Is a Dream: A Documentary History of Women in the Episcopal Church* (New York: Church Publishing, Inc., 2002), 146.

82. Sheryl A. Kujawa-Holbrook, "Women and Vocation in the Episcopal Church: Reflections on Our History," *Anglican and Episcopal History*, 79 (June 2010), 113.

83. Miriam U. Chrisman, *"To Bind Together": A Brief History of the Society of the Companions of the Holy Cross* (Byfield, MA: Society of the Companions of the Holy Cross, 1984), 69–70.

84. Hopkins, *The Rise of the Social Gospel*, 106.

85. Hopkins, *The Rise of the Social Gospel*, 175, 177.

86. Henry May, *Protestant Churches and Industrial America* (New York: Harper and Brothers, 1949), 246.

87. May, *Protestant Churches and Industrial America*, 186.

88. See, e.g., John Hutchinson, ed., *Christian Faith and Social Action* (New York: Charles Scribner's Sons, 1953).

Chapter 13

Visions

The Future(s) of Mission and Ministry in the Anglican Tradition

The rupture between the Church of England and the Pope set in motion in the first half of the sixteenth century proved to be decisive in the development of a distinctively English approach to the Church's ministry. Most of the Church's clergy made their peace with the new ecclesiastical regime, with the result that in many ways day-to-day ministry on the level of the congregation continued as it had before. But as the course of the English Reformation proceeded under the leadership of Thomas Cranmer, European Protestant influences became more pronounced. Yet the unique aspects of the Reformation in England, particularly its insistence that the monarch is the "head" (Henry and Edward) or "supreme governor" (Elizabeth) of the Church, determined that from early times the "ministry of Word and Sacrament" as Anglicans practiced it would have its own characteristics that set it apart from both its Roman Catholic forebears and its Reformed "sister churches."

The long history of the evolution of ministry in the Anglican tradition has proceeded by a dialectic process in which Catholic, Reformed and uniquely Anglican impulses have jostled for dominance, often through bitter and sometimes violent conflict. Once England became a global power, its form of Christianity and its practice of ministry made their way overseas, following the Union Jack and attempting to replicate in new contexts the English understanding of the Church's ministry and its relationship to the society in which it was attempting to take root.

But once Anglican Christianity and the ministry that fostered it were transplanted to other parts of the world, it inevitably underwent profound changes. The role of the clergy, the relationship between ordained and lay ministry, and the place of the church in the new society, all were challenged in multiple ways. Sometimes gradually and at other times dramatically, ministry in the Anglican tradition broadened to reflect its new contexts.

Unfortunately, in many settings, Anglican ministry was colored by the colonial and imperial power that often undergirded it. The practice of ministry was tainted and often inhibited by assumptions of superiority and a failure to recognize that, as the old hymn had it, "new occasions teach new duties."[1] One of the early critics of the ways in which Anglican Christianity adapted, and failed to adapt, to new settings was Roland Allen, whose brief service as a CMS missionary in China at the turn of the twentieth century convinced him that the Church had failed to adapt its ministry to the demands of its new settings. As evidence, he cited the fact that "it still remains true that Christianity in the lands of our missions is still a foreign religion." Furthermore, he noted that mission churches remained dependent: "Day by day and year by year there comes to us an unceasing appeal for men and money for the last fifty or sixty years . . . " Finally, he lamented the fact that "everywhere we see the same types. . . . If we read the history of a mission in China, we have only to change a few names and the same history will serve as the history of a mission in Zululand. There has been no new revelation. There has been no new discovery of new aspects of the Gospel, no new unfolding of new forms of Christian life." These failures, Allen believed, were the result of permitting "racial and religious pride to direct our attitude towards those whom we have been wont to call 'poor heathen.'" Nor did the missionary community trust "native independence," asking for obedience rather than leadership.[2]

Allen was convinced that if the Church were to adapt the missionary methods found in the New Testament, and particularly in the work of St. Paul, these failings could be overcome. Ministry in missionary situations as Allen conceived it would draw new Christians into close collaboration with the missionary, trusting the local leaders with finances, education, administration, incorporation of new members and the community's own discipline. Furthermore, missionaries should plan to retire from the newly established church as soon as is possible.[3]

From the vantage point of the twenty-first century, Allen's analysis seems remarkably prophetic and illuminates many of the ways in which Anglican ministry in a global context emerged in the century now behind us.

The English-speaking churches found themselves called to exercise their ministry in the face of violence unlike that of any previous century, first in World War I, when the easy relationship between Church and State seemed more problematic than ever, and only two decades later in another World War which re-made the map of Europe and Asia. The Russian Revolution and the subsequent growth of a bloc of Communist states that stretched from central Europe to the Pacific, and for a while included much of the world's population, affected the ways in which ministry and culture understood each other.

But no twentieth century movement affected the practice of ministry in the Anglican tradition more profoundly than the struggle of peoples, colonized (and evangelized) in the context of the British and American Empires, to liberate themselves. Across Asia and Africa, and from the Rio Grande to the tip of South America, Anglicans participated in the process of achieving not only political independence but control of their own expressions of Christian faith in the Anglican way. The second half of the twentieth century witnessed previously colonial churches receiving their independence as autonomous member churches of a Communion that grew precipitously, especially in those parts of the world where previously colonial churches at last dared to practice their faith in ways more closely expressive of local culture.

But that process has not always been smoothly executed. The relationship between the church culture imported with the missionaries—or with English-speaking immigrants—and the culture of the local context has often proved to require delicate negotiation, and misunderstanding and mistrust are all too common. Furthermore, in many places where Anglican Christianity has been "at home" for nearly two centuries, it continues to look to its English-speaking forebears for guidance, support and approval. The legacy of complex institutions—hospitals, schools and colleges, and church structures—created by the missionaries sometimes proves to be a burden difficult or impossible to maintain when support from overseas is not forthcoming. And where English-speaking Anglicanism has interacted most with local cultures, the result is a "hybrid" form of ministry which combines the patterns inherited from abroad with more local expressions to create a new style of ministry neither strictly contextualized nor entirely "foreign."

The rapid social changes that have been experienced in the countries of the North Atlantic inevitably affect other parts of the world, but interactions have not only a social and political dimension but also touch religious and ecclesial relationships. The nature of Anglican worship has been influenced by the work of liturgical renewal in which Anglican scholars have worked in dialogue with their Roman Catholic and Protestant colleagues. The role of the clergy, the liturgical participation of laypeople, and church music have been significantly re-shaped by the Liturgical Movement; the *Book of Common Prayer* which once served as an important instrument of Anglican unity has been revised in many directions, and while the *shape* of Anglican worship remains similar across much of the Communion, its *forms* no longer display conformity with the products of Thomas Cranmer in the sixteenth century.[4]

The appearance of a theology of ministry based on baptism rather than ordination, which emerged from the Liturgical Movement at mid-century, has had considerable effect in the English-speaking churches as the "ministry of all the baptized" has called into question the traditional Anglican roles of the clergy and spawned experiments with "total" or "mutual ministry," especially in those parts of the Church where numbers and resources are limited and congregations are widely separated.[5] But this model is viewed with alarm in some postcolonial churches as it also challenges not only traditional authority structures but also the sometimes autocratic practices inherited from the missionaries and which have been incorporated into the churches' institutional life.

In the United States, the civil rights movement which began with the demand by African Americans for all the prerogatives of citizenship reinvigorated Black congregations and provided the impulse for many churches to become centers for programs designed to empower racial and ethnic minorities. Just as urban churches had responded to poverty in the nineteenth century, so many African American churches provided the primary link between the Episcopal Church and the movement for civil rights. The tactics and perceptions of that movement also strengthened similar demands for other minorities, and the decades of the sixties and seventies saw Native and Latinx congregations taking on new ministries of education and empowerment. As Anglicans in many parts of the world focus more deeply on the implications of the Baptismal Covenant and its commitment to "respect the dignity of every person," the overtones of paternalism and elitism that often accompanied a church identified with the political, economic and social Establishment are gradually being replaced by principles of solidarity and equity.

The changing role of women and the increasing acceptance of gay and lesbian persons in the life of the Church and its lay and ordained ministry in the English-speaking world have also been felt in other parts of the Communion, but again often conflict with both traditional mores and the imported morality taught by an earlier generation of missionaries. The effect on the relationship among member churches across the Anglican Communion has been severe, in both the older churches and in its more recently autonomous members.

Among the newer churches of the Communion, remarkable new developments in ministry have emerged in the twentieth century. In 1948, the year in which the long struggle of the Indian people for political independence reached fruition, Anglicans in southern India became the first to achieve union with a number of other Christian denominations to form the Church of South India, a success replicated later in both North India and Pakistan. In China, following the Revolution in 1949, the Chung Hua Sheng Kung Hui (Holy Catholic Church of China), an autonomous member of the Anglican Communion since 1912, gave up its independent existence to join with other Chinese churches from a wide variety of traditions to form the "Three-Self Patriotic Movement," based on the principles of self-government, self-propagation and self-support first articulated by Henry Venn in the mid-nineteenth century and advocated by Roland Allen half a century later.

In Africa, the East African Revival unleashed a powerful wave of Evangelical fervor in the 1930s which has still not abated and is responsible for much of the rapid growth of Anglican churches on the African continent in the last century. Its impulses have contributed greatly to re-shaping ministry, affirming the importance of laypeople as the primary agents of mission and evangelism, and incorporating elements of local spiritual practices into traditional Anglican understanding of the Church's life.[6]

Anglican ministry has been called to respond to perksecution and violence in a variety of settings. In Sudan, the Anglican Church has provided support for the victims of a devastating civil war. Anglicans in Ruanda, Burundi and Congo have been deeply affected by war. The political conflict in Zimbabwe has divided Anglicans and brought persecution to many. Some Anglican ministry takes place in situations where the church's status is tenuous and where Christian participation is dangerous. In the Middle East, Anglicans have found their ministry impeded by both Israeli and Arab governments. The Bishop of Iran was forced into exile when the Shah was overthrown in 1979. Archbishop Janani Luwum was killed by the murderous regime of Idi Amin in Uganda. Anglicans in Myanmar have lived for decades with nearly constant threats from a hostile military government.

The ongoing situations of warfare, violence and political conflict have also influenced the practice of ministry in a number of contexts. The threat of nuclear war brought many American and British Anglicans to engage in protest against their governments' continuing reliance on a nuclear deterrent to prevent war. In particular, the Vietnam War led many Anglicans on both sides of the Atlantic to see protesting against the war as an integral part of the Church's ministry. In Japan, the Nippon Sei Ko Kai has been involved not only in the campaign to outlaw nuclear weapons but to assure that Japan never again becomes a military power. Korean Anglicans have been in the forefront of the grassroots movement to demilitarize the Korean peninsula and foster the reunion of North and South Korea. In South Africa, under the tireless leadership of its Nobel Prize-winning primate, Desmond Tutu, the Anglican Church participated fully in the struggle which finally led to the downfall of the brutal *apartheid* regime of racial segregation and oppression in that country.

Latin American Anglicans have found their ministries challenged from a number of distinct directions. As the Roman Catholic Church responded to the impulses of Vatican Council II with a liberation theology based on the reign of God and its demand for justice, Christians of other traditions—including Anglicans—often embraced its starting point, God's "preferential option for the poor." This required revising their practice of ministry to give priority to solidarity with the poor who make up the majority of the population. The Anglican Episcopal Church of Brazil has been especially active in this regard, establishing missions in the *favelas* of Brazilian cities and in the undeveloped reaches of the Amazonian rainforest, defending the indigenous tribal people against the encroachment of corporations and land-hungry farmers alike, and experimenting with forms of worship designed to engage and communicate with illiterate congregations. The retired bishop of Rio de Janeiro pioneered a regular celebration of the Eucharist on a street corner for a large community of the homeless, and a priest in the city of Campo Grande established a ministry with transgendered people.

As the twentieth century drew to a close and the twenty-first century began, the breadth of diversity with which Anglicans around the world engaged in the practice of ministry became more obvious as its differences widened. Michael Poon, a Hong Kong Chinese priest now working in Singapore, has questioned the nature of the relationship between Anglicans and Christians of other churches and challenged the traditional Anglican understanding of the role of bishops in the Church's ministry.[7] Saw Shee Sho, now bishop of the diocese of Toungoo, Myanmar, has argued for re-thinking the Church's theology using concepts derived from Buddhism rather than Western philosophical traditions; the Anglican Church of Myanmar has developed a Eucharistic liturgy in which the Service of the Word incorporates the structure of Buddhist gatherings.[8] Sungkonghoe (Anglican) University in Korea has provided the context for several Anglican scholars to explore the relationship between Buddhist and Christian scriptures as well as the ways in which elements of Korean folk religion can illuminate Christian spirituality. Lee Joo-Yup, a Korean Anglican priest, has written on the ways in which aspects of Buddhist piety can enrich Anglican worship and spiritual practices, and has incorporated them into his own parish's ministry.[9]

Meanwhile, the older Anglican churches in the English-speaking world have found their ministry challenged by shrinking resources as the religious landscape of the West has changed. The number of participants has dropped, in response to changing demographics and the increasingly secular nature of most Western societies. The so-called "Fresh Expressions" or "Emerging Church" movement has attempted to structure ministry in a way more congruent with contemporary Western culture, while continuing to incorporate elements of the Anglican tradition such as Eucharistically centered worship and, in some cases, the formation of intentional communities of prayer and community ministry. Many of these experimental ministries are housed in cathedrals or otherwise enjoy the support of congregations or dioceses.[10]

The Lambeth Conferences of 1998 and 2008 revealed many fault-lines running through each of the member churches and between them. It is clear that the Church of England, and for that matter the other English-speaking churches which long enjoyed a privileged position within the Communion, can no longer dictate how Anglicans approach the practice of their faith; the overwhelming majority of Anglicans engage in ministries that are clearly identified with the newer Churches and the term "Anglican" no longer necessarily points to an allegiance that accepts direction from Canterbury.[11]

The enormous diversity of ministries, the cultural distinctions that they reflect and the theological differences that support them have led some Anglicans to wonder if the relationship of communion that has bound them together can survive. Certainly those diversities and differences are real and significant. But many of the bonds that held Anglicans together in past centuries remain intact today, none stronger than a common sense of responsibility for their community and its people and a shared belief that every Christian people has the right to practice its faith in ways rooted in the context in which they live.

Perhaps what will bind the Anglicans of a global Communion together most deeply in the twenty-first century will be the shared perception of the threat to the planet we share. Christians of many traditions have responded to the dangers unleashed by a rapidly forming vision of a planet in deep distress. Contemporary descriptions of the nature of ministry and mission increasingly emphasize the common responsibility to care for the earth which lies—often forgotten—at the heart of any Christian doctrine of creation. Anglicans in the industrialized world have called on Christians to tackle both their own excessive use of the world's resources and the profligate habits of their culture. Anglicans in the developing world have cried for an end to the destruction of the ecosystems on which whole nations depend. Theologians have already pointed to the importance of eco-theology for contemporary Christians; perhaps it is past time to focus as well on *eco-ministry*, the development of a style of ministry that takes seriously the vocation of stewardship which belongs to us all.[12]

Meanwhile, the call to bring the Church's ministry to bear on the poorest among us—a call which helped to shape Anglican ministry of Anglicans in Britain and the United States more than a century ago—continues to be heard, but now it comes not only from within each of our societies and cultures but from Anglicans in other parts of the world, where a globalized economy has improved the lot of a few while deepening the misery of the majority. Surely addressing that misery and the structures and institutions that cause it remains an aspect of the Church's calling that can foster unity among Anglicans and draw them even closer together.

The churches of the Anglican Communion live and work under the shadow of two contrary visions. On one hand, there is the vision of the world as it is, with all its pain, misery and death. On the other, there is the vision of the world as God would have it be, a place of joy, abundance, compassion, and justice, the reign of God we pray for every time we pray as Jesus taught,

"Your kingdom come, your will be done on earth as in heaven." Ministry has always happened when Christians are aware of those two visions and the contradiction between them. The vision of "the way things are" is never far from us; but ministry is our response to the second, the vision of the world as it might be, for as long as it remains an unfulfilled dream.

NOTES

1. The words of the hymn "Once to Every Man and Nation" were written in 1845 by the poet James Russell Lowell to protest the American war with Mexico. "Joint Commission on the Revision of the Hymnal of the Protestant Episcopal Church in the USA," *The Hymnal 1940 Companion* (New York: The Church Pension Fund, 1951), 312.

2. Roland Allen, *Missionary Methods: St. Paul's Or Ours?* (London: World Dominion Press, 1960), 141–143.

3. Allen, *Missionary Methods,* 154–159. In his concern that missionaries not remain permanently in new churches, Allen reflects the perspective which Henry Venn worked unsuccessfully to instill in the work of the CMS.

4. See *Unbound! Anglican Worship Beyond the Prayer Book*, a series of papers delivered at the Church Divinity School of the Pacific in 1999 and published in the *Anglican Theological Review*, 82 (Winter 2000).

5. See John L. Kater, Jr., "Alternative Patterns for Ministry: North and South America," in A. Wingate, K. Ward, C. Pemberton and W. Sitshebo, eds., *Anglicanism: A Global Communion* (New York: Church Publishing, 1998), 124–131 and Kevin Thew Forrester, *I Have Called you Friends: An Invitation to Ministry* (New York: Church Publishing, 2003).

6. See Ward, *A History of Colonial Anglicanism*, 175–179.

7. Michael Nai-Chiu Poon, "Authority for Ministry and Mission in an East Asian Context," *Anglican and Episcopal History*, LXII (March 1992).

8. Saw Shee Sho, "Doing Theology in Myanmar's Context," *Madang* 7 (15 June 2007), 7–18.

9. Joo-Yup Lee, "Entering the Kingdom Within," Berkeley, CA: Church Divinity School of the Pacific, unpublished D. Min. thesis, 2007.

10. Steven Croft, Ian Mobsby and Stephanie Spellers, eds., *Ancient Faith, Future Mission: Fresh Expressions in the Catholic Tradition* (New York: Seabury Press, 2010).

11. John L. Kater, Jr., "Faithful Church, Plural World: Diversity at Lambeth 1998," in *Anglican Theological Review*, 81 (Spring 1999), 235–260.

12. John L. Kater, Jr., "Tending This Fragile Earth, Our Island Home: The Pope's Encyclical in Dialogue with Anglican Theology," *Anglican Theological Review* 100 (Fall 2018), 721–743.

Bibliography

Abell, Aaron I. *The Urban Impact on American Protestantism 1865–1900.* Cambridge: Harvard University Press, 1943.

Addison, James Thayer. *The Episcopal Church in the United States, 1789–1931.* New York: Charles Scribner's Sons, 1951.

Allen, Anne Beiser. *And the Wilderness Shall Blossom: Henry Benjamin Whipple, Churchman, Educator, Advocate for the Indians.* Afton, MN: Afton Historical Society Press, 2008.

Allen, J. W. *Political Thought in the Sixteenth Century.* London: Methuen, 1928.

Allestree, Richard. *The practice of Christian graces, or, The Whole Duty of Man, laid down in a plain and familiar way for the use of all, but especially the meanest sort . . .* London: SPCK, 1870.

Anderson, Owanah. *400 Years: Anglican/Episcopal Mission Among American Indians.* Cincinnati: Forward Movement Publications, 1997.

Anderson, Owanah. *Jamestown Commitment: The Episcopal Church and the American Indian.* Cincinnati: Forward Movement Publications, 1988.

Ashdown, Paul G. "Commission from a Higher Source: Church and State in the Civil War," *Historical Magazine of the Protestant Episcopal Church,* XLVII, September 1979.

Ashton, Rosemary. *142 Strand: A Radical Address in Victorian London.* London: Vintage Books, 2008.

Avis, Paul. *Church, State and Establishment.* London: SPCK, 2001.

Avis, Paul. *The Church in the Theology of the Reformers.* London: Marshall Morgan and Scott, 1981.

Balda, Wesley. "Ecclesiastics and Enthusiasts: The Evangelical Emergence in England 1760 – 1800," *Anglican and Episcopal History,* 49 (September 1980).

Balia, Daryl and Kirsteen Kim. *Edinburgh 2010, Volume II: Witnessing to Christ Today.* Oxford: Regnum Books International, 2010.

Barnhart, William C. "Anglican Volunteerism, Ecclesiastical Politics, and the Bath Church Missionary Association Controversy, 1817–1818," *Anglican and Episcopal History,* 77 (March 2008).

Barstow, Anne Llewellyn Barstow. "The First Generations of Anglican Clergy Wives: Heroines or Whores?" *Anglican and Episcopal History,* 52 (March 1983).

Beasley, Nicholas. "Domestic Rituals: Marriage and Baptism in the British Plantation Colonies, 1650 – 1780," *Anglican and Episcopal History*, 76 (September 2007).
Benson, Richard M. *The Religious Vocation*. London: A. R. Mowbray & Co., 1939.
Bilson, Thomas. *The Perpetual Government of Christ's Church* (Oxford: Oxford University Press, 1842).
Black, Robert M. "Stablished in the Faith: The Church of England in Upper Canada 1780–1867," in Alan L. Hayes, ed., *By Grace Co-Workers: Building the Anglican Diocese of Toronto 1780 – 1989*. Toronto: Anglican Book Centre, 1989.
Bloxam, Matthew. "On Chantry Altars," in *Transactions of the Cambridge Camden Society: A Selection from the Papers Read at the Ordinary Meetings in 1839–1841*. Cambridge: T. Stevenson, 1841.
Blunt, John Henry. *Directorium Pastorale: The Principles and Practice of Pastoral Work in the Church of England*. London: Rivingtons, 1872.
Bolton, F. R. *The Caroline Tradition of the Church of Ireland: With Particular Reference to Bishop Jeremy Taylor*. London: SPCK, 1958.
Bond, Edward L. "Colonial Virginia Mission Attitudes toward Native Peoples and African-American Slaves," in Amos Yong and Barbara Brown Ziklund, eds., *Remembering Jamestown: Hard Questions About Christian Mission*. Eugene, OR: Pickwick Publications, 2010.
The Book of Common Prayer and Administration of the Sacraments and Other Rites and Ceremonies of the Church. New York: The Seabury Press, 1979.
Booty, John E. "The English Reformation: A Lively Faith and Sacramental Confession," in Paul Elmen, ed., *The Anglican Moral Choice*. Harrisburg, PA: Morehouse Publishing, 1983.
Booty, John, ed. *Richard Hooker, Of the Laws of Ecclesiastical Polity: Attack and Response*. Cambridge: Cambridge University Press, 1982.
Bosher, Robert Bosher. *The American Church and the Formation of the Anglican Communion, 1823–1853*. Evanston, Illinois: Seabury-Western Theological Seminary, 1962.
Bosher, Robert S. *The Making of the Restoration Settlement: The Influence of the Laudians 1649–1662*. London: Dacre Press, 1951.
Brander, Michael. *The Country Divine*. Edinburgh: The St. Andrew Press, 1981.
Bray, William, ed. *The Diary of John Evelyn*. New York: M. Walter Dunne, 1901, I.
Brethren of the Epiphany. *A Hundred Years in Bengal: A History of the Oxford Mission 1880–1980*. Delhi: S.P.C.K., 1979.
Brotherhood of St. Andrew. "A Brief History of the Brotherhood of St. Andrew," http://www.brotherhoodstandrew.org/aboutus2.html
Bryson, Bill. *At Home: A Short History of Private Life*. New York: Doubleday, 2010.
Bullock, F. W. B. *A History of Training for the Ministry of the Church of England in England and Wales*. St. Leonard's-on-Sea: Budd and Gillatt, 1955.
Burgess, Clive. "London Parishioners in Times of Change: St. Andrew Hubbard, Eastcheap, c. 1450 – 1570." *Journal of Ecclesiastical History*, 53 (January 2002).
Callaghan, Moeawa. *Theology in the Context of Aotearoa New Zealand*. Unpublished thesis, Graduate Theological Union: Berkeley, CA, 1999.

Calvani, Carlos. "Eclesiologia em mudança: Uma leitura da Igreja Episcopal Anglicana do Brasil," *Inclusividade*, 9 (April 2010).
Carlton, Charles. *Archbishop William Laud.* London: Routledge and Kegan Paul, Ltd., 1987.
Carpenter, S. C. *Church and People, 1989 – 1889: A History of the Church of England from William Wilberforce to "Lux Mundi."* London: SPCK, 1933.
Caswall, Henry. *America and the American Church.* London: J. G. and F. Rivington, 1839.
Cavieses, Guillermo. *¡ANGLICANOS! Latin American Anglicanism: A Study of the Ecclesiology and Identity of the Anglican Churches of Latin America.* Unpublished thesis, Uppsala University, 2010.
Chadwick, Henry. "The Quadrilateral in England," in J. Robert Wright, ed., *Quadrilateral at One Hundred: Essays on the Centenary of the Chicago-Lambeth Quadrilateral 1886–88 – 1986–88.* Oxford: A. R. Mowbray and Co., 1988.
Chadwick, Owen. "The Lambeth Conference: An Historical Perspective," *Anglican and Episcopal History,* 58 (September 1989).
Chadwick, Owen. *The Victorian Church: An Ecclesiastical History of England, Vol. I and II.* London: Adam and Charles Black, 1966.
Cheshire, Joseph. *The Church in the Confederate States: A History of the Protestant Episcopal Church in the Confederate States.* New York: Longmans, Green and Co., 1912.
Chiu, Patricia Pok-Kwan."'A Position of Usefulness': Gendering of Girls' Education in Colonial Hong Kong (1850s-1890s)," *History of Education,* 37 (November 2008).
Chrisman, Miriam U. *"To Bind Together": A Brief History of the Society of the Companions of the Holy Cross.* Byfield, MS: Society of the Companions of the Holy Cross, 1984.
Clark, J. C. D. *English Society 1688–1832: Ideology, social structure and political practice during the ancient regime.* Cambridge: Cambridge University Press, 1985.
CMS MissionUpdateOnline: http://mission.typepad.com/church_mission_society_cm/2009/08/index.html
Collett, Henry. *Little Gidding and Its Founder: An Account of the Religious Community Established by Nicholas Farrer in the XVIIth Century.* London: SPCK, 1925.
Collins, Brenda. *Victorian Country Parsons.* London, Book Club Associates, 1977.
Constant, Joseph M. *No Turning Back: The Black Presence at Virginia Theological Seminary.* Brainerd, MN: Evergreen Press, 2009.
Corfe, Charles John. *The Anglican Church in Corea.* London: Rivington, 1906.
Cornick, David. "Pastoral Care in England: Perkins, Baxter and Burnet," in G. R. Evans, ed., *A History of Pastoral Care.* New York: Cassell, 2000.
Cornwall, Obert D. "Divine Right Monarchy, Henry Dodwell's Critique of the Reformation and Defense of the Deprived Nonjuror Bishops," *Anglican and Episcopal History* 68 (March 1999).
Cort, John C. *Christian Socialism: An Informal History.* Maryknoll, NY: Orbis Books, 1988.

Cranmer, Thomas. "ARTICLES to be inquired of in the visitations to be had within the Diocese of Canterbury . . . ," 1548. Quoted in Cox, ed., *Miscellaneous Writings and Letters of Thomas Cranmer.* Cambridge: Cambridge University Press, 1846.

Cranmer, Thomas. "*De Ordine*, Injunctions given by the most Excellent Prince, Edward the Sixth . . . in earth under Christ of the Church of England and of Ireland the Supreme Head . . .," in J. E. Cox, ed., *Miscellaneous Writings and Letters of Thomas Cranmer.* Cambridge: Cambridge University Press, 1846.

Cranmer, Thomas. "Injunctions given by the most Excellent Prince Edward the Sixth . . . in earth under Christ of the Church of England and Ireland the Supreme Head . . . ," in Cox. ed., *Miscellaneous Writings and Letters of Thomas Cranmer.* Cambridge: Cambridge University Press, 1846.

Cranmer, Thomas. "Letters Missive from the Council to the Bishops of the Realm Concerning the Communion to be ministered in both Kinds," in Cox, ed., *Miscellaneous Writings and Letters of Thomas Cranmer.* Cambridge: Cambridge University Press, 1846.

Cranmer, Thomas. "Reasons why the Lord's Board should be rather after the form of a Table . . . than of an altar," in Cox, ed., *Miscellaneous Writings and Letters of Thomas Cranmer*, Cambridge: Cambridge University Press, 1846.

Cressy, David. *Agnes Bowker's Cat: Travesties and Transgressions in Tudor and Stuart England.* Oxford: Oxford University Press, 2000.

Croft, Steven Croft, Ian Mobsby and Stephanie Spellers, eds. *Ancient Faith, Future Mission: Fresh Expressions in the Catholic Tradition.* New York: Seabury Press, 2010.

Cuattingius, Hans. *Bishops and Societies: A Study of Anglican Colonial and Missionary Expansion 1698–1850.* London: SPCK, 1952.

Curthoys, Patricia. "State Support for Churches," in Kaye, ed., *Anglicanism in Australia: A History,* Melbourne: Melbourne University Press, 2002.

Daeley, J. I. "Pluralism in the Diocese of Canterbury during the Administration of Matthew Parker, 1559–1575," *Journal of Ecclesiastical History,* 18, 1967.

Davidson, Harriet E. "The Rise and Fall of Kemper College," *The Historiographer,* 47 (September 2009).

Davidson, Randall T., ed. *Origin and History of the Lambeth Conferences of 1867 and 1878, With the Official Reports and Resolutions.* London: SPCK, 1888.

Davies, E. T. *Episcopacy and the Royal Supremacy in the Church of England in the XVI Century.* Oxford: Basil Blackwell, 1950.

Donne, John. "*Nunc lento somitu dicunt, morieris,* XVII. MEDITATION," *Devotions Upon Diverse Occasions,* in Robert Coffin and Alexander Witherspoon, eds., *Seventeenth Century Prose and Poetry.* New York: Harcourt Brace, 1957.

Donovan, Mary S. *A Different Call: Women's Ministries in the Episcopal Church 1850 – 1920.* Wilton, CT: Morehouse-Barlow, 1986.

Donovan, Mary S. "Women Missionaries in Utah," *Anglican and Episcopal History,* 66 (June 1997).

Doran, Susan and Christopher Durston. *Princes, Pastors and People: The Church and Religion in England 1529–1689.* London: Routledge, 1991.

Douglas, Ian T. *Fling Out the Banner: The National Church Ideal and the Foreign Mission of the Episcopal Church.* New York: Church Hymnal Corp., 1996.

Drake, George. "The Ideology of Oliver Cromwell," *Church History,* 35 (September 1966).

Duffis, Ennis. "Capellanía en Centroamérica," in Ashton Jacinto Brooks, ed., *Eclesiología: presencia anglicana en la Región Central de América.* San José, Costa Rica: DEI, 1990.

Duffy, Eamon. *The Stripping of the Altars: Traditional Religion in England, 1400–1580.* New Haven: Yale University Press, 2005.

Duffy, Eamon. *The Voices of Morebath: Reformation and Rebellion in an English Village.* New Haven: Yale University Press, 2001.

Dunch, Ryan. *Fuzhou Protestants and the Making of a Modern China 1857 – 1927.* New Haven: Yale University Press, 2001.

Dunch, Ryan. "Science, Religion, and the Classics in Christian Higher Education to 1920," in Daniel H. Bays and Ellen Widmer, eds., *China's Christian Colleges, Cross-Cultural Connections, 1900–1950.* Stanford, CA: Stanford University Press, 2009.

Dunscombe, Edward S. "The Northern Arapahoe Experience of Episcopal Mission Work and United States Policy, 1883–1925, Part I: Background," *Anglican and Episcopal History*, 66 (June 1997).

Echlin, Edward P. *The Story of Anglican Ministry.* Slough: St. Paul Publications, 1974.

Emerson, N. D. "Church Life in the Nineteenth Century," in Walter A. Phillips, ed., *History of the Church of Ireland from the Earliest Times to the Present Day,* III. Oxford: Oxford University Press, 1933.

Emery, Julia C. *A Century of Endeavor 1821 – 1921: A Record of the First Hundred Years of the Domestic and Foreign Missionary Society.* New York: Department of Missions, 1921.

England, Frank. "Tracing Southern African Anglicanism," in Frank England and Torquil Paterson, eds., *Bounty in Bondage: The Anglican Church in Southern Africa.* Johannesburg: Ravan Press, 1989.

Evans, Gillian R. "Permanence in the Revealed Truth and Continuous Exploration of Its Meaning," in J. R. Wright, ed., *Quadrilateral at One Hundred: Essays on the Centenary of the Chicago-Lambeth Quadrilateral 1886–88 – 1986–88.* Oxford: A. R. Mowbray and Co., 1988.

Evans, John H. "The Constitution of The Church of the Province of New Zealand," *Anglican and Episcopal History*, 66 (June 1987).

Faught, Brad. "Tractarianism on the Zambezi: Bishop Mackenzie and the Beginnings of the Universities Mission to Central Africa," *Anglican and Episcopal History*, 66 (June 1987).

Fincham, Kenneth. *Prelate As Pastor: The Episcopate of James I.* Oxford: Clarendon Press, 1990.

Fincham, Kenneth and Peter Lake. "The Ecclesiastical Policies of James I and Charles I," in K. Fincham, ed., *The Early Stuart Church, 1603–1642.* London: The Macmillan Press, 1993.

The First and Second Prayer-Books of King Edward the Sixth. London: J.M. Dent & sons, 1927.

Fletcher, Brian. "The Anglican Ascendancy 1788–1835," in Bruce Kaye, ed., *Anglicanism in Australia: A History.* Melbourne: Melbourne University Press, 2002.

Fletcher, Brian H. *The Place of Anglicanism in Australia: Church, Society and Nation.* Mulgrave, Australia: Broughton Publishing, 2008.

Foribo, Obuo. *A History of the Niger Delta Diocese (Anglican Communion) 1864–1980.* No publisher, 1990.

Forrester, Duncan B. *Caste and Christianity: Attitudes and Policies on Caste of Anglo-Saxon Protestant Missions in India.* London: Curzon Press, 1980.

Foster, Roland. "Seabury and the Anglican Communion," in Robert G. Carroon, ed., *A New Heart, A New Spirit: Sermons and Addresses Commemorating the Bicentennial of the Consecration of Samuel Seabury, First Bishop of the American Episcopal Church.* Wilton, CT: Morehouse-Barlow, 1988.

Frame, Tom. "Local Differences, Social and National Identity 1930–1966," in Bruce Kaye ed., *Anglicanism in Australia: A History.* Melbourne: Melbourne University Press, 2002.

Franks, Kenny A. "Missionaries in the West: An Expedition of the Protestant Episcopal Church In 1844," *Historical Magazine of the Protestant Episcopal Church,* 44 (September 1975).

Frykenberg, Robert Eric. *Christianity in India: From Beginnings to the Present.* London: Oxford University Press, 2008.

Garnett, Jane and Colin Matthew, eds. *Revival and Religion Since 1700: Essays for John Walsh.* London: The Humbledon Press, 1992.

Gibson, William, ed. *Religion and Society in England and Wales, 1989–1800.* Leicester: Leicester University Press, 1998.

Glasson, Travis. *Mastering Christianity: Missionary Anglicanism and Slavery in the Atlantic World.* Oxford: Oxford University Press, 2012.

Glen, Robert, ed. *Mission and Moko: Aspects of the Work of the Church Missionary Society in New Zealand 1814–1832.* Christchurch, NZ: Latimer Fellowship, 1992.

Goedhals, Mandy. "From Paternalism to Partnership," in Frank England and Torquil Paterson, eds., *Bounty in Bondage: The Anglican Church in Southern Africa.* Johannesburg: Ravan Press, 1989.

González, Justo L. and Ondina E. González. *Christianity in Latin America.* Cambridge: Cambridge University Press, 2008, 190–191.

Gott, John. *The Parish Priest of the Town: Lectures Delivered in the Divinity School Cambridge.* London: SPCK, 1887.

Grau, Marion. *Rethinking Mission in the Postcolony: Salvation, Society and Subversion.* New York: T. and T. Clark, 2011.

Gray, G. F. S., revised by Martha Lund Smalley. *Anglicans in China: A History of the Zhonghua Shenggong Hui (Chung Hua Sheng Kung Huei).* Episcopal China Mission History Project, 1996.

Gregory, Jeremy. *Restoration, Reformation and Reform 1660–1828: Archbishops of Canterbury and their Diocese.* Oxford: Clarendon Press, 2000.

Grimes, Cecil John. *Towards an Indian Church: Two Centuries of the Growth of the Church in India in Constitution and Life.* London: SPCK, 1946.
Hall, Joseph. "Columba Noae, with a Translation," in Philip Wynter, ed., *The Works of the Right Reverend Joseph Hall, D.D.,* X. Oxford: Oxford University Press, 1843.
Hammond, Peter C. *The Parson and the Victorian Parish.* London: Hodder and Stoughton, 1977.
Hanciles, Jehu J. "Bishop Crowther and Archdeacon Crowther," *International Bulletin of Mission Research,* 28 (October 2004).
Hanciles, Jehu J. "Bishop Crowther and Archdeacon Crowther: Inter-Generational Challenge and Opportunity in the African Christian Encounter," in Chima J. Korieh and G. Ugo Nwokeji, eds., *Religion, History and Politics in Nigeria: Essays in Honor of Ogbu U. Kalu.* Kanham, MD: University Press of America, 2005.
Hanson, Peter F., revised and edited by A. W. Campbell. *The Call of the Cloister: Religious Communities and Kindred Bodies in the Anglican Communion.* London: SPCK, 1964.
Harrison, Charles H. *The Religious Orders of the Anglican Communion,* unpublished dissertation, Divinity School, University of Chicago, 1932.
Hart, A. Tindal. *The Man in the Pew: 1558–1660.* London: John Baker, 1966.
Hartley, Brian T. "The Liturgical Reordering of the *Ecclesia Anglicana:* Faithful Understanding of the Elizabethan Homilies of 1563," *Anglican and Episcopal History,* 76 (December 2007).
Hawkins, J. Barney, IV. "International Students at Virginia Seminary: A Long History with a Rich and Transformative Practice," in Richard J. Jones and J. Barney Hawkins IV, eds., *Staying One, Remaining Open: Educating Leaders for a Twenty-First Century Church.* New York: Morehouse Publishing, 2010.
Heal, Felicity. *Reformation in Britain and Ireland.* Oxford: Oxford University Press, 2003.
Heaney, Robert S. "Coloniality and Theological Method in Africa," *Journal of Anglican Studies,* 7 (May 2009).
Hebb, Ross N. "Bishop Charles Inglis and Bishop Samuel Seabury: High Churchmanship in Varying New World Contexts," *Anglican and Episcopal History,* 76 (March 2007).
Herbert, George. *A Priest to the Temple or The Country Parson with Selected Poems.* Ronald Blythe, ed. London: SCM-Canterbury Press, Ltd., 2003.
Herklots, H. G. G. *Frontiers of the Church: The Making of the Anglican Communion.* London: Ernest Benn, 1961.
Hogge, Alice. *God's Secret Agents: Queen Elizabeth's Forbidden Priests and the Hatching of the Gunpowder Plot.* London: Harper Perennial, 2005.
Holmes, David L. *A Brief History of the Episcopal Church.* Valley Forge, PA: Trinity Press International, 1993.
Holmes, David L. "The Episcopal Church and the Revolution," *Historical Magazine of the Protestant Episcopal Church,* 57 (September 1978).
Hooker, Richard. *Of the Laws of Ecclesiastical Polity.* Cambridge: Cambridge University Press, 1977.

Hooker, Richard. "Virtus Sacramenti et Dei gratia," Dublin Fragments, 16–17, in John Booty, ed., *Richard Hooker, Of the Laws of Ecclesiastical Polity: Attack and Response.* Cambridge, Cambridge University Press, 1982.

Hopkins, Alberta Pualani. "The Challenge of the Future: Creating a Place Called Home," in John L. Kater, ed., *The Challenges of the Past, The Challenges of the Future: Essays on Mission in the Light of Five Hundred Years of Evangelization in the Americas.* Berkeley, CA: Church Divinity School of the Pacific, 1994.

Hopkins, Charles H. *The Rise of the Social Gospel in American Protestantism 1865 – 1915.* New Haven: Yale University Press, 1940.

Hough, Brend. "The Archives of the Society for the Propagation of the Gospel," *Historical Magazine of the Protestant Episcopal Church,* 46 (September 1977).

Houlbrooke, Ralph. "The Family and Pastoral Care," in G. R. Evans, ed., *A History of Pastoral Care.* London: Cassell, 2000.

Hudson, D. Dennis. *Protestant Origins in India: Tamil Evangelical Christians, 1706–1835.* Grand Rapids: William B. Eerdmans, 2000.

Huntington, William Reed. *The Church-Idea: An Essay toward Unity.* New York: E. P. Dutton and Co., 1870.

Hutchinson, John, ed. *Christian Faith and Social Action.* New York: Charles Scribner's Sons, 1953.

Hylson-Smith, Kenneth. *High Churchmanship in the Church of England from the 16th Century to the Late Twentieth Century.* Edinburgh: T. and T. Clark, 1993.

Jacob, W. M. "George Augustus Selwyn, First Bishop of New Zealand and the Origins of the Anglican Communion," *Journal of Anglican Studies,* 9 (May 2011).

Jacob, W. M. *The Making of the Anglican Church Worldwide.* London: SPCK, 1997.

James I. "Directions Concerning Preachers" (1622) in Henry Gee and William Hardy, eds., *Documents Illustrative of English Church History.* New York: The Macmillan Company, 1896.

Jameson, J. Parker. "The Sunday School in the National Period," *Historical Magazine of the Protestant Episcopal Church,* 51 (June 1982).

Jelley, Philip M. "Power, Authority and Conflict: How the Virginia Colonists secured, exercised and defended the right of their local Church of England Parish Vestries to select their clergy," unpublished paper, 2007.

Jernegan, Marcus W. "Slavery and Conversion in the American Colonies," *American Historical Review,* 21 (April 1916).

Jessett, Thomas E. "Anglican Indians In the Pacific Northwest Before the Coming of White Missionaries," *Anglican and Episcopal History,* 45 (December 1976).

Jewel, John. *An Apology, or Answer, In Defense of the Church of England, with a brief and plain declaration of the true religion professed and used in the same* (1567 English edition), in J. Ayre, ed., *The Works of John Jewel, Bishop of Salisbury.* Cambridge: Cambridge University Press, 1848, III.

Johnson, Richard. "An Address to the Inhabitants of the Colonies, Established in New South Wales and Norfolk Island," printed by the author, 1792.

Joint Commission on the Revision of the Hymnal of the Protestant Episcopal Church in the USA. *The Hymnal 1940 Companion.* New York: The Church Pension Fund, 1951.

Jones, Elwood. "Reaching Out for Two Hundred Years: Church Growth and Church Extension 1780–1989," in Alan L. Hayes, ed., *By Grace Co-Workers: Building the Anglican Diocese of Toronto 1780 – 1989*. Toronto: Anglican Book Centre, 1989.

Jones, Richard J. and J. Barney Hawkins IV, eds. *Staying One, Remaining Open: Educating Leaders for a Twenty-First Century Church*. Harrisburg, PA and New York: Morehouse Publishing, 2010.

Journal of the Proceedings of the Bishops, Clergy and Laity of the Protestant Episcopal Church in the United States of America. New York: Protestant Episcopal Press, 1835.

Kater, John L., Jr. "Alternative Patterns for Ministry: North and South America," in A. Wingate, K. Ward, C. Pemberton and W. Sitshebo, eds., *Anglicanism: A Global Communion*. New York: Church Publishing, 1998.

Kater, John L., Jr. "The Beginnings of the Episcopal Church in Panama, 1852–1904," *Anglican and Episcopal History*, 57 (June 1988).

Kater, John L., Jr. "Faithful Church, Plural World: Diversity at Lambeth 1998," *Anglican Theological Review*, 81 (Spring 1999).

Kater, John L., Jr. "Under Fire: Faith, Prejudice, and Compassion in a Virginia Parish, 1861–1865," *Anglican and Episcopal History*, 71 (March 2002).

Kaye, Bruce. "The Emergence and Character of Australian Anglican Identity," in Bruce Kaye, ed., *Anglicanism in Australia: A History*. Melbourne: Melbourne University Press, 2002.

Keable, Robert. *Darkness or Light: Studies in the History of the Universities' Mission to Central Africa*. London: UMCA, 1914.

Keble, John. *The Christian Year: Thoughts in verse for the Sundays and holydays through the year*. London: Frederick Stakes and Co., 1827.

Keely, Karen A. "'Let the Children have their part': *The Young Christian Soldier* and the Domestic Missionary Army," *Anglican and Episcopal History* 79 (September 2010).

Kennedy, Gerald Studder F. "Theology and Authority, Constitution and Improvisation: The Colonial Church in India," in Judith M. Brown and Robert E. Frykenberg, eds., *Christians, Cultural Interactions, and India's Religious Traditions*. Grand Rapids: William B. Eerdmans, 2002.

Kent, Eliza F. *Converting Women: Gender and Protestant Christianity in Colonial South India*. New York: Oxford University Press, 2004.

Kings, Graham. "Abdul Masih: Icon of Indian Ingenuity," *International Bulletin of Missionary Research*, 23 (April 1999).

Kip, William Ingraham. *The Early Days of My Episcopate*. New York: Thomas Whittaker, 1892.

Kirby, Ethyn W. "The Cromwellian Establishment," *Church History*, 10 (June 1941).

Koschorke, Klaus, Frieder Ludwig, Mariani Delgado, eds. *A History of Christianity in Asia, Africa and Latin America, 1450–1990: A Documentary Sourcebook*. Grand Rapids: William B. Eerdmans Publishing Company, 2007.

Kujawa-Holbrook, Sheryl A. *Freedom Is a Dream: A Documentary History of Women in the Episcopal Church*. New York: Church Publishing, Inc., 2002.

Kujawa-Holbrook, Sheryl A. "Women and Vocation in the Episcopal Church: Reflections on Our History," *Anglican and Episcopal History,* 79 (June 2010).

Kverndal, Roald. *Seamen's Missions: Their Origin and Early Growth.* Pasadena, CA: William Carey Library, 1986.

Kverndal, Roald. *The Way of the Sea: The Changing Shape of Mission in the Seafaring World.* Pasadena, CA: William Carey Library, 2008.

Lammers, Anne C. "The Rev. Absalom Jones and the Episcopal Church: Christian Theology and Black Consciousness in a New Alliance," *Historical Magazine of the Protestant Episcopal Church,* 51 (June 1982).

Latourette, Kenneth Scott. *A History of Christian Missions in China.* New York, Russell and Russell, 1929, 1967.

Lautz, Terrill E. "The SVM and Transformation of the Protestant Mission in China," in Daniel H. Bays and Ellen Widmer, eds., *China's Christian Colleges: Cross-Cultural Connections, 1900–1950.* Stanford, CA: Stanford University Press, 2009.

Law, William. *A Serious Call to a Devout and Holy Life.* New York: Paulist Press, 1978.

Lawson, John Parker. *The Episcopal Church of Scotland.* Edinburgh: Gallie and Bayley, 1844.

Lee, Mary Greenhow. *Diary,* unpublished manuscript, Archives Room, Handley Regional Library, Winchester, Virginia.

Lee, Sidney, ed. *Dictionary of National Biography, LXII.* London: Smith, Elder, 1900.

Lee, Sidney, ed. "John Gott," *The Dictionary of National Biography [Supplement January 1901 – December 1911].* Oxford: Oxford University Press, 1912.

Lee, Joo-Yup. "Entering the Kingdom Within." Berkeley, CA: Church Divinity School of the Pacific, unpublished D. Min. thesis, 2007.

Lewis, Harold T. *Yet With a Steady Beat: The African American Struggle for Recognition in the Episcopal Church.* Valley Forge, PA: Trinity Press International, 1996.

Liu, Judith and Donald P. Kelly. "'An Oasis in a Heathen Land': St. Hilda's School for Girls, Wuchang, 1928–1936," in Daniel H. Bays, ed., *Christianity in China: From the Eighteenth Century to the Present.* Stanford: Stanford University Press, 1996.

Luckock, H. M. *The Church in Scotland.* London: Wells, Gardner, Barton & Co., 1892.

MacCulloch, Diarmaid. *All Things New: The Reformation and Its Legacy.* Oxford: Oxford University Press, 2016.

MacCulloch, Diarmaid. "Henry the Eighth and the Reform of the Church," in D. MacCulloch, ed., *The Reign of Henry VIII: Politics, Policy and Piety.* New York: Palgrave Macmillan, 1995.

MacCulloch, Diarmaid. *The Later Reformation in England 1547–1603.* London: MacMillan Press, 1990.

MacCulloch, Diarmaid. *The Reformation: A History.* New York: Viking, 2004.

MacCulloch, Diarmaid. *Tudor Church Militant: Edward VI and the Protestant Reformation.* London: Allen Lane, 1999.

Maltby, Judith. "'By the Book': Parishioners, the Prayer Book and the Established Church," in Kenneth Fincham, ed., *The Early Stuart Church, 1603–1642.* Stanford: Stanford University Press, 1997.

Manross, William W. *A History of the American Episcopal Church.* New York: Morehouse-Gorham Co., 1950.

Markwell, Bernard K. *The Anglican Left: Radical Social Reformers in the Church of England and the Protestant Episcopal Church, 1846 – 1954.* Brooklyn: Carlson Publishing, Inc., 1991.

Marshall, Peter. *Reformation England 1480–1642.* London: Arnold, 2003.

Marshall, Peter, ed. *The Impact of the English Reformation 1500–1640.* New York: Oxford University Press, 1997.

Mattia, Joan Plubell. "Walking the Rift: The Missionary Art of Bishop Alfred Robert Tucker," *Anglican and Episcopal History*, 80 (September 2011).

Maurice, Frederick, ed. *The Life of Frederick Denison Maurice, chiefly told in his own letters.* London: Macmillan and Co., 1884, I.

Maurice, Frederick Denison. *Reconstructing Christian Ethics: Selected Writings,* Ellen K. Wondra, ed. Louisville: Westminster John Knox Press, 1995.

May, Henry. *Protestant Churches and Industrial America.* New York: Harper and Brothers, 1949.

McAdoo, H. R. *The Structure of Caroline Moral Theology.* New York: Longmans, Green and Co., 1949.

McGinnis, Timothy Scott. *George Gifford and the Reformation of the Common Sort: Puritan Priorities in Elizabethan Religious Life.* Kirksville, MO: Truman State University Press, 2004.

McGrath, Alister. *In the Beginning: The Story of the King James Bible and How It Changed a Nation, a Language and a Culture.* New York: Random House, 2001.

McIlhiney, David B. *A Gentleman in Every Slum: Church of England Missions in East London 1837 – 1914.* Allison Park, PA: Pickwick Publications, 1988.

Meade, William. *Sermons Addressed to Masters and Servants, and Published in the Year 1743, by the Rev. Thomas Bacon . . . Now Republished with Other Tracts and Dialogues on the Same Subject, and Recommended to All Masters and Mistresses to Be Used in their Families.* Winchester, VA: John Heiskell, Printer, 1813.

Merrard, André, and Jorge Pavez. *Mapuche y Anglicano: Vestigios fotográficos de la Misión Araucana de Kepe, 1896 – 1908.* Santiago: Ocho Libros Editores, 2007.

Merritt, J. F. "The Cradle of Laudianism? Westminster Abbey, 1558–1630," *Journal of Ecclesiastical History*, 52 (October 2001).

Meyer, Lucy Rider. *Deaconesses, Biblical, Early Church, European, American: The Story of the Chicago Training School for City, Home and Foreign Missions, and The Chicago Deaconess House.* Chicago: The Message Publishing Co., 1889.

Michael, Charles D. *James Hannington, Bishop and Martyr: The Story of a Noble Life.* London: S. W. Partridge and Co., 1886.

Miller, Spencer, Jr., and Joseph F. Fletcher. *The Church and Industry.* New York: Longmans Green and Co., 1930.

Mills, Frederick V., Sr. "The Protestant Episcopal Churches in the United States 1783–1789: Suspended Animation of Remarkable Recovery?" *Historical Magazine of the Protestant Episcopal Church,* 46 (June 1977).
Moore, Herbert. *The Christian Faith in Japan.* London: SPG, 1904.
Moore, Willis H. A. "'Ehā ali'i wahine: Four royal women," *The Historiographer,* 43 (Lent 2005).
Moyse, Cordelia. *A History of the Mothers' Union: Women, Anglicanism and Globalization 1876–2008.* Woodbridge, Suffolk: Boydell Press, 2009.
Murray, Jocelyn. *Proclaim the Good News: A Short History of the Church Missionary Society.* London: Hodder and Stoughton, 1985.
Murray, Julio E. "The Episcopal Church in Costa Rica: Its First Century," *Anglican and Episcopal History,* 60 (September 1991).
Neill, Stephen. *A History of Christian Missions.* London: Penguin Books, 1986.
Newman, Henry Stanley. *Days of Grace in India: A Record of Visits to Indian Missions.* London: G. W. Partridge and Co., 1880.
Nicolson, Adam. *God's Secretaries: The Making of the King James Bible.* New York: HarperCollins, 2003.
Norbeck, Mark Douglas. "False Start: The First Three Years of Episcopal Missionary Endeavor in the Philippine Islands, 1898–1901," *Anglican and Episcopal History,* 62 (June 1993).
"North Carolina commemorates baptisms of Manteo and Virginia Dare," *The Historiographer,* 19 (Fall 2008).
O'Connor, Daniel et al. *Three Centuries of Mission: The United Society for the Propagation of the Gospel 1701–2000.* London: Continuum, 2000.
O'Day, Rosemary. *The English Clergy: The Emergence and Consolidation of a Profession, 1558–1642.* Leicester: Leicester University Press, 1979.
O'Day, Rosemary and Felicity Heal, eds. *Continuity and Change: Personnel and Administration in the Church of England 1500–1642.* Leicester: Leicester University Press, 1976.
Orens, John Richard. "Christ, Communism and Chorus Girls: A Reassessment of Stewart Headlam," *Anglican and Episcopal History,* 49 (September 1980).
Owadayo, M. O. "Bishop Samuel Adjai Crowther (1810–1891)," in Joseph Akinyele Omoyajowo, ed., *Makers of the Church in Nigeria.* Lagos: CSS Bookshops, 1995.
Painter, Borden W., Jr. "The Vestry in Colonial New England," *Historical Magazine of the Protestant Episcopal Church,* 44 (December 1975).
Perry, William Stevens, ed. *Journals of General Conventions of the Protestant Episcopal Church in the United States of America,* III: Historical Notes and Documents. Claremont, NH: The Claremont Manufacturing Co., 1874.
Pickard, Stephen. "Church of the In-Between God: Recovering an Ecclesial Sense of Place Down-Under," *Journal of Anglican Studies,* 7 (May 2009).
Poon, Michael Nai-Chiu. "Authority for Ministry and Mission in an East Asian Context," *Anglican and Episcopal History,* 62 (March 1992).
Postles, Dave. "Penance and the Market Place: A Reformation Dialogue with the Medieval Church c.1250-c.1600," *Journal of Ecclesiastical History,* 54 (July 2003).

Pounds, N. J. G. *A History of the English Parish: The Culture of Religion from Augustine to Victoria.* Cambridge: Cambridge University Press, 2000.

Pui-Lan, Kwok. *Chinese Women and Christianity 1860–1927.* Atlanta: Scholars Press, 1992.

Putney, Clifford. "Men and Religion: Aspects of the Church Brotherhood Movement, 1880–1920," *Anglican and Episcopal History*, 63 (December 1994).

Rajalakshmi, Theodore. *Anglicanism in Madras.* Madras: CLS, 2006.

Reeves, Thomas C. "James Lloyd Breck and the Founding of Nashotah House," *Anglican and Episcopal History*, 65 (March 1996).

Reid, John Sheldon. *Glorious Battle: The Cultural Politics of Victorian Anglo-Catholicism.* Nashville: Vanderbilt University Press, 1996.

Renouf, Robert W. "Anglicanism in Nicaragua 1745–1985," *Anglican and Episcopal History,* 65 (March 1996).

Reventlow, H. G. *The Authority of the Bible and the Rise of the Modern World.* London: SCM, 1984.

Rex, Richard. *Henry VIII and the English Reformation.* New York: St. Martin's Press, 1993.

Rhodes, Nancy L. *Revolutionary Anglicanism: The Colonial Church of England Clergy during the American Revolution.* New York: New York University Press, 1999.

Robbins, William G. "Against Indian Culture," Oregon Historical Society, Online Oregon History Project, http://www.ohs.org/the-oregon-history-project/narratives/this-land-oregon/political-economic-culture/against-indian-culture.cfm.

Robinson, Mary Judith. *From Gold Rush to Millennium: 150 Years of the Episcopal Diocese of California 1849–2000.* San Francisco: Episcopal Diocese of California, 2001.

Roper, Henry. "The Anglican Episcopate in Canada: An Historical Perspective," in *Frontiers Then and Now: The Canadian Anglican Episcopate 1787 – 1987.* Toronto: Anglican Book Centre, 1989.

Ross, Andrew. "Christian Missions and the Mid-Nineteenth Century Change in Attitudes to Race: The African Experience" in Andrew Porter, ed., *The Imperial Horizons of British Protestant Missions, 1880–1914.* Grand Rapids: William B. Eerdmans, 2003.

Rowlands, J. H. L. *Church, State and Society: The Attitudes of John Keble, Richard Hurrell Froude and John Henry Newman, 1827–1845.* Worthing, UK: Churchman Publishing Ltd., 1989.

Ruggle, Richard E. "The Saints in the Land," 1867–1939, in Alan L. Hayes, ed., *By Grace Co-Workers: Building the Anglican Diocese of Toronto 1780–1989.* Toronto: Anglican Book Centre, 1989.

Russell, Edward Francis, ed. *Alexander Heriot Mackonochie: A Memoir.* New York: E. & J. B. Young & Co,. 1890.

Sachs, William L. *The Transformation of Anglicanism: From State Church to Global Communion.* Cambridge: Cambridge University Press, 1993.

Sanneh, Lamin. "The CMS and the African Transformation," in Kevin Ward and Brian Stanley, eds., *The Church Mission Society and World Christianity, 1799 – 1999.* Grand Rapids: William Be. Eerdmans Publishing Co., 2000.

Sanneh, Lamin. *West African Christianity: The Religious Impact.* Maryknoll, NY: Orbis Books, 1983.

Schneider, Helen. "The Professionalization of Chinese Domesticity: Ava B. Milam and Home Economics at Yenching University," in Daniel H. Bays and Ellen Widmer, eds., *China's Christian Colleges: Cross-Cultural Connections, 1900–1950.* Stanford, CA: Stanford University Press, 2009.

Schutz, John A. "Christopher Codrington's Will: Launching the S.P.G. into the Barbadian Sugar Business," *Pacific Historical Review,* 15 (March 1946).

Shannon, Richard Shannon. *Gladstone: Volume II, 1865–1898.* London: Penguin, 1999.

Shattuck, Gardiner H., Jr. *Episcopalians and Race: Civil War to Civil Rights.* Lexington, KY: The University Press of Kentucky, 2000.

Sheldrake, Philip. "George Herbert and *The Country Parson*," in Evans, ed., *A History of Pastoral Care.* New York: Cassell, 2000.

Sheldrake, Philip. *Love Took My Hand: The Spirituality of George Herbert.* Cambridge, MA: Cowley Publications, 2000.

Sho, Saw Shee. "Doing Theology in Myanmar's Context," *Madang,* 7 (15 June 2007).

Smith, Larry Douglas. "FitzRoy and the Fuegians: A Clash of Cultures," *Anglican and Episcopal History,* 59 (September 1990).

Speilmann, Richard M. "The Beginning of Clerical Marriage in the English Reformation: The Reigns of Edward and Mary," *Anglican and Episcopal History,* 56 (September 1987).

Steed, W. T., ed. *The Last Will and Testament of C. J.Rhodes,* 1902; quoted in Klaus Koschorke, Frieder Ludwig, Mariani Delgado, eds., *A History of Christianity in Asia, Africa and Latin America, 1450–1990: A Documentary Sourcebook.* Grand Rapids: William B. Eerdmans Publishing Company, 2007.

Steiner, Bruce. *Samuel Seabury 1729–1796: A Study in the High Church Tradition.* Athens, OH: Ohio University Press, 1971.

Stock, Eugene. *The History of the Church Missionary Society: Its Environment, Its Men and Its Work,* II, III. London: Church Missionary Society, 1899.

Stone, Lawrence. *The Family, Sex and Marriage in England in England 1500–1800.* New York: Weidenfeld and Nicolson, 1977.

Stowe, Walter H. "A Turning Point: The General Convention of 1835," *Historical Magazine of the Episcopal Church,* 4 (September 1935).

Strong, L. A. G. *Flying Angel: The Story of the Mission to Seamen.* London: Methuen and Co., Ltd., 1956.

Strong, Rowan. *Episcopalianism in Nineteenth Century Scotland: Religious Response to a Modernizing Society.* Oxford: Oxford University Press, 2002.

Stubbs, John. *John Donne: The Reformed Soul: A Biography.* London: Viking Press, 2007.

Sugeno, Frank E. "The Establishmentarian Ideal and the Mission of the Episcopal Church," *Historical Magazine of the Protestant Episcopal Church,* 53 (December 1984).

Summerscale, Kate. *The Suspicions of Mr. Whicher or The Murders at Road Hill House.* London: Bloomsbury, 2008.

Sykes, Norman. *Old Priest and New Presbyter: Episcopacy and Presbyterianism in the Reformation with especial relation to the Churches of England and Scotland.* Cambridge: Cambridge University Press, 1956.

Takeda, John M. "Public and Private Church: The Experience of Japanese Anglicans, Past and Future," *Anglican and Episcopal History,* 65 (December 1996).

Tasie, G. O. M. *Christian Missionary Enterprise in the Niger Delta 1864–1918.* Leiden: E.J. Brill, 1978.

Tavard, George. *The Quest for Catholicity: A Study in Anglicanism.* New York: Herder and Herder, 1964.

Taylor, A. A. *The Negro in the Reconstruction of Virginia.* Washington: Association for the Study of Negro Life and History, 1924.

Taylor, Jeremy. *The Rule and Exercise of Holy Living.* New York: Harper and Row, 1970.

TePaa, Jenny Plane. "Leadership Formation for a New World: An Emergent Indigenous Anglican Theological College," in Ian T. Douglas and Kwok Pui-Lan, eds., *Beyond Colonial Anglicanism: The Anglican Communion in the Twenty-First Century.* New York: Church Publishing Inc., 2001.

Thew Forrester, Kevin. *I Have Called you Friends . . . An Invitation to Ministry.* New York: Church Publishing, 2003.

Thomas, Philip H. E. "Unity and Concord: An Early Anglican 'Communion,'" in Henry St. George Tucker, *The History of the Episcopal Church in Japan.* New York: Charles Scribner's Sons, 1938.

Transactions of the Cambridge Camden Society: A Selection from the Papers Read at the Ordinary Meetings in 1839–1841. Cambridge: T. Stevenson, 1841.

Trask, Haunani-Kay. "The Taking of Hawaiian Sovereignty: Manifest Destiny and Sugar-Planter Capitalism," in *Hawaiian Sovereignty: Myth and Reality.* Center for Hawaiian Studies, University of Hawai'i at Mānoa, undated.

Tucker, Beverley D. "Channing Moore Williams (1829–1910): Apostle to Japan," *Anglican and Episcopal History,* 66 (September 1997).

Tuttle, Daniel Sylvester. *Missionary to the Mountain West: Reminiscences of Bishop Daniel S. Tuttle 1866–1886.* Salt Lake City: University of Utah Press, 1987.

Tyacke, Nicholas. "Archbishop Laud," in K. Fincham, ed., *The Early Stuart Church, 1603 – 1642.* London: The Macmillan Press, 1993.

Tyers, John. "Not a Papal Conspiracy but a Spiritual Principle: Three Early Anglican Apologists for the Practice of Retreat," *Journal of Anglican Studies,* 8 (November 2010).

Unbound! Anglican Worship Beyond the Prayer Book, a series of papers delivered at the Church Divinity School of the Pacific in 1999 and published in the *Anglican Theological Review,* 82 (Winter 2000).

Valense, Deborah. "Charity, Custom and Humanity: Changing Attitudes towards the Poor in Eighteenth-Century England," in Jane Garnett and Colin Matthew, eds., *Revival and Religion Since 1700: Essays for John Walsh.* London: The Humbledon Press, 1992.

Vines, Stephen. The Story of St. John's Cathedral. Hong Kong: FormAsia, undated.

Wakefield, Gordon. "John and Charles Wesley: A Tale of Two Brothers," in Geoffrey Rowell, ed., *The English Religious Tradition and the Genius of Anglicanism.* Oxford: Ikon Productions, Ltd. 1992.

Wand, J. W. C., ed. *The Anglican Communion: A Survey.* London: Oxford University Press, 1948.

Ward, Kevin. *A History of Global Anglicanism.* Cambridge: Cambridge University Press, 2006.

Ward, Kevin and Brian Stanley, eds. *The Church Mission Society and World Christianity, 1799–1999.* Grand Rapids: William B. Eerdmans Publishing Co., 2000.

Warren, Max, ed. *To Apply the Gospel: Selections from the Writings of Henry Venn.* Grand Rapids: William B. Eerdmans Publishing Co., 1971.

Webster, C. A. "The Reconstruction of the Church," in Walter A. Phillips, ed., *History of the Church of Ireland from the Earliest Times to the Present Day,* III. Oxford: Oxford University Press, 1933.

Welsh, Ian. "Mission, Murder and Diplomacy in Late 19th Century China: A Case Study," unpublished paper, 2nd Annual ANU Missionary History Conference, 2006.

Wesley, John. "The Nature, Design, and General Rules of the United Societies, in London, Bristol, Kingswood, Newcastle-upon-Tyne, etc., 1743," in *John and Charles Wesley: Selected Prayers, Hymns, Journal Notes, Sermons, Letters and Treatises.* New York: Paulist Press, 1981.

Whaling, Frank. "Introduction," *John and Charles Wesley: Selected Prayers, Hymns, Journal Notes, Sermons, Letters and Treatises.* New York: Paulist Press, 1981.

Whiting, Robert. "Local Responses to the Henrician Reformation," in D. MacCullough, ed., *The Reign of Henry VIII: Politics, Policy and Piety.* New York: MacMillan and Co., 1995.

Wickeri, Philip. "Clergy Training and Theological Education: The Anglican-Episcopal Experience in China," Conference Paper, Yale-Edinburgh, History of the Missionary Movement and World Christianity, June 30—July 2, 2011.

Wickeri, Philip. *Reconstructing Christianity in China: K. H. Ting and the Chinese Church.* Maryknoll, NY: Orbis Books, 2007.

Wickeri, Philip. *Seeking Common Ground: Protestant Christianity, the Three-Self Movement and China's United Front.* Maryknoll: Orbis, 1988.

Wickham, E. R. *Church and People in an Industrial City.* London: Lutterworth Press, 1957.

Wilberforce, Samuel. *A History of the Protestant Episcopal Church in America.* London: James Burns, 1844.

Wilberforce, William. Speech to Parliament, May 12, 1789, in Klaus Koschorke, Frieder Ludwig, and Marianne Delgado, eds., *A History of Christianity in Asia,*

Africa, and Latin America, 1450–1990: A Documentary Sourcebook. Grand Rapids, MI: William B. Eerdmans Publishing Co., 2007.

Williams, Thomas Jay. *Priscilla Lydia Sellon: The Restorer After Three Centuries of the Religious Life in the English Church.* London: SPCK, 1950.

Williamson, Hugh Ross. *The Beginning of the English Reformation.* New York: Sheed and Ward, 1957.

Wilson, Daniel. *Sermons Delivered in India during the Course of the Primary Visitation.* London: J. Hatchard and Son, 1838.

Wilson, David H. *King James VI and I.* London: Jonathan Cape Ltd, 1963.

Wilson, George Herbert. *History of the Universities' Mission to Central Africa.* New York: New World Book Manufacturing Co., 1971.

Wolf, William J., ed. "Frederick Denison Maurice," in W. Wolf, ed., *The Spirit of Anglicanism: Hooker, Maurice, Temple.* Wilton, CT: Morehouse-Barlow Co., Inc., 1979.

Woodhouse, H. F. *The Doctrine of the Church in Anglican Theology 1547–1603.* London: SPCK, 1954.

Woolverton, John. *Colonial Anglicanism in North America.* Detroit: Wayne State University Press, 1984.

Wright, J. Robert. "Heritage and Vision: The Chicago-Lambeth Quadrilateral," in J. R. Wright, ed., *Quadrilateral at One Hundred: Essays on the Centenary of the Chicago-Lambeth Quadrilateral 1886–88 – 1986–88.* Oxford: A. R. Mowbray and Co., 1988.

Xu, Edward Yihua. "Liberal Arts Education in English and Campus Culture at St. John's University," in Daniel H. Bays and Ellen Widmer, eds., *China's Christian Colleges: Cross-Cultural Connections, 1900–1950.* Stanford, CA: Stanford University Press, 2009.

Yuill, Allan. "William Meade, 1789 – 1862: Third Bishop of Virginia, the 'Beloved Diocesan.'" *The Churchman,* 77 (Fall 1963).

Zacek, Natalie. "West Indian echoes: Dodington House, the Codrington family and the Caribbean heritage," in Madge Dresser, ed., *Slavery and the British Country House.* London: English Heritage, 2013.

Index

Aboriginal population, 107–8, 163–67, 208, 211
Act of Settlement (1701), 68
Act of Supremacy (1534), 5
Act of Supremacy (1559), 21
Act of Toleration (1689), 66
Act of Uniformity (1559), 21–22, 30
Act of Union, 68
advowson (right of nomination), 26
Africa: Anglican ministry in, 285; baptism in, 159–60, 204; clergy from, 159, 198–200, 203–4; CMS for, 156, 197–98, 201–4; conversion in, 143–44, 176, 198–99, 204; East African Revival in, 285; Niger Delta Pastorate of, 159, 198–200; Rhodes, C., on, 197; synod in, 175. *See also* Central Africa; East Africa; South Africa
African American congregations, 143–45
Allen, Roland, 231, 282, 284, 288n3
altars: destruction of, 11–12, 22; support for, 22, 122
America: American Episcopal and white settlers of, 259–63; Anglo-Catholicism in, 270–71; baptism in, 85–87, 89–90, 92, 99, 108n1, 145; bishops for, 94, 103–4, 214–15, 259–62; business interests on Hawaii, 243–44; civil rights movement in, 284; Civil War in, 90, 249–53; clergy as Black, 253–55; clergy behavior in, 88, 91; clergy education in, 136–37; Confederate prayer book in, 250; conversion in, 262; English Church in, 98–99; English clergy to, 140–41; Evangelical Movement of, 136–37; government and American Episcopal, 258; House of Bishops, 214–15; laity and parishes of, 89, 101, 103–4; Manifest Destiny of, 240–42, 255; Mexico and imperial, 241, 259, 282, 288n1; monastic orders in, 268–71; no national church for, 100–101, 138–40; on Native populations, 146–47, 150–51; Oxford movement in, 137–38; parish on clergy, 89–91; on Philippine Islands, 242; religious diversity in, 88; women on poverty and, 274. *See also* Protestant Episcopal Church
American Bible Society, 135–37
American Episcopal. *See* Protestant Episcopal Church
American Revolution, 76–81, 96, 136; Anglican ministry and, 98–100,

307

110n44; English Church after, 100–104, 113
Anderson, Owanah, 96, 256, 258
Andrewes, Lancelot, 45–47
Anglican Communion, 204; as Anglo-Catholicism, 122–23; BSA and, 267; global churches of, 85, 210, 212–14, 216, 283–84, 286–88; Hooker of, 32; Lambeth Conference (1930) and, 35; monastic orders and, 189, 263; SPG and, 92
Anglican ministry. *See specific subjects*
Anglicans: on Article 34, 15; as Catholic-minded, 13, 283; on Communion, 43, 64n10; Cromwell, O., on, 53–54; on diversity, 287; on eco-theology, 287; on Elizabethan Reformed religion, 21; of Elizabethan times, 28, 34; English, 34–35, 104; exiled, 59–60; Lambeth Conference (1888) on, 214–16; on Puritanism, 34; spirituality of, 50
Anglo-Catholicism: in Africa, 176; in America, 270–71; in Australia, 208, 210; for Canada, 149; Evangelicals or, 129–30, 138, 149, 210, 270; in Korea, 236; on Mothers' Union, 185; Ritualist movement as, 122–23, 191–93, 270–71; on seamen mission, 132n16; Victoria on, 190
Anne (Queen), 68
Apology (Jewel), 31–32
Apostles' Creed, 8, 42, 93, 122, 176, 215

The Arminian Nunnery, 50

Arminius, Jacob, 42–43, 46, 59
Article 34, of Thirty-nine Articles, 14–15
Ashton, Rosemary, 128
Aspenwall, William A., 172
Australia: Anglo-Catholicism in, 208, 210; convicts of, 107–8, 164–65; English Church in, 107–8, 165–66; laity in, 164–66, 208; missionaries in, 206, 208–9; national church in, 163–65
Avis, Paul, 12, 34–35
Ayres, Anne, 268–69

Bacon, Francis, 22, 93
Bacon, Thomas, 93
baptism, 28, 214; in Africa, 159–60, 204; in America, 85–87, 89–90, 92, 99, 108n1, 145; Apostles' Creed as, 215; in Canada, 106; in China, 222; in England, 183, 190, 194; English Church on, 39, 52; freed slaves and, 89–90; as global, 283–84; in Hawaii, 244; in India, 161, 206; in Japan, 235; in Korea, 237; in New Zealand, 166–67; Puritans and, 29; slaves and, 86–87, 90, 92, 94, 145
Baptismal Covenant, 283–84
Barstow, Anne, 24
Baycroft, John, 210
Bazley, Barbara, 238
Beagle, 171
Beasley, Nicholas, 89–90
Benson, Richard M., 188
Bentham, Thomas, 29–30
Bettelheim, Bernard John, 231
Beveridge, William, 94

the Bible: English translation of, 2, 7; reading of, 9; Reformation on, 11–12

Bickersteth, Edward, 234
Bilson, Thomas, 34
bishops: for America, 94, 103–4, 214–15, 259–62; America and house of, 214–15; Andrewes as, 45–47; in Australia, 166, 208; for Canada, 104–5, 209; Chicago Quadrilateral and, 214–16; confirmation and, 9, 25, 41, 60, 115; on Elizabeth, 30; English Church on, 13–14, 30; English Ordinal and, 10; induction and *collation* by, 26–27; James

I on, 41–42; as missionaries, 201–2, 261–62; Parliament and, 13–14, 120; on reform, 118–19; on Savoy Conference, 60; slave holdings by, 118
"Black Rubric," 13, 22
Bliss, William, 275
Blunt, John Henry, 184
Boleyn, Anne (Queen), 17
Bolton, F. R., 130
"Bonnie Prince Charlie," 68
Book of Common Order (Knox), 40, 51
Book of Common Prayer: Chinese translation of, 223; for Confederate US states, 250; Hawaiian translation of, 243; for Ireland, 130; for Korea, 236
Book of Common Prayer (1549), 38n59; Christ and, 13; on clergy clothing, 10; on Confirmation, 9; of Cranmer, 50–51, 69, 283
Book of Common Prayer (1552): on 1549 Prayer Book, 13; abolishment of, 51–52; Act of Uniformity for, 21–22, 30; on "Black Rubric," 13, 22; Charles I imposing, 50–51; Christ and, 13; on Communion, 12; of Cranmer, 50–51, 69, 283; Herbert on, 47–50; laity demanding, 56n10; Puritans on, 60; revision of, 61; on right action, 49; on sacrifices, 9; as second edition, 12–13, 22
Book of Common Prayer (1662), 61, 102, 115, 130, 165
Book of Common Prayer of America (1789), 103
Book of Homilies, 9, 22–23, 42
Boone, William James, 173, 222, 229
Booth, William, 189
Bosher, Robert, 59–61, 103–4
Boxer Rebellion, 230–31
Bray, Thomas, 91–93, 108
Brazil, 171, 240–41, 285–86
Breck, James Lloyd, 146
Brent, Charles Henry, 242–43

Brotherhood of St. Andrew (BSA), 267–68
Broughton, William G., 165–66
Bryson, Bill, 191
BSA. *See* Brotherhood of St. Andrew
Burden, J. S., 223
Burnet, Gilbert, 66–67

C.A.I.L. *See* Church Association for the Advancement of the Interests of Labor
California, 172–73, 259–60
Calvani, Carlos, 240
Calvin, John: Cromwell, O., and, 53–54; English on, 40; Laud on, 46–47, 51; Scottish people for, 50; teachings of, 23, 33, 41–43, 59, 63–64, 98–99, 136–37, 151, 174
Cambridge Camden Society, 122
Cambridge colleges, 27–28
Canada: bishops for, 104–5, 209; church in western, 150–51; clergy and, 98, 106; English Church on, 106, 147–52; laity of, 106, 149, 209; missionaries in, 149, 209–11; Native populations of, 150–51, 211, 218n48; synod in, 148–49, 177, 209, 211
Canadian Church, 210–11, 232
Carlile, William, 189
Caroline theologians, 50

The Case of the Episcopal Churches in the United States Considered (White), 100–101

caste system, 160–61, 163, 205
Caswall, Henry, 138–41
Catherine of Aragon, 5
Catholic Relief Act, 118
Canterbury shrine, 2
Central Africa, 200–201
Chadwick, Henry, 215
Chadwick, Owen, 118–19, 123–24, 128, 182–83, 186, 190
Charles I (King), 45–46, 50–52

Charles II (King), 45, 55, 60, 63–64
Chartist movement, 125–26
Chase, Philander, 139
Cheshire, Joseph, 250–51
Chicago Quadrilateral, 214–16
China: American Episcopal on, 170, 222, 224, 227–30; Anglican ministry to, 173–74, 222–31; *Book of Common Prayer* for, 223; clergy of, 222–24; CMS and, 173–74, 222–23, 227; conversion in, 174, 222, 226; education in, 224–27; evangelism and, 221, 230; Hong Kong and, 173–74, 186, 221–23, 226–28, 286; imperialism of, 173, 221, 230–31, 233; Kucheng Massacre in, 230; Opium Wars and, 173, 221, 224; Three-Self Patriotic Movement in, 284; Victoria Diocese of, 173, 221, 223, 227; Ward on, 173, 222–23, 230; women in, 227–30
Chiu, Patricia Pok-Kwan, 227
Christianity, 1; female nature in, 266–67; India violence and, 204; Japan on, 232, 234–35; male nature in, 267
Christianity Not Mysterious (Toland), 73
Christian Socialist movement, 125–27, 192–94, 271, 274–75
"church-ale," 43
Church and People in an Industrial City (Wickham), 123–24
Church and Stage Guild, 194
Church Army, 189
Church Association for the Advancement of the Interests of Labor (C.A.I.L.), 270, 272–73
Church Commission for Work Among Colored People, 253–54
churches: altars in, 11–12, 22, 122; in Australia, 165; Communion tables in, 12, 16, 46; layout of, 149, 165, 233, 260, 267; pew renting in, 43, 74, 90, 106, 122, 165, 210–11, 273; poor rejecting, 186; shrines and, 2, 6, 8–9; vestments and dress in, 3, 10, 13, 22, 27, 47, 60, 122, 172, 235, 241; women roles in, 1, 4, 147, 158, 169, 183–84, 186–87, 210–11, 223–24

The Church-Idea (Huntington, W.), 214

Church Missionary Society (CMS), 107, 209; Africa and, 156, 197–98, 201–4; Ceylon controversy and, 205–6; China and, 173–74, 222–23, 227; English Church and, 157, 159; in India, 158; in Japan, 232; for laity, 157–58; on Lutherans, 156–57; on polygamy, 159–61, 167, 175; in South Africa, 174
Church of England (English Church), 8; in America, 87–88, 98–99; after American Revolution, 100–104, 113; in Australia, 107–8, 165–66; on baptism, 39, 52; on bishops, 13–14, 30; on Canada, 106, 147–52; in Central America, 239; on child poverty, 116–17; CMS and, 157, 159; on conversions, 86–87; Cromwell, O., on, 53–55; deaconesses in, 263; for divine right of kings, 65; of Elizabeth, 34–36; emancipation and, 94; for English settlers, 159; on English society, 120, 183; Evangelical Movement in, 81–82; as global, 85, 210, 212–14, 216, 283–84, 286–88; Great Awakening challenging, 94–96; Henry VIII on, 4–5; India and, 160–63, 205; India self-government and, 206–7; on indigenous women, 163, 205, 227–30, 233, 263–71, 274, 285; Jewel and middle way for, 30–33; laity and, 1–2, 61, 74; *Of the Laws of Ecclesiastical Polity* on, 32, 37n45, 137; on Methodists, 80; national church and, 34–35, 39, 95, 108, 123–24, 208; New Zealand and, 167–68; on Niger Delta Pastorate, 159, 198–200; Oxford movement on, 119–20;

Parliament for, 60; as Presbyterian, 52; Puritans and, 29–31, 34; Royal Supremacy over, 5, 16–17, 30–31, 120–21; science and, 123, 127–30, 164, 182–83, 276; slaves on, 93; on slave trade, 89; social dislocation failures of, 75–76; social reform and, 116–19; transitioning ministry of, 113–16; urban ministry of, 189–94; *The Whole Duty of Man* as, 62, 70; working class and, 123–24
Church of Ireland, 130–31
Church of Scotland (Scottish Church), 40, 50, 62–64, 67–68, 102. *See also* Non-Jurors
Church of South India, 284
Claggett, Thomas, 103
Clapham Sect, 80–81, 156
clergy: *advowson* for, 26; African, 159, 198–200, 203–4; America inappropriate behavior by, 88, 91; in American Civil War, 250–51; American education of, 136–37, 139, 145–46; American parish choice in, 89–91; on American Revolution, 98–100, 110n44; Andrewes as, 45–47; of Australia, 208; Black, 253–55; of Canada, 98, 106; of China, 222–24; *collation* for, 26–27; Cuddesdon College educating, 182; disdain for, 116–17, 119; Donne shaping, 44–45, 47; education of, 27–28, 44, 66–67, 91–92, 116, 174, 182–84; Elizabethan Settlement on, 23–24; to England, 98; English to America, 140–41; *Essays and Reviews* by, 129; financial support for, 25, 27, 70–71, 114–15, 119; Five-Mile Act on, 61; Herbert on, 47–50; homes of, 44, 114; Hooker on, 32–35, 37n45, 39, 46, 69, 137; induction for, 26–27; James I restricting, 42, 44; James II and Scottish, 65–66; of Japan, 233–35; Jewel on, 30–33; as justices, 13–14, 30, 114; laity distance from, 28–29, 210; laity with, 35, 38n59, 183–84; marriage for, 10–11, 23–25, 270–71; on Mary and Catholicism, 17; missionaries or, 158; monastic rules for, 191–92; as Native American, 256–57; Non-Jurors and oath refusal by, 66; novelists on, 181; Panama left by, 239; for public penance, 28–29; as Puritans, 23; as rural, 186; for sacraments and salvation, 1; science and, 73, 127, 224; social backgrounds of, 61, 70, 114; as social group, 27, 44; as spies, 242; as Tamil, 207; with trading merchants, 85; vestments and dress for, 3, 10, 13, 22, 27, 47, 60, 122, 172, 235, 241; work load of, 33, 71–73
CMS. *See* Church Missionary Society
Codrington, Christopher, 94–95
Coke, Thomas, 80
Cole, William, 72
Colenso, John William, 174–77, 212
collation (responsibility granting), 26–27
College of William and Mary, 97
Collins, Brenda, 186
Colton, Calvin, 138
common land, 11, 74, 113–14
common land enclosure, 11, 74, 113–14
Communion: Andrewes for, 45–47; Anglicans emphasizing, 43, 64n10; confirmation and, 232; Elizabethan Settlement on, 22; Quadrilateral on, 216; Reformation on, 12; slaves and, 93; tables for, 12, 16, 46; timing of, 73, 115; in Virginia, 88–89; warnings on, 9–10
confession: elimination of, 7, 10; Ritualist movement for, 123
confirmation, 28; bishops and, 9, 25, 41, 60, 115; Communion and, 232; preparation for, 73, 149, 190
Congregational church, 90
constitutional monarchy, 65

Conventicle Act (1664), 61
conversion: in Africa, 143–44, 176, 198–99, 204; in America, 262; in Asia, 237; in Australia, 107; in China, 174, 222, 226; education and, 127; English Church and, 86–87; of enslaved, 93; in India, 161–62, 205; in Japan, 232–34; of Jews, 223, 225, 231; in Korea, 237; in Latin America, 170–71, 241; by missionaries, 158–59, 210; Mothers' Union and, 185; of Native populations, 86–87, 92, 94, 96, 147, 151, 256–57; polygamy and, 160, 175; poverty and, 189; Roman Catholics and, 51, 64, 85, 131; by SPG, 92
convicts, 107–8, 164–65, 278n44
Convocation, 14, 123, 148; of Canterbury, 21, 182, 189, 213, 263; of Church, 68; of York, 21
Cooper, Anthony Ashley, 117
Cooper, James Fenimore, 100
Copleston, R. S., 205–6
Corfe, Charles, 236–37
Corporation Act, 61, 118
Corrie, Daniel, 161, 163
Cranmer, Thomas, 121; criticisms of, 69–70; on English Church and imperial model, 5; on "Forty-Two Articles of Religion," 14; as Henry VIII advisor, 4, 281; Mary executing, 17; *Prayer Books* of, 50–51, 69, 283
Cressy, David, 27–29
Cromwell, Oliver, 52–55, 59
Cromwell, Thomas, 4, 8
Crowther, Dandeson, 198–200
Crowther, Samuel Adjai, 159–60, 198–200
Cuddesdon College, 182
Curthoys, Patricia, 166

Daily Mattins, 9
Daniel, Paul, 162–63
Daniel O'Connor, 94
Darwin, Charles, 129, 171, 182, 238

Davies, E. T., 34
Davies, James, 189
deaconesses, 263, 265, 268
Dering, Edward, 30
Dickens, Charles, 74–75
Diocesan Native Female Training School, 227–28
"Directions Concerning Preachers," 42
Directory of Public Worship, 51
Dissenters, 70, 118; Charles II on, 63–64; CMS and, 157; Ireland Church excluding, 130; Methodists as, 80; as Protestant, 69
divine right of kings, 34, 40, 42, 50–51, 65, 120–122
Doane, George, 142
Dodwell, Henry, 70
Domestic and Foreign Missionary Society (1820), 141, 169–70
Domestic Missionary Army of the Young Soldiers of Christ, 266
Donne, John, 44–45, 47
Donovan, Mary, 263–65
Duffy, Eamon, 11

East Africa, 201–4
East African Revival, 285
Eastern Equatorial Africa Mission, 202
East India Company, 64, 160
Echlin, Edward, 13
eco-theology, 286–87
education: of American clergy, 136–37, 139, 145–46; American Episcopal on urban, 276; in American West, 262; Canada forcing, 211, 218n48; for caste system, 160–61, 163, 205; in China, 224–27; of clergy, 27–28, 44, 66–67, 91–92, 116, 174, 182–84; conversion and, 127; Cuddesdon College for clergy, 182; of freed slaves, 253–54; in Hawaii, 243; in Japan, 232–33; in Latin America, 238; missionaries using, 161–62, 198, 210, 224–26; of Native

Americans, 257–58, 265; Sunday School for poverty, 141–42
Edward VI (King), 8–16
election doctrine, 42–43
Elizabeth (Queen), 17; Anglicans of, 28, 34; on bishops, 30; English Church of, 34–36; Hooker on, 32–35, 37n45, 39, 46, 69, 137; on national church, 21, 39; "neighbourly scrutiny" under, 28; on prophesyings, 30; Puritans and, 23, 31; Reformation consolidation by, 21
Elizabethan Settlement: Act of Uniformity and, 21–22, 30; advocates for, 31–34; common ground for, 23–29; on Communion, 22; consequences of, 34–36; on marriage, 23–24; Puritan laity on, 29; Travers on, 33–34, 39
Ellison, Thomas, 100
Ely, Richard, 275–76
Emery, Julia Chester, 264
Emery, Margaret Theresa, 264
Emery, Mary Abbot, 264
England: Act of Union and, 68; baptism in, 183, 190, 194; clergy to, 98; English Church on, 120, 183; imperialism of, 5, 64, 95, 169, 185–86, 282; on India, 160–63; laity to, 100; for Latin America, 170–71; Non-Jurors in, 67–68; for Scottish church government, 51
English: Anglican as, 34–35, 104; on Calvin, 40; church union among, 214–15; clergy to America, 140–41; common law and Cromwell, 4; English Church and settlers as, 159; on non-national church, 138–40; society of, 184; superiority assumptions by, 159, 164, 166, 176, 190, 197, 209, 282
English Bible translation, 2
English Bill of Rights, 65
English Church. *See* Church of England
English Ordinal, 10

Enmegabowh, John Johnson, 256
Episcopal Church in the Confederate States of America, 250–55
Essays and Reviews, 129
European Reformation, 1, 7
Evangelical Movement, 8; of America, 136–37; on Anglo-Catholicism, 129–30, 138, 149, 210, 270; in Australia, 208; for Canada, 149; China and, 221, 230; CMS in, 107; East African Revival in, 285; East India Company discouraging, 160; in English Church, 81–82; high church or, 136–38, 156, 167, 210; H.M.S. Beagle for, 171; in Ireland, 130–31; Japan and Korea with, 221; as middle and upper class, 80; Mother's Union for, 114–15, 183–84; numbers of, 124; on poverty, 117, 193; on seamen's chapel, 118, 132n16; on slaves, 81, 93–95; on Sunday Schools, 142; Victoria on, 190
Evans, Gillian, 215
Evans, John, 97
Evelyn, John, 54–55, 59
Evensong, 9

Farrer, Nicholas, 49–50
Father Ignatius, 187–88
Ferard, Catherine, 261
financial support: for clergy, 25, 27, 70–71, 114–15, 119; for medieval Church, 1–2; for parishes, 43–44; pluralities in, 72–73
Five-Mile Act, 61
Fletcher, Brian, 108, 164–65, 208
Fletcher, Wendy, 211
"Forty-Two Articles of Religion" (1553), 14
freed slaves: American Episcopal on, 143, 249; baptism and, 89–90; civil liberty erosion for, 254–55; as clergy, 253–54; emigration by, 144
French Revolution, 100, 104, 113, 116–17, 194

Froude, Anthony, 128
Froude, R. H., 121

Gardiner, Allen, 171–72, 238
Garry, Spokan, 150–52
gay and lesbian persons, 284
George, Henry, 270
George IV (King), 119
Georgia, 76–77, 107, 249
Gladstone, William Ewart, 124
global church, 85, 210, 212–14, 216, 282–84, 286–88
Godwyn, Morgan, 93
Goedhals, Mandy, 176
Goldsmith, A. G., 227
Gott, John, 189–90
Grau, Marion, 168–69
Gray, Robert, 96, 175–76, 180n70, 201
Great Awakening, 94–96
Gregory, Jeremy, 61
Grey, Jane (Lady), 15–16
Grimes, Cecil John, 206–7
Grindal, Edmund, 30
Grubb, W. Barbrooke, 238
Gunpowder Plot (1605), 40–41

Hall, Joseph, 44
Hannington, James, 202
Hansen's Disease, 227, 233
Hare, William Hobart, 257
Harris, Sayre, 147
Hartley, Brian, 22–23
Hawai'i, 241–43
Headlam, Stewart, 193–94
Henry VIII (King), 2–8, 70, 130, 146, 281
Herbert, George, 47–50
Herklots, H. G. G., 90–91
Hickes, George, 69
Hicks, Robert, 97
high church, 45–46, 123; evangelical or, 136–38, 156, 167, 210; as political, 61, 176
Hills, George, 210
Hinman, Samuel, 256–57

Hoadley, Benjamin, 73
Hobart, John Henry, 135–38, 145
Hoffman, Eugene Augustus, 137
Holly, James T., 144
Holmes, David, 98–99
Hong Kong: Anglican ministry in, 220, 224–26, 284; British controlling, 173–74, 221, 223; Mothers' Union in, 186
Hooker, Richard, 32–35, 37n45, 39, 46, 69, 137
Hopkins, Pualani, 244
Houghteling, James, 267
Huang Kuang-tsai, 222
Hudson, Winthrop, 96
Hudson's Bay Company, 64
Hunt, Robert, 86
Huntington, Frederick Dan, 272
Huntington, James O. S., 269–70
Huntington, William Reed, 216
Huxley, Thomas, 182
Hymns on the Lord's Supper (Wesley, C.), 78

imperialism: of China, 173, 221, 230–31, 233; of England, 5, 64, 95, 169, 185–86, 282; of Japan, 221, 234–35; Manifest Destiny as, 240–42, 255; Mexico on American, 241, 259, 282, 288n1; struggle against, 283; superiority assumptions as, 159, 164, 166, 176, 190, 197, 209, 282
Independents, 51–53
India: Anglican self-government in, 206–7; baptism in, 161, 206; caste system of, 160–61, 163, 205; Christianity and violence in, 204; Church of South India in, 284; CMS and, 158; conversion in, 161–62, 205; English Church on, 160–63, 205; laity of, 206; society or Anglicanism, 205; SPG in, 204–5; Ward on, 207–8
Indian Commission, 258
indulgences, 7

Industrial Revolution, 114, 116, 123–24, 190, 272
Inglis, Charles, 105–6
Ireland, 51, 120, 130–31

Jacob, W. M., 85, 91
James I (King), 39–42, 44, 86–87
James II (King), 64–66
Jane Bohlen School for Girls, 228–29
Japan, 221, 231–36, 285
Jarrett, Devereux, 96
Jewel, John, 30–33
Jewish conversions, 223, 225, 231
Johnson, Richard, 107–8, 163
Jones, Absalom, 143–44
Jowett, Benjamin, 129
"justification by grace through faith," 7, 10

Kamehameha III (King), 243
Kaye, Bruce, 208
Keble, John, 120–21, 200
Keely, Karen, 266
Kemper, Jackson, 141–42, 145–46
King, Bryan, 122
Kingsley, Charles, 125–26, 189
Kingsley, William, 186
Kinsolving, Lucien Lee, 240–41
Kip, William Ingraham, 259–60, 262
Knox, John, 40, 51
Korea, 221, 236–37, 285–86
Kucheng Massacre, 230
Kwok Pui-Lan, 229–30

laity: in American Civil War, 251, 253; in American parishes, 89, 101, 103–4; in Australia, 164–66, 208; for *Book of Common Prayer*, 56n10; of Canada, 106, 149, 209; with clergy, 35, 38n59, 183–84; clergy distance from, 28–29, 210; clergy marriage guiding, 24–25; CMS for, 157–58; devotion manuals for, 50; to England, 100; English Church and, 1–2, 61, 74; faith practice by, 3–4; of India, 206; as lectors, 26; mandatory church attendance for, 28; Methodists and, 76, 78–80; against monastic disbanding, 6; as Native Americans, 257; Pearsall as missionary, 262–64; preachers from, 79; Reformation impact on, 11; religious instruction by, 33; on "ruined" Church, 74; Social Gospel movement for, 275
Lambeth Conference: in 1867, 177, 212–13; in 1878, 213–14; in 1888, 214–16; in 1897, 236, 271; in 1930, 35; in 1978, 206; in 1988, 234; in 1998, 286–87; in 2008, 286–87
Langley (Archbishop), 212–13
Laning, Henry, 233
Latimer, Hugh, 17
Latin, 4, 8
Latin America, 170–73, 238–41
Latitudinarians, 66–69, 98, 128
Laud, William, 45–47, 51
Law, William, 69–70, 75–76
Lee, Mary Greenhow, 251–52
Lee, Joo-Yup, 286
Lewis, Harold, 144–45, 253–54
Liberia, 143–44, 169–70
Liggins, John, 231–32
Lili'uokalani (Queen), 243–44
Lincoln, Abraham, 256
Little Gidding community, 49–50
Liturgical Movement, 283–84
Livingstone, David, 200–201
Locke, Clinton, 137–38
Locke, John, 73
Lollards (movement), 2
Longley, John Thomas, 177
Ludlow, J. M., 124–26
Luther, Martin, 2–3, 7
Lutherans, 6–7, 9, 120, 161, 263; CMS and SPCK supporting, 156–57; with deaconesses, 268
Luwum, Janani, 285
Lyne, Joseph, 187–88

MacCulloch, Diarmaid, 4, 11, 13

Machonochie, Alexander Heriot, 192
Machray, Robert, 210
Mackenzie, Charles, 201
Madison, James, 103
Malthy, Judith, 64n10
Manifest Destiny of America, 240–42, 255
Mann, Horace, 124
Manross, William, 87–89

A Manual of Private Devotions (Andrewes), 45–47

Maori people, 166–68, 209
Markwell, Bernard, 192
marriage: for clergy, 10–11, 23–25, 270–71; Cranmer and, 4–5
Marsden, Samuel, 163–64, 166–67
Mary (Queen), 15–17
Maryland, 91, 103, 109n20
Mary Stuart (Queen), 39
Massachusetts, 90
Matthew, Tobias, 41
Maurice, Frederick Denison, 124–27, 189, 192, 194, 214
May, Henry, 276
McAdoo, H. R., 50
Meade, William, 93, 136–37, 142
Men's Service, 193
Methodists, 76, 78–81
Mexico, 241, 259, 282, 288n1
Middleton, Thomas, 160
Milligan, Elizabeth, 169
Mills, Frederick, 100
Milnor, James, 141–42
missionaries: of American Episcopal, 135, 139, 141, 169–70, 265–68; in Australia, 206, 208–9; *Beagle* for, 171; bishops as, 201–2, 261–62; in Canada, 149, 209–11; to China, 173–74; clergy or, 158; conversion by, 158–59, 210; Domestic and Foreign Missionary Society for, 141, 169–70; education by, 161–62, 198, 210, 224–26; India with women, 158; to Latin America, 170–73; on native independence, 282; New Zealand, 168–69, 206, 209; in nineteenth century, 155–56, 181–84; Oxford ceremony or India, 206; Pearsall as laity, 262–64; Philippines, 242–43; on race, 257; SAMS as, 238; to South Africa, 174–77; in South Asia, 204–8; in South Pacific, 163–69; SPG for English, 92; women as, 263–64
monastic orders, 4; Anglican Communion and, 189, 263; clergy and, 191–92; criticism of, 270–71; Henry VIII against, 5–6, 146; men and women in, 1, 268–71; in nineteenth century, 186–89
Montgomery, Henry, 208
Moore, Herbert, 235
Moravian Brethren, 77
Morgan, Emily Malbone, 274
Morgan, J. Pierpont, 273
Morris, James Watson, 240–41
Mother's Union, 114–15, 183–85, 186
Mountain, Jacob, 106, 147–48
Muhlenberg, William A., 138, 268–69, 271–72
Mullin, Robert Bruce, 138
Mwanga II, 202, 204
Myanmar, 285–86

national church, 14, 46, 51, 121; America as not, 100–101, 138–40; Anglican as, 34–35, 39, 95, 108, 208; in Australia, 163–65; Avis on, 12, 34–35; Cromwell, O., on, 54; Elizabeth on, 21, 39; English Church and, 34–35, 39, 95, 108, 123–24, 208; Ireland on, 130; in Korea, 237; Oxford movement on, 119–20; Scottish Non-Jurors on, 67; SPG and, 94
Native Church, 158–60, 199–200, 203–4, 207, 209, 233; growth of, 284, 288n3

Native populations, 88; Aboriginal population as, 107–8, 163–67, 208, 211; American Episcopal on, 145–47, 255–58; American laity in, 257; America on, 146–47, 150–51; of Canada, 150–51, 211, 218n48; civilization of, 96–97; Colenso for, 175–77, 212; conversion of, 86–87, 92, 94, 96–97, 147, 151, 256–57; defense of, 285–86; Diocesan Native Female Training School and, 227–28; education of American, 257–58, 265; Maori as, 166–68, 209; missionaries on independence and, 282; slaves ownership by, 146; western medicine for American, 258, 264–65

A Necessary Doctrine and Erudition for any Christian Man, 7
"neighbourly scrutiny," 28

Neill, Stephen, 155
Newfoundland, 85
Newman, Henry Stanley, 207
Newman, John Henry, 121, 270
New Order Army, 52
New Zealand, 166–69, 206, 209
Nicene Creed, 8, 139, 214–15, 234, 237
Nicolson, Adam, 41
Niger Delta Pastorate, 159, 198–200
Nightingale, Florence, 187
Nippon Sei Ko Kai, 235–36, 285
Non-Jurors, 66–70, 75–76, 101–2

oath refusal, 66
O'Day, Rosemary, 24, 26–27, 29, 43–44, 128
Of the Laws of Ecclesiastical Polity (Hooker), 32, 37n45, 137
O'Neill, S. W., 188
Opium Wars, 173, 221, 224
Orens, John Richard, 194
Otey, James H., 147, 249–50
Oxford and Cambridge Mission to Central Africa, 200

Oxford movement: in America, 137–38; in India, 205–6; on national church, 119–20; Pusey and, 116, 120–21, 186–87, 192–93, 200

Paley, William, 71
parishes: in Canada, 106; functions in, 43; Hobart and American, 136; income sources in, 43–44
Parker, Matthew, 25–26, 30
Parliament, 9; bishops and, 13–14, 120; Charles I on, 50–51; on clergy marriage, 10–11; Cromwell, O., on, 52–53; on Elizabethan Settlement, 21; for English Church, 60; Gunpowder Plot against, 40–41; Ireland and English Church, 120; on James I, 42; against king, 34; on national church, 119–20; against reconciliation, 60–61; as re-convened, 55; for Scottish Church, 51–52; slave trade outlawed by, 117
Parr, Katherine (Queen), 8
Payne, John, 170
Pearsall, Emily, 262–64
Pelly, Kootenay, 150
Pennsylvania, 101

The Pentateuch and the Book of Joshua Critically Examined (Colenso), 176–77

people. *See* laity

The Perpetual Government of Christ's Church (Bilson), 34

Perry, Matthew C., 219
Philippine Islands, 242–43, 268
Philipse, Frederick, 99
pilgrimages, 6
Plubell Mattia, Joan, 203
Polk, Leonidas, 250
polygamy, 159–61, 167, 175
Poon, Michael, 286

Pott, Hawks, 225
Potter, Alonso, 173
Potter, Henry Codman, 272–74
poverty, 8–9; American Episcopal on, 269–76, 282; Anglican ministry to, 190–94, 285–86; children working in, 116–17; Christian Socialists on, 125–27, 192–94, 271, 274–75; church rejected by, 186; Clapham Sect on, 80–81, 156; in eighteenth century, 74–75, 113–14; English Church on, 116–17; Evangelicals on, 117, 193; Maurice on, 124–27, 189, 192, 194, 214; Muhlenberg on, 138, 268–69, 271–72; Sunday School for, 141–42; in twenty-first century, 287; urban ministry on, 189–94; women on American, 274

A Practical View of the Prevailing Religious System (Wilberforce, W.), 81

Prayer Book. *See Book of Common Prayer*
preaching: *Book of Homilies* for, 9, 42; of Donne, 44–45, 47; Herbert on, 47–50; James I on, 42; laity and, 79; license revoked, 8–9, 25; Puritans emphasizing, 43
predestination, 42–43, 78
Presbyterians, 51–53, 62–63, 67

A Priest to the Temple or The Country Parson (Herbert), 47

prophesyings, 29–30
Protestant (Anglican) Ascendancy, 130–31
Protestant Episcopal Church (American Episcopal), 100; African American congregations and, 143–45; American civil rights movement and, 282; American government and, 258; American settlers and, 259–63; in China, 170, 220, 224, 227–30; Confederate States and, 250–53; deaconesses in, 263, 265; on English Church, 103–4; on freed slaves, 143, 249; in Japan, 231–32; missionaries of, 135, 139, 141, 169–70, 265–68; on Native populations, 145–47, 255–58; overseas missions of, 169–70; on poverty, 269–76, 284; Scotland on Church and, 102–3; services in, 139–40; on slavery, 144, 249–51, 254; on society, 272–74; structure of, 102–4; on urban education, 276; women missionaries in, 262–64
Protestantism, 7–8, 69. *See also* high church
Provoost, Samuel, 102
public penance, 28–29
purgatory, 7–8
Puritans, 23, 27–31, 43, 51–52, 60–61; Hooker on, 32–35, 37n45, 39, 46, 69, 137
Pusey, Edward, 116, 120–21, 187, 192–93, 200

Quakers, 66

racism, 198–99; after American Civil War, 254–55; missionaries and, 257; segregation in, 174–75, 254, 285; in South Africa, 285
Rainsford, William, 273
Reasonableness of Christianity (Locke, J.), 73
Reformation, 1–2; Dodwell on, 70; by Edward VI, 8–15; Elizabeth consolidating, 21; Hooker on, 32–35, 37n45, 39, 46, 69, 137; on household, 23, 25. *See also* Cranmer, Thomas
Reformed Church of Ireland, 130
religious instruction, 33
religious orders. *See* monastic orders
Remarks on the Proper Treatment of Polygamy (Colenso), 175

responsibility granting. *See collation*
Restoration: Anglican ministry after, 59–81, 90, 121–22; Bosher on, 59–61, 103–4; Church of Scotland and, 62–64; of monarchy, 118
Rex, Richard, 11
Rhodes, Cecil, 197
Rhodes, Nancy, 98–99
Ridley, Nicholas, 17
right of nomination. *See advowson*
Ritualist movement, 122–23, 191–94, 270–71
Roman Catholic Christianity, 1–2; Act of Settlement and, 68; Act of Toleration on, 66; Anglicans and, 13, 283; in Australia, 164, 208; Ayres on, 268–69; on Brazil missionaries, 240–41; Charles II for, 63–64; conversion and, 51, 64, 85, 131; Cromwell, O., on, 54; Ireland Church excluding, 130; Ireland with, 51, 130–31; James II for, 64–65; in Korea, 221; Latin America with, 170–71; Manifest Destiny on, 240; Mary reestablishing, 15–17; on western America and Canada, 151; William of Orange on, 66
Roper, Henry, 148–49, 210–11
Royal Supremacy, 5, 16–17, 30–31, 34, 120–21

The Rule and Exercise of Holy Dying (Taylor), 50
The Rule and Exercise of Holy Living (Taylor), 50

Sacrament. *See* Communion
saints, 8
Salvation Army, 189
SAMS. *See* South American Missionary Society
Sarum (Salisbury) Use, 3
Savoy Conference, 60
Saw Shee Sho, 284

Schereschewsky, Samuel Joseph Isaac, 223, 225
science: China and, 230; clergy and, 73, 127, 224; Darwin and, 129, 171, 182, 238; English Church and, 123, 127–30, 164, 182–83, 276; Japan and, 234; Latitudinarians on, 66, 128
Scotland, 50–51, 62–63, 66–68, 101–3
Scottish Church. *See* Church of Scotland
Scottish Episcopal Church, 67–68
Scottish Prayer Book, 50–51
Scottish Reformation, 40
Scudder, Vida, 274–75
Seabury, Samuel, 100–103, 105
seamen's chapel, 117–18, 132n16, 227
Secher, Thomas, 73
Sellon, Priscilla Lydia, 187
Selwyn, George, 167–68, 212–14

A Serious Call to a Devout and Holy Life (Law), 69–70

Sharp, James, 63
Shaw, A. C., 233–34
Sheldrake, Philip, 49
shrines, 6, 8–9
Sisterhood of the Holy Cross, 187
slave trade, 129; abolition of, 118; by Afrikaners, 174; America and, 88; American Episcopal on, 143–44, 249–51, 254; American Natives and, 146; by Arab traders, 201–2; baptism and, 86–87, 90, 92, 94, 145; Clapham Sect on, 80; emancipation and, 94; English Church and, 89; Evangelical Movement on, 81, 93–95; Parliament outlawing, 117; SPG on, 92–95, 110n29, 110n31. *See also* freed slaves
Slave Trade Act (1807), 81

The Social Aspects of Christianity (Ely), 275–76

Social Gospel movement, 275

Societas Sanctae Crucis (Society of the Holy Cross), 122–23
society, 80; American Episcopals on, 272–74; Chartist movement on, 125–26; clergy as group in, 27, 44; clergy backgrounds in, 61, 70, 114; of English, 184; English Church and reform of, 116–19; English Church failures on, 75–76; English Church on English, 120, 183; of India, 205; Maurice on, 124–27, 189, 192, 194, 214; urban ministry on, 189–94; of working class, 123–24
Society for Propagation of the Gospel in Foreign Parts (SPG), 96–98, 100–102, 105, 108, 135; Canada and, 147–49; differentiation from, 156, 159; in India, 204–5; in Japan, 232–33; in Korea, 236–37; national church and, 94; slaves of, 92–95, 110n29, 110n31; in South Africa, 174
Society for the Promotion of Christian Knowledge (SPCK), 92, 94, 135, 156–57
Society of the Holy Cross. *See Societas Sanctae Crucis*
Solemn League and Covenant, 51
South Africa, 174–77, 285
South American Missionary Society (SAMS), 238
South Asia, 204–8
South Pacific, 107–8, 163–69, 208, 211
SPCK. *See* Society for the Promotion of Christian Knowledge
SPG. *See* Society for Propagation of the Gospel in Foreign Parts

The Spirit of Missions, 265

Staley, Thomas, 243
Stanley, David, 202
Stock, Eugene, 159, 209
Stone, Lawrence, 23, 28
Strachan, John, 148
Strong, Rowan, 95–96, 169

Student Volunteer Movement for Foreign Missions (SVM), 224
Sugeno, Frank, 100
Sumner, Mary, 114–15, 184–85
Sunday School, 141–42
SVM. *See* Student Volunteer Movement for Foreign Missions
synod: in Africa, 175; in America, 248; in Australia, 208; in Canada, 148–49, 177, 209, 211; in Japan, 234; of Lambeth, 212, 214; in New Zealand, 166–68; in Scotland, 62–63; of Westminster, 129

Tait (Archbishop), 213
Takeda, John, 235
Taylor, Jeremy, 50
Temple, Frederick, 182
The Temple (Herbert), 47
Ten Articles, 7
Thackara, Eliza, 265
Thirty-Nine Articles of Religion (1563), 13–15, 21–22, 235
Thomas, Josiah, 157
Thornton, Henry, 80
Toland, John, 73
Tozer, William, 201
Tractarians, 138
Tracts for the Times, 120–21
transubstantiation, 3, 5, 45–46, 118, 137
Travers, Walter, 33–34, 39
Trollope, Anthony, 181–82
Tucker, A. R., 203
Tuttle, Daniel S., 260–62
Tutu, Desmond, 285

Uganda martyrs, 202
UMCA. *See* Universities Mission to Central Africa
Unitarians, 66
United States of America. *See* America
Universities Mission to Central Africa (UMCA), 200–201

urban ministry: by American Episcopals, 269–76, 284; in nineteenth century, 189–94
Usagers, 69

Valense, Deborah, 75
Venn, Henry (grandfather), 81
Venn, Henry (grandson), 81; Native Church of, 158–60, 199–200, 203–4, 207, 209, 233, 284, 288n3; on polygamy, 159–60
Venn, John (son), 81, 156
Verbeck, G. F., 232
vestments and dress, 27; Japan and, 235; Latin America and, 172, 241; proscription of, 13, 22, 60; use of, 3, 10, 27, 47, 122
Victoria (Queen): as period, 123–24, 174, 182, 184, 186–89, 203–6, 210, 228; as person, 119, 167, 173, 183–84, 186, 189–90, 243
Vietnam War, 285
Vincent, Boyd, 215
Virgin, Peter, 73
Virginia, 85–89, 103, 108n1, 109n20

Wadleigh, George, 264
Wakefield, Gordon, 79
Walsingham shrine, 2
Ward, Kevin, 239, 241; on China, 173, 222–23, 230; on India, 207–8; on South Pacific, 163–64
Watts-Ditchfield, John Edwin, 193
Webster, C. A., 131
Wesley, Charles, 76–81, 96
Wesley, John, 76–81, 96
West, Emily, 256–57
western medicine, 269; in American West, 262; in China, 227; on Hansen's Disease, 227, 233; in Japan, 231, 233; in Latin America, 238; for Native Americans, 258, 264–65
Westminster, 51, 129

Whipple, Henry B., 255–56
White, William, 100–103, 141, 143
Whitefield, George, 77–78, 96

The Whole Duty of Man (anonymous), 62, 70

Wickeri, Philip, 226–27
Wickham, E. C., 123–24
Wilberforce, Samuel, 104, 129, 160, 188
Wilberforce, William, 80–81, 107, 118, 129, 163
William of Orange (King), 65–68
Williams, Channing Moore, 231–33
Williams, Peter, Jr., 144
Wilson, Daniel Thomas, 160–61
Woman's Auxiliary to the Board of Missions, 264–65
women: American Episcopal missionaries as, 262–64; on American poverty, 274; in Anglican ministry, 263–65, 284; in China, 227–30; as Christian Socialists, 274–75; church roles for, 1, 4, 147, 158, 169, 183–84, 186–87, 210–11, 223–24; convicts as, 278n44; as deacons, 263, 265, 268; English Church on indigenous, 163, 205, 227–30, 233, 263–71, 274, 285; India missionaries as, 158; of Japan, 233; as missionaries, 263–64; monastic orders with, 1, 268–71; Mother's Union for, 114–15, 183–85, 186; restrictions for, 7, 49, 123; Sisterhood of the Holy Cross and, 187
Wondra, Ellen, 127
Woodforde, James, 71
Woodhouse, H. F., 32
Woolverton, John, 91
Workhouse Test Act (1723), 74
World Church, 169
Wright, Robert, 215
Wycliffe, John, 2

Xu, Edward Li-Hua, 225–26

Yen Yűn-ching, 224–25

The Young Christian Soldier, 266

About the Author

John L. Kater is a native of Virginia and holds degrees from Columbia University, The General Theological Seminary, and McGill University. He is an ordained priest of the Episcopal Church and began his ministry as a parish priest in Poughkeepsie, New York. He has taught at Marist College, Vassar College and served as Education Officer for the diocese of Panama. For twenty-seven years he was Professor of Ministry Development at the Church Divinity School of the Pacific in Berkeley, California, where he also directed the Center for Anglican Learning and Leadership. He has been teaching at Ming Hua Theological College in Hong Kong since 2007. He has taught or lectured in twelve countries throughout the Americas and in East Asia. He has published widely in the areas of Anglican studies and the history and practice of ministry and is also the author of two books for children and one for teenagers.

www.ingramcontent.com/pod-product-compliance
Lightning Source LLC
Chambersburg PA
CBHW020836020526
44114CB00040B/1062